The Biopolitical Animal

Animalities

Series Editor
Matthew Chrulew, Curtin University

Editorial Advisory Board
Brett Buchanan, Laurentian University
Vinciane Despret, Université de Liège
Donna Haraway, University of California, Santa Cruz
Jean Langford, University of Minnesota
Dominique Lestel, École normale supérieure
Stephen Muecke, Flinders University
Stephanie Posthumus, McGill University
Isabelle Stengers, Université libre de Bruxelles
Thom van Dooren, University of Sydney
Cary Wolfe, Rice University

Books available
Deborah Bird Rose, *Shimmer: Flying Fox Exuberance in Worlds of Peril*
Robert Briggs, *The Animal-to-Come: Zoopolitics in Deconstruction*
Dinesh Joseph Wadiwel, *Animals and Capital*
Felice Cimatti and Carlo Salzani (eds), *The Biopolitical Animal*

Forthcoming books
Dominique Lestel, *Animality: An Essay on the Status of the Human*, together with *Animalities* by Matthew Chrulew

Visit the series website at edinburghuniversitypress.com/series-animalities

The Biopolitical Animal

Edited by

Felice Cimatti and Carlo Salzani

EDINBURGH
University Press

Edinburgh University Press is one of the leading university presses in the UK. We publish academic books and journals in our selected subject areas across the humanities and social sciences, combining cutting-edge scholarship with high editorial and production values to produce academic works of lasting importance. For more information visit our website: edinburghuniversitypress.com

© editorial matter and organisation Felice Cimatti and Carlo Salzani, 2024
© the chapters their several authors, 2024

Edinburgh University Press Ltd
13 Infirmary Street
Edinburgh EH1 1LT

Typeset in 10/14pt Warnock Pro and Gill Sans
by Cheshire Typesetting Ltd, Cuddington, Cheshire

A CIP record for this book is available from the British Library

ISBN 978 1 3995 2598 5 (hardback)
ISBN 978 1 3995 2600 5 (webready PDF)
ISBN 978 1 3995 2601 2 (epub)

The right of Felice Cimatti and Carlo Salzani to be identified as the editors of this work has been asserted in accordance with the Copyright, Designs and Patents Act 1988, and the Copyright and Related Rights Regulations 2003 (SI No. 2498).

Contents

Notes on Contributors   vii

Introduction: What is a Biopolitical Animal?   1
Felice Cimatti and Carlo Salzani

PART I: THE ANIMAL OF BIOPOLITICS

1. Turning Back to Nature: Foucault and the Practice of Animality   23
   Matthew Calarco

2. Community and Animality in the Ancient Cynics   40
   Vanessa Lemm

3. Biopolitics of Covid-19 and the Space of Animals: A Planetary Perspective   58
   Miguel Vatter

4. How to Chirp like a Cricket: Agamben and the Reversal of Anthropogenesis   76
   Sergei Prozorov

5. Animality and Inoperativity: Interspecies Form-of-Life   92
   Sherryl Vint

PART II: TALES OF BIOPOLITICS AND ANIMALITY

6. Restraining Biopolitics: On Dino Buzzati's Living Animals   113
   Timothy Campbell

7. Cages and Mirrors: Mr. Palomar and the Albino Gorilla 132
   Serenella Iovino

8. Bunnies and Biopolitics: Killing, Culling and Caring for Rabbits 151
   David Redmalm and Erica von Essen

9. Deading Life and the Undying Animal: Necropolitics After the Factory Farm 175
   James K. Stanescu

10. Factory Farms for Fishes: Aquaculture, Biopolitics and Resistance 190
    Dinesh Wadiwel

PART III: RECONCEPTUALISING BIOPOLITICS

11. Imagining Liberation beyond Biopolitics: The Biopolitical 'War against Animals' and Strategies for Ending It 215
    Zipporah Weisberg

12. Animal Magnetism: (Bio)Political Theologies Between the Creature and the Animal 234
    Diego Rossello

13. Creaturely Biopolitics 252
    Carlo Salzani

14. A Dog's Life: From the Biopolitical Animal to the Posthuman 274
    Felice Cimatti

Afterword: Locating Race and Animality amidst the Politics of Interspecies Life 295
Neel Ahuja

Index 299

Notes on Contributors

Neel Ahuja is Professor in the Harriet Tubman Department of Women, Gender, and Sexuality Studies at the University of Maryland, College Park, where he is Director of Undergraduate Studies. Neel teaches a variety of courses in critical race and ethnic studies, feminist science studies, disability studies and environmental humanities. His research explores the relationship of the body to the geopolitical, environmental and public health contexts of colonial governance, warfare and security. Neel is the author of two books, *Bioinsecurities: Disease Interventions, Empire, and the Government of Species* (2016) and *Planetary Specters: Race, Migration, and Climate Change in the Twenty-First Century* (2021).

Matthew Calarco is Professor of Philosophy at California State University, Fullerton, where he teaches courses in continental philosophy, history of philosophy, animal studies and environmental philosophy. He is author of *The Boundaries of Human Nature* (Columbia University Press, 2021), *Beyond the Anthropological Difference* (Cambridge University Press, 2020) and *Thinking Through Animals: Identity, Difference, Indistinction* (Stanford University Press, 2015). He is currently completing a monograph on the inhumanist philosophy of Robinson Jeffers.

Timothy Campbell teaches courses in philosophy and film in the Department of Romance Studies at Cornell University. In addition to his translations of Roberto Esposito's *Bios: Biopolitics and Philosophy* (Minnesota, 2008), *Communitas: The Origin and Destiny of Community* (Stanford, 2009), as well as Carlo Diano's *Form and Event: Principles for an Interpretation of the Greek World* (with Lia Turtas), he is the author of *Improper Life: Technology and*

Biopolitics from Heidegger to Agamben (Minnesota, 2011), *The Techne of Giving: Cinema and the Generous Form of Life* (Fordham, 2017) and *The Comic Self: Towards Dispossession* (Minnesota, 2023), co-authored with Grant Farred.

Felice Cimatti is Professor of Philosophy of Language at the University of Calabria. The semiological study of animal languages leads to questions about how language relates to biology in humans, and this is where his current research on the relationship between the body, language and society comes from. His latest books include *Bio-semiotic Ontology: The Philosophy of Giorgio Prodi* (2018), *Unbecoming Human: Philosophy of Animality after Deleuze* (2020) and, co-edited with Carlo Salzani, *Animality in Contemporary Italian Philosophy* (2020). His new book *Il postanimale. La natura dopo l'Antropocene* (2021) is being translated into English.

Erica von Essen is a nondisciplinary human–animal researcher who specialises in hunting, ethics of wildlife killing, wildlife conflict and problem animals in society. She is widely published on controversies in wildlife management, including poaching, resistance movements, trophy hunting and wildlife tourism. Von Essen currently leads three projects on changing human–wildlife relations.

Serenella Iovino is Professor of Italian Studies and Environmental Humanities at the University of North Carolina at Chapel Hill. She is author and editor of twelve volumes and over a 150 essays and articles. Her most recent publications are *Gli animali di Calvino: Storie dell'Antropocene* (Treccani, 2023, 1st ed. *Italo Calvino's Animals: Anthropocene Stories,* Cambridge University Press, 2021) and *Paesaggio civile: Storie di ambiente, cultura e resistenza* (Il Saggiatore, 2022, 1st ed. *Ecocriticism and Italy: Ecology, Resistance, and Liberation*, Bloomsbury, 2016, winner of the MLA Prize and AAIS Book Prize). A philosopher by training and a public intellectual, she is among the leading animators of the international debate on humanities and the environment.

Vanessa Lemm is Professor of Political Philosophy, Pro Vice-Chancellor and Executive Dean of the Faculty of Liberal Arts and Science at the University of Greenwich, London, UK. She is an Honorary Professorial Fellow at the University of Melbourne, Australia. She has published widely on the philosophy of Friedrich Nietzsche, contemporary political thought, biopolitics, and animal and plant studies. She is the author of *Homo Natura: Friedrich Nietzsche, Philosophical Anthropology and Biopolitics* (Edinburgh University Press, 2020) and *Nietzsche's Animal Philosophy: Culture, Politics and the Animality of the*

Human Being (Fordham University Press, 2009). She is currently working on a book manuscript on ancient Cynicism.

Sergei Prozorov is Professor of Political Science at the Department of Social Sciences and Philosophy, University of Jyväskylä. His research interests include contemporary political theory, continental philosophy, biopolitics, democracy and totalitarianism, crisis studies and post-truth politics. He is the author of nine monographs, the most recent being *Biopolitics After Truth: Knowledge, Power and Democratic Life* (2021), *Democratic Biopolitics: Popular Sovereignty and the Power of Life* (2019) and *Agamben and Politics: A Critical Introduction* (2014).

David Redmalm is an associate professor of Sociology at the School of Health, Care and Social Welfare at Mälardalen University, Sweden. He works within the field of human–animal studies with a special focus on how life is made valuable and grievable on the one hand, and replaceable and expendable on the other. He has published articles and book chapters on, among other things, the grief for companion animals, presidential pets, chihuahuas in popular culture, riding schools and the biopolitics of pet keeping.

Diego Rossello is an Associate Professor at the Department of Philosophy, Universidad Adolfo Ibáñez, in Santiago, Chile. His work has appeared in journals such as *Síntesis, Revista de Filosofía, Ideas y Valores, New Literary History, Philosophy Today, Society and Animals, Politics and Animals, Political Theology, Contemporary Political Theory,* and *Political Theory,* among others. He is co-editor, with Matías Bascuñán, of *Derrida: el arte de leer* (Buenos Aires: Katz, 2023), and with José Antonio Valdivia of *Filosofía, teología y política en un mundo post-secular* (Valencia: Tirant lo blanch, 2023). His book *La teoría política en el Antropoceno: animalidad, soberanía, dignidad* is forthcoming.

Carlo Salzani is Research Fellow in the Department of Philosophy of the University of Innsbruck, Austria, Guest Scholar at the Messerli Research Institute of Vienna, Austria, and faculty member of the Paris Institute for Critical Thinking. His research interests focus on animal ethics, posthumanism and biopolitics. Among his recent publications are the edited volumes *A Responsibility to the World: Saramago, Politics and Philosophy* (2023) and *Animality in Contemporary Italian Philosophy* (2020), and the books *Agamben and the Animal* (2022) and *Walter Benjamin and the Actuality of Critique: Essays on Violence and Experience* (2021).

James K. Stanescu is an Assistant Professor of Communication Studies at Mercer University (USA). He is the co-editor of *The Ethics and Rhetoric of Invasion Ecology* (Lexington Books, 2017) and founder of the early influential animal studies blog, *Critical Animal*. He publishes widely in the intersections of animal and environmental studies, continental philosophy and American pragmatism. He is currently working on a project about how weird and radical empiricisms can force us to communicate with the more-than-human-world.

Miguel Vatter is Professor of Politics at the Alfred Deakin Institute for Citizenship and Globalisation at Deakin University, Australia. His main areas of research are Machiavelli and republicanism, biopolitics and political theology. His most recent book is *Living Law: Jewish Political Theology from Hermann Cohen to Hannah Arendt* (Oxford 2021) and he is co-editor with Vanessa Lemm of *The Viral Politics of Covid-19: Nature, Home and Planetary Health* (Palgrave Macmillan, 2022).

Sherryl Vint is Professor of Media and Cultural Studies and Chair of the Department of English at the University of California, Riverside, where she directs the Speculative Fictions and Cultures of Science programme. She has published widely on science fiction, including, most recently, *Biopolitical Futures in Twenty-First Century Speculative Fiction* (2021) and *Programming the Future: Speculative Television and the End of Democracy* (2022, co-authored with Jonathan Alexander). She was a founding editor of *Science Fiction Film and Television* and is an editor for the journal *Science Fiction Studies* and the book series *Science in Popular Culture*.

Dinesh Joseph Wadiwel is Associate Professor in Socio-Legal Studies and Human Rights at the University of Sydney. His research interests include theories of violence, critical animal studies and disability rights. He is author of *The War against Animals* (Brill, 2015), *Animals and Capital* (Edinburgh UP 2023) and is co-editor, with Matthew Chrulew of *Foucault and Animals* (Brill, 2016).

Zipporah Weisberg is an independent scholar currently living in Vienna, Austria. Her academic areas of specialisation include critical animal studies, the critical theory of the early Frankfurt School and existentialism and phenomenology. In 2013, Zipporah completed her PhD in Social and Political Thought at York University in Toronto, Canada. From 2013 to 2015, Zipporah was the Abby Benjamin Postdoctoral Fellow in Animal Ethics in the Department of Philosophy at Queen's University, under the supervision of Will Kymlicka, Canada Research

Chair in Political Philosophy. Zipporah's postdoctoral research focused on the ethics of biotechnology and the phenomenology of animal life. In March 2021, Zipporah was awarded a Culture and Animals Foundation grant for her project on animal agency in animal sanctuaries. Zipporah is currently working on a book on the psychopathology of animal extermination.

Introduction: What is a Biopolitical Animal?
Felice Cimatti and Carlo Salzani

What *Was* the Political Animal?

The 'primal scene' of Western political theory,[1] Aristotle's famous definition of 'man'[2] as a *politikon zōon*, a 'political animal', set the coordinates of the frame that would determine and organise Western politics and subjectivity for two and a half millennia. It already displayed all the problems that would plague this frame from the very beginning and that would come to a head in late modernity, when its too fragile pillars would collapse, opening the gates to other possible forms of politics and subjectivity. A revisiting of this primal scene, even if brief and cursory, therefore seems to be a good starting point to lay out the terms and stakes of the question about politics and animality.

In book I of his *Politics*, Aristotle purports to demonstrate that the polis is a 'natural' institution, and he begins by tracing its origins in other 'natural' forms of community such as the household and the village. Aristotle scholars have pointed out, however, that the 'naturality' of the political is not limited to human beings, and in fact the definition 'political animal' occurs already in book I of *The History of Animals* (though many translations render here *politikon* as 'social' rather than properly 'political'), probably the first of Aristotle's zoological works, where it designates a sub-group of the gregarious animals that includes 'man, the bee, the wasp, the ant, and the crane' (I.1, 488a, 8–13).[3] The defining characteristic of this group is cooperation in some common enterprise (*ergon*). In *Politics*, however, the statement that 'man is by nature a political animal' (I.2, 1253a, 2) is complemented by the corollary that he is so 'in a higher degree than bees or other gregarious animals' (I.2, 1253a, 7), and this is because, as it is well known, 'man alone of the animals is furnished with the faculty of language'. If all animals are endowed with the 'making of sounds' (*phōnē*), which 'serves to indicate pleasure and pain', the peculiarity of man is language (*logos*), which 'serves to declare what is advantageous and what is the reverse' and provides thereby the 'perception of good and evil, of the just and the unjust' (I.2, 1253a, 10–18).[4]

On the one hand, Aristotle notes the *continuity* between human and (some) nonhuman animals: the political is a *biological* feature humans share with other animals, and the difference between these species is thus one of degree and not of kind. This is a point worth stressing, since it is frequently missed by the current debate on biopolitics: for Aristotle, and hence for the Western philosophical tradition, politics and biology are always already intertwined.[5] On the other hand, the political in the Aristotelian definition works as an apparatus of exclusion: twice Aristotle states that 'He who is without a city [. . .] is either a poor sort of being, or a being higher than man: he is like the man of whom Homer wrote in denunciation: Clanless and lawless and hearthless is he' (I.2, I253a, 4–8); and a little later: 'The man who is isolated, who is unable to share in the benefits of political association, or has no need to share because he is already self-sufficient, is no part of the city, and must therefore be either a beast or a god' (I.2, 1253a, 28–32). Moreover, treating *logos* as the faculty by which to discriminate between good and bad and between just and unjust further excludes *phōnē* – and with it all *aloga zōa*, the animals without *logos* or the 'irrational' animals, but also *human* biological life – from the polis. Agamben will famously argue that this very exclusion is what founds the human polis as such.[6] And it did indeed found the whole Western political tradition, which chose to downplay or forget the continuity of the political across many species and to emphasise instead its exclusionary logic, transforming the Aristotelian difference of degree into a difference of kind, thereby asserting human exceptionality.[7]

This 'topology' of the political is what, according to biopolitical theories, collapses at the inception of modernity.[8] Foucault famously claimed that 'a society's "threshold of modernity" has been reached when the life of the species is wagered on its own political strategies', and concluded: 'For millennia, man remained what he was for Aristotle: a living animal with the additional capacity for a political existence; modern man is an animal whose politics places his existence as a living being in question'.[9] When the separation/co-implication between biological life and political life collapses, not only does politics become (the previously oxymoronic crasis of) bio-politics,[10] but the very definition of 'political animal' becomes ultimately untenable. The subjects of biopolitics are, beyond species barriers, *all* biopolitical animals: the biopolitical turn, then, allows for a revisiting of the Aristotelian definition that emphasises how animality, human and nonhuman alike, is not only excluded from the polis but also constitutes its fundamental and inescapable ground – and finally also its destiny that returns today with a vengeance.[11]

What this means is not that the definition of Political Animal should be revised and enlarged to include (some) other social animals, as proposed in some quarters,[12] but rather that other forms of politics and subjectivity must be imagined, experienced and lived beyond and without the exclusionary logic of the Political Animal, beyond the apparatus that places politics on the side of *Homo sapiens* and nature and biology on that of nonhuman animality. What is at stake is precisely to imagine a thus-far unexperienced *humanimality*, that is, a way of being human, and therefore political, that is intrinsically connected to animality. In this sense, the biopolitical animal is that living being whose life can be – for the first time in human history – *naturally political*. The main goal of this volume is to contribute to this reimagining of the relationship between politics and animality.

Biopolitics and Animality

Cary Wolfe has compellingly shown that, within a biopolitical frame, the distinction human/animal is a 'discursive resource, not a zoological designation', and that humans and non-humans alike are, therefore, 'all always already (potential) "animals" before the law'.[13] In other words, all animals, humans included, are biopolitical animals. The major biopolitical theories, however, have almost exclusively focused on what this has meant for human beings: if, as Wolfe again argued, the animal works as the 'ur-form' or archetype of biopolitical subjectivity,[14] this emphasises the 'nightmarish' face of biopolitics, the subjection, instrumentalisation and violence that the 'animal' has always experienced and suffered and that now, importantly and on an unprecedented scale, affect human beings as well. Dehumanisation and animalisation have always been fundamental mechanisms to produce the 'Western subject' (the Political Animal), whereby what was dehumanised and 'expelled' from the human 'proper' (not only nonhuman animals but also women, children, 'barbarians', racialised 'others', and so on) was – legitimately – exposed to domination and violence. With the 'progressive animalization of man'[15] in biopolitical modernity the same treatment is extended to humans in a common 'control over life and death' in general.[16]

It is not, therefore, only (cruelly) 'ironic' that the main biopolitical theories 'forgot' to consider the place of nonhuman beings within this frame, as Wolfe argues[17]; this is indeed tragic, and not only because this forgetfulness perpetuates the exclusionary logic of the Political Animal – with all the violence and suffering it entails – but, more importantly, because it prevents a true understanding of what biopolitics truly is and means. Animality lies at the very heart of biopolitics, hence the relationships between human and nonhuman animals are fundamental to understanding the mechanisms and the essence of biopolitics itself. Animality is central to biopolitical theories not only, as has been mostly the case, because it is *human* animality itself (what the prefix *bio-* denotes, or the Aristotelian *zōon* to which the *politikon* is added) that becomes subject to the biopolitical calculation.[18] Historically speaking, as Foucault has showed in *Discipline and Punish* and in many lecture courses at the Collège de France, perfecting the control and mastery over the human body – with the consequent 'animalization of man' – was both a condition and a consequence of the capitalist system, which needs a tame 'tool' adequate to its political-economic apparatuses.[19] But animality is central in a much more fundamental way, namely because it constitutes the 'limit possibility' of life, human and nonhuman, in the grip of this very biopolitical calculation.[20]

The 'species blindness'[21] of the major biopolitical approaches can perhaps be corrected using Foucault's own theorisation: in *Society Must Be Defended*, Foucault identified racism as the apparatus through which power can introduce a break between what can live and what must die and can thus continue to exercise the sovereign right to kill.[22] There is no biopolitics without the 'corrective' of racism, and this schema can be easily applied to species, which is ultimately what construes biological difference in terms of a (post-)sovereign right to kill.[23] Richard Twine notes that this theorisation of racism can broadly be interpreted as a 'dominant approach to difference, one which is to an extent applicable to the naturalization of gender, class, race and species hierarchy'.[24] What is probably the most interesting facet of the contemporary theorisation of biopolitics takes place at the intersection of all these different but interdependent streams: the crossing of biopolitics and animality generates in turn a rich and fruitful multiplication of intersectional analyses from feminist, antiracist, queer and decolonial perspectives that question the Euro-white-masculinist identity of the Political Animal – but also of the traditional biopolitical theories.[25]

The right to kill is however only one aspect of the problem: if the true essence of biopolitics is 'to make live' – the focus on, and management of, life – then animality is the key to understanding it. Several scholars have convincingly shown how the technologies and rationality of biopower are nothing but the progressive extension to human beings of the technologies of management of animal life.[26] Therefore, Dinesh Wadiwel argues, the paradigm of biopolitics is not the concentration camp (Agamben) or the colony (Mbembe), but rather animal domestication as the ensemble of technologies of management, control, regulation and killing that have shaped human relationships with animals throughout the millennia.[27] This is also the argument put forward by Peter Sloterdijk: the 'taming' of humans into good citizens has always been the goal of politics and the docile 'herd' is the paradigm toward which we've been always inexorably tending, today more so than ever.[28] Pastoral power is the telling example: Foucault theorised it as a form of power, adopted first by the church and then by the modern state, which is characterised by the 'care' the good shepherd takes of his flock.[29] For Foucault this was only a metaphor, but if we take off the species blinders what becomes evident is not only that the biopolitical subject is first and foremost an animal (beyond all species barriers), but also that this 'care' manifests itself as deception, control, instrumentalisation and domination.[30]

In the past few decades, many thinkers have worked to correct the anthropocentrism of the main biopolitical theories and to emphasise and clarify the role that animality and animals did and should play. Biopolitics remains nonetheless a 'concept in flux'[31] and an often-inconsistent field of inquiry: the meanings of life and politics are constantly evolving, and their interaction is not, therefore, necessarily condemned to the *negative* connotation that has been briefly sketched above, but can also be opened to an *affirmative* dimension that could lead to a positive and constructive politics of life beyond the barrier of the species.

Beyond the Species

If there is something that the COVID-19 pandemic that spread across the planet in late 2019 has definitively shown, it is that the contemporary politics of life cannot and does not work along species lines but rather operates on 'biopolitical collectives',[32] acting *collectively* on macro social groups comprising many different kinds of entities: living beings of many species, but also non-sentient forms of life (e.g., viruses) and, if we adopt the Latourian actor–network perspective, even inanimate beings. This has of course been the case for a long time (viruses and pandemics have accompanied the evolution of the human species[33]), but the COVID-19 pandemic – a biopolitical dream (or rather nightmare) come true[34] – has brought this fact into the spotlight: the various lockdowns around the world 'imprisoned' human beings into the 'cages' of their homes and partially also 'liberated' the space that was reappropriated (for a brief time) by nonhuman animals, inverting in a sense the usual topology of power, but above all unveiling its mechanics. Power controls bodies and lives, human and nonhuman alike. We are all biopolitical animals.

The task we are confronted with today is a re-specification and reclaiming of biopolitics, that is, a redefinition of the relationship between the prefix 'bio-' and 'politics' beyond the negative combination delineated above. A redefinition has already been at work even within the traditional, mostly still anthropocentric biopolitical frames: Antonio Negri and Roberto Esposito, among others, have been elaborating forms of liberating or affirmative biopolitics that, in Esposito's words, aim at being 'no longer over life but *of* life'.[35] As well as shifting its focus from the technologies of control and management of bodies, and the 'progressive animalization of man', to re-centring on animality and corporeality as *lively potentials* and *creative forces*, this new politics *of* life must be further anthropo-*de*centralised so that it will also open up to new concepts and forms of expanded communities of the living, such as those we find already imagined and sketched, for example, in the work of Donna Haraway and in the multispecies ethnography of Anna Tsing, Thom van Dooren and others.[36] This anthropo-decentralisation will have to be accompanied by, or rather is an integral part of, an andro-decentralisation and Euro-decentralisation that institute a cross-species biopolitics along race, gender and decolonial lines as well.

Important work has been already been done to 'open up' traditional biopolitical theories (especially as articulated by Foucault and Agamben[37]) to the animal question, and new labels have even been proposed for these 'expanded' forms of biopolitics, such as 'trans-biopolitics'[38] or what Derrida (ironically) called 'zoo-politics', which has been appropriated and redefined many times.[39] Further possibilities also exist, as some chapters in the present volume propose: a different frame that goes beyond the limits of biopolitics itself.[40]

Whatever option one choses, the redefinition of the relationship between 'bios' and 'politics' entails, first of all, a redefinition of the relationship between *phōnē* and *logos* that for twenty-five centuries has structured the Political Animal and 'his' polis. The Political Animal was constructed around and inseparable from the primacy of articulated language, which, according to Aristotle, is alone that which gives access to the 'perception of good and evil, of the just and the unjust'.[41] There is no politics without language and, as Benveniste argued, without language there is no (human) subjectivity either, no psychological 'I'.[42] Politics, (human) subjectivity and language are inextricably bound together in the Political Animal. The overcoming of this construction implies therefore a sort of 'demotion' of language, which in the past few decades, and not only in the field of animal studies, has taken the form of a 'counter-linguistic turn'.[43] This 'turn' presents multiple and diverse manifestations, but in the biopolitical debate it can be summarised by the striking conclusion of Agamben's *The Sacrament of Language*:

It is perhaps time to call into question the prestige that language has enjoyed and continues to enjoy in our culture, as a tool of incomparable potency, efficacy, and beauty. And yet, considered in itself, it is no more beautiful than birdsong, no more efficacious than the signals insects exchange, no more powerful than the roar with which the lion asserts his dominion. The decisive element that confers on human language its peculiar virtue is not in the tool itself but in the place it leaves to the speaker, in the fact that it prepares within itself a hollowed-out form that the speaker must always assume in order to speak – that is to say, in the ethical relation that is established between the speaker and his language. *The human being is that living being that, in order to speak, must say 'I', must 'take the word', assume it and make it his own.*[44]

Conversely, the biopolitical animal will not wager its whole existence as individual and as community on this 'hollowed-out form' and will find its place beyond language and subjectivity[45] (i.e. beyond the human: as post-human). The prefix 'post-', just like 'bio-', deactivates the markers of traditional subjectivity and of traditional politics and opens them up to new possibilities that remain to be imagined and invented. Maybe the time has come for imaging a politics no longer based on the taming of animal (human and nonhuman) life. A politics in which the human cannot not be a post-human 'subject' and the animal will be a post-animal, that is, a living being no longer constructed as the mere opposite of the human.

On the Structure of This Book

The present volume aims to contribute to the contemporary debate on biopolitics and animality with chapters by leading authors in the fields of biopolitics and animal studies exploring the issues we have briefly sketched in this introduction. The volume is divided into three parts. Part One, 'The Animal of Biopolitics', includes five chapters focusing on how some traditional biopolitical theories have approached the question of the animal, and the place and function the animal has taken or could take within this framework. In Chapter 1, 'Turning Back to Nature: Foucault and the Practice of Animality', Matthew Calarco remarks on Foucault's mainly dismissive attitude toward the more-than-human world and his disregard for how the systems of power he analysed affects animals. However, in his 1984 (and last) lecture course, *The Courage of Truth*, Foucault showed a new appreciation for the importance of animals and animality, especially through an intriguing analysis of the ancient Cynics' philosophy and way of life: Cynic practices of living according to animals and nature (κατά φύσιν) represent an important means for countering the biopolitical capture of life in modernity and a novel way of proceeding through and beyond the anthropocentrism of Foucault's biopolitical analysis.

This point is taken up and expanded by Vanessa Lemm in Chapter 2, 'Community and Animality in the Ancient Cynics'. Lemm argues that the Cynics' rethinking of the human being, its relation to nature and its role within the community of the cosmos, may provide us with some hints towards a new understanding of community and immunity. Lemm shows that the Cynic's way of thinking and living in relation to the environment articulates a vision of communities of life that are inherently trans-species and provides an example of what it means to live in common or communicate with forms of non-human life without being able to exchange either words or reasons. In Chapter 3, 'Biopolitics of Covid-19 and the Space of Animals: A Planetary Perspective', Miguel Vatter focuses instead on the adoption of spatial/ecological terms in biopolitical discourses. From Uexkull and Plessner's *Umwelt* to Foucault's notion of 'milieu' as the space at the level of which biopolitics operates, from Deleuze and Guattari's idea of 'territorialisation' and 'de-territorialisation' to Sloterdijk's motif of 'spheres', *space* is a central notion for biopolitics. Vatter problematises this centrality from the viewpoint of the recent 'animal turn' in political theory, applying in particular some of the results of the critical analysis to think about the phenomenon of zoonosis and its relation to the Covid-19 pandemic.

In Chapter 4, 'How to Chirp like a Cricket: Agamben and the Reversal of Anthropogenesis', Sergei Prozorov addresses the relation between language and anthropogenesis in Agamben's work. From the early 1980s, Agamben posited the process of entering into language as unique to human beings' subjectivation, but in his diagnosis of the late-modern condition this process appears to be running on empty, as discourse becomes devoid of both truth and meaning. This seems to imply that the process of anthropogenesis is also rendered inoperative, and there is no longer any difference between the human experience of language and the animal dwelling in language. Prozorov explores these implications, posing the question of what kind of being emerges from this reversal of anthropogenesis. Finally, in Chapter 5, 'Animality and Inoperativity: Interspecies Form-of-Life', Sherryl Vint shows how in his later work Agamben frequently turns to the figure of the animal as a living being that makes use of its body without this 'use' falling into the problematic binaries that have so troubled Western metaphysics. Agamben's interest in thinking subjectivity outside the property relation it takes in liberal theory opens a space through which we might recognise that new articulations between the animal and the human *must* be a part of a reinvented metaphysics through which this new kind of self can emerge via an inoperativity of Being, what Agamben calls *form-of-life*.

Part Two, 'Tales of Biopolitics and Animality', proposes five multispecies stories or narratives of the intertwining of biopolitics and animality, beginning with two literary chapters. In Chapter 6, 'Restraining Biopolitics: On Dino Buzzati's Living Animals', Timothy Campbell reads the works of the Italian twentieth-century author, Dino Buzzati, as exemplary of the biopolitical animal as thought within the modern project. Buzzati's short stories and novels become for Campbell seismographs for measuring when the Italian 'biological threshold of modernity' has been crossed. Often these moments are linked to the collective murder of diverse species such that the biopolitical animal emerges only when and where other animals do not. Buzzati's writings, Campbell argues, theorise the biopolitical event as the moment when a certain kind of animal wagers in favour of its own existence and against another's life. Analogously, in Chapter 7, 'Cages and Mirrors: Mr. Palomar and the Albino Gorilla', Serenella Iovino analyses an episode from Italo Calvino's last novel, *Mr Palomar*, in which the title character visits the Barcelona Zoo and observes the albino gorilla Copito de Nieve. Palomar perceives the gorilla as a brother, sharing a dimension of solitude and need for a meaning, but the story also prompts a discussion on the very institution of zoological gardens and the parallel oppression of human and nonhuman subaltern subjects. Using biosemiotics, multispecies ethnography and postcolonial studies as theoretical coordinates, Iovino elicits the connections between Calvino's literary animals and the crisis of the Anthropocene biosphere.

A different kind of story is told by David Redmalm and Erica von Essen in Chapter 8, 'Bunny and Biopolitics: Killing, Culling and Caring for Rabbits'. Redmalm and von Essen analyse the human response to the increase of feral rabbits in the Stockholm area, 'profaning' the mythological tale of the human as the guardian of nature and highlighting the many dilemmas inherent to humans' attempt to maintain law and order in the chaos of nature. Synthesising Agamben's conceptualisation of the relationship between biopolitics and thanatopolitics with Esposito's affirmative biopolitics, Redmalm and von Essen examine the issues at stake when the interests of human and nonhuman populations collide in multispecies landscapes, and when humans ostensibly kill for conservation. Another tale of the thanatopolitical side of biopolitics is told by James K. Stanescu in Chapter 9, 'Deading Life and the Undying Animal: Necropolitics After the Factory Farm'. Starting off from the recent 'unproductive' killing of thousands of farm animals that could not be 'processed' due to the COVID-19 epidemic, Stanescu explores what he calls the ontology of 'deading life', that is, the 'necropolitics' of the biopolitical animals that should be alive but are somehow already dead, as in the factory farm. The alternative to deading life is finally identified in the 'undying', the life that always escapes the stratagems and violence of necropolitics.

The tales of biopolitics and animality are closed by Dinesh Wadiwel, who, in Chapter 10, 'Factory Farms for Fishes: Aquaculture, Biopolitics and Resistance', analyses the relatively new phenomenon of fish farms. In just a few decades, aquaculture has changed and refined the modalities of biopolitical domination over animals: intensification of domesticated fish production required the development of biopolitical techniques in the management of nonhuman life to extract, contain, regulate and slaughter sea animals, with attendant technological developments around fish pumps, sea pens, 'barcoding' and behavioural control. These changes, however, also opened different problems for power and resistance. Wadiwel finally examines the way in which the intensification of fish production within sea pens creates new problematics of visibility and control, and thus establishes different patterns for animal resistance and insubordination within the production system.

Finally, Part Three, 'Reconceptualising Biopolitics', includes four chapters focusing on how the animal question pushes the boundaries and redefines the scope of traditional biopolitical theories, calling for a reconceptualisation that might even lead us beyond biopolitics itself. In Chapter 11, 'Imagining Liberation beyond Biopolitics: The Biopolitical "War against Animals" and Strategies for Ending It', Zipporah Weisberg calls for a left-humanist self-overcoming and reconciliation with 'nature'. Weisberg argues that, to develop a robust politics of liberation, it could be useful to depart from Foucauldian and posthumanist approaches and turn instead to radical left humanist traditions (especially Marxist and socialist humanisms) and the critical theory of the early Frankfurt School. Whereas biopolitical theories highlight, among other things, the management of bodies, radical humanisms and critical theory redirect our focus to the *subject* who, as a self-unified (but not self-identical) entity, in negative (dialectical) relationship to the prevailing ideology, can, individually and collectively, forge a path to freedom (*from* violence and *to* self-actualisation).

In Chapter 12, Animal Magnetism: (Bio)Political Theologies Between the Creature and the Animal', Diego Rossello explores alternative accounts of political theology in the works of Eric Santner and Jacques Derrida, where the creature and the animal take centre stage. Whereas Santner explores the pressures and excitations of sovereignty over life, which render human beings creaturely, Derrida offers a genealogical account of the role played by the animal in the philosophical foundations of sovereign authority. Close as they are, the two accounts also differ insofar as the creature ultimately refers to a Creator, whereas the animal seems to remain naturalistic. A possible point of intersection between Santner's creature and Derrida's animal, Rossello argues, lies in the notion of 'animal magnetism'.

The category of 'creature' is also mobilised by Carlo Salzani in Chapter 13, 'Creaturely Biopolitics'. Noting that an immemorial geometry of verticality, named here the 'biopolitics of rectitude', captures and manages life through the opposition straight/crooked, and thus through exclusion, rejection, submission and normalisation, Salzani construes a counterproposal of a politics that deactivates instead the dichotomous opposition straight/crooked and proposes a politics of life that is inclusive and eludes dualisms and contrapositions. A 'creaturely biopolitics' would be a politics that approaches life, human and nonhuman alike, not to straighten it up or reject its crookedness, but rather by caring for its playful multiplicity of forms. Finally, in Chapter 16, 'A Dog's Life: From the Biopolitical Animal to the Posthuman', Felice Cimatti argues that the recent Covid-19 pandemic has shown that the traditional notion of biopolitics should be modified and refocused on a notion of corporeality that emphasises the vulnerability and fragility of the body, human and nonhuman alike. Drawing, like Calarco and Lemm, from Foucault's final theme of cynical life, Cimatti calls for a radical immanence that overcomes species barriers. The time that opens with the pandemic, he argues, is the time of a *humanimal* life, and the biopolitical animal is thus properly the posthuman, the condition of a subjectivity no longer defined by anthropocentrism and its sovereign logic.

Notes

1. Dinesh Wadiwel, 'Three Fragments from a Biopolitical History of Animals: Questions of Body, Soul, and the Body Politic in Homer, Plato, and Aristotle', *Journal for Critical Animal Studies* 6, no. 1 (2008): 19.
2. The masculine form (though Aristotle uses the neutral term *anthropos* and not the masculine *anèr*) is appropriate insofar as it emphasises the exclusionary logic that marks, from the very beginning, the construction of Western politics and subjectivity, which are based on the exclusion of women (here in Aristotle as in most of Western tradition) as also of many other categories.
3. Aristotle, *Historia Animalium*, Volume 1: Books I-X, ed. D. B. Balme (Cambridge: Cambridge University Press, 2002). See for example, R. G. Mulgan, 'Aristotle's Doctrine That Man Is a Political Animal', *Hermes* 102, no. 3 (1974): 438–45; David J. Depew, 'Humans and Other Political Animals in Aristotle's *History of Animals*', *Phronesis* 40, no. 2 (1995): 156–81; Cheryl E. Abbate, '"Higher" and "Lower" Political

Animals: A Critical Analysis of Aristotle's Account of the Political Animal', *Journal of Animal Ethics* 6, no. 1 (2016): 54–66; Refik Güremen, 'In What Sense Exactly Are Human Beings More Political According to Aristotle?', *Philosophy and Society* 29, no. 2 (2018): 153–316.
4. Aristotle, *Politics*, trans. Ernest Barker, ed. R. F. Stalley (Oxford: Oxford University Press, 1998). *Logos* denotes of course both conceptual abstraction and symbolic speech, both reason and language, so a possible translation could be 'rational language' (and not *any* language), or 'rational speech'.
5. For many critics but also for many supporters of biopolitical theories, this means that politics is always already biopolitics. Whereas for the critics this point invalidates the heuristic value of the concept itself, for the supporters it helps with reconceptualising the Western political tradition beyond Foucault's historically limited theorisation.
6. Giorgio Agamben, *Homo Sacer: Sovereign Power and Bare Life*, trans. Daniel Heller-Roazen (Stanford, CA: Stanford University Press, 1998), 7–8.
7. The brute who lives outside the polis is a human being who lives is a non-human way, that is, without *logos*. *Logos* means in fact a particular kind of relations with other human beings, a form of life centred around the 'perception of good and evil, of the just and the unjust', and the brute lives beyond these distinctions. Hence, the brute lives beyond ethics, is not an ethical subject, that is, she is not a *subject* at all, since what defines Western subjectivity are precisely the attributes of the Political Animal. The brute offers therefore also a glimpse into a possible different form of humanity – a glimpse that some chapters of this book will develop by analysing the Cynics' critique of the Political Animal.
8. Thomas Lemke, *Biopolitics: An Advanced Introduction*, trans. Eric Frederick Trump (New York: New York University Press, 2011), 32.
9. Michel Foucault, *The History of Sexuality, Volume I: An Introduction*, trans. Robert Hurley (New York: Pantheon Books, 1978), 143.
10. Lemke, *Biopolitics*, 2.
11. Wadiwel, 'Three Fragments from a Biopolitical History of Animals', 19. In his last seminar, *The Beast and the Sovereign* (vol. 1, trans. Geoffrey Bennington (Chicago, IL: The University of Chicago Press, 2009), 348–9), Derrida briefly returned to Aristotle's definition of 'political animal' in his criticism of Agamben's famous distinction between *zoē* and *bios*, biological life and political life (*Homo Sacer*, 1–2) – and of the concept of biopolitics more generally. Aristotle's passage shows for Derrida that life (*zōon*) has always been at the centre of politics, that politics has always been therefore *zoo-politics* (rather than bio-politics), a point also made by many critics of biopolitics. This does not invalidate, however, the exclusionary logic that structures Western politics and subjectivity as such – whatever one wants to

call it – a structure that Derrida was well aware and fiercely critical of (though he called it 'sacrificial logic').
12. For example, Abbate, '"Higher" and "Lower" Political Animals'.
13. Cary Wolfe, *Before the Law: Humans and Other Animals in a Biopolitical Frame* (Chicago, IL: University of Chicago Press, 2013), 10.
14. Wolfe, *Before the Law*, 46. See also Dinesh Wadiwel, *The War Against Animals* (Leiden: Brill – Rodopi, 2015), 27.
15. This expression has been often attributed to Foucault, notably by Agamben (*Homo Sacer*, 3), who misattributes it to the presentation of Foucault's 1977–8 course *Security, Territory, Population* as collected in the third volume of *Dits et écrits*, but is not to be found there or anywhere in his oeuvre. Jeffrey Nealon ('The Archaeology of Biopower: From Plant to Animal Life in *The Order of Things*', in *Biopower: Foucault and Beyond*, eds. Vernon W. Cisney and Nicolae Morar (Chicago, IL: The University of Chicago Press, 2016), 156–7, n26) shows that Agamben in fact quotes from the French translation of Hubert Dreyfus and Paul Rabinow's *Michel Foucault: Beyond Structuralism and Hermeneutics* (1982, trans. 1984), who refer to a question and answer session at Stanford where Foucault allegedly used this expression. It is interesting to note that in his translation of *Homo Sacer* Daniel Heller-Roazen renders the Italian '*animalizzazione*' as 'bestialisation', whereas Dreyfus, Rabinow and their French translator (Fabienne Durand Bogaert) all have 'animalisation/animalization'.
16. Wolfe, *Before the Law*, 46.
17. Wolfe, *Before the Law*, 10.
18. Nicole Shukin, *Animal Capital: Rendering Life in Biopolitical Times* (Minneapolis, MN: University of Minnesota Press, 2009), 9–10.
19. If we follow the idea that politics has always already been biopolitics, then this control of and mastery over the human biological body can be read as the very process of subjectivation, that is, the production of the Political Animal: it is by controlling the body and splitting it from the 'mind' that the human animal becomes a subject, a psychological 'I'. That is, the originary splitting between nature and culture is *internal* to the human itself (what Agamben (*The Open: Man and Animal*, trans. Kevin Attell (Stanford, CA: Stanford University Press, 2004)) has called the 'anthropological machine'). Cf. Felice Cimatti, *Unbecoming Human: Philosophy of Animality after Deleuze* (Edinburgh: Edinburgh University Press, 2020).
20. Wadiwel, *The War Against Animals*, 95.
21. Species blindness mirrors the gender blindness that has plagued Western (political) thought from the very beginning. Both are traditional, ingrained and very powerful biases construed upon the exclusionary logic of the Political Animal.
22. Michel Foucault, '*Society Must Be Defended*'. *Lectures at the Collège de France 1975–76*, trans. David Macey (New York: Picador, 2003), 255.

23. Cf. Wolfe, *Before the Law*, 43; Wadiwel, *The War Against Animals*, 52. In *Security, Territory, Population* (*Lectures at the Collège de France 1977–78*, trans. Graham Burchell (Basingstoke: Palgrave Macmillan, 2007, 75), Foucault marks the crossing of the 'threshold of modernity' precisely with the passage, in the common use, from defining humanity as *le genre humaine* (the human *genus*, usually translated into English as 'humankind') to *l'espèce humaine*, the human 'species'. The first to precisely describe the species in biological terms, as Foucault remarks in a note, was the English naturalist John Ray, who in his 1686 *Historia plantarum* defined the species as a 'set of individuals who, through reproduction, engender other individuals similar to themselves' (quoted in Foucault *Security, Territory, Population*, 85–6, n34). But it is with the Darwinian revolution that this terminology stabilised and the term entered common use. This means that species is, by definition, a biopolitical concept – perhaps the biopolitical concept par excellence.
24. Richard Twine, *Animals as Biotechnology: Ethics, Sustainability and Critical Animal Studies* (London: Routledge, 2015), 85.
25. The discussions of biopolitics and animality in feminist, antiracist, queer and decolonial contexts are rich and diversified and here we cannot offer more than a brief and incomplete exemplary list: Noreen Giffney and Myra J. Hird (eds.), *Queering the NonHuman* (Aldershot: Ashgate Press, 2008); Kalpana Seshadri, *HumAnimal: Race, Law, Language* (Minneapolis, MN: University of Minnesota Press, 2012); Mel Chen, *Animacies: Biopolitics, Racial Mattering, and Queer Affect* (Durham, NC: Duke University Press, 2012); Neel Ahuja, *Bioinsecurities: Disease Interventions, Empire, and the Government of Species* (Durham, NC: Duke University Press, 2016); Krithika Srinivasan, 'Posthumanist Animal Studies and Zoöpolitical Law', in *Critical Animal Studies: Towards Trans-species Social Justice*, eds. John Sorenson and Atsuko Matsuoka (Lanham, MA: Rowman & Littlefield International, 2018), 234–53; Zakiyyah Iman Jackson, *Becoming Human: Matter and Meaning in an Antiblack World* (New York: NYU Press, 2020).
26. For example, Wadiwel, *The War Against Animals*; Alex Mackintosh, 'Foucault's Menagerie: Cock Fighting, Bear Baiting, and the Genealogy of Human-Animal Power', in *Foucault and Animals*, eds. Matthew Chrulew and Dinesh Wadiwel (Leiden: Brill, 2017), 161–89.
27. Wadiwel, *The War Against Animals*, 94.
28. Peter Sloterdijk, 'Rule for the Human Park: A Response to Heidegger's "Letter on 'Humanism'"', in *Not Saved: Essays After Heidegger*, trans. Ian Alexander Moore and Christopher Turner (Cambridge: Polity Press, 2017), 193–216.
29. It is no accident that Heidegger uses the very same metaphor for a future, no longer humanistic 'Man': the 'shepherd of Being'. In both cases the point is to tame nature and animality.

30. See Wadiwel, *The War Against Animals*, 109–20. There is another Foucauldian concept that can be interpreted this way: *parrēsia*, saying the truth about oneself. The main function of this apparatus is simultaneously to institute the conscious self and to tame the animal body. From this perspective, *parrēsia* becomes the first internal biopolitical apparatus, whereby a living being 'learns' how to consider itself as a divided entity, separating the soul from the sinful and tempting flesh. It is also at this primordial level that a different relationship between animality and politics should be developed.
31. Rick Elmore, 'Biopolitics', in *The Edinburgh Companion to Animal Studies*, eds. Lynn Turner, Undine Sellbach and Ron Broglio (Edinburgh: Edinburgh University Press, 2017), 80.
32. Kristin Asdal and Tone Druglitrø, 'Modifying the Biopolitical Collective: The Law as a Moral Technology', in *Humans, Animals and Biopolitics: The More-than-human Condition*, eds. Kristin Asdal, Tone Druglitrø and Steve Hinchliffe (London: Routledge, 2017), 66–84.
33. Cf. Felice Cimatti, *Il postanimale. La natura dopo l'Antropocene* (Rome: DeriveApprodi, 2021); also Natalie Porter, 'One Health, Many Species: Towards a Multispecies Investigation of Bird Flu', in *Humans, Animals and Biopolitics*, eds. Asdal, Druglitrø and Hinchliffe, 136–51.
34. Philipp Sarasin, 'Mit Foucault die Pandemie verstehen?', *Geschichte der Gegenwart*, 25 March 2020, available at https://geschichtedergegenwart.ch/mit-foucault-die-pandemie-verstehen/ (accessed July 8, 2021).
35. Antonio Negri, *Reflections on Empire*, with contributions from Michael Hardt and Danilo Zolo, trans. Ed Emery (Cambridge: Polity Press, 2008), 60–78; Roberto Esposito, *Bios: Biopolitics and Philosophy*, trans. Timothy Campbell (Minneapolis, MN: University of Minnesota Press, 2008), 184–94, quotation at 181, emphasis in the original.
36. For example, Donna J. Haraway, *When Species Meet* (Minneapolis, MN: University of Minnesota Press, 2008); and Haraway, *Staying with the Trouble: Making Kin in the Chthulucene* (Durham, NC: Duke University Press, 2016); Anna Tsing, *Friction: An Ethnography of Global Connection* (Princeton, NJ: Princeton University Press, 2004); and Tsing, *The Mushroom at the End of the World: On the Possibility of Life in Capitalist Ruins* (Princeton, NJ: Princeton University Press, 2015); Thom van Dooren, *Flight Ways: Life and Loss at the Edge of Extinction* (New York: Columbia University Press, 2016); and van Dooren, *The Wake of Crows: Living and Dying in Shared Worlds* (New York: Columbia University Press, 2019).
37. For example, Matthew Chrulew and Dinesh Wadiwel, eds., *Foucault and Animals* (Leiden: Brill, 2017); Carlo Salzani, *Agamben and the Animal* (Newcastle upon Tyne: Cambridge Scholars, 2022).

38. Gwendolyn Blue and Melanie Rock, 'Trans-Biopolitics: Complexity in Interspecies Relations', *Health* 15, no. 4 (2010): 353–68. Cf. also the important queer and trans reconceptualisation of biopolitics: for example, Harlan Weaver, 'Trans Species', *Trans*gender Studies Quarterly* 1, nos. 1–2 (2014): 253–4; Eva Hayward and Jami Weinstein, 'Tranimalities in the Age of Trans* Life', *TSQ: Transgender Studies Quarterly* 2, no. 2 (2015): 195–208; Hyaesin Yoon, 'Feral Biopolitics: Animal Bodies and/as Border Technologies', *Tranimacies: Intimate Links between Animal and Trans* Studies*, special issue of *Angelaki: Journal of the Theoretical Humanities* 22, no. 2 (2017): 135–50.

39. Derrida, *The Beast and the Sovereign*, vol. 1, 348–9; see for example, Shukin, *Animal Capital*; Matthew Chrulew, 'Animals as Biopolitical Subjects', in *Foucault and Animals*, eds. Chrulew and Wadiwel, 222–38.

40. Cf. also Patricia Ticineto Clough and Craig Willse (eds.), *Beyond Biopolitics: Essays on the Governance of Life and Death* (Durham, NC: Duke University Press, 2011); James Stanescu, 'Beyond Biopolitics: Animal Studies, Factory Farms, and the Advent of Deading Life', *PhaenEx* 8, no. 2 (2013): 135–60; Alastair Hunt and Stephanie Youngblood (eds.), *Against Life* (Evanston, IL: Northwestern University Press, 2016).

41. Recent research in ethology and animal psychology seems to put into question this point, showing that some nonhuman animals are also able thereby to implicitly distinguish between just and unjust, fair and unfair and, importantly, that they base their social behaviours on these distinctions (for a brief overview of a by-now solid literature in relation to Aristotle, see Abbate, '"Higher" and "Lower" Political Animals'). But this is beside the point we want to make, which is not that the 'circle' of the Political Animal should be 'expanded' – by stating for example that some nonhuman beings possess the same capabilities and thus also 'qualify' as political animals – but rather that these premises should be disregarded and the entire structure dismantled.

42. Émile Benveniste, *Problems in General Linguistics: An Expanded Edition*, vol. 1, trans. Mary Elizabeth Meek (London: Hau Books, 2021).

43. Kari Weil, *Thinking Animals: Why Animal Studies Now?* (New York: Columbia University Press, 2012), 11–16.

44. Giorgio Agamben, *The Sacrament of Language: An Archaeology of the Oath*, trans. Adam Kotsko (Stanford, CA: Stanford University Press, 2011), 71.

45. It can be and has been argued that biopolitics entails different forms of subjectivation (e.g., Chrulew, 'Animals as Biopolitical Subjects'), but the discussion of this point exceeds the scope of this brief introduction.

Works Cited

Abbate. Cheryl E. '"Higher" and "Lower" Political Animals: A Critical Analysis of Aristotle's Account of the Political Animal'. *Journal of Animal Ethics* 6, no. 1 (2016): 54–66.

Agamben, Giorgio. *Homo Sacer: Sovereign Power and Bare Life*. Translated by Daniel Heller-Roazen. Stanford, CA: Stanford University Press, 1998.

Agamben, Giorgio. *The Open: Man and Animal*. Translated by Kevin Attell. Stanford, CA: Stanford University Press, 2004.

Agamben, Giorgio. *The Sacrament of Language: An Archaeology of the Oath*. Translated by Adam Kotsko. Stanford, CA: Stanford University Press, 2011.

Ahuja, Neel. *Bioinsecurities: Disease Interventions, Empire, and the Government of Species*. Durham, NC: Duke University Press, 2016.

Aristotle. *Politics*. Translated by Ernest Barker, edited by R. F. Stalley. Oxford: Oxford University Press, 1998.

Aristotle. *Historia Animalium*. Volume 1: Books I-X. Edited by D. B. Balme, prepared for publication by Allan Gotthelf. Cambridge: Cambridge University Press, 2002.

Asdal, Kristin, and Tone Druglitrø. 'Modifying the Biopolitical Collective: The Law as a Moral Technology'. In *Humans, Animals and Biopolitics: The More-than-human Condition*, edited by Kristin Asdal, Tone Druglitrø and Steve Hinchliffe, 66–84. London: Routledge, 2017.

Benveniste, Émile. *Problems in General Linguistics: An Expanded Edition*, Volume 1. Translated by Mary Elizabeth Meek. London: Hau Books, 2021.

Blue, Gwendolyn, and Melanie Rock. 'Trans-Biopolitics: Complexity in Interspecies Relations'. *Health* 15, no. 4 (2010): 353–68.

Chen, Mel. *Animacies: Biopolitics, Racial Mattering, and Queer Affect*. Durham, NC: Duke University Press, 2012.

Chrulew, Matthew. 'Animals as Biopolitical Subjects'. In *Foucault and Animals*, edited by Matthew Chrulew and Dinesh Wadiwel, 222–38. Leiden: Brill, 2017.

Chrulew, Matthew, and Dinesh Wadiwel, eds. *Foucault and Animals*. Leiden: Brill, 2017.

Cimatti, Felice. *Unbecoming Human: Philosophy of Animality after Deleuze*. Edinburgh: Edinburgh University Press, 2020.

Cimatti, Felice. *Il postanimale. La natura dopo l'Antropocene*. Rome: DeriveApprodi, 2021.

Depew, David J. 'Humans and Other Political Animals in Aristotle's *History of Animals*'. *Phronesis* 40, no. 2 (1995): 156–81.

Derrida, Jacques. *The Beast and the Sovereign*, volume 1. Translated by Geoffrey Bennington. Chicago, IL: The University of Chicago Press, 2009.

Elmore, Rick. 'Biopolitics'. In *The Edinburgh Companion to Animal Studies*, edited by Lynn Turner, Undine Sellbach and Ron Broglio, 80–93. Edinburgh: Edinburgh University Press, 2017.

Esposito, Roberto. *Bios: Biopolitics and Philosophy*. Translated by Timothy Campbell. Minneapolis, MN: University of Minnesota Press, 2008.

Foucault, Michel. *The History of Sexuality, Volume I: An Introduction*. Translated by Robert Hurley. New York: Pantheon Books, 1978.

Foucault, Michel. *Discipline and Punish: The Birth of the Prison*. Translated by Alan Sheridan. New York: Vintage Books, 1995.

Foucault, Michel. *'Society Must Be Defended'. Lectures at the Collège de France 1975–76*. Translated by David Macey. New York: Picador, 2003.

Foucault, Michel. *Security, Territory, Population. Lectures at the Collège de France 1977–78*. Translated by Graham Burchell. Basingstoke: Palgrave Macmillan, 2007.

Giffney, Noreen, and Myra J. Hird, eds. *Queering the NonHuman*. Aldershot: Ashgate Press, 2008.

Güremen, Refik. 'In What Sense Exactly Are Human Beings More Political According to Aristotle?' *Philosophy and Society* 29, no. 2 (2018): 153–316.

Haraway, Donna J. *When Species Meet*. Minneapolis, MN: University of Minnesota Press, 2008.

Haraway, Donna J. *Staying with the Trouble: Making Kin in the Chthulucene*. Durham, NC: Duke University Press, 2016.

Hayward, Eva, and Jami Weinstein. 'Tranimalities in the Age of Trans* Life'. *TSQ: Transgender Studies Quarterly* 2, no. 2 (2015): 195–208.

Hunt, Alastair, and Stephanie Youngblood, eds. *Against Life*. Evanston, IL: Northwestern University Press, 2016.

Jackson, Zakiyyah Iman. *Becoming Human: Matter and Meaning in an Antiblack World*. New York: NYU Press, 2020.

Lemke, Thomas. *Biopolitics: An Advanced Introduction*. Translated by Eric Frederick Trump. New York: New York University Press, 2011.

Mackintosh, Alex. 'Foucault's Menagerie: Cock Fighting, Bear Baiting, and the Genealogy of Human-Animal Power'. In *Foucault and Animals*, edited by Matthew Chrulew and Dinesh Wadiwel, 161–89. Leiden: Brill, 2017.

Mulgan, R. G. 'Aristotle's Doctrine That Man Is a Political Animal'. *Hermes* 102, no. 3 (1974): 438–45.

Nealon, Jeffrey T. 'The Archaeology of Biopower: From Plant to Animal Life in *The Order of Things*'. In *Biopower: Foucault and Beyond*, edited by Vernon W. Cisney and Nicolae Morar, 138–57. Chicago, IL: The University of Chicago Press, 2016.

Negri, Antonio. *Reflections on Empire*. With Contribution from Michael Hardt and Danilo Zolo. Translated by Ed Emery. Cambridge: Polity Press, 2008.

Porter, Natalie. 'One Health, Many Species: Towards a Multispecies Investigation of Bird Flu'. In *Humans, Animals and Biopolitics: The More-than-human Condition*, edited by Kristin Asdal, Tone Druglitrø and Steve Hinchliffe, 136–51. London: Routledge, 2017.

Salzani, Carlo. *Agamben and the Animal*. Newcastle upon Tyne: Cambridge Scholars, 2022.

Sarasin, Philipp. 'Mit Foucault die Pandemie verstehen?' *Geschichte der Gegenwart*, 25 March 2020, https://geschichtedergegenwart.ch/mit-foucault-die-pandemie-verstehen/ (accessed July 8, 2021).

Seshadri, Kalpana. *HumAnimal: Race, Law, Language*. Minneapolis, MN: University of Minnesota Press, 2012.

Shukin, Nicole. *Animal Capital: Rendering Life in Biopolitical Times*. Minneapolis, MN: University of Minnesota Press, 2009.

Sloterdijk, Peter. 'Rule for the Human Park: A Response to Heidegger's "Letter on 'Humanism'"'. In *Not Saved: Essays After Heidegger*, translated by Ian Alexander Moore and Christopher Turner, 193–216. Cambridge: Polity Press, 2017.

Srinivasan, Krithika. 'Posthumanist Animal Studies and Zoöpolitical Law'. In *Critical Animal Studies: Towards Trans-species Social Justice*, edited by John Sorenson and Atsuko Matsuoka, 234–53. Lanham, MA: Rowman & Littlefield International, 2018.

Stanescu, James. 'Beyond Biopolitics: Animal Studies, Factory Farms, and the Advent of Deading Life'. *PhaenEx* 8, no. 2 (2013): 135–60.

Ticineto Clough, Patricia, and Craig Willse, eds. *Beyond Biopolitics: Essays on the Governance of Life and Death*. Durham, NC: Duke University Press, 2011.

Tsing, Anna. *Friction: An Ethnography of Global Connection*. Princeton, NJ: Princeton University Press, 2004.

Tsing, Anna. *The Mushroom at the End of the World: On the Possibility of Life in Capitalist Ruins*. Princeton, NJ: Princeton University Press, 2015.

Twine, Richard. *Animals as Biotechnology: Ethics, Sustainability and Critical Animal Studies*. London: Routledge, 2015.

van Dooren, Thom. *Flight Ways: Life and Loss at the Edge of Extinction*. New York: Columbia University Press, 2016.

van Dooren, Thom. *The Wake of Crows: Living and Dying in Shared Worlds*. New York: Columbia University Press, 2019.

Wadiwel, Dinesh. 'Three Fragments from a Biopolitical History of Animals: Questions of Body, Soul, and the Body Politic in Homer, Plato, and Aristotle'. *Journal for Critical Animal Studies* 6, no. 1 (2008): 17–31.

Wadiwel, Dinesh. *The War Against Animals*. Leiden: Brill – Rodopi, 2015.

Weaver, Harlan. 'Trans Species'. *Trans*gender Studies Quarterly* 1, nos. 1–2 (2014): 253–4.

Weil, Kari. *Thinking Animals: Why Animal Studies Now?* New York: Columbia University Press, 2012.

Wolfe, Cary. *Before the Law: Humans and Other Animals in a Biopolitical Frame.* Chicago, IL: University of Chicago Press, 2013.

Yoon, Hyaesin. 'Feral Biopolitics: Animal Bodies and/as Border Technologies'. *Tranimacies: Intimate Links between Animal and Trans* Studies*, special issue of *Angelaki: Journal of the Theoretical Humanities* 22, no. 2 (2017): 135–50.

PART I
THE ANIMAL OF BIOPOLITICS

1 | Turning Back to Nature: Foucault and the Practice of Animality
Matthew Calarco

Introduction

Early in his intellectual career and before becoming an established figure in his own right, Michel Foucault helped prepare a translation of Swiss psychiatrist Ludwig Binswanger's *Traum und Existenz* with his colleague Jacqueline Verdeaux.[1] Foucault had just recently come to Paris at this time to teach classes at the Ecole Normale at Louis Althusser's behest, and Verdeaux – a longtime friend of the Foucault family – was tasked with looking out for Michel.[2] Verdeaux, who had an independent and longstanding interest in psychiatry, began the translation of Binswanger's text on her own. As she pursued the project in more depth, though, Verdeaux realised that rendering its dense philosophical vocabulary into French would require outside assistance. It was in view of such assistance that she turned to Foucault, as she knew he had a serious interest in the theoretical and philosophical figures with which Binswanger's text was in dialogue (thinkers ranging from Sigmund Freud and Carl Jung to Martin Heidegger and Karl Jaspers). Foucault was delighted to help and worked regularly with Verdeaux on the translation (although Verdeaux is the only one officially credited as translator). Published in 1954, the translated volume was accompanied by notes and a lengthy Introduction written by Foucault.

While working on the translation, Verdeaux and Foucault took trips together and travelled to visit Binswanger during his vacation in the scenic southern Alps. Verdeaux and Foucault became close friends during these travels (Foucault would refer to Verdeaux as his 'wife' when queried); they studied artworks together and visited sites dotted with magnificent landscapes and scenery.

Verdeaux recalls, however, that while Foucault showed a great interest in the art, he was utterly uninterested in the natural world. Whenever Verdeaux urged Foucault to look at a particularly beautiful landscape or a bit of natural scenery, he disregarded her plea. Verdeaux goes so far as to say that Foucault 'detested nature', and that when pressed to look at natural scenery he would turn around and make a 'great show of walking off toward the road, saying "My back is turned to it"'.[3]

This general distaste and disregard for the more-than-human world characteristic of the young Foucault is clearly on display in the bulk of Foucault's later activism and published writings as well. Whether we examine the archaeologies, the genealogies or the final texts on practices of the self, Foucault's writings and activism remain by and large anthropocentric in orientation. In employing the term anthropocentric here, I intend more than a mere 'illogical prejudice' in favour of *Homo sapiens*.[4] Anthropocentrism denotes, rather, an entire system and form of life predicated on a strong opposition and hierarchical ranking of the human (understood as a subject position rather than as a biological reality) over and against the animal and other Others (including the nonhuman natural world as well as de-humanised and sub-humanised human beings). More than just an ideology or set of beliefs, this oppositional and hierarchical schema derives from and reinforces a wide range of practices, institutions and structures that enact and sustain complex relations of power between the human and its Others. That Foucault's work should be characterised as being 'by and large' anthropocentric but not entirely or dogmatically so, speaks to the fact that his work stands in a complicated relationship to anthropocentrism. For, even as Foucault often turned his back on both the ontological reality and violence carried out against nature and animals, his work also indicates a keen awareness of the ways in which those human beings who do not accede to the subject position of the human (and it would be fair to say that this 'set' of beings constitutes his primary concern) exist in a series of complex and overlapping relations with nonhuman others of various sorts.

Governing Animals

Unfortunately, however, Foucault rarely developed his central concepts or critical frameworks primarily in view of examining such connections. With regard to his work on disciplinary power and biopolitics in particular, Foucault explicitly frames his approach in exclusively human-centred terms. Consider, for example, the classic statements in which Foucault examines the subtle distinctions and relations between modern forms of discipline and biopower.[5]

In describing the transition from sovereign power (with its characteristic trait of taking life and letting live) to the emergence of discipline and biopower (with their contrasting characteristic traits of controlling and regulating life), Foucault famously discerns a fundamental change in how power circulates throughout human society. He suggests that, with the advent of regimes of discipline and biopower, killing human individuals or letting them live still serve as ways in which political power is exercised, but that the interests of power shift increasingly in the direction of fostering human life, taking charge of it, and trying to master and form it towards certain ends.

Although the interest that modern forms of power exhibit in controlling and regulating life has by no means been restricted to human bodies (a point to which I will return below), Foucault's analysis almost always remains strictly within that anthropocentric frame. Thus, when articulating the precise mechanisms whereby discipline and biopower circulate, he underscores the point that it is *human* lives in particular that are the focus of his analysis. As power becomes increasingly interested in the control of life, the disciplinary pole of this process, Foucault suggests, centres on

> the body as machine: its disciplining, the optimization of its capabilities, the extortion of its forces, the parallel increase of its usefulness and its docility, its integration into systems of efficient and economic controls, all this was ensured by the procedures of power that characterized the *disciplines:* an *anatomo-politics of the human body.*[6]

In terms of the second, biopolitical pole of development, Foucault suggests that it emerges 'somewhat later' and is

> focused on the species body, the body imbued with the mechanics of life and serving as the basis of the biological processes: propagation, births and mortality, the level of health, life expectancy and longevity, with all the conditions that can cause these to vary. Their supervision was effected through an entire series of interventions and *regulatory controls: a biopolitics of the population.*[7]

Thus, instead of being aimed solely at individual human bodies, biopolitics shifts the exercise of power to the administering, 'massifying' and 'regularising' of large groups of human beings, extending its purview even to whole populations – or, to use the language of the lecture course *'Society Must Be Defended'*, to 'man-as-species'.[8] Despite the important shift in the locus and mechanisms of power that Foucault highlights here, the frame within which he operates remains focused exclusively in both instances on human beings and the varied process of their subjectification.

While few readers would dispute the importance of examining the ways in which discipline and biopower function among human individuals and populations, many critics have persuasively argued that an exclusive focus on how power circulates in the human register alone is insufficient for understanding either the source or extent of such power. In this vein, theorists and activists who work in the field of critical animal studies have recently taken an acute interest in reconsidering the scope and extent of biopolitics in particular, as it is clear that a focus on controlling and regulating large animal populations is of crucial importance for understanding how contemporary animal industries function and how they prefigure and reinforce the deployment of biopolitics among human populations. To this end, Richard Twine has demonstrated the widespread presence of biopower in the exploitation and manipulation of animal genetics in the biotechnology industry[9]; Matthew Chrulew has shown how biopolitical logic is operative in the management of the reproductive practices of endangered species[10]; and Stephen Thierman[11] and Chloë Taylor[12] have examined the biopolitical dimensions of factory farming and the agricultural industry. The examples could be multiplied.[13] What the bulk of this research on animal biopolitics underscores is the manner in which biopower extends its malignant reign far beyond the sphere of interhuman relations and deep into the lives and deaths of animals. Just as biopolitics on Foucault's analysis marks a shift in modernity toward the management of human populations toward the administrative ends of the state and economy, much of this work on animal biopolitics suggests a similar shift can be marked in the treatment of animals. No longer are animals merely hunted in the wild or farmed in small numbers in domesticated settings; today, animals are managed in massive numbers in highly technical, scientific ways in order to extract maximum profit from their lives, flesh and even their left-over body parts.[14]

Other theorists have sought a more complicated and equivocal engagement with biopolitics, noting its negative effects on animals and human beings but also suggesting that biopolitics might be reconstituted in more affirmative terms. The most influential work of this sort derives from Cary Wolfe.[15] In line with the approach on animal biopolitics just discussed, Wolfe hopes to place consideration of both human and animal existence squarely at the core of biopolitical thought. In situating both groups within what he refers to as a 'biopolitical frame', Wolfe demonstrates that biopolitics captures human beings and animals in sometimes overlapping, sometimes distinct ways. Correlatively, he suggests there can be no single, unified way of developing resistance to biopolitical violence. To be effective, biopolitical resistance must be differentiated and strategically refined. Toward this end, Wolfe experiments with the idea of an affirmative biopolitics that views the joint capture of human and animal life as a challenge and an opportunity to think through a more expansive ethics, one that heals some of the fractures that harmful biopower creates within and among human and animal life.

Wolfe's point about the importance of accounting for the differing effects of biopolitics on human beings and animals can be extended in a different direction to suggest that a biopolitical approach is, by itself, an insufficient framework for scholars and activists interested in understanding how power and resistance circulate among animals. James Stanescu argues in this vein that even though biopolitical frameworks uncover important ways in which biopower is applied to animals, it is equally crucial to attend to the specific history of the capture and control of animal populations.[16] Stanescu thus calls for

> more theorizing from the specific horror of the lives of other animals. For a long time now, we have analogized violence to animals to intrahuman violence. We have talked of murder, genocide, and slavery, and surely these terms have great rhetorical value. At the same time, philosophically, it is not enough to say that concepts produced to understand intrahuman violence can simply have the anthropocentrism removed and deployed for animal studies. The agricultural power and thanatonomy of the factory farm fabricate a new mode of being, a new production of death and life.[17]

In brief, then, even if we accept that amending the Foucauldian notion of biopolitics to include the capture of animal life is an essential task, such an amendment should (if we follow Stanescu's suggestion) be understood as but a partial and limited strategy for diagnosing how animals are affected by systems of power in contemporary society. In order to grasp the workings of power in the dominant human institutions in which animal life and death unfold today, it will be necessary to develop frameworks that are not restricted in advance to a biopolitical frame.

Resisting Animals

I take it, though, that the ultimate point of Foucault's various diagnoses of power (whether disciplinary, biopolitical or otherwise) is to discern points of resistance in regard to those power regimes, such that other possibilities for living well might come into view. It would thus be equally important for us to attend to this 'counter' register of his thought and consider both its anthropocentric limitations as well as its nonanthropocentric promise. In general, in regard to techniques of resistance (as with his critical diagnoses of power) Foucault tended to overlook the specificity of animals and their particular modes of resistance. Yet, there is an important exception to this anthropocentric trend found in Foucault's late work on the Cynics that I want to focus on at more length in what follows. But in order to appreciate how this late analysis forms an exception to the general thrust of Foucault's work on this theme, it will be helpful to consider briefly the basic contours of his more common, more anthropocentric approach.

Foucault is perhaps best known (and notoriously so, to some) for denying that there is an outside to power; furthermore, he suggests that any form of resistance to the established order which claims it is completely removed from or stands above power's machinations would be in bad faith. Thus, even as Foucault is clearly sympathetic to and actively involved in a number of radical and liberatory struggles, he always insists that one should never uncritically align oneself with such struggles but should instead always maintain a willingness to interrogate their presuppositions and tendencies to reassert problematic forms of power. Politics for Foucault is fundamentally a matter of deploying one form of power against another, not as a way of seeking a pure space outside the play of agonistics, but rather in view of playing that agonistic game in a way that minimises domination and maximises potentialities as much as possible. Yet Foucault also recognises that the play of power and the general *agon* that irreducibly structures human political life can sometimes take forms that are so restrictive and so dominating that one has little choice (if any meaningful notion of agency and living well are at stake) but to seek to abolish or radically limit them. The point of resistance to total domination of this sort is thus not to get outside of power but to deploy alternative kinds of power against those forms in order to return living beings to the contest or 'game' of life. Seeking a return to the game of life does not, from a Foucauldian perspective, aim at guaranteeing individuals a secure and safe existence, but it does aim at making possible the pursuit of worthwhile ways of life that are precluded by mechanisms and institutions of total domination.

Foucault's important notions of counter-conduct and collective resistance are intended, in part, to explore how overturning such forms of domination might be possible. Although Foucault never examined contemporary pro-animal politics in this vein, it is useful to consider such politics as an effort to abolish (or at least radically limit the presence of) institutions that try to bring animals under regimes of total domination. Much of what happens in institutions such as factory farms, zoos, experimental laboratories, breeding facilities and so on can be rightly understood as an attempt to achieve such domination over animals.[18] Animal rights activists, coupled with the discourses and organisations that have arisen around critical animal studies and related approaches, aim (I believe correctly and justly) to abolish and limit these institutions and modes of power as much as is possible, under the assumption that there is little to salvage in these forms of human–animal interactions.

In seeking to abolish these institutions of domination, it is sometimes suggested that pro-animal activists are effectively relegating the animals that populate them to the status of mere museum pieces, kept alive and on display for human onlookers but deprived of any meaningful or purposeful role to play with their lives. Following Foucauldian logic, however, the obvious response to this sort of critique of liberatory activism is: (1) to deny the naturalisation of institutionalised forms of human–animal relations (there is nothing inevitable about our using animals as objects of research, as commodities and so on), and (2) to reject the notion that animals have a fixed *telos* (there is no reason to assume that animals can live their lives and die their deaths in only one fixed, reductive way). To militate against institutions of absolute domination can be more fairly and more accurately described, I would suggest, as a version of Foucault's counter-conduct – that is, as an attempt to allow animals to return to the game of life and its agonistics. Radical pro-animal activists are not generally asking for a sanitised or utterly secure future for living animals, but are instead trying to open up additional potentials for animal life and death beyond the reductive and one-dimensional modes of life and death offered by the established order.

The Practice of Animality

The other major approach to resistance, developed most fully in Foucault's last works, concerns what he calls an *aesthetics of existence*. This set of strategies concerning self-formation has the effect of inverting our perspective on Foucault's earlier analyses of discipline and biopolitics, allowing us to see the flip-side or counter-side to these modes of power. Whereas Foucault understood disciplinary power and biopower to constitute the very being of human subjects from within, he was also interested in the processes whereby subjects came to counter-constitute or counter-form new modes of subjectivity that allowed for resistance to normalisation. Consistent with Foucault's general approach to the machinations of power, these latter processes of re-subjectification are situated in and among discourses and regimes of power and are not to be found in a site totally pure of power's effects. Rather, re-subjectification uses whatever tools and potentials are at hand in order to craft an alternative way of life that is, to be sure, constrained and shaped by power but not utterly determined by its reigning modes.

It is in his consideration of historical practices of re-subjectification that Foucault changes course from his previous work and turns back to nature in a certain way. In considering ancient Greek philosophical practices of the self and the art of living, Foucault begins to glimpse the ways in which reconstituting relations with the more-than-human world might play a critical role in our becoming something other than compliant subjects of discipline and biopower. We see this shift towards a nonanthropocentric (or perhaps less anthropocentric) approach most visibly in Foucault's very last lecture course, *The Courage of Truth*, and particularly in the latter part of the course focusing on the Cynics.[19]

Readers familiar with Foucault's previous courses at the Collège de France will recognise that in this final lecture course he is extending his previous analyses of *parrēsia* (frank speech) as they appear in the context of ancient practices of the self. More precisely, this lecture course belongs to the general trajectory of Foucault's work in which he aims to interweave his analyses of modes of veridiction, techniques of governmentality and practices of care of the self in order to better understand the co-constitution of power and resistance.[20] The Cynics belong to the trajectory Foucault has traced in previous lecture courses inasmuch as they place *parrēsia* at the very centre of the philosophical life;[21] furthermore, they stand in fundamental agreement with the ancient tradition in viewing the philosophical life as a pursuit of the 'true life' (*alethēs bios*). The true life in this context is a life that goes well beyond a search for truth in the epistemological sense, and even beyond speaking frankly and boldly in the face of the reigning doxa. The true life is a far more expansive ideal and includes committing to an entire way of life that is 'true' in the sense of living a life that is, as Foucault notes, unconcealed, unadulterated, direct and unwavering in both its form and content.[22] Foucault tracks these four aspects of the true life throughout various dialogues of Plato in order to show that they are by no means original with the Cynics; and we could, to be sure, easily find parallels among the Peripatetics, Epicureans, Stoics and other ancient philosophical schools. All of this serves to suggest, then, that the Cynic quest for the true life is a well-worn theme in the ancient context and that the Cynics themselves should not be characterised (as is sometimes suggested by their more dismissive philosophical critics) as being situated entirely outside the boundaries of philosophy 'proper'.

At the same time, Foucault wants to impress upon his audience that the Cynics and their specific practice of the true life constitute something distinctive in relation to the preceding philosophical tradition as well as to the contemporary milieu in which it emerges; thus, rather than marking a complete rupture or absolute break with the tradition, Foucault suggests that the Cynic way of life establishes a certain 'carnivalesque' continuity with it.[23] For the Cynics enact a simultaneously dual and somewhat contradictory gesture of identification and dis-identification with the tradition: on the one hand, as we have noted they take up in a fairly straightforward and continuous manner classical themes and motifs surrounding frank speech, reason, the true life and so on; on the other hand, they push these familiar themes and motifs 'to their extreme consequence', up to the point where they seem to morph into their exact opposite.[24] This is why Foucault suggests that Cynics make traditional philosophy 'grimace', make it smirk dismissively and squirm embarrassedly, in an effort to avoid the consequences of its own commitments when those commitments are pushed to their utmost logical consequence.[25]

One clue that the Cynics are engaged in this carnivalesque and paradoxical relation to the tradition is that, even as they gladly accept the name and calling of being philosophers, they do so *as* dogs. Whatever the ultimate origin of the label of 'Cynic', there is no doubt that Cynic philosophers were routinely characterised as dogs and that they came to assume and even affirm this label even though it was clearly intended by its users as an epithet.[26] Thus, with the Cynics we encounter the scandalous gesture of linking the practice of philosophy directly and tightly with dogs and with animal life more generally. In making this connection, what the Cynics claim to discern, and what other philosophical schools would seem to overlook by Cynic standards, is the fact that the true and good life is to be found most clearly, most exemplarily not among one's fellow human beings (neither among the *kaloi kagathoi* nor with the individual sage) but among dogs and other animals.

Foucault clearly recognises and underscores the tight link that Cynics establish between dog-ness (and animality in general) and the true life. In assuming the *bios kunikos*, the dog life, Foucault notes that the Cynic philosopher takes up the task of living the true life in a way that she or he believes to be the fullest, most genuine way to do so. Thus, in choosing a dog's life, the Cynic is not simply choosing a lifestyle for its shock value or to be deliberately ironic; rather, at bottom, the Cynic believes – and this is the profound insight that lies at the heart of their philosophy – that dogs and other animals have something to teach us about what it means to live true and good lives. To rephrase this notion in Foucault's terminology, the Cynics would have us think about practicing the art of life and re-subjectification by looking for exemplars not just (or even primarily) among our fellow human beings or interhuman relations, but among dogs, animals, animality and the more-than-human world more broadly. In practicing a 'dog's life' beyond the dictates of the dominant culture, the Cynic philosopher encourages those individuals who are oriented primarily toward human culture (*nomos*) and who have turned their backs on nature (*physis*), to turn back to nature and to find the energies, relations and potentials for living well within that alternative register.

Foucault further underscores these close connections between philosophy and animality in his discussion of the third aspect of the true life, that is, the true life in the sense of living a direct or straight life. As Foucault notes, the directness of the true life was generally understood by most ancient philosophical schools, as it was by the Cynics, to be found in living *kata physin*, according to nature – but the meaning of *physis*, or nature, varies considerably, depending on the school. Among the Stoics, for example, living according to nature generally meant living according to the proper nature *of the human*, a nature that was indexed to the divine *logos* that providentially structures the cosmos. For the Cynics, however, living according to nature meant something more akin to living according to the rhythms and dictates of more-than-human nature – which is to say, to animals and to the natural world that trouble the boundaries of the all-too-human *polis* and its institutions. Thus, the Cynics reject nearly all common cultural conventions and taboos as anti-natural and as being in opposition to the true life. Questions about how best to eat, have sex, dress, spend one's days and nights and so on were, for the Cynics, to be answered not by cultural tradition or by convention (*nomos*) but by examining how animals carry out these actions and experimenting with their ways of life in order to discern which ones allowed them to flourish.

Here we can see more clearly why the Cynics are by no means recommending a simple return to some 'original' or 'pure' human nature but are instead advocating a transformative aesthetics of existence that re-forms our 'second', culturally acquired natures. This process of re-formation and re-subjectification both (a) turns us *inside out* (in the sense of taking what is on hand with our current form of subjectivity and developing ascetic practices modelled on animal life that can transform that subjectivity in the direction of a true, genuine and flourishing life), and (b) turns us *outward* (in the sense of shifting our perceptions, loyalties and loves towards animals, animality and the more-than-human world). Foucault is correct to suggest, then, that the Cynic disposition towards animality, while making use of familiar philosophical themes having to do with the true life, flourishing and living according to nature, is ultimately 'odd and scandalous' in the ancient context.[27] Here, again, he demonstrates his keen awareness that what we today call 'anthropocentrism' was already operative and explicit in ancient Greek culture at the time of the Cynics, and that animals and animality represent one of the key sites of exclusion upon which the human is founded. As Foucault explains:

in ancient thought animality played the role of absolute point of differentiation for the human being. It is by distinguishing itself from animality that the human being asserted and manifested its humanity. Animality was always, more or less, a point of repulsion for the constitution of man as a rational and human being.[28]

What makes the Cynics' form of life particularly scandalous is not just their affirmation of the irreducible animality of the human, since recognition of the embodied existence we share with animals was not uncommon in philosophical and cultural discourses of that time (or in our own, for that matter). Rather, what made the Cynics scandalous for the ancients, and why they remain scandalous for us today, is that they give priority of place to animals in terms of the locus of life's meaning, value and orientation. For the Cynics, animals recall us to our animality, of course, but they also call us out of ourselves and towards another, inhuman and more-than-human world and set of ideals. In order to live true lives – truly flourishing, truly good lives – the Cynics believe we must become something other than human, other than who have become as human subjects; in brief, we must become-animal. In one of Foucault's most insightful comments on the Cynics, he notes that such becoming-animal is not something to which we revert but is instead presented to us by the Cynics as a challenge and as an ideal, as something we have to strive to attain through ascetic practices:

> Animality is not a given; it is a duty. Or rather, it is a given, offered to us directly by nature, but at the same time it is a challenge to be continually taken up. [. . .] Animality is a way of being with regard to oneself, a way of being which must take the form of a constant test. Animality is an exercise. It is a task for oneself and at the same time a scandal for others.[29]

**

Foucault's extended engagement with the Cynics in his final lecture course – an engagement that is animated by a manifest and profound admiration for this philosophy and way of life[30] – can be read, with some justice, as marking an opening onto a rather different philosophical orientation from the anthropocentric one that structured most of his career. As I mentioned at the outset of this chapter, although Foucault's anthropocentrism is never entirely dogmatic and shows moments of keen insight into its machinations, at no point in his work does he approach anything like the enthusiastic engagement with a thought of animals and animality we find in this final course. In these lectures, it is as if

Foucault glimpsed an entire field of research – a set of potentials for contesting the biopolitical present and for living differently – that had largely eluded him up to this point. The Cynic way of life is one of the earliest and most profound attempts to live in radical opposition to the dominant social order; and perhaps more than any other philosophy in the West, the Cynics were among the first to recognise just how thoroughly mainstream culture tries to capture and constitute our souls and how rigorous and sustained the effort must be to twist free (even minimally) from its effects. These were matters of profound importance to Foucault, and he was no doubt taken both by the Cynic diagnosis of the ills of *nomos* as well as their unique understanding and practice of how to bring *physis* (in the form of animality and animal life) to bear on those limits.

We have no way of knowing what the effects of discovering these alternative registers of resistance and existence might have had on Foucault's subsequent thought. How might Cynic philosophy have informed and altered his historical analyses of governmentality and related modes of power? What possibilities might he have uncovered for reconstituting and redeploying Cynic *askēsis* in the present? I will not endeavour to answer these questions on Foucault's behalf, but I would like to venture my own suggestion about how these themes might be taken up in our own time. If we bear in mind the terrain of biopolitics and the forms of counter-conduct and practices of the self that Foucault studied as possible modes of resistance; and if we do so in view of the insights Foucault achieved with regard to the ancient Cynics and possible variations on Cynic philosophy in a contemporary context, then I would suggest that one of the most pressing tasks today is not so much the formulation of an affirmative biopolitics (a project that certainly has its merits) as the articulation and practice of a *generalised ethology*. As we have seen, what the Cynics practiced, and what made their way of life so shocking for their contemporaries, is a radical turn outward in terms of attention, love and loyalty to the animal and more-than-human world. The Cynics indexed their sense of self, sociality and place to radically inhuman referents; and they did so in such a way as to displace the dominance and significance of the established order. In this sense, the Cynics were (at least in the received philosophical tradition of the West[31]) the inaugurators of a 'deep' ethological approach to the good life that seeks to rebuild human individuals from the ground up and to re-form and re-orient their most basic social and existential relations in view of other animals.[32]

To characterise the Cynic way of life as a generalised ethology (from the Greek, *ēthos* + *logia*) is particularly fitting, as the term *ēthos* and the closely related notion of *ethos* carry the senses of the various philosophical and existential registers of life on which the Cynics most concentrated.[33] They were interested in an aesthetics of existence that functioned to re-form and reconstitute: (a) one's individual *ethos*, or character and sense of self; (b) our collective *ēthos* in the form of shared social customs and form of life; and (c) our *ēthos* in the sense of the abode we inhabit. The term ethology also means for us, today, the careful study of animals not in a laboratory setting but in their natural habitats and in and among their kin. The Cynics believed that it was through just such observation of animals in their own abodes and habitats, in their own natural ways of life and daily rhythms, that we might learn how to resist the dominant culture and learn to live otherwise. Whether it was through observing the frugality of a mouse or the fiercely loyal friendship of a dog, the Cynics found continuing inspiration for a life lived counter to the dominant culture among animals and nature. To resist the biopolitical present in which we find ourselves, we will no doubt have to experiment with a range of tactics, strategies and forms of counter-conduct. But in carrying out these experiments, there must also be a thorough reckoning with a culture that has encouraged us to detest the more-than-human world and turn our backs on it. With the Cynics and with the late Foucault in mind, we might see our task today as one of turning back to nature and seeking, in the words of Michel Serres, to 'reinvent the contemporary meaning' of living *kata physin*.[34]

Notes

1. Ludwig Binswanger, *Le rêve et l'existence*, trans. Jacqueline Verdeaux (Paris: Desclée de Brouwer, 1954). A full account of the publishing details of this volume can be found in Stuart Elden, 'Foucault as Translator of Binswanger and von Weizsäcker', *Theory, Culture & Society* (2020): 1–26. https://doi.org/10.1177/0263276420950459.
2. I am indebted to Didier Eribon, *Michel Foucault*, trans. Betsy Wing (Cambridge, MA: Harvard University Press, 1991) for the biographical details in these opening paragraphs.
3. Eribon, *Michel Foucault*, 46.
4. The concept of speciesism in its classical form (as articulated, for example, by Richard Ryder and Peter Singer) is typically defined as an 'illogical prejudice' in favour of the human species over other animal species. I use the concept of anthropocentrism in contradistinction to speciesism in order to highlight what I take to be a series of phenomena and relations that include but go well beyond prejudice.
5. Here I have in mind the remarks made in Part Five ('Right of Death and Power over Life') of Michel Foucault, *The History of Sexuality, vol. 1*, trans. Robert Hurley (New York: Random House, 1978).

6. Foucault, *The History of Sexuality*, vol. 1, 139.
7. Foucault, *The History of Sexuality*, vol. 1.
8. Michel Foucault, *'Society Must Be Defended': Lectures at the Collège de France 1975–1976*, trans. David Macey (New York: Picador, 2003), 242. It is worth noting that the various passages in which Foucault uses this language of 'man-as-species' in *'Society Must Be Defended'* demonstrate that neither the deployment of biopower nor its contestation are grounded on a simple 'speciesism' – which is to say, despite the fact that biopolitics on Foucault's account circulates at the meta-levels of human populations and of human beings as a whole, the ways in which such modes of power operate in those registers is anything but uniform across the species as a whole.

    Thus, when Foucault notes that 'unlike discipline, which is addressed to bodies, the new nondisciplinary power [of biopolitics] is applied not to man-as-body but to the living man, to man-as-living-being; ultimately, if you like, to man-as-species' (242), we might be tempted to think that biopolitics is indiscriminately and uniformly applied to the human species. But in later passages, Foucault refines his notion of biopolitics and complicates this picture in order to underscore the point that power which operates on large groups and populations is entirely consistent with – and even serves as the precondition for – fragmenting these groups and populations in various ways. Along these lines, Foucault writes that biopolitics allows power to treat a given 'population as a mixture of races, or to be more accurate, to treat the species, to subdivide the species it controls, into the subspecies known, precisely, as races. That is the first function of racism: to fragment, to create caesuras within the biological continuum addressed by biopower' (255). It is in such passages that Foucault, despite his general anthropocentric tendencies with regard to nonhuman others, clearly recognises that racism is (paradoxically) an anthropocentrism.

9. Richard Twine, *Animals as Biotechnology: Ethics, Sustainability, and Critical Animal Studies* (Washington, DC: Earthscan, 2010).
10. Matthew Chrulew, 'Managing Love and Death at the Zoo: The Biopolitics of Endangered Species Preservation', *Australian Humanities Review* (2011), accessed 1 November, 2022, http://australianhumanitiesreview.org/2011/05/01/managing-love-and-death-at-the-zoo-the-biopolitics-of-endangered-species-preservation. See also Chrulew's 'Animals in Biopolitical Theory: Between Agamben and Negri', *New Formations* 76 (2012): 53–67.
11. Stephen Thierman, 'Apparatuses of Animality: Foucault Goes to a Slaughterhouse', *Foucault Studies* 9 (2010): 89–110.
12. Chloë Taylor, 'Foucault and Critical Animal Studies: Genealogies of Agricultural Power', *Philosophy Compass* 8, no. 6 (2013): 539–51.

13. For an expert overview of this scholarship, see Dinesh Wadiwel, 'Biopolitics', in *Critical Terms for Animal Studies*, ed. Lori Gruen (Chicago, IL: University of Chicago Press, 2018), 79–98.
14. Nicole Shukin, *Animal Capital: Rendering Life in Biopolitical Times* (Minneapolis: University of Minnesota Press, 2009).
15. Cary Wolfe, *Before the Law: Humans and Other Animals in a Biopolitical Frame* (Chicago, IL: University of Chicago Press, 2013).
16. James Stanescu, 'Beyond Biopolitics: Animal Studies, Factory Farms, and the Advent of Deading Life', *PhaenEx* 8, no. 2 (2013): 135–60.
17. Stanescu, 'Beyond Biopolitics', 155.
18. That such attempts can and often do fail suggests that animals have their own forms of resistance and agency worth considering. Taking animal resistance and agency into account also serves to recast the stakes of pro-animal politics, challenging the widespread notion that this politics is little more than a paternalistic gesture that seeks to help animals who 'have no voice' (as the saying goes) and allowing it instead to be seen as a form of support for and alliance with more-than-human resistance and agency. On these points, see Jason Hribal, *Fear of the Animal Planet: The Hidden History of Animal Resistance* (Oakland, CA: AK Press, 2010).
19. Michel Foucault, *The Courage of Truth. The Government of Self and Others II: Lectures at the Collège de France 1983–1984*, trans. Graham Burchell (New York: Palgrave Macmillan, 2011).
20. Foucault, *The Courage of Truth*, 8.
21. See, for example, the oft-cited *chreia* involving Diogenes: 'Asked what was the most beautiful thing in the world, he said, "Freedom of speech"'. [ἐρωτηθεὶς τί κάλλιστον ἐν ἀνθρώποις, ἔφη, 'παρρησία'.] (Diogenes Laertius, *Lives of the Eminent Philosophers*, trans. Pamela Mensch (New York: Oxford University Press, 2018), 6.69).
22. Foucault, *The Courage of Truth*, 218–19.
23. Foucault, *The Courage of Truth*, 228.
24. Foucault, *The Courage of Truth*, 227.
25. Foucault, *The Courage of Truth*, 227.
26. For more on the use of the dog label among the Cynics, see Marie-Odile Goulet-Cazé, *Cynicism and Christianity in Antiquity*, trans. Christopher R. Smith (Grand Rapids, MI: Eerdmans Publishing, 2019), 29–31; and Luis E. Navia, *Diogenes of Sinope: The Man in the Tub* (Westport, CT: Greenwood Press, 1998), 50–4. For more on the status of dogs in ancient Greek culture, see Cristiana Franco, *Shameless: The Canine and the Feminine in Ancient Greece*, trans. Matthew Fox (Oakland, CA: University of California Press, 2014).
27. Foucault, *The Courage of Truth*, 264.
28. Foucault, *The Courage of Truth*, 264.

29. Foucault, *The Courage of Truth*, 265.
30. Thomas Flynn, 'Foucault as Parrhesiast', in *The Final Foucault*, ed. James Bernauer and David Rasmussen (Cambridge: MIT Press, 1988), 102–18.
31. For a broader historical and cultural perspective on this tradition, see Claire Huot, 'Chinese Dogs and French Scapegoats: An Essay in Zoonomastics', in *Foucault and Animals*, ed. Matthew Chrulew and Dinesh Joseph Wadiwel (Boston: Brill, 2017), 37–58.
32. I borrow the term deep ethology from Marc Bekoff, 'Deep Ethology, Animal Rights, and the Great Ape/Animal Project: Resisting Speciesism and Expanding the Community of Equals', *Journal of Agricultural and Environmental Ethics* 10 (1998): 269–96.
33. For a fuller discussion of the relations and differences between *ēthos* (spelled with an eta) and the correlative term *ethos* (spelled with an epsilon) in the ancient Greek context, see: Thomas E. Corts, 'The Derivation of Ethos', *Speech Monographs* 35 (1968): 201–2; and Charles Chamberlain, 'From "Haunts" to "Character": The Meaning of *Ēthos* and Its Relation to Ethics', *Helios* 11 (1984): 97–108.
34. 'Live in conformity with nature, the Ancients used to say. It behooves us to reinvent the contemporary meaning of this conformity' (Michel Serres, '*Feux et Signaux de Brume*: Virginia Woolf's Lighthouse', trans. Judith Adler, *SubStance* 37 [2008]: 110–31, 129).

Works Cited

Binswanger, Ludwig. *Le rêve et l'existence*. Translated by Jacqueline Verdeaux. Paris: Desclée de Brouwer, 1954.

Chrulew, Matthew. 'Animals in Biopolitical Theory: Between Agamben and Negri'. *New Formations* 76 (2012): 53–67.

Chrulew, Matthew. 'Managing Love and Death at the Zoo: The Biopolitics of Endangered Species Preservation'. *Australian Humanities Review* 50 (2011). Accessed November, 1 2022. http://australianhumanitiesreview.org/2011/05/01/managing-love-and-death-at-the-zoo-the-biopolitics-of-endangered-species-preservation.

Elden, Stuart. 'Foucault as Translator of Binswanger and von Weizsäcker'. *Theory, Culture & Society* (2020): 1–26. https://doi.org/10.1177/0263276420950459.

Eribon, Didier. *Michel Foucault*. Translated by Betsy Wing. Cambridge, MA: Harvard University Press, 1991.

Flynn, Thomas. 'Foucault as Parrhesiast'. In *The Final Foucault*, edited by James Bernauer and David Rasmussen, 102–18. Cambridge, MA: MIT Press, 1988.

Foucault, Michel. *'Society Must Be Defended': Lectures at the Collège de France 1975–1976*. Translated by David Macey. New York: Picador, 2003.

Foucault, Michel. *The Courage of Truth. The Government of Self and Others II: Lectures at the Collège de France 1983–1984*. Translated by Graham Burchell. New York: Palgrave Macmillan, 2011.

Foucault, Michel. *The History of Sexuality*, volume 1: *An Introduction*. Translated by Robert Hurley. New York: Random House, 1978.

Franco, Cristiana. *Shameless: The Canine and the Feminine in Ancient Greece*. Translated by Matthew Fox. Oakland, CA: University of California Press, 2014.

Goulet-Cazé, Marie-Odile. *Cynicism and Christianity in Antiquity*. Translated by Christopher R. Smith. Grand Rapids, MI: Eerdmans, 2019.

Hribal, Jason. *Fear of the Animal Planet: The Hidden History of Animal Resistance*. Oakland, CA: AK Press, 2010.

Huot, Claire. 'Chinese Dogs and French Scapegoats: An Essay in Zoonomastics'. In *Foucault and Animals*, edited by Matthew Chrulew and Dinesh Joseph Wadiwel, 37–58. Boston, MA: Brill, 2017.

Laertius, Diogenes. *Lives of the Eminent Philosophers*. Translated by Pamela Mensch. New York: Oxford University Press, 2018.

Navia, Luis E. *Diogenes of Sinope: The Man in the Tub*. Westport, CT: Greenwood Press, 1998.

Serres, Michel. '*Feux et Signaux de Brume*: Virginia Woolf's Lighthouse'. Translated by Judith Adler. *SubStance* 37 (2008): 110–31.

Shukin, Nicole. *Animal Capital: Rendering Life in Biopolitical Times*. Minneapolis, MN: University of Minnesota Press, 2009.

Stanescu, James. 'Beyond Biopolitics: Animal Studies, Factory Farms, and the Advent of Deading Life'. *PhaenEx* 8, no. 2 (2013): 135–60.

Taylor, Chloë. 'Foucault and Critical Animal Studies: Genealogies of Agricultural Power'. *Philosophy Compass* 8, no. 6 (2013): 539–51.

Thierman, Stephen. 'Apparatuses of Animality: Foucault Goes to a Slaughterhouse'. *Foucault Studies* 9 (2010): 89–110.

Twine, Richard. *Animals as Biotechnology: Ethics, Sustainability, and Critical Animal Studies*. Washington, DC: Earthscan, 2010.

Wadiwel, Dinesh. 'Biopolitics'. In *Critical Terms for Animal Studies*, edited by Lori Gruen, 79–98. Chicago, IL: University of Chicago Press, 2018.

Wolfe, Cary. *Before the Law: Humans and Other Animals in a Biopolitical Frame*. Chicago, IL: University of Chicago Press, 2013.

2   Community and Animality in the Ancient Cynics
Vanessa Lemm

Returning to the Cynics

It is common knowledge that we know the ancient Cynics only by sayings, that is, by what has been transmitted about their philosophy and way of life through other sources. The most famous and important work for understanding Diogenes of Sinope, for example, is the *Lives of Eminent Philosophers* by Diogenes Laertius.[1] Diogenes Laertius retells the life of Diogenes of Sinope ('the Dog'), and in his biography, he provides a list of the works written by his namesake (DL 6.80). None of these have survived.[2] Even in antiquity there were debates regarding what exactly the most famous Cynic wrote: Diogenes Laertius, after listing works, goes on to write that several are of disputed authorship and that Diogenes the Dog may have written nothing at all. This example is typical for any investigation of the Cynics.[3] Source survival and transmission aside, the main reason that we must rely on the reports of others is that the Cynics believed that philosophical truth must be reflected in the true philosophical life and embodied in the way of life of the philosopher rather than in their academic production. These two reasons have produced the curious fact that the philosophy of the Cynics is inseparable from the history of their reception.[4] There is no complete text to which we can return or against which we can test the veracity of our interpretations. Instead, the philosophy and way of life of the Cynics is radically exteriorised and dispersed in the continuous history of their interpretation. By leaving no written trace of his life and thought, Diogenes of Sinope successfully undermines any attempt to appropriate his philosophy, to reduce the common dimension of his life and thought to something that could be attributed to him as his own or proper. Furthermore, the intimate relationship between ancient Cynicism and the history of their interpretation produces the curious effect that by studying the Cynics and the multiple ways in which their philosophy has been received, we also discover their readers. As such the Cynics successfully dissolve any attempt to distinguish between self and other, identity and plurality, immunity and community.

Both ancient and contemporary appropriations of Cynic philosophy illustrate this idea, for example, when interpreters point to the similarities between Diogenes and Socrates, Diogenes and Alexander the Great, Diogenes and Diderot and so on, to reveal affinities between their respective philosophical ideals.[5] This may also explain why the history of Western philosophy is populated with a multiplicity of interpretations, interpretations that are both complementary and contradictory to each other. One might examine the Cynics and note their association with an ideological force (poverty);[6] consider it as a pagan model for early Christian communities;[7] as a practice of telling truth to power[8]; as a universal ethical model of freedom and autonomy;[9] as a philosophical critique devoted to defacing the false values of the dominant culture[10] and so forth.

However, in general terms, one can distinguish between two divergent readings of the Cynics in the history of their reception: on the one hand, we have those who see in Diogenes the embodiment of the highest philosophical virtue and, on the other hand, those who see in Diogenes and the Cynics nothing but primitivism, animalism and the rejection of humanity. Rather than seeing in these two interpretations a dualism between negative and affirmative readings of Diogenes and the Cynics, I argue that this history reflects a history of increasing immunisation where the various interpretations of the Cynics function as means of protection against the threat of undifferentiated community reflected in Diogenes's example of life and thought. Just as modern political philosophy erects an enormous apparatus of immunisation against the claims of community, as Esposito remarks, the history of the reception of the Cynics reflects an attempt to protect us (philosophy) from their thinking of community.[11] On my view, the history of reception of the Cynics reflects an increasing interiorisation of their philosophy that culminates in the figure of the Cynic as an advocate of individual freedom where freedom is understood as an inalienable property of the modern individual. From this perspective, it comes as no surprise that the Cynic's idea of individual freedom is rendered as an exaggerated and hyper-immunitary individualism that translates into self-interested egoism and cynicism. Today, the true meaning of Cynic freedom has been forgotten, and when we speak of cynicism, we mean nothing but 'a person who believes all people are motivated by selfishness'.[12] What has been lost in both instances is the intimate connection between freedom and community in the way of life and thought of the ancient Cynics. The purpose of my reading of the Cynics is to bring back their powerful thinking of community.

More-Than-Human Communities[13]

A renaissance of ancient Cynicism is called for in a time when the question of community has come again to the foreground in debates in contemporary thought. In the traditional understandings of community as *Gemeinschaft* and *Gesellschaft*,[14] the common bond is constituted primarily by language, independently of whether by language we mean a given, spoken and lived practical idiom or whether by language we understand an ontological entity (language as the 'house' of being, as in Heidegger), or more simply a coded exchange of information that establishes a basis for systematic (predictable) behaviour (as in Luhmann).[15] Whether we are talking about community in contemporary French and Italian philosophy or in the recent Anglo-American debates, what is striking is that in both cases the fact of community is conceived through the shared fact of language.[16] As a result, in both debates we are dealing with largely humanistic and anthropocentric conceptions of community. Whether we centre our attention on the phenomenon of naming, as in the Heideggerian tradition, or on the phenomenon of justification, as in the pragmatic tradition, in both cases language is what distinguishes, rather than includes, human beings from other living species.

In his last lecture course, Jacques Derrida pointed out that in *Genesis*, even prior to human fallenness and guilt, language is already an instrument of domination linked with man's presumption to name other animals.[17] But it is unclear whether the Western tradition of philosophy can do any better since there is an intrinsic speciesism in the identification of the human being as the animal with reason, the animal that employs arguments. From my perspective, all conceptions of the communal bond that are based on the belief – so predominant during the last century – that language alone can make sense of the world, that the world is linguistically constructed, prove themselves to be insufficient insofar as they are incapable of providing an answer to the need for communal relationships with other forms of species life.

In the age of the Anthropocene, it has become evident that the human species needs to create communities and learn to be in community with other forms of species life, including the life of animals, plants and other more complex assemblages of life such as rivers, seas and mountains.[18] These communities can no longer be based on the assumption that all participants share the same human language. Instead, it is a shared biological and geological life[19] that provides the link between human and other-than-human life. But what does community now mean when the relationship to another becomes 'more-than-human'? When it is a question of relating to other-than-human forms of life? How do we live in common or communicate with other-than-human forms of life without being able to exchange either words or reasons?

An example of this predicament is given every day by the industrial production and processing of food. In industrial farms, animals are treated in completely 'inhuman' ways.[20] In particular, what causes us to say, paradoxically, that animals are treated inhumanly is the fact that their living conditions are such that animals can have no possible community or common form of life. In the case of chicken, for example, animals are so crowded that the proverbial 'pecking order' is destroyed. As a result of these inhuman conditions for animals, animal diseases have developed, from mad cow disease to avian flu, that begin in other species but turn out to be easily transmissible and affect in deadly ways our own species.[21] By destroying the possibility of community of and with other species, it seems, we generate diseases that destroy us. In this new understanding of what it means to live in community with other, there is a shift in the presupposition of community from the fact of language to the fact of life, because it is this last fact that allows us to think about forms of community that engage with other-than-human living species.[22] This paradigm shift leads us to the question of the meaning of 'the human' in the Anthropocene and of how to rethink community in relation to other-than-human forms of life.[23]

In my view, we need to work towards a more-than-human conception of community where the question of community is investigated from the perspective of life rather than of language, and perhaps even allow us to question the value of language for life, rather than the other way around. In this respect, there may be something for us to learn from the Cynics: the Cynics questioned language on the basis that language is incapable of capturing singularity and also that it cannot articulate the relationship between singularity and community, in particular, when the members of the community understand themselves as inhabitants of the cosmos, that is, of a world that belongs to all and none.

The Cynics point us to the shortcomings of a community founded on *logos* (reason and language) that protect the individual members of the *polis* against the claims of nature. By contrast, the Cynics advocate a 'return to nature' to recover a genuine sense of community according to which all forms of life are interrelated to and interdependent on each other.[24] For the Cynics, it is the community of life and nature that ultimately protects each and every individual's life rather than the unnatural customs of the Greek *polis*. According to the Cynics, we learn from the animals what it means to live in common with others without having to rely on the immunitary exchange of words or reasons. To become a Cynic requires living according to nature by adopting the way of life of the dogs. The affirmation of nature as the highest source of value and truth, in the Cynics, comes hand in hand with the search for a community that is not based on the immunising separation between nature and culture. This idea culminates in the figure of the philosopher and the political significance of the embodiment of truth in the Cynics.[25] The Cynics are biopolitical animals that break with the immunitary practices of the *polis* orienting human life towards a cosmopolis that affirms the wealth of the community of life. As such, a return to the Cynics produces a new perspective on today's debate on community, animality and biopolitics.

Singular Bodies

In order to understand the Cynics' thinking of community, we need to begin with their belief that the universe is made up of singulars that are irreducible to each other. This belief has important implications for their use and understanding of language and is reflected in their adherence to Antisthenes's logic. According to Antisthenes, the function of language is to identify without elaboration the objects of the physical world.[26] Following Antisthenes, the Cynics accepted only ostensive definitions: if something cannot be shown (that is, literally pointed at) then it cannot be spoken. For the Cynics, language takes on meaning only where meaning is derived from direct referencing. The question of the relation between meaning and referencing is still at the centre of current debates in analytical philosophy. Saul Kripke, for example, distinguishes between meaning (indirect referencing) and naming (direct referencing).[27] He would agree with the Cynics that only names can adequately reflect the singularity of each and every thing or person that makes up our world, but would disagree with them on the source of meaning. Whereas for the Cynics only names are meaningful, and language should be restricted to naming, for Kripke names alone cannot generate meaning.

In contrast to contemporary debates on the question of meaning and referencing, for the Cynics, a philosophical idea or truth is meaningful only to the extent that it translates directly into action. This is why following their philosophical insights some Cynics practiced silence and refrained from speaking altogether (namely Secundus).[28] The practice of silence reflected an enactment of their philosophical conviction that the world is made up of singulars and that language cannot adequately capture this singularity. In a universe of singulars, contradiction is impossible for every existing thing is inherently singular and irreducible to anything else. Therefore, the Cynics thought that a truthful and authentic use of language must overcome the dualism of opposition and contradiction. The Cynics were looking for a language that reveals the singularity of the physical world and rejected one that was made up of nothing but falsifying generalisations. Nietzsche addresses the same problem when he distinguishes between first and second metaphors in *On Truth and Lies in an Extra-Moral Sense*. Nietzsche contrasts intuition, pictures and dreams (first metaphors) with concepts, metaphors and schemes (second metaphors).[29] While the former relies on pictorial thinking to generate a world of first impressions, the latter uses conceptual thinking to create an abstract world of regulating and imperative linguistic laws. Whereas first metaphor is the name Nietzsche gives to an idea of truth as singularity, second metaphors are always already dead metaphors that are falsifying reflections of the world.[30] The problem of the authenticity of language is that language is primarily made up of second metaphors and thus reflects a falsifying relation to the world.

For Nietzsche – and also the Cynics – the problem with language is not merely an epistemological one but a practical problem that is reproduced on the social and also political level. If language is the basis of communication with others, then our social interactions with others is falsifying and inauthentic. Given this problem of language, within a community, the question remains how to generate a meaningful relationship to the other that genuinely reflects the singularity of its members. In response to this dilemma of language, the Cynics were constantly seeking ways to break with the traditional and customary frameworks of conceptual reference by inventing new metaphors, coining new words which capture the singularity of their way of thinking and living in a world shared with others (e.g., the word *cosmopolites*: DL 6.63). It is therefore not surprising that throughout the history of Western thought, the Cynics are known for their literary imagination and creativity. Desmond, for example, acknowledges that while the influence of language on subjective experience is more a modern than an ancient theme, 'many Cynics stretch the language, making puns, coining new words, cobbing new metaphors, and even inventing new poetic meters and literary genres, as if they were struggling to burst through the bonds of customary speech to fashion their own, Cynic forms of communication'.[31]

Diogenes's own rhetoric and performance needs to be understood within this context of the radical innovation of language based on the rejection of traditional logic and the privileging of the ostensive use of language. However, Diogenes's rhetoric and performance also reflect an attempt to move beyond a merely theoretical stance in philosophy bound by the limits of formal logic towards philosophy as a way of life and form of action. With the Cynics, philosophy undergoes what could be called a turn towards practice, or what Michel Foucault refers to as the care of the self: the Cynics no longer understand philosophy as a metaphysical discourse on being. Instead, philosophical truth is reflected in the philosophers' practice of (self)experimentation, her pursuit of the true philosophical life which for the Cynics is the only meaningful life.[32]

Cynic rhetoric and performance mark a point of rupture and discontinuity with the established philosophical discourses and practices of their time. While ancient Cynicism is typically regarded as deeply embedded in classical culture, some commentators have emphasised that their philosophy and way of life reflects a break in classical philosophy and history.[33] As Peter Sloterdijk convincingly argues, Cynic gesture and bodily language is a means to escape the 'hegemony of *logos*, science, morality and self-justifying ideologies'.[34]

Despite Diogenes's rejection of standard habits of living, it is said that he was well-groomed (DL 6.81) and that he had a 'radiant complexion' which would attract the attention of the people by the very appearance of his body (Epict. *Disc.* 3.22.88).[35] Diogenes's physical appearance and body is without comparison and as such demonstrates the singularity of the philosophical truths he embodies. Diogenes' singularity best illustrates the discontinuity between his way of life and the established customs and norms of his time. This point of discontinuity has been noted by several commentators who have emphasised the uniqueness of Diogenes's body: Navia writes that Diogenes is 'vastly different from those who in astonishment surround him' and claims that Diogenes is not a human being, not a citizen, but a creature.[36] Branham draws a similar conclusion and compares Diogenes to a 'freak, a monster, like every violator of taboos'.[37] In both cases, Diogenes is depicted as a living creature that falls outside of the conceptual framework of the human. By means of his physical and bodily appearance Diogenes questions what it means to be human.

Diogenes's body is the material reflection of his philosophical thought; it stands out as singular and unique.[38] What is striking about Diogenes is the material embodiment of his philosophy which lead Foucault to the insight that in the Cynics we find an idea of the philosophical life in which truth is revealed or manifest in the material body of life.[39] Against the philosophical discourse of his time dominated by Platonic ideas, Diogenes upheld the materiality of the human body. The Cynics rejected the construction of human nature or reason as something that transcends the physical world. Instead, they thought that human reason is immanent to the body and hence needs to be understood as an aspect of the material world. Their preoccupation with the physical world and the body is by no means a sign of their 'gross materialism', as pointed out by Navia, but reflects their concern for the here and now exemplified in the numerous anecdotes about Diogenes's body, hands, performance and actions (up to and including his death).[40] Diogenes's philosophy became embodied in a series of performances that may appear at first enigmatic and irrational but which in fact are very well staged and thought through as part of a more general attempt to overturn the established norms and value systems of his time.[41]

The Cynics overcome a philosophical discourse that prioritises reason and language over life and the body towards an embodied example of truth worthy of imitation. From the standpoint of Platonic reason, Diogenes is a Socrates gone mad (DL 6.54) – all his actions scandalously undermine the authority of reason. The Cynics' philosophy is disconcerting and unsettling precisely because their actions continuously question the universal validity of reason and language. However, according to the Cynics, reason does not provide a privileged access to the world: it obfuscates our vision of reality. This is why Navia argues that the Cynics and Diogenes in particular stand for a higher sense of reason. For Navia, Diogenes's madness is a sign of his higher rationality. Navia turns around the claim that Diogenes was mad, by saying that after all Diogenes is the only truly rational human being in a world that has gone mad. He praises Diogenes's relentless commitment to reason and concludes that Diogenes's actions were not for nothing: 'for even if the battle against the insanity of the world may only succeed within the confines and in the privacy of his tub'.[42]

However, by reducing Diogenes's singularity and the singularity of his reasoning to the private and individual, Navia misses what I take to be the major innovation of ancient Cynicism, namely, their thinking of community. For the Cynics, nothing can be confined to the private: everything is public and held in common. From the perspective of their thinking of community, a Diogenes who enjoys his individual freedom within the private sphere of his tub is a contradiction in terms and irreconcilable with their practice of public life. Against, the universal language of reason, Diogenes upholds the singularity of embodied life as a reflection of the community of life. The singularity of embodied life reflects the interrelatedness and interdependence of human and other-than-human life exemplified by the Cynics' way of life and thought. For the Cynics, the singularity of embodied life in community with others is not a simple given but the fruit of a particular practice requiring one to literally become a Cynic.

Becoming (Biopolitical) Animals

In my reading of the Cynics, I distinguish between three constitutive features of ancient Cynicism. These constitutive features of their philosophy do not take the form of principles or dogmas, but instead call for a way of life that one needs to adopt to become a Cynic. First, to become a Cynic requires embracing exile. Leading a nomadic and wandering way of life in exile stands for an affirmation of singularity over and above the particularities of a given city state or a given culture one may have been born into. For the Cynics, community does not define one's identity, a place to which one returns or from which one emerges, rather community designates a place of non-belonging that unites all those who are excluded and do not submit to the immunitary logic of their political organisations. Secondly, to become a Cynic requires giving up all one's material wealth and adopting a life of radical poverty. The Cynics reject property for they believe that community is not a property or an entitlement but rather that we are all free to use what is at hand and that the wealth of nature is due to all the inhabitants of the world.[43] Thirdly, to become a Cynic requires living according to nature by adopting the way of life of the dogs. The affirmation of nature as the highest source of value and truth, in the Cynics, comes hand in hand with the search for a community that is not based on the immunising separation between nature and culture. All three constitutive features culminate in the final aspect of ancient Cynicism, namely, the embodiment of truth in the philosopher. To become a Cynic requires the courage to speak the truth without reservations and is reflected in the figure of the philosopher and the political significance of the embodiment of truth.[44] For reasons of space, I will not be able to develop all four aspects of ancient Cynicism and its relevance for the question of community today and will therefore restrict myself to a few broad comments on Cynic asceticism and the becoming animal of the Cynics which in my view has been falsely interpreted by commentators as a becoming self-sufficient of the Cynics sage.

In contrast to standard readings of the Cynic practice of asceticism, the objective of Cynics *askesis* is not, in my view, mastery over what nature requires but the maximum exposure to the contingencies of life. The Cynics seek to develop a relationship to nature that does not build on mastery and domination. It is through the individual's radical externalisation, its maximum exposure to others, its heightened vulnerability that it becomes part of a network of relationships, a community of life that 'paradoxically' ends up preserving and protecting it.[45] Through the practice of asceticism, the Cynics seek to show that the community of life is more powerful than the social and political relationships instituted in the *polis*. The embrace of ascetic practice is a transformative experience which does not reflect an immunitary internalisation of the external world where self-sufficiency rests on a separation between the individual and the other. Rather the Cynic's renunciation of the privileges associated with the life of the *polis* reflects a radical externalisation and opening of the individual to the human and more-than-human.[46]

This is also how I understand the Cynics' becoming animal. Rather than seeing in their becoming animal a reduction of one's physical and bodily needs to a minimum required for the preservation of life, I see in their adoption of animality as a model of life an affirmation of the community of life. In the Cynics, wealth passes through radical externalisation which is achieved through an imitation of nature and animal life. Accordingly, the Cynic conception of wealth is not subjective and closed onto itself, as Desmond argues, but cosmic and open to the common use of goods generously provided by nature for the satisfaction of everybody's needs. The Cynic is rich insofar as he partakes in nature and the community of life.

On Desmond's account, the Cynics believed that what one can learn from nature is how to live a simple, happy and fulfilled life:

> For them, the natural life is one of complete simplicity, free of all unnecessary, all-too-human contrivances. It is unburdened by needless cogitation and mental distraction. Living fully in the moment, without great hopes or fears, is for the Cynic the only way to become virtuous and happy: natural living brings the greatest pleasures, and the right pleasures.[47]

On this view, the Cynics' interpretation of a simple, happy and fulfilled life is entirely centred on the notion of the virtuous subject exemplified by the philosopher: 'through contemplation, the philosopher becomes at least psychologically more self-sufficient, less dependent on community'.[48] According to Desmond's interpretation of the Cynic's anthropology, 'a human being is not naturally so sociable and dependent on others: therefore, one does not need to live as citizens of cities or subject oneself to a mass of burdensome laws, taboos and social expectations, to actualize one's potential'.[49] As a consequence of this anthropology, achieving the Cynic's ideal of individual virtue is simple: all we need to do is use only what is immediately available and live here and now. We need to follow 'the wisdom of the animals that eat what is nearby, drink from the closest stream or pond, hide in a cave or hole or whatever is available and copulate when nature urges'.[50] The only thing that is holding us back from a return to a simple, happy and fulfilled natural life, so Desmond argues, is degenerate custom.[51] Desmond argues that the philosopher is successful in regaining a truly natural life, by withdrawing himself from the life of the *polis* and dedicating himself entirely to the life of the spirit: the philosopher approaches divine self-sufficiency by means of spiritual contemplation and 'he needs others only for bodily needs' (Desmond 2006: 39). Furthermore, he holds that '[b]odily needs are finite and easily satisfied, but moral and intellectual ends require constant attendance. Therefore, the ambitious thinker "works" constantly towards his chosen goals of self-sufficiency and self-actualization. Only by such "work" can one escape the body's inalienable poverty'.[52]

There are several problems with Desmond's interpretation of the philosophical life in the Cynics. First of all, Desmond understands freedom in the Cynics as a spiritual experience that is entirely disconnected from the body and embodied life. The problem with this view is that it does not sufficiently appreciate the Cynics' reversal of the Platonic worldview. It undermines the importance of the Cynics' assertion of embodiment and embodied life as a way of re-establishing nature as a source of value against the Socratic and Platonic tradition which sets reason over and above the material world. On Desmond's account, the Cynics would be nothing but 'despisers of the body', to borrow a phrase from Nietzsche's *Thus Spoke Zarathustra*, in pursuit of a contemplative life that is superior to the life of the body. Desmond articulates a hyper-spiritualist conception of Cynicism which cannot, in my view, be reconciled with their affirmation of life and their giving themselves over to the materiality of nature and the community of life.

In contraposition to the Platonic tradition, for the Cynics, the body is not poor in the first place and their philosophy is not a means to escape the 'inalienable poverty' of the body as Desmond claims. Rather, the example of the life of the animals shows that nature has equipped us with everything we need to protect ourselves against external circumstances and to satisfy our needs. As such, the Cynics recover the wealth of their bodies by living a life in accordance with nature. For the Cynics, nature is generous and full of resources for those who know how to use them. The Cynics draw their wealth not from mastery and domination over the body (by satisfying only the most necessary needs) but from their creative use of the body. They are constantly inventing and reinventing their form of life inspired by their appreciation of the resources they find in nature. For example, it is being said that the idea to live in a tub came to Diogenes when he was observing a snail carrying its house. And, also, 'after observing a mouse running around in the marketplace, unconcerned about luxuries and unafraid of dark places, Diogenes learned one of the fundamental lessons of Cynicism, namely, to dispense with superfluous things and to adapt oneself to all sorts of situations' (DL 6.22). Cynic asceticism is therefore not about the control and mastery over the body, but about developing a transformative, perhaps freer, relationship to one's body: the Cynics were constantly experimenting with their physical needs responding to them in unexpected and unpredictable ways, challenging themselves to adapt to continuously changing life situations. As such, their relationship to nature is inherently playful and creative questioning the established religious and cultural norms that commonly regulate our relationship to nature, for example, through dietary prescriptions, where and what to eat and so on, which, as is well known, Diogenes was highly critical of contesting the separation of nature and culture, *physis* and *nomos* reflected in the (religious and political) customs instituted in the *polis*.

The Cynics ascetic *ponoi* creatively engage with the materiality of embodied life, not teaching us how to become more spiritual and withdrawn from others but how to be more in our bodies and use our bodies like the animals is the purpose of ascetic practice in the Cynics: 'My prayer is that my feet be just like hooves as Chiron's were said to be; that I need bedclothes no more than do lions; expensive food no more than dogs. Let the whole world be bed large enough for me, let me call the universe my home'.[53] Rather than responding to the lack of freedom associated with (bodily) needs by instituting mechanisms of domination (i.e., the rule of the household and the idea of work), the Cynics celebrate the satisfaction of needs as liberating by emulating the creativity of animal life. Whereas in Aristotle, freedom requires a separation of the sphere of the household (need) from the sphere of politics (freedom), the Cynics publicly celebrate the satisfaction of their bodily needs transforming the dependency on others into the wealth of interrelated and interdependent forms of life that make up the community of life. As such, living in accordance with nature becomes a source of creativity which inspires a different use of the body, one that is not subject to the conventional idea of the sphere of work and the household that conceive of the body as an instrument of the preservation of life. Rather, the Cynics follow the animals in quest for a free use of the body teaching us how to transform our bodies into 'pure means'.[54]

Notes

1. Ancient sources are cited by the abbreviations list of Simon Hornblower and Antony Spawforth (eds.), *The Oxford Classical Dictionary*, 3rd edition (Oxford: Oxford University Press, 2003). Diogenes Laertius, *Lives of Eminent Philosophers*, 2 vols, trans. R. D. Hicks, Loeb Classical Library (Cambridge, MA: Harvard University Press, 1959), here abbreviated as DL.
2. On the evidence for Diogenes of Sinope, see Donald R. Dudley, *A History of Cynicism from Diogenes to the 6th Century A.D.* (London: Methuen, 1937), 17–20 and 53, n1.
3. For an accessible collection of the surviving texts on Cynicism, see Robert Dobbin, *The Cynic Philosophers: From Diogenes to Julian*, trans. Robert Dobbin (London: Penguin, 2012).

4. R. Bracht Branham and Marie-Odile Goulet-Cazé, 'Introduction', in *The Cynics: The Cynic Movement in Antiquity and Its Legacy*, eds. R. Bracht Branham and Marie-Odile Goulet-Cazé (Berkeley: University of California Press, 1996), 14.
5. For an example of the issues at play in such anecdotes (and how they might be navigated), consider P. R. Bosman, 'King Meets Dog: The Origin of the Meeting between Alexander and Diogenes', *Acta Classica* 50 (2007): 51–63.
6. William D. Desmond, *The Greek Praise of Poverty: The Origins of Ancient Cynicism* (Notre Dame, IN: University of Notre Dame Press, 2006); cf. Heinrich Niehus-Proebsting, 'The Modern Reception of Cynicism: Diogenes in the Enlightenment', in *The Cynics: The Cynic Movement in Antiquity and its Legacy*, 329–65.
7. Marie-Odile Goulet-Cazé, *Cynicme et christianisme dans l'Antiquité* (Paris: Vrin, 2014).
8. Michel Foucault, *The Courage of Truth (The Government of Self and Others II): Lectures at the Collège de France 1983–1984*, trans. Graham Burchell (Basingstoke/ New York: Palgrave Macmillan, 2011).
9. Luis E. Navia, *Diogenes the Cynic: The War against the World* (Amherst, NY: Humanity Books, 2005).
10. Heinrich Niehus-Proebsting, *Der Kynismus des Diogenes und der Begriff des Zynismus* (Frankfurt: Suhrkamp, 1988).
11. Roberto Esposito, *Immunitas: The Protection and Negation of Life*, trans. Zakiya Hanafi (Cambridge: Polity, 2011).
12. The definition is provided by *The American Heritage Dictionary of the English Language* s.v. Cynic, cited by R. Bracht Branham, 'Defacing the Currency: Diogenes' Rhetoric and the Invention of Cynicism', in *The Cynics: The Cynic Movement in Antiquity and Its Legacy*, 82. See also the discussion of the distinction between 'Zynismus' and 'Kynismus' in Heinrich Niehus-Proebsting, *Der Kynismus des Diogenes und der Begriff des Zynismus* (Frankfurt: Suhrkamp, 1988). Niehus-Probesting shows that 'Zynismus' is typically associated with a reduction of the human being to the animal, the absence of a value proposition as well as the escape from morality towards the power of politics as the only way to preserve oneself. He also discusses the meaning of Zynismus in psychology where interestingly it is defined as a means of protection and immunity of the individual, a defensive reaction and way of assimilating oneself to an inhuman system that surrounds us. Friedrich Nietzsche is among the few modern readers of the Cynics who has detected this trend and warns against the misappropriation of the Cynics' idea of a return to nature in the Stoics. See Friedrich Nietzsche, *Beyond Good and Evil: Prelude to a Philosophy of the Future*, ed. Rolf-Peter Horstmann and Judith Norman, trans. Judith Norman (Cambridge: Cambridge University Press, 2001), aphorisms 9 and 227. The same could be said of ancient Epicureanism which in modernity has been flattened

into the celebration of hedonistic pleasure. See Jean-Maria Guyau, *The Ethics of Epicurus and its Relation to Contemporary Doctrines* (London: Bloomsbury, 2021).

13. This section draws on a previous publication on the notion of community, Vanessa Lemm, "Nuevas direcciones en el pensamiento sobre la comunidad", *Revista Instantes y Azares – Escrituras nietzscheanas* 13 (2015): 207-220.

14. On the distinction between the two concepts, see Ferdinand Tönnies, *Community and Civil Society*, trans. Margaret Hollis (Cambridge: Cambridge University Press, 2001). Zygmunt Bauman, *Community: Seeking Safety in an Insecure World* (Cambridge: Polity, 2000).

15. See Heidegger's 'Letter on Humanism' in Martin Heidegger, *Basic Writings: Key Selections from Being and Time to The Task of Thinking* (New York: Harper Perennial Modern Thought, 2008), 213–66; Niklas Luhmann, *Social Systems*, trans. John Bednarz Jr. and Dirk Baecker (Stanford, CA: Stanford University Press, 1996).

16. See for example, Charles Taylor, *Multiculturalism and the 'Politics of Recognition'* (Princeton, NJ: Princeton University Press, 1992); Jürgen Habermas, *The Theory of Communicative Action*, trans. Thomas McCarthy, 2 vols. (Boston: Beacon Press, 1985) and *Inclusion of the Other: Studies in Political Theory* (Cambridge, MA: MIT Press, 2000).

17. Jacques Derrida, *The Beast and the Sovereign, Volume 1*, trans. Geoffrey Bennington (Chicago, IL: University of Chicago Press, 2009).

18. Donna J. Haraway, *When Species Meet* (Minneapolis, MN: University of Minnesota Press, 2008).

19. See Elizabeth A. Povinelli, *Geontologies: A Requiem to Late Liberalism* (Durham, NC: Duke University Press, 2016).

20. The same could be said of the industrial production of plants. See Jeff T. Nealon, *Plant Theory: Biopower and Vegetable Life* (Stanford, CA: Stanford University Press, 2016), and also Dinesh Joseph Wadiwel, *The War against Animals* (Leiden: Brill, 2015).

21. On the problem of zoonosis and speculations regarding the animal 'origin' of the COVID pandemic, see Vanessa Lemm and Miguel Vatter, eds., *The Viral Politics of Covid-19: Nature, Home and Planetary Health* (London: Palgrave Macmillan, 2022).

22. See Bruno Latour, *Facing Gaia: Eight Lectures on the New Climatic Regime* (Cambridge: Polity Press, 2017).

23. See Rosi Braidotti, *The Posthuman* (Cambridge: Polity Press, 2013).

24. Arthur O. Lovejoy and George Boas, *Primitivism and Related Ideas in Antiquity* (New York: Octagon Books, 1965).

25. Foucault, *The Courage of Truth*.

26. Navia, *Diogenes the Cynic*, 116–17; Luis E. Navia, *Classical Cynicism: A Critical Study* (Westport, CT: Greenwood, 1996), 63–4.

27. Saul Kripke, *Naming and Necessity* (Malden, MA: Wiley-Blackwell, 1991).
28. On Secundus, see Ben E. Perry, *Secundus, the Silent Philosopher: The Greek Life of Secundus* (Chapel Hill, NC: American Philological Association, 1964). See also S. P. Brock, 'Secundus the Silent Philosopher: Some Notes on the Syriac Tradition', *Rheinisches Museum für Philologie* 121 (1978): 94–100 for a corrected English translation of the Syriac Life of Secundus the Silent Philosopher. Cf. DL 6.31.
29. See Friedrich Nietzsche, *Sämtliche Werke*, Kritische Studienausgabe in 15 Bänden, vol. 1, eds. Giorgio Colli and Mazzino Montinari (Berlin: De Gruyter, 1988); English trans. in *The Portable Nietzsche*, ed. and trans. Walter Kaufmann (London: Penguin, 1977).
30. Vanessa Lemm, *Nietzsche's Animal Philosophy: Culture, Politics and the Animality of the Human Being* (New York: Fordham University Press, 2009), chapter 6.
31. William Desmond, *Cynics* (Berkeley, CA: University of California Press, 2008), 122.
32. Foucault, *The Courage of Truth*.
33. Desmond, *Cynics*, 122.
34. Desmond, Cynics, 123; Peter Sloterdijk, *Kritik der zynischen Vernuft*, 2 vols. (Frankfurt: Suhrkamp, 1983).
35. Epictetus, *Discourses*, in *The Cynic Philosophers: From Diogenes to Julian*, trans. Robert Dobbin (London: Penguin, 2012), abbreviated as Epict. *Disc.*
36. Navia, *Diogenes the Cynic*, 65.
37. R. Bracht Branham, 'Defacing the Currency: Diogenes' Rhetoric and the Invention of Cynicism', in *The Cynics: The Cynic Movement in Antiquity and Its Legacy*, 103.
38. Navia, *Diogenes the Cynic*, 65; see also 74.
39. Foucault, *The Courage of Truth*, 159.
40. Navia, *Diogenes the Cynic*, 48–9, 148–9.
41. Navia, *Diogenes the Cynic*, 85.
42. Navia, *Diogenes the Cynic*, 196.
43. See also Giorgio Agamben, *The Highest Poverty: Monastic Rules and Form-of-Life*, trans. Adam Kotsko (Stanford, CA: Stanford University Press, 2013). Agamben's book is centred on the Franciscans and does not discuss the Cynics.
44. Foucault, *The Courage of Truth*.
45. On the paradox of the practice of Cynic asceticism, see Foucault, *The Courage of Truth*.
46. This externalisation is reflected in the Cynic's renouncing of ownership including ownership over their own body. Epictetus remarks that Diogenes 'has personally surrendered his body to be used or abused however anyone likes' (Epict. *Disc.* 3.22.45ff.).
47. Desmond, *Cynics*, 134.
48. Desmond, *The Greek Praise of Poverty*, 28. Desmond's individualistic reading of the Cynics culminates in his understanding of Cynics' cosmopolitanism: 'The Cynics

are unusual, however, in utterly internalising that ideal [self-sufficiency] and applying it solely to the individual. For Plato and Aristotle, the accomplished philosopher or great-souled man may not need the friendship or companionship of others, but he remains physically dependent on society's exchange of service; he who lives outside the city is either an animal or a god, or he will not live long. Cynic rhetoric, on the other hand, proclaims the sage as city unto himself. [. . .] he needs nothing but himself because he is his own world' (*The Greek Praise of Poverty*, 40).

49. Desmond, *Cynics*, 147.
50. Desmond, *Cynics*, 151.
51. Desmond, *Cynics*, 155.
52. Desmond, *The Greek Praise of Poverty*, 83.
53. *The Cynic Philosophers*, 9.
54. Giorgio Agamben, *Means without End: Notes on Politics*, trans. Vincenzo Binetti and Cesare Casarino (Minneapolis, MN: University of Minnesota Press, 2000).

Works Cited

Agamben, Giorgio. *The Coming of Community*. Translated by Michael Hardt. Minneapolis, MN: University of Minnesota Press, 1993.

Agamben, Giorgio. *Means without End: Notes on Politics*. Translated by Vincenzo Binetti and Cesare Casarino. Minneapolis, MN: University of Minnesota Press, 2000.

Agamben, Giorgio. *The Highest Poverty: Monastic Rules and Form-of-Life*. Translated by Adam Kotsko. Stanford, CA: Stanford University Press, 2013.

Bataille, Georges. *The Accursed Share*. Translated by Robert Hurley. 3 vols. New York: Zone Books, 1991.

Blanchot, Maurice. *The Unavowable Community*. Translated by Pierre Joris. Barrytown, NY: Station Hill Press, 2006.

Bosman, P. R. 'King Meets Dog: The Origin of the Meeting between Alexander and Diogenes'. *Acta Classica* 50 (2007): 51–63.

Braidotti, Rosi. *The Posthuman*. Cambridge: Polity, 2013.

Branham, R. Bracht. 'Defacing the Currency: Diogenes' Rhetoric and the Invention of Cynicism'. In *The Cynics: The Cynic Movement in Antiquity and Its Legacy*, edited by R. Bracht Branham and Marie-Odile Goulet-Cazé, 81–104. Berkeley, CA: University of California Press, 1996.

Branham, R. Bracht, and Marie-Odile Goulet-Cazé. 'Introduction'. In *The Cynics: The Cynic Movement in Antiquity and Its Legacy*, edited by R. Bracht Branham and Marie-Odile Goulet-Cazé, 1–27. Berkeley, CA: University of California Press, 1996.

Brock, S. P. 'Secundus the Silent Philosopher: Some Notes on the Syriac Tradition'. *Rheinisches Museum für Philologie* 121 (1978).

Derrida, Jacques. *L'animal que donc je suis*. Paris: Galilé, 2006.

Derrida, Jacques. *The Beast and the Sovereign, Volume 1*. Translated by Geoffrey Bennington. Chicago, IL: University of Chicago Press, 2009.

Desmond, William D. *The Greek Praise of Poverty: The Origins of Ancient Cynicism*. Notre Dame: University of Notre Dame Press, 2006.

Desmond, William. *Cynics*. Berkeley, CA: University of California Press, 2008.

Diogenes Laertius. *Lives of Eminent Philosophers*. 2 vols. Translated by R. D. Hicks. Cambridge, MA: Harvard University Press, 1959.

Dobbin, Robert. *The Cynic Philosophers: From Diogenes to Julian*. Translated by Robert Dobbin. London: Penguin, 2012.

Dudley, D. R. *A History of Cynicism from Diogenes to the 6th Century A.D.* London: Methuen, 1937.

Epictetus, *Discourses*. In *The Cynic Philosophers: From Diogenes to Julian*. Translated by Robert Dobbin. London: Penguin, 2012.

Esposito, Roberto. *Bios: Biopolitics and Philosophy*. Minneapolis, MN: University of Minnesota Press, 2008.

Esposito, Roberto. *Communitas: The Origin and Destiny of Community*. Translated by Timothy Campbell. Stanford, CA: Stanford University Press, 2010.

Esposito, Roberto. *Immunitas: The Protection and Negation of Life*. Translated by Zakiya Hanafi. Cambridge: Polity, 2011.

Foucault, Michel. *The Courage of Truth (The Government of Self and Others II): Lectures at the Collège de France 1983–1984*. Translated by Graham Burchell. Basingstoke: Palgrave Macmillan, 2011.

Goulet-Cazé, Marie-Odile. *Cynicme et christianisme dans l'Antiquité*. Paris: Vrin, 2014.

Guyau, Jean-Marie. *The Ethics of Epicurus and its Relation to Contemporary Doctrines*. London: Bloomsbury, 2021.

Habermas, Jürgen. *The Theory of Communicative Action*. Translated by Thomas McCarthy. 2 vols. Boston, MA: Beacon Press, 1985.

Habermas, Jürgen. *Inclusion of the Other: Studies in Political Theory*. Cambridge, MA: MIT Press, 2000.

Haraway, Donna J. *When Species Meet*. Minneapolis, MN: University of Minnesota Press, 2008.

Heidegger, Martin. *Basic Writings: Key Selections from Being and Time to The Task of Thinking*. New York: Harper Perennial Modern Thought, 2008.

Hornblower, S. and A. Spawforth (eds.). *The Oxford Classical Dictionary*. 3rd edition. Oxford: Oxford University Press, 2003.

Kripke, Saul. *Naming and Necessity*. Malden, MA: Wiley-Blackwell, 1991.

Latour, Bruno. *Facing Gaia: Eight Lectures on the New Climatic Regime*. Cambridge: Polity Press, 2017.

Lemm, Vanessa. *Nietzsche's Animal Philosophy: Culture, Politics and the Animality of the Human Being*. New York: Fordham University Press, 2009.

Lemm, Vanessa and Miguel Vatter, eds. *The Viral Politics of Covid-19: Nature, Home and Planetary Health*, London: Palgrave Macmillan, 2022.

Long, Anthony A. 'The Socratic Tradition: Diogenes, Crates and Hellenistic Ethics'. In *The Cynics: The Cynic Movement in Antiquity and Its Legacy*, edited by R. Bracht Branham and Marie-Odile Goulet-Gaze, 28–46. Berkeley, CA: University of California Press, 1996.

Lovejoy, A. O., and G. Boas. *Primitivism and Related Ideas in Antiquity*. New York: Octagon Books, 1965.

Luhmann, Niklas. *Social Systems*. Translated by John Bednarz Jr. and Dirk Baecker. Stanford, CA: Stanford University Press, 1996.

Navia, Luis E. *Diogenes the Cynic: The War against the World*. Amherst: Humanity Books, 2005.

Navia, Luis E. *Classical Cynicism: A Critical Study*. Westport, CT: Greenwood, 1996.

Nealon, J. T. *Plant Theory: Biopower and Vegetable Life*. Stanford, CA: Stanford University Press, 2016.

Niehus-Proebsting, Heinrich. *Der Kynismus des Diogenes und der Begriff des Zynismus*. Frankfurt: Suhrkamp, 1988.

Niehus-Proebsting, Heinrich. 'The Modern Reception of Cynicism: Diogenes in the Enlightenment'. In *The Cynics: The Cynic Movement in Antiquity and its Legacy*, edited by R. Bracht Branham and Marie-Odile Goulet-Cazé, 329–65. Berkeley, CA: University of California Press, 1996.

Nietzsche, Friedrich. *Beyond Good and Evil: Prelude to a Philosophy of the Future*. Edited by Rolf-Peter Horstmann and Judith Norman, translated by Judith Norman. Cambridge: Cambridge University Press, 2001.

Nietzsche, Friedrich. *Sämtliche Werke*, Kritische Studienausgabe in 15 Bänden. Edited by Giorgio Colli and Mazzino Montinari. Berlin: De Gruyter, 1988.

Perry, Ben E. *Secundus, the Silent Philosopher: The Greek Life of Secundus*. Chapel Hill: American Philological Association, 1964.

Povinelli, Elizabeth A. *Geontologies: A Requiem to Late Liberalism*. Durham, NC: Duke University Press, 2016.

Sloterdijk, Peter. *Kritik der zynischen Vernuft*. 2 vols. Frankfurt: Suhrkamp, 1983.

Taylor, Charles. *Multiculturalism and the Politics of Recognition*. Princeton, NJ: Princeton University Press, 1992.

Tönnies, Ferdinand. *Community and Civil Society*. Translated by Margaret Hollis. Cambridge: Cambridge University Press, 2001.

Wadiwel, Dinesh Joseph, *The War against Animals*. Leiden: Brill, 2015.

3 Biopolitics of Covid-19 and the Space of Animals: A Planetary Perspective[1]

Miguel Vatter

Introduction

The global governance of the Covid-19 pandemic, despite widely divergent approaches and heavily parasitic on extant socio-economic conditions and inequalities, generally led to a proliferation of new controls on human and nonhuman mobility, and the erection of new borders (international, national, subnational, local and even at the individual level). The government policies of lockdowns, with heightened surveillance and controls, were often justified by appealing to the 'right to health' of citizens that trumped, in this case, their 'right to freedom of movement'. What threatened the 'right to health' of citizens was the superior motility of a virus whose immediate or mediate origins – as seems likely, although the matter remains contested – were zoonotic. The very possibility of zoonosis, that is, of a viral strain that jumps across animal species in mutations that are highly contagious and damaging for our species, signals the need to reconceive the divide between veterinary and human medicine. Indeed, the Covid-19 pandemic signalled a shift from global to planetary health approaches, in which the health of the environment, of other-than-human life and of human beings are inextricably interconnected.[2] Essential to the governmental responses to containing the epidemic was a complex deployment of spatial logics that reflect a deep imbrication between ecosphere and technosphere in our globalised societies, what has recently been termed the 'environmentality' of biopower.[3]

In this chapter, I propose to consider some aspects of the biopolitics of Covid-19 through the perspective of an emerging discourse on spheres, or spherology, that is deeply tied up with the biological conception of space as milieu or habitat. This spherology can be employed to establish the possibility of a right-less control of our free movements, but it can also open towards a new discourse on rights established on the basis of the internal normativity of all life. In what follows, I rehearse how the spatiality of biological life has been employed in order to develop new forms of governmentality, and suggest some paths forward through which these developments can be contested.

Planetary Health and Zoe-Egalitarianism

The blueprints for the idea of planetary health were set out nearly twenty years before the Covid-19 pandemic by the 'Manhattan Principles' of One World One Health (2004).[4] The principles of One Health, as a model for a planetary understanding of health, can be understood as a 'posthuman' turn in medicine. Rosi Braidotti has defined the posthuman as 'technologically mediated emphasis on life as zoe-centered system of species egalitarianism' (Braidotti 2013: 60).[5] The principles of One Health presuppose a life-based 'system of species egalitarianism' in which human beings do not stand above and apart from the other living kingdoms, including that of bacteria, fungi and viruses that contribute to our genetic makeup.[6] At the same time, One Health and in general the new conception of planetary health, articulates this 'system of species egalitarianism' in a 'technologically mediated' way. For example, the fifth Manhattan principle calls for 'devising adaptive, holistic and forward-looking approaches to the prevention, surveillance, monitoring, control and mitigation of emerging and resurging diseases that fully account for the complex interconnections among species'.[7] These same technologies of surveillance and tracking worked hand in hand with governmental controls on the mobility of persons as potential carriers of the Covid-19 virus.

In his study on the origins of the 'reproduction number', R0, and why it seemed for some time to be the sole criterion governments used to determine when to decree the state of emergency, Warwick Anderson has come to the conclusion that 'disease modelling is thus a story of how mosquitoes briefly became humans and humans lastingly became mosquitoes'.[8] Anderson argues that by using this kind of modelling as the sole source to determine public health policy entailing the suspension of rights, 'epidemiologists effectively were reimagining human societies and communities as elementary biological collectives or herds'. This illustrates what is at stake in the idea of biological citizenship where differential health status may grant differential recognition of rights.[9] More generally, the clash between rights to health and rights to mobility that characterised a great deal of the public debate on Covid measures were articulated, often unconsciously, within the framework of neoliberal biopolitics, in accordance to which governments are expected by their citizens to work under the imperative to 'make live' the populations under their care, by raising the 'quality of life', by keeping the economy 'growing' and by keeping the citizens 'healthy'.[10] Situated in this context, one should reconsider Giorgio Agamben's suspicion that the requirement to show vaccine passes to enter most places of social interaction was less a case of 'nudging' citizens into getting vaccinated and more a case of using the drive to vaccinate in order to deploy and normalise the use of vaccine passes and a new practice of bordering.[11] On this pessimistic hypothesis, Covid-19 governance employed a vision of 'planetary health' in order to accelerate the subsumption of the biosphere into the technosphere.

Vaccine Passes and Bodies as New Borders

The need to transition from pandemic to endemic viral spread, and the systemic global pressures that condition the growth of wealth and welfare to the 'free movement' of peoples and things, required governments to look for ways to make compatible hard, quasi-sovereign bordering with soft, differential regulation of flows associated with a biopolitical concept of security.[12] Throughout this process of generating an adequate pandemic governance, the employment of an animal spatial imaginary was essential. Thus, Anderson has shown the essential importance of spatial concepts in modelling the reproduction number (R0). Predictions based on the value of R0 as applied to the infectiousness of the virus in a human population were based on the assumption of 'a homogeneous animal population *distributed across uniform space*' garnered from previous experience of viral spread in animal husbandry.[13] The predictive model operationalised a concept of contact and contagion 'as if there is no such thing as society': 'the places where we congregate thus wither into plain and meager spaces of contamination shorn of any sociological and ecological diversity'.[14] Once lived spaces are reconceived as 'spaces of contamination', it is not surprising that public health orders adopted on the basis of the reproduction number alone brought to the fore older elements of sovereign and disciplinary power, not just biopolitical power, that 'have involved centrifugal expansion of juridical processes, which punish and exclude, as well as disciplining strategies, which codify what is forbidden and permitted in daily life, drilling and correcting populations'.[15]

The use of the spaces of animals to model human conduct in Covid governmentality was not only a reflection of a return towards sovereign and disciplinary power. True, the new bordering of bodies that Ayelet Shachar and others have identified in the securitisation of Covid-19 show that the sovereign 'power of states to regulate movement across international bodies and within countries of residence has ballooned to unprecedented proportions', but the way in which 'public officials have unleashed biometric "eyes" and "ears" to monitor human mobility – or conversely to mandate its immobility'[16] suggests also the possibility of a distinct deployment of animal spatiality that problematises the typical sovereign decision between those who are in a legal order and those who are excluded from it. The phenomena to which Shachar draws attention is the fact that 'the unit of analysis for mobility control was traditionally reserved to the territorial border, [and] today it is gradually grafting into the body itself'.[17] Dispositifs like vaccine passes, through which 'a body marked as suspect, let alone infected, is barred from participating in society, from entering public spaces, and from engaging with the full extent of rights and protections that other members take for granted',[18] or so I shall suggest, is less a matter of internalising the sovereign border into civil society, at 'the perimeter of shops, salons, and cultural institutions', and more the sign of a new deployment of a biopolitical conception of milieu and habitat, the 'dwelling-shell' of the animal body, outward into society in a novel articulation of ecological and technological spheres.

Genealogy of Biopolitical Spherology

As Bruno Latour and Peter Sloterdijk have pointed out, the shift from a 'global' perspective to one that is 'planetary' entails a meta-discourse not only on 'globes' but, more primordially, on 'spheres'.[19] In particular, what poses a crucial problem is how to think critically about the interactions between the bio-sphere and the technosphere in the Anthropocene, not forgetting that the concept of the Anthropocene itself has undergone severe critique from the perspective of multi-species ethnology as well as de-colonial discourses.[20] Thomas Lemke's recent work on Foucault's expression of the 'government of things' thematises the ubiquity of technologies of power by emphasising the centrality of the 'spherical' moment, that is, what in biology is called the 'milieu' within which all life on earth takes place.

According to Lemke's reconstruction, with the idea of 'government of things' Foucault was after 'a relational and self-reflexive mode of power that takes into account mechanisms of self-regulation and self-control'[21] that are originally drawn from living systems and are then modelled in terms of feedback control and homeostatic systems that underpin the discourse of cybernetics.

Cybernetics refers to the idea of 'government' (*kybernetike* as art of governing a vessel), and Foucault saw it as applicable across medicine, politics and ethics.[22] For Foucault, modern biopolitics emerges when 'politics has to work in the element of a reality that the physiocrats called, precisely, physics, when they said economics is a physics'.[23] But this is the 'physics' of homeostatic systems that derives from biology. According to Lemke, Foucault's genealogy of biopolitics was particularly influenced by the developments of biology after the genetic revolution, when life is no longer explained by vitalist forces but by 'an informational understanding of the body and life'[24] in terms of programme and code, and where 'genes and cells are material-semiotic entities: they are organic systems as well as "small machines" and "calculators". This "cybernetic" account of genetics is encapsulated in the surprising idea of a "biology without life"'.[25] Although the possibility of an indistinction between living being and calculating machine would be decisive for the possibility of a government of human beings in and through a government of things, I am not convinced Foucault understood it that way, since it is equally crucial to note that organic systems are essentially beings composed of parts that form self-maintaining structures, and that do so in their interaction with their environments, and it is this latter aspect that seems to me to be key in determining the dangers as much as the opportunities of spherology in biopolitics.

The problem of critically investigating the relation between biosphere and technosphere turns on understanding the uses of the concept of 'milieu'. Foucault followed Canguilhem in taking up the latter's understanding of the biological concept of milieu in order to develop his own idea of governmentality. Governmentality assumes that human beings (but not only them) live by disposing and regulating things around them, in a milieu conceived of as 'an interactive space, a relational network that constitutes the elements of which it consists as much as it is itself their endpoint or outcome'.[26] The crucial idea of the milieu is that it 'conceives of organisms as actively creating and transforming the milieus they inhabit',[27] and so provides the biological side to the political aspect focused on cybernetics and on problems of 'circulation' of humans and things. Lemke argues that governmentality becomes truly an 'environmentality' when it realizes that 'while the milieu is the object of regulations and adjustments, it also exhibits self-regulatory capacities that have to be respected and fostered. It defines an "intersection between a multiplicity of living individuals working and coexisting with each other in a set of material elements that act on them and on which they act in turn"'.[28] For Lemke, this biological idea of a self-regulating milieu, in and through which living beings attempt to regulate their own lives, that is, engage in the conduct of their own conduct, is what grounds his claim that Foucault had already taken a kind of 'planetary' and 'other-than-human' turn: 'Foucault quite clearly recognizes the idea that agency is not exclusively a property of humans; rather, agential forces originate in relations between human and nonhuman entities'.[29]

It is interesting to note that the use of the concept of milieu for neoliberal biopolitics emphasises both the inner normativity of living beings or living matter and the problem of mobility: neoliberal governmentality operates on the 'vital norms' of individuals[30] and 'liberalism sets in motion a very specific concept of freedom that privileges mobility and movement and is utterly dependent on mechanisms of security: "Freedom is nothing else but the correlative of the deployment of dispositives of security [...] it is in terms of this option of circulation that we should understand the word freedom"'.[31] To have a critical purchase on neoliberal environmentality, it is necessary to cast a glance at the history of the concept of milieu from a genealogical point of view.

This history points to a back and forth between mechanical and living understandings of the milieu, which helps to explain how their conflation in cybernetics comes about, and at the same time points to the emergence of a 'planetary' discourse of the emergence of life on earth.[32] Canguilhem's discussion of the concept of milieu in his famous 1946 essay 'The Living and Its Milieu' was decisively influenced by the work of John Scott Haldane.[33] Haldane and the Russian geochemist Vladimir Vernadsky were the first to propose a conception of the biosphere as creating and maintaining homeostatically its own environment.[34] Haldane's key axiom is that there exists an internal or 'dialectical' relation between organism and environment, between inside and outside: 'the environment is thus expressed in the structure of each part of the organism, and conversely'.[35] I believe that Canguilhem adopted Haldane's 'dialectical' conception of the milieu or habitat.

For Canguilhem, habitat is the most favourable surrounding for an organism, but it is not simply 'given' to organisms as much as 'sought' by them (as one looks for certain places on a map, with a certain intention behind this search), and eventually also 'moulded' by them as a function of their spread in given geographical zones. Thus, Canguilhem gives as primary example of the biological idea of the milieu: 'the whole set of these plant species [which spread themselves out, each limiting the other species to a place on a map] ends up constituting its own milieu. In this way exchanges between the plants and the atmosphere end up creating a sort of screen of water vapor around the plant kingdom that ends up limiting the effects of radiation'. The same principle of course applies to the human species, so that a decade or so before Lovelock came up with the Gaia hypothesis, Canguilhem already said that 'man becomes a creator of the geographical configuration: he is a geographical factor'. This entails the idea that organisms move on the planet with a kind of map, looking out for certain places, and this movement is also one that creates landscapes, that 'moulds' the habitat as a function of the spread of life forms in given geographical zones. As Canguilhem says, 'if the living does not go looking for something, it gets nothing',[36] and to look for something requires orienting oneself, having an image of one's surrounding world.

Canguilhem credits Uexküll with the discovery of this dialectical conception of the milieu: 'from the biological point of view, one must understand that between organism and environment there is the same relationship that exists between parts and whole within the organism itself'. This is Uexkull's idea of *Umwelt* which is not simply the physical surroundings of an organism (*Umgebung*) and even less the 'scientific world' (*Welt*) but the set of stimuli that signal to the organism what to do, that is, that turn the organism into an actant.[37] The idea of a signal (more generally, of semiotics) is tied to meaning, and the main point of the *Umwelt* is that an organism 'notices' stimuli because it is 'interested' in them – it is 'looking out' for specific stimuli which signal it into action.[38] 'The animal's *Umwelt* is nothing other than a milieu centred around the subject of life values that makes up the essential part of what constitutes the living'.[39] For Canguilhem it is the 'subject of life' that disposes its milieu, or for whom its milieu is disposed in a certain way as a result of what can perhaps best be understood as a debate or dialogue (hence 'dialectical') that each organism has with its milieu. In this debate, the organism brings to the 'middle' or 'milieu' its own values or norms for appreciating the situation or surroundings; the milieu 'responds' to this laying out of a position or standpoint by indicating where the organism is best suited to spread. From this, Canguilhem derives one of his definitions of life: 'to live is to spread out; it is to organize a milieu starting from a central reference point that cannot itself be referred to without losing its original meaning' (Canguilhem 2001: 21).[40] Thus, each living being is characterised by a drive to 'spread out' which is not so much Darwin's struggle for the survival of the fittest as, instead, the effort by life to make its environment habitable, turning it into a dwelling place.[41]

Furthermore, this 'spreading out' or 'inhabiting' is always already normative: the disposition of a habitat is done by living beings around themselves as centres of value. Based on this dialectical relation between organism and milieu (nature as a signifying pluriverse) Canguilhem gives his definition of the living: 'a living thing is not a machine that responds by movement to stimuli, it is a machinist who responds to signals by operations'.[42] The milieu is thus a 'map' that signals to the organism when to turn off and on a series of switches to move and get to where it wants to get, namely, to what satisfies a need. The constitution of a milieu allows for the movement of the organism to be the result of *normative choices* that all living organisms make. It is in this sense that, from a bio-planetary perspective, freedom of movement is a fundamentally normative conception while at the same time being a more-than-human attribute. This offers one normative basis for so-called 'rights of nature'. In the case of rights for rivers, one has in mind the right of the river not to be interfered with or even dominated with respect to its freedom to flow, where it is understood that this 'flow' is itself de-signed by a complex 'dialogue' between the river and the other agents, some of whom may also be human, that are habitat-fashioning in that given place on the planet.[43]

Canguilhem's analogy of the living being with a machinist employs and deconstructs the analogy between life and machine, thus providing a theoretical platform from which to think the imbrication of biosphere and technosphere. In the next section I shall also address further the connection between mapping a territory, the mobility on earth that characterises globalisation and the use of spherical thinking in the thought of Sloterdijk. The internal connection between biospheres and technospheres is thematised in a series of articles by Florian Sprenger on Haldane's theory of environment. Since for Haldane 'an organism and its environment are one', and assuming, with thinkers from Helmuth Plessner to Rosi Braidotti, that living beings are characterised by an 'originary technicity', Sprenger shows how for Haldane the technological control of the environment becomes a feature of life itself.[44] Indeed, Sprenger believes that Haldane anticipated Sloterdijk's hypothesis of an 'environmental inversion [*Umwelt-Umkehrung*]' – which Sloterdijk dates to the use of gas warfare in World War I – in which the technological modulation of environments becomes essential for the maintenance of life (viz., breathing) under stress conditions. As Sloterdijk will say later: 'air-conditioning is destiny'. That is, when habitats come under stress, and the habitability of certain areas comes into question, then the technosphere becomes part of our living environment as an 'artifact of design'.[45]

The construction of the technosphere both relies on and imitates the semiotic features of biological habitats highlighted by Haldane, Uexküll and Canguilhem. The design of the technosphere emphasises the role of sensors 'that are capable of registering information about their surroundings' and act on organisms and their mobility as a consequence. Sprenger calls it 'environmental media' that generates 'calculated and calculating environments' based on digital networks that map geographical locations: 'as populations move through those spaces using mobile media or other devices, they simultaneously generate knowledge and represent object of knowledge'.[46] As Sprenger notes, this development was identified by Foucault as essential to the idea of 'security' as the set of *dispositifs* that seek to assure homeostasis in populations of living beings.

In this case, the *Umwelt* no longer signals to living beings as machinists, but rather it becomes an englobing space within which all our significant movements are tracked in order to 'conduct' or 'nudge' our conduct. These developments have been implemented by Covid-era technologies like the vaccine passes and QR codes to give or bar access to certain areas depending on one's bio-medical status discussed above. When Foucault speaks of governmentality as a form of 'environmentality', he means thereby the possibility of technological modulation of the milieu in the sense that the milieu is altered through security *dispositifs* in order to affect the *centre of values* of the subjects of life.[47] At this point, governmentality becomes a practice of subjection, in which the milieu 'disposes' things in such a way that the subject of life believes it is doing the disposing, it is pursuing its needs, while at the same it is actually deposed from being an evaluator into being a value, a variable, what Deleuze calls a 'chiffre',[48] and thus becomes the object of a calculus of government (a calculus that can easily be carried through by machine-learning and AI algorithms, key components of the contemporary technosphere).

Cartographies, Global and Planetary

In his genealogy of the concept of 'milieu' or 'habitat', Canguilhem takes an interesting detour through the nineteenth-century history of geography; this detour indicates that the spherological discourse on milieu had always already had a planetary dimension.[49] Canguilhem refers to the work of Carl Ritter, according to whom 'human history is unintelligible without understanding the connection of humanity to the land and to the whole earth. The terrestrial globe, considered as a whole, is the stable support for the vicissitudes of history'. Although with the entrance of the Anthropocene concept we no longer believe in the last assertion, the first one still retains a fundamental importance for an ecological or environmental approach to the human species. Canguilhem next refers to Alexander von Humboldt, who might have been among the first to bring attention to the internal, dialectical relation between life and its physical milieu: 'doing history consists in reading a map, if we understand by map the configuration of a set of metric, geodesic, geological, climatological and description of biogeographical data'. Humboldt here appears as the father of what would become Earth systems science, but he also spatialises history, or perhaps one can say that human history is 'mapped out' in analogy to how life reads space as if it were a map, so as to spread out to places that are most favourable for its inner development.

Humboldt plays an important role also in Sloterdijk's genealogy of globalisation. Sloterdijk finds the key to globalisation, driven by European colonialism and imperialism, in the modern discovery of 'empty space', which does away with the 'the mythical enclosure of the firmament' in pre-Copernican cosmology.[50] The connection between empty space and a new 'planetary' approach to the Earth was sealed by Humboldt's *Kosmos*: 'physical cosmography, or picture of the universe, should begin therefore not with the earth but with regions of space'.[51] For Sloterdijk, there is a close relation between the 'nautical circumnavigation' of the Earth and its 'cosmic dismantling'.[52] What makes Sloterdijk's account of globalisation 'planetary' is not so much his emphasis on circumnavigation and mapping of the seas, but that this process was made possible by a prior act of bringing the infinite 'emptiness' of post-Copernican conception of astronomical space to bear down on Earth, where the Earth is conceived as just another planet orbiting in empty space. This is what Sloterdijk calls the 'primacy of the outside' in early modern thought that gives 'a radically altered sense of human localisation. The earth now became the planet to which one returns; the outside of the general From-where of all possible returns'.[53] Basically, the localisation in the modern conception of the global is any point (on a map) to which humans make a return from a voyage to the outside: 'the map [guiding the trip to the outside] absorbs the land [the original dwelling place]'.[54] But the additional key is that this 'outside' is terrestrial: it is not super-lunary, as in the ancients, but emerges 'from the development of the physical-technical, aero- and astronautical imagination'.[55]

What Sloterdijk means is that the modern conception of space as a pure 'outside' is made possible in and through the experience of navigating the world's oceans on ships. 'The location is the point in the imagined world at which the natives grasp themselves as grasped from the outside; it is what enables the circumnavigated to return to themselves'; thus, for Sloterdijk 'globalization burst open, layer by layer, the dream shells of grounded, housed, internally oriented and autonomously salvific collective life'.[56] The new terrestrial 'globe', mapped out thanks to seafarers and geographers, 'embodied the new doctrine of a precedence of the outside, in which Europeans advanced into this outside as discoverers, merchants and tourists, but simultaneously withdrew into their artfully wallpapered inner spaces'.[57]

In this sense, one can say that the connection between the biological spread of life and the inner cartography of organisms that I discussed above in relation to Uexküll's and Canguilhem's conceptions of the natural milieu is turned around in European modernity: territory is no longer a function of what Uexküll calls the 'dwelling-shell' of all living organisms,[58] but territorial expansion becomes a function of a use of cartography as a way to map exteriority as entirely deprived of dwelling-shells. Thus 'overseas territories were considered ownerless things as long as the discoverers-occupiers felt unhindered and unchallenged in the mapping of new areas, be they inhabited or uninhabited'.[59] Likewise, 'for the pirate's and the liberal's eye, it is no longer true that it inhabits being "as a man lives in his house" [. . .]. The other viewed as a body in external space is no cohabitant of a shared lifeworld sphere [. . .] but rather an arbitrary component of welcome or unwelcome external circumstances'.[60] For Sloterdijk, 'the agents of globalization are never active as inhabitants of their own property; they are unleashed actors who no longer respect the house rules of culture anywhere'.[61] But it would perhaps be more accurate to say that globalisation becomes possible once human beings are disconnected from the task of the living, namely, to spread out as a function of making their planet more, not less, habitable.

Given the priority of a home-less exteriority, the resulting conception of habitat or milieu in globalisation can only be a hyper-immunitary one:

> It is therefore not as the Existentialists claimed, only a matter of giving oneself a direction and a project in the senseless space through a freely chosen commitment; rather, after the general exposure of humans on the surfaces of the earth and the systems, it is a matter of inhabiting the indifferent outside as if ensouled bubbles could achieve longer-term stability within it. [. . .] Only in such self-producing vessels can the withered word 'solidarity' be fulfilled in the most radical layer of its meaning: the living-arts of modernity aimed to establish the non-indifferent within the indifferent.[62]

This sentence encapsulates Sloterdijk's general viewpoint: by 'evacuating' space of any internal relation to normativity, by bringing us face to face with the 'horror' of the pure outside, modernity can only understand normativity in terms of self-withdrawal into protected 'bubbles' that give rise to the 'living-arts' of self-fashioning, but equally deprives the human species of a sense of the planet as their home.

Conclusion: Towards a Planetary *Nomos*

With Latour, Dipesh Chakrabarty argues that a planetary conception of politics in the Anthropocene must be one that 'helps humans to be at home on earth beyond the time of the living'.[63] The question is how one should understand this sense of the Earth as home. Is the idea of the planetary home here an auto-immunitary one, a designed sphere within which we can control atmospheric factors and protect ourselves from a threatening exterior, following upon Sloterdijk's dictum that only 'explicit climate policy will be the foundation of the new ecumene. [. . .] Airconditioning is destiny. [. . .] Humans create their own climate'?[64] Or should one not rather think about a planetary 'home' in terms of the idea of 'habitability', where the latter is the product of a 'dialectical' relation between organisms and their milieu in which there exists no longer a 'pure exterior' or 'white space' like the one mobilised since early modernity for the purpose of establishing the capitalist and liberal *nomos* of globalisation? And where should one draw inspiration for a new planetary *nomos* if not from the ancestral *nomoi* that were nearly obliterated by European expansion, for which nature never appears as an 'indifferent' outside, but quite the opposite, as that 'inside' without exteriority from within which everything that lives draws its life?[65]

Notes

1. Parts of this essay draw on Miguel Vatter, 'Planetary Health and the Biopolitics of Home', in *The Viral Politics of COVID-19: Nature, Home and Planetary Health*, eds Vanessa Lemm and Miguel Vatter (Basingstoke: Palgrave Macmillan, 2022), 221–46.
2. For discussion of these matters, I refer now to Lemm and Vatter (eds), *The Viral Politics of COVID-19*. On the shift towards a planetary level of analysis of politics, see Dipesh Chakrabarty, *The Climate of History in a Planetary Age* (Chicago, IL: University of Chicago Press, 2021) and Nigel Clark and Bronislaw Szerszynski, *Planetary Social Thought: The Anthropocene Challenge to the Social Sciences* (Cambridge: Polity, 2020).
3. See Thomas Lemke, *The Government of Things: Foucault and the New Materialisms* (New York: New York University Press, 2021).
4. On One Health, see Marilyn Walton (ed.), *One Planet, One Health* (Sydney: University of Sydney Press, 2019). On the transition from global to planetary approaches to health, see in particular Lyle Fearnley, 'From Global to Planetary Health: Two Morphologies of Pandemic Preparedness', in *The Viral Politics of COVID-19*, eds. Lemm and Vatter, 15–31.
5. Rosi Braidotti, *The Posthuman* (Cambridge: Polity, 2013). For discussion, see Simon Susen, 'Reflections on the (Post-)Human Condition: Towards New Forms of Engagement with the World?', *Social Epistemology* 36, no. 1 (2022): 63–94.
6. Donna Haraway, *When Species Meet* (Minneapolis, MN: The University of Minnesota Press, 2007) and Eben Kirksey, 'The Emergence of COVID-19: A Multispecies Story', *Anthropology Now* 12, no. 1 (2020): 11–16.

7. See the text of the principles found at https://oneworldonehealth.wcs.org/About-Us/Mission/The-Manhattan-Principles.aspx.
8. Warwick Anderson, 'The model crisis, or how to have critical promiscuity in the time of Covid-19', *Social Studies of Science* 51, no. 2 (2021): 172.
9. Nikolas Rose, *The Politics of Life Itself: Biomedicine, Power, and Subjectivity in the Twenty-First Century* (Princeton, NJ: Princeton University Press, 2007); Didier Fassin, 'Another Politics of Life is Possible', *Theory, Culture and Society* 26, no. 5 (2009): 44–60.
10. Miguel Vatter, *The Republic of the Living: Biopolitics and the Critique of Civil Society* (New York: Fordham University Press, 2014).
11. See Giorgio Agamben, *Where Are We Now?: The Epidemic as Politics* (Lanham, MD: Rowman & Littlefield, 2021) and for a polemical response Benjamin Bratton, *The Revenge of the Real: Politics for a Post-Pandemic World* (London: Verso, 2021) inter alia.
12. Sandro Mezzadra and Brett Neilson, *Border as Method, Or the Multiplication of Labor* (Durham, NC: Duke University Press, 2013).
13. Anderson, 'The Model Crisis, or How to Have Critical Promiscuity in the Time of Covid-19', 174, emphasis added.
14. Anderson, 'The Model Crisis, or How to Have Critical Promiscuity in the Time of Covid-19', 177.
15. Anderson, 'The Model Crisis, or How to Have Critical Promiscuity in the Time of Covid-19', 177.
16. Ayelet Shachar and Acquib Mahmood 'The Body as Border: A New Era', *Historical Social Research* 46, no. 3 (2021): 125.
17. Shachar and Mahmood 'The Body as Border', 147.
18. Shachar and Mahmood 'The Body as Border', 147.
19. Bruno Latour, *Facing Gaia. Eight Lectures on the New Climate Regime* (Cambridge: Polity Press, 2017); Peter Sloterdijk, *Globes. Spheres II: Macrospherology* (New York: Semiotext(e), 2014).
20. See the discussion in Chakrabarty, *The Climate of History in a Planetary Age*, 4ff, of the technosphere introduced by Peter Haff ('Humans and Technology in the Anthropocene: Six rules', *The Anthropocene Review* 1, no. 2 [2014]: 126–36). For critical takes on the Anthropocene, see Donna Haraway, *Staying with the Trouble: Making Kin in the Chthulucene* (Durham, NC: Duke University, 2016), and Kathryn Yusoff, *A Billion Black Anthropocenes or None* (Minneapolis, MN: University of Minnesota Press, 2018) among many others.
21. Lemke, *The Government of Things*, 117.
22. Lemke, *The Government of Things*, 119.
23. Michel Foucault, *Security, Territory, Population: Lectures at the Collège de France 1977–1978* (New York: Picador, 2009), 47.

24. Lemke, *The Government of Things*, 123.
25. Lemke, *The Government of Things*, 125.
26. Lemke, *The Government of Things*, 131.
27. Lemke, *The Government of Things*, 129.
28. Foucault, *Security, Territory, Population*, 22; Lemke, *The Government of Things*, 131.
29. Lemke, *The Government of Things*, 131.
30. Lemke, *The Government of Things*, 134.
31. Foucault, *Security, Territory, Population*, 48–9; Lemke, *The Government of Things*, 135.
32. In what follows, I make use of formulations I used in my 'Planetary Health and the Biopolitics of Home'.
33. Georges Canguilhem, 'The Living and Its Milieu', *Grey Room* 3 (2001): 7–31.
34. See Vladimir Vernadsky, *The Biosphere* (New York: Springer, 1997) and Lynn Margulis and Dorion Sagan *Slanted Truths* (New York: Springer, 1997).
35. John Scott Haldane, *The Philosophical Basis of Biology* (London: Hodder & Straughton, 1931), 15.
36. Canguilhem, 'The Living and Its Milieu', 19.
37. Jacob von Uexküll, *Foray Into the Worlds of Animals and Humans: With A Theory of Meaning* (Minneapolis, MN: University of Minnesota Press, 2010).
38. 'All the organs of plants as well as of animals owe their form and their distribution of materials to their meaning as utilizers of the meaning factors which come to them from the outside. The question as to meaning must therefore have priority in all living beings' (Uexküll, *Foray Into the Worlds of Animals and Humans*, 151). For the whole discussion in relation to Heidegger, see Giorgio Agamben, *The Open: Man and Animal*, trans. Kevin Attell (Stanford, CA: Stanford University Press, 2004). On Uexküll's influence on philosophy, see now Francesca Michelini and Kristian Köchy (eds.), *Jacob von Uexküll and Philosophy: Life, Environments, Anthropology* (London: Routledge, 2019).
39. Canguilhem, 'The Living and Its Milieu', 20.
40. Canguilhem, 'The Living and Its Milieu', 21.
41. See the discussion in Dorion Sagan, 'Umwelt After Uexküll', introduction to Uexküll, *Foray into the Worlds of Animals and Human*, 1–34. Sloterdijk uses the Heideggerian word-play: *Da-sein* is 'De-sign'. Here we can use this word play as well, provided it is clear that such de-signing of habitats is done by all living beings, beyond the organic and inorganic distinction, and that there is no specific priority assigned to human de-sign/da-sein. For a discussion of Sloterdijk on de-sign and its Stoic antecedents, see Kurt Lampe and Andrew Benjamin (eds.), *German Stoicisms: From Hegel to Sloterdijk* (London: Bloomsbury, 2020). I discuss Sloterdijk's spherology below.

42. Canguilhem, 'The Living and Its Milieu', 19.
43. For rights of nature construed in this way see Miguel Vatter, 'Nature's Law or Law's Law? Community of Life, Legal Personhood, and Trusts', in *Personhood in the Age of Biolegality*, eds. Marc de Leeuw and Sonja van Wichelen (New York: Palgrave Macmillan, 2020), 225–45, and for flows, see now Margaret Davies, *EcoLaw. Legality, Life, and the Normativity of Nature* (New York: Routledge, 2022), chapter 4. But see also the view on planetary biopolitics as a neoliberalisation of nature in Federico Luisetti, 'Geopower. On the States of Nature of Late Capitalism', *European Journal of Social Theory* 22, no. 3 (2019): 343–62.
44. Florian Sprenger, 'Zwischen Umwelt und milieu: Zur Begriffgeschichte von environment in der Evolutionstheorie', *Forum interdisziplinare Begriffsgeschichte* 3, no. 2 (2014): 7.
45. Florian Sprenger, 'Environments of Experimentation and Epistemologies of Surroundings. John Scott Haldane's Physiology and Biopolitics of the Living', *Grey Room* 75 (2019): 26.
46. Sprenger, 'Environments of Experimentation and Epistemologies of Surroundings', 27.
47. Foucault, *Security, Territory, Population*, 261.
48. Gilles Deleuze, 'Postscript on the Societies of Control', *October* 59 (1992): 3–7.
49. Christophe Bonneuil, 'Der Historiker und der Planet. Planetaritätsregimes an der Schnittstelle von Welt-Ökologien, ökologischen Reflexivitäten und Geo-Mächten', in *Gesellschaftstheorie im Anthropozän*, ed. Frank Adloff and Sighard Neckel (Frankfurt: Campus, 2020), 55–92.
50. Sloterdijk, *Globes*, 769.
51. qtd. in Sloterdijk, *Globes*, 776.
52. Sloterdijk, *Globes*, 763.
53. Sloterdijk, *Globes*, 777.
54. Sloterdijk constantly polemises with what he considers to be Heidegger's nostalgic and anti-modernist conception of 'dwelling', not unrelated to Schmitt's primacy of the 'home' in his conception of the *nomos*.
55. Sloterdijk, *Globes*, 779.
56. Sloterdijk, *Globes*, 790.
57. Sloterdijk, *Globes*, 792.
58. Uexküll, *Foray into the Worlds of Animals and Human*, 102ff.
59. Sloterdijk, *Globes*, 877.
60. Sloterdijk, *Globes*, 891.
61. Sloterdijk, *Globes*, 892.
62. Sloterdijk, *Globes*, 827.
63. Chakrabarty, *The Climate of History in a Planetary Age*, 12.

64. Sloterdijk, *Globes*, 961.

65. To employ the terms of Esposito, ancestral *nomoi* articulate the fundamental *munus* of life on the planet, the basis of a community that does not recognise species-differences. For senses of the ancestral that can be employed to develop a new planetary biopolitics, see Elizabeth Povinelli, *Between Gaia and Ground: Four Axioms of Existence and the Ancestral Catastrophe of Late Liberalism* (Durham, NC: Duke University Press, 2021) and Eduardo Viveiros de Castro, *Cannibal Metaphysics: For a Post-Structuralist Anthropology* (Minneapolis, MN: Univocal, 2014).

Works Cited

Agamben, Giorgio. *The Open: Man and Animal*. Translated by Kevin Attell. Stanford, CA: Stanford University Press, 2004.

Agamben, Giorgio. *Where Are We Now? The Epidemic as Politics*. Lanham, MD: Rowman & Littlefield, 2021.

Anderson, Warwick. 'The Model Crisis, or How to Have Critical Promiscuity in the Time of Covid-19'. *Social Studies of Science* 51, no. 2 (2021): 167–88.

Bonneuil, Christophe. 'Der Historiker und der Planet. Planetaritätsregimes an der Schnittstelle von Welt-Ökologien, ökologischen Reflexivitäten und Geo-Mächten'. In *Gesellschaftstheorie im Anthropozän*, edited by Frank Adloff and Sighard Neckel, 55–92. Frankfurt: Campus, 2020.

Braidotti, Rosi. *The Posthuman*. Cambridge: Polity, 2013.

Bratton, Benjamin. *The Revenge of the Real. Politics for a Post-Pandemic World*. London: Verso, 2021.

Canguilhem, Georges. 'The Living and Its Milieu'. *Grey Room* 3 (2001): 7–31.

Chakrabarty, Dipesh. *The Climate of History in a Planetary Age*. Chicago, IL: University of Chicago Press, 2021.

Clark, Nigel, and Bronislaw Szerszynski. *Planetary Social Thought. The Anthropocene Challenge to the Social Sciences*. Cambridge: Polity, 2020.

Davies, Margaret. *EcoLaw. Legality, Life, and the Normativity of Nature*. New York: Routledge, 2022.

Deleuze, Gilles. 'Postscript on the Societies of Control.' *October* 59 (1992): 3–7.

Fassin, Didier. 'Another Politics of Life is Possible'. *Theory, Culture and Society* 26, no. 5 (2009): 44–60.

Fearnley, Lyle. 'From Global to Planetary Health: Two Morphologies of Pandemic Preparedness'. In *The Viral Politics of COVID-19: Nature, Home and Planetary Health*, edited by Vanessa Lemm and Miguel Vatter, 15–31. Basingstoke: Palgrave Macmillan, 2022.

Foucault, Michel. *Security, Territory, Population: Lectures at the Collège de France 1977–1978*. New York: Picador, 2009.
Haff, Peter. 'Humans and Technology in the Anthropocene: Six Rules'. *The Anthropocene Review* 1, no. 2 (2014): 126–36.
Haldane, John Scott. *The Philosophical Basis of Biology*. London: Hodder & Stoughton, 1931.
Haraway, Donna. *When Species Meet*. Minneapolis, MN: The University of Minnesota Press, 2007.
Haraway, Donna. *Staying with the Trouble: Making Kin in the Chthulucene*. Durham, NC: Duke University, 2016.
Kirksey, Eben. 'The Emergence of COVID-19: A Multispecies Story'. *Anthropology Now* 12, No. 1 (2020): 11–16.
Lampe, Kurt, and Andrew Benjamin, eds. *German Stoicisms: From Hegel to Sloterdijk*. London: Bloomsbury, 2020.
Latour, Bruno. *Facing Gaia. Eight Lectures on the New Climate Regime*. Cambridge: Polity Press, 2017.
Lemke, Thomas. *The Government of Things. Foucault and the New Materialisms*. New York: New York University Press, 2021.
Lemm, Vanessa, and Miguel Vatter, eds. *The Viral Politics of COVID-19: Nature, Home and Planetary Health*. Basingstoke: Palgrave Macmillan, 2022.
Luisetti, Federico. 'Geopower. On the States of Nature of Late Capitalism'. *European Journal of Social Theory* 22, no. 3 (2019): 343–62.
Margulis, Lynn, and Dorion Sagan. *Slanted Truths*. New York: Springer, 1997.
Mezzadra, Sandro, and Brett Neilson. *Border as Method, Or the Multiplication of Labor*. Durham, NC: Duke University Press, 2013.
Michelini, Francesca, and Kristian Köchy, eds. *Jacob von Uexküll and Philosophy: Life, Environments, Anthropology*. London: Routledge, 2019.
Povinelli, Elizabeth. *Between Gaia and Ground. Four Axioms of Existence and the Ancestral Catastrophe of Late Liberalism*. Durham, NC: Duke University Press, 2021.
Rose, Nikolas. *The Politics of Life Itself. Biomedicine, Power, and Subjectivity in the Twenty-First Century*. Princeton, IL: Princeton University Press, 2007.
Sagan, Dorion. 'Umwelt After Uexküll'. In Jacob von Uexküll, *Foray into the Worlds of Animals and Humans: With a Theory of Meaning*, 1–34. Minneapolis, MN: University of Minnesota Press, 2010.
Shachar, Ayelet, and Acquib Mahmood. 'The Body as Border: A New Era'. *Historical Social Research* 46, no. 3 (2021): 124–50.
Sloterdijk, Peter. *Globes. Spheres II: Macrospherology*. New York: Semiotext(e), 2014.
Sprenger, Florian. 'Zwischen Umwelt und milieu: Zur Begriffsgeschichte von environment in der Evolutionstheorie'. *Forum interdisziplinare Begriffsgeschichte* 3, no. 2 (2014): 7–18.

Sprenger, Florian. 'Environments of Experimentation and Epistemologies of Surroundings. John Scott Haldane's Physiology and Biopolitics of the Living'. *Grey Room* 75 (2019): 6–35.

Susen, Simon. 'Reflections on the (Post-)Human Condition: Towards New Forms of Engagement with the World?' *Social Epistemology* 36, no. 1 (2022): 63–94.

Uexküll, Jacob von. *Foray Into the Worlds of Animals and Humans: With A Theory of Meaning*. Minnesota, MN: University of Minnesota Press, 2010.

Vatter, Miguel. *The Republic of the Living. Biopolitics and the Critique of Civil Society*. New York: Fordham, 2014.

Vatter, Miguel. 'Nature's Law or Law's Law? Community of Life, Legal Personhood, and Trusts'. In *Personhood in the Age of Biolegality*, edited by Marc de Leeuw and Sonja van Wichelen, 225–45. New York: Palgrave Macmillan, 2020.

Vatter, Miguel. 'Planetary Health and the Biopolitics of Home'. In *The Viral Politics of COVID-19: Nature, Home and Planetary Health*, edited by Vanessa Lemm and Miguel Vatter, 221–46. Basingstoke: Palgrave Macmillan, 2022.

Vernadsky, Vladimir. *The Biosphere*. New York: Springer, 1997.

Viveiros de Castro, Eduardo. *Cannibal Metaphysics: For a Post-Structuralist Anthropology*. Minneapolis: Univocal, 2014.

Walton, Marilyn, ed. *One Planet, One Health*. Edited by Marilyn Walton. Sydney: University of Sydney Press, 2019.

Yusoff, Kathryn. *A Billion Black Anthropocenes or None*. Minneapolis, MN: University of Minnesota Press, 2018.

4 How to Chirp Like a Cricket: Agamben and the Reversal of Anthropogenesis
Sergei Prozorov

This chapter addresses the relation between language and anthropogenesis in Agamben's work. From his writings of the early 1980s onwards Agamben has posited the process of entering language as unique to human beings. While animals always already find themselves within their natural languages, human beings must enter language, begin to speak, say 'I'. This experience is not merely linguistic but also ethico-political, insofar as it initiates the process of subjectivation, in which the speaking subject assumes responsibility for its own enunciations. In Agamben's diagnosis of the late-modern condition, this process of subjectivation now appears to be running on empty, as discourse becomes devoid of both truth and meaning. Yet, if this diagnosis is accepted, it must imply that the process of anthropogenesis is also rendered inoperative and there is no longer any difference between the human experience of language and the animal dwelling in language, the chirping of the cricket or the braying of the donkey. The chapter addresses these implications, posing the question of what kind of being emerges from this reversal of anthropogenesis.

Introduction

The relationship between language and humanity is a key focus of Agamben's philosophy. In the preface to his *Infancy and History*, Agamben speaks of an unwritten work to which that book serves as a kind of a prologue, entitled *The Human Voice*. This work would address the specificity of the human experience of language, posing the question of whether there is such a thing as 'a human voice, a voice that is the voice of man as the chirp is the voice of the cricket or the bray is the voice of the donkey? And, if it exists, is this voice language?'[1]

While this problem was subsequently posed in the sequel to *Infancy and History*, called *Language and Death*, Agamben returned to the question of the human experience of language throughout his work, most notably in *The Sacrament of Language*, which addressed this question from the perspective of the oath and its decline in contemporary culture.[2] The parallel with the cricket and the donkey is present in this later text as well, forming something like a red line throughout Agamben's work on language.

In this chapter, I shall venture to understand the significance of this parallel for Agamben's understanding of the process of *anthropogenesis*, becoming human. In his early work on language this process was described as heterogeneous to animal experience of language: in contrast to the cricket and the donkey that always already find themselves within their natural languages of chirping and braying, the human being was defined as having to *enter* language, begin to speak from the position of not-speaking (*infancy*). The entry into language is therefore never merely linguistic but is also an ethico-political experience, insofar as it initiates the process of subjectivation, in which the speaking subject assumes responsibility for its own enunciations. The answer of the early Agamben to the question posed in the unwritten *Human Voice* is clearly that the human voice is quite unlike the chirping of the cricket and the braying of the donkey.

However, in his later work on the oath things become rather more complicated. The ethico-political experience of subjectivation through language finds its clearest manifestation in the oath and its attendant phenomenon of the curse, in which the subject takes responsibility for their words and is prepared to suffer the consequences if their words prove false or hollow. Yet, in his analysis of the transformations of the apparatus of the oath in modernity Agamben observes that this apparatus has been rendered inoperative and is now running on empty, producing nothing but vain speech with no truth or meaning. This diagnosis, all too familiar to us from myriad critiques of popular culture, acquires a rather uncanny significance in the context of Agamben's account of anthropogenesis. If human beings were constituted as subjects by entering language and taking responsibility for their enunciations, then the vacuity of oaths and curses in contemporary culture manifests nothing less than a reversal of anthropogenesis, whereby our voice stops being specifically human and becomes strictly analogous to the chirping of the cricket. The question posed in the unwritten *Human Voice* thus receives a new answer: our language, purged of oaths and curses, is our voice.

My analysis will begin by addressing Agamben's understanding of anthropogenesis as the entry into language. I shall then analyse Agamben's argument on the oath as the apparatus of subjectivation and its decline in contemporary culture. Thirdly, I shall discuss the implications of this decline in the context of Agamben's earlier work on the experience of language devoid of all negativity. Finally, I shall address the implications of approaching this experience of language as a reversal of anthropogenesis.

Entering Language: On Anthropogenesis

In *Infancy and History* Agamben defines infancy as the experience of the human being's entry into language, which presupposes its not having language at that point in time (hence, *in-fancy*, 'not speaking'). While this condition evidently characterises the human infant at a certain developmental stage, Agamben generalises this specifically neo-natal experience as a 'transcendental origin', which is not chronologically separate and prior to the object but is rather constitutive of and coextensive with it:

> What we must renounce is merely a concept of origin cast in a mould already abandoned by the natural sciences themselves, one which locates it in a chronology, a primary cause that separates in time a before and an after. Such a concept of origins is useless to the human sciences whenever what is at issue is not an 'object' presupposing the human already behind it, but is instead itself constitutive of the human. The origin of a 'being' of this kind cannot be *historicized* because it is itself *historicizing*, and itself founds the possibility of there being any history.[3]

The origin is not something that has occurred once in the past but rather that which *keeps occurring* in the present and thereby renders intelligible that of which it is the origin. Agamben's favourite example of the transcendental origin is the Indo-European root, 'reinstated through philological comparison of the historical languages, a historically unattested state of the language, yet still real'.[4] Other examples include 'the child of psychoanalysis exerting an active force within the psychic life of the adult, or the big bang which is supposed to have given rise to the universe but continues to send toward us its fossil radiation'.[5]

Infancy is yet another example of a transcendental origin, a moment of not speaking that survives in every act of speech as the gap between the speaker and language that makes it necessary for us to enter language. It is this gap that separates the human experience of language from that of other animals.

Animals might have infants, but they do not have an infancy. In Agamben's reading, animals, however young, are always already *inside* language and hence incapable of *entering* it: 'Animals are not in fact denied language; on the contrary, they are always and totally language. Animals do not enter language, they are already inside it. Man, instead, by having an infancy, by preceding speech, splits this single language and, in order to speak, has to constitute himself as the subject of language – he has to say "I"'.[6]

Thus, only human language is split between the *semiotic* dimension of a closed and self-referential system of signs existing prior to the speaker and the *semantic* dimension of actual discourse. It is this split that constitutes anthropogenesis and grants human existence a historical dimension: if one were always already within language, one would remain united with one's nature and there would be no place where the discontinuity of history could enter. Thus, contrary to the traditional belief since Aristotle, a human being is not an animal *having* language but rather an animal originally deprived of it and hence having to enter it, thereby effecting the transition from the semiotic to the semantic. Agamben does not define the human condition in terms of plenitude or 'added value' (animal *plus* language) but rather in terms of lack, as the originary being-without-language that must be overcome through a subjectivising practice of entry into language.

Yet, this lack is immediately converted into a kind of plenitude, not an actual plenitude of possessing more than the animal but the plenitude of potentiality that in Agamben's view the animal lacks as such. The human being does not possess language as such but rather a faculty of language, a potentiality for speech that logically presupposes its obverse, the potentiality not to speak, to remain in infancy. The passage from language to discourse and from a natural being to a human subject remains radically contingent and hence a matter of freedom, which is once again denied to the animal. And yet, this freedom comes at a price, lending the human experience of language the kind of gravity that we cannot observe in the chirping of the cricket and the braying of the donkey.

Speaking in Vain: The Oath and its Decline

The subjectivation involved in the human entry into language does not stop with the overcoming of originary infancy and beginning to speak. What matters is also how human beings speak and what consequences their speech carries. The entry into language entails our taking responsibility for our enunciations: '[The] living being, who has discovered itself speaking, has decided to be responsible for his words, and, devoting himself to the *logos*, to constitute himself as the "living being who has language"'.[7]

Having entered into language, human beings sought to stabilise their dwelling in it, ensuring that names refer to the same things each time they are used and that the use of certain words leads to the same kinds of actions. From now on, the speaking subject would not simply speak but would speak either truly or falsely and could be held responsible for the content of their enunciations. '[For] the living human being, who found himself speaking, what must have been decisive is the problem of the efficacy and truthfulness of his word, that is, of what can guarantee the original connection between names and things, and between the subject who has become a speaker – and thus capable of asserting and promising – and his actions'.[8] Entering into language no longer merely means gaining freedom to speak or not to speak but also entails the speaker's assumption of responsibility for what they say, '[responding] with its life for its words, to testify in the first person for them'.[9]

Agamben approaches oaths and curses as two of the earliest historical apparatuses of linguistic subjectivation, whereby the speaker is bound to their enunciations. An oath establishes a connection between words and things, language and reality, affirming that what is said is indeed (or will indeed be) so and specifying the sanction that would follow if one does not act as one said (i.e., the curse that would accompany a broken oath).[10] Every act of speech either confirms the efficacy of language when the oath is kept or undermines it when it is betrayed. The subject is thus held responsible not merely for their individual words and actions but for the state of language as such: a broken oath does harm not only to the individuals affected by it but to language itself, rendering it ineffective and unreliable.

It is clear that with this dimension of responsibility we are far from the animal experience of language. While for the animal language is inseparable from its life, the human experience of language separates life and language only to articulate them again in the form of an oath. For an oath to be possible in the first place,

> [it] is necessary to be able to distinguish and articulate together in some way, life and language, actions and words, and this is precisely what the animal, for which language is still an integral part of its vital practice, cannot do. The first promise is produced by means of this division, in which man, opposing his language to his actions, can put himself at stake in language, can promise himself to the logos.[11]

The originary oath is thus an act in which the speaker affirms that she is serious about her use of language, that her words will be linked to actions and that what she says is not in vain. Every actual oath, promise, guarantee, commitment and other performative speech act that we practice on a daily basis are, in Agamben's view, 'the relics in language of this constitutive experience of speech – veridiction – that exhausts itself with its utterance, since the speaking subject neither pre-exists it nor is subsequently linked to it but coincides integrally with the act of speech'.[12] It is not a coincidence that all these performative formulae must be uttered in the first person and lose their performative efficacy when used in reporting on the activities of others. One can report on the oaths made by others, but one can only make an oath in one's own name. The oath is thus an apparatus that binds the subject to their enunciations, rendering it responsible for them and threatening sanction in the form of a curse if the oath ends up broken. One thereby becomes a speaking subject not merely in the sense of being an agent that speaks but also in the sense of being subjected to one's speech acts.

In Agamben's reading, religion and law subsequently ritualise and technicalise the anthropogenic experience, 'separating and opposing point by point truth and lie, true name and false name, efficacious formula and incorrect formula'.[13] The performative force of language is thus ordered and routinised in familiar formulae, reserved for specific speakers endowed with particular authority. What began as the establishment of a relation between living beings and their acts of speech ends up split into a myriad of institutions and authorities, dogmata and rituals, ceremonies and routines that all seek to stabilise 'the originary performative force of the anthropogenic experience'.[14] J. L. Austin's speech act theory, which highlights the importance of 'conventional procedures' as a guarantee of the efficacy or 'felicity' of speech acts, is founded on this institutionalisation of performativity that effaces the originary experience of language.[15]

At the end of the book, having offered a lengthy genealogy that traces our current experience of the performative force of language back to ancient oaths and even further to the first human experience of language, Agamben draws a striking conclusion that throws a different light on the entire preceding discourse:

> [We] are today the first generations to live our collective life without the bond of the oath. Humanity finds itself today before a disjunction or at least a loosening of the bond that, by means of the oath, united the living being to its language. On the one hand, there is the living being, more and more reduced to a purely biological reality and to bare life. On the other hand, there is the speaking being, artificially divided from the former, through a multiplicity of technico-mediatic apparatuses, in an experience of the word that grows ever more vain, for which it is impossible to be responsible,

and in which anything like a political experience becomes more and more precarious. When the ethical – and not simply cognitive – connection that unites words, things and human actions is broken, this in fact promotes a spectacular and unprecedented proliferation of vain words on the one hand and on the other, of legislative apparatuses that seek obstinately to legislate on every aspect of that life on which they seem no longer to have any hold. The age of the eclipse of the oath is also the age of blasphemy, in which the name of God breaks away from its living connection with language and can only be uttered 'in vain'.[16]

At first glance, Agamben's claim appears to be self-evident. Oaths and especially curses certainly appear in decline in contemporary culture, often reduced to official rituals devoid of any meaning. Yet, if we agree with Agamben's genealogy, then the decline of the oath has far-reaching consequences for the very experience of being human. If the living being and the speaking being no longer coincide in the oath but dwell in the separate dimensions of bare life and communication technology, then it is no longer possible for the human being to place itself at stake in language and speak either truly or falsely. The result is proliferation of 'vain words' and, what amounts to the same, blasphemy.

Blasphemy is traditionally understood as uttering the name of God in vain (e.g., saying 'Oh my God!', 'Gosh!' or 'Jesus Christ!') in trivial settings without actually appealing to the deity in question in a petition or a prayer. It is therefore a diametrical opposite of the oath, in which the name of God is relied on to produce the sought performative effect:

> Blasphemy presents us with a phenomenon that is perfectly symmetrical to the oath. Blasphemy is an oath, in which the name of a god is extracted from the assertorial or promissory context and is uttered in itself, in vain, irrespectively of a semantic content. The name, which in the oath expresses and guarantees the connection between words and things and which defines the truthfulness and force of the logos, in blasphemy expresses the breakdown of this connection and the vanity of human language.[17]

While in the oath the name of God is used to fortify the performative efficacy of the statement, in blasphemy its use serves to undermine any such efficacy. Yet, if the performative efficacy of language functions in the process of anthropogenesis to subjectivise the living being as human by putting its life at stake in its discourse, what happens when oaths and curses lose their efficacy and all that remains is blasphemy, which is no longer even recognised as such, precisely because there is no longer any other way to speak than in vain? What remains of the human being that can no longer be held responsible for what it says?

It is important to emphasise that Agamben does not lament the decline of oaths and curses in the manner of conservative cultural criticism. Any revival of the oath would only amount to bringing back or propping up the remaining apparatuses of religion and law, whose prior technicalisation and routinisation of the performativity of language led to the decline of the oath in the first place. Instead, Agamben argues, quite provocatively, that

> it is perhaps time to call into question the prestige that language has enjoyed and continues to enjoy in our culture, as a tool of incomparable potency, efficacy and beauty. And yet, considered in itself, it is no more beautiful than birdsong, no more efficacious than the signals insects exchange, no more powerful than the roar with which the lion asserts his dominion.[18]

We are back to the parallel between human and animal experiences of language, which, however, is no longer presented as a rigorous distinction but as something rather more fragile. In itself, human language is not that different from the languages of birds, insects or lions. What distinguishes human language is only the place it assigns for the subject to be constituted: '[The] decisive element that confers on human language its peculiar virtue is not in the tool itself but in the place it leaves to the speaker, a hollowed out form that the speaker must always assume in order to speak'.[19] Yet, if the speaker can no longer assume responsibility for their enunciations by means of oaths and curses, what kind of subject could possibly emerge in this hollowed out form?

The Trite Words of Habit

Agamben's final words in *The Sacrament of Language* carry a strong and somewhat unexpected resonance with his earlier work, especially *Language and Death*, in which he sought to overcome the negativity at work in the human experience of language, the negation of the (animal) voice that is the presupposed foundation of language as the system of signification: 'Man is the living being who removes himself and preserves himself at the same time – as unspeakable – in language; negativity is the human means of *having* language'.[20]

The removal of the animal voice leaves the human being in a purely negative, 'hollowed out' structure that Agamben terms Voice. This capitalised Voice should not be confused with the natural sound of animal voice, which it negates. Instead, it is a presupposition that can never be itself brought to speech itself, but only indicated through deictic markers, known in linguistics as shifters, that refer to the taking place of discourse: 'I', 'this', 'here'. It is only thanks to these shifters that human beings can enter language and begin to speak, as opposed to animals which are always already within language: 'If language were immediately the voice of man, as braying is the voice of the ass and chirping the voice of the cicada, man could not experience the taking place of language or the disclosure of being. But if, on the other hand, man radically possessed no voice (not even a negative Voice), every shifter and every possibility of indicating the event of language would disappear equally'.[21]

At first glance, the negativity of the Voice appears to be necessary and inescapable for the human experience of language. However, Agamben's critical project in *Language and Death* ventures nothing less than the complete liquidation of the figure of the Voice. '[Only] if language no longer refers to any Voice, is it possible for man to experience a language that is not marked by negativity and death'.[22] It is important to stress that this liquidation of the Voice is not an attempt to return to a somehow purer or more originary human experience of language. As we have seen, the infantile entry into language *is* the origin of being human, hence the Voice is as originary as origins get. Moreover, to recall Agamben's understanding of origin as transcendental, the negative foundation of the Voice is not an event in the distant past but something that remains at work in contemporary linguistic practices. The liquidation of the Voice would therefore not return us to the way humanity once was but rather take us to what humanity has never been but is on the verge of becoming due to the decline of the apparatuses of linguistic subjectivation such as the oath.

But what sort of language would the liquidation of the Voice result in? If the negative foundation of the Voice is produced by the 'removal' or negation of 'animal voice' or natural sound, then the negation of that negation should presumably restore the natural immediacy of language, akin to the braying of the donkey or the chirping of the cricket. In his frequent reference to these examples Agamben seeks to describe precisely an immediate experience of language devoid of any split, discontinuity or difference that characterises the human mode of having language. The liquidation of the Voice would thus make human language entirely indistinct from the human voice, with no negative presupposition separating them any longer.

Yet, is this liquidation of the Voice even possible? Its possibility is established by the transcendental nature of infancy that produced this negative foundation in the first place. Since infancy as the threshold of anthropogenesis is not crossed once and for all at some moment in the past but must be traversed in every act of speech, it can also be deactivated or even reversed in these acts. If we keep becoming human by continuing to assume responsibility for our discourse, then the increasingly evident vanity and inefficacy of this discourse points to the reversal of this process. Thus, the scene of the contemporary degradation of language that Agamben observes in *Language and Death* becomes the site of a new experience of language whose direction is diametrically opposed to anthropogenesis:

> Perhaps in the age of absolutely speakable things, whose extreme nihilistic furour we are experiencing today, the age in which all the figures of the Unspeakable and all the masks of ontotheology have been *liquidated*, or released or spent in words that merely show the nothingness of their foundation; the age in which all human experience of language has been redirected to the final negative reality of a willing that means nothing – perhaps this age is also the age of man's in-fantile dwelling in language.[23]

In the process of anthropogenesis, infancy was a point of departure that was subsequently negated by our beginning to speak, entering language and saying 'I'. How is it then possible to dwell in language in an 'infantile manner'? Presumably, this does not mean a simple cessation of speech, since this would entail our no longer dwelling in language at all. Instead, infantile dwelling in language might be read as suspending not the acts of speech themselves but only the subjectivation that is at work in them, which ties human beings to their enunciations. Yet, what remains of our experience of language in the absence of this subjectivation and the negativity of the Voice that it implies? In the final pages of *Language and Death* Agamben alludes to this new mode of dwelling in language in the following manner: '[is] it possible that being is not up to the level of the simple mystery of humans' having, of their habitations or their habits? What if the dwelling to which we return beyond being were neither a supercelestial place nor a Voice, but simply the *trite* words that we *have*?'[24]

What are these trite words? Agamben speaks of a 'language without Voice, a word that is not grounded in any meaning' as something that 'we must still learn to think',[25] which suggests that this vision of language is something esoteric, akin to Benjamin's pure language that, in Agamben's description, 'does not mean anything, but simply speaks'.[26] Alternatively, Agamben might be interpreted as intending a particular mode of using language (e.g., in (modernist) poetry, which he has extensively analysed as a mode of discourse that bears within itself the deactivation of the signifying function).[27]

We would nonetheless like to suggest a more literal interpretation. It is not a matter of the introduction of either a new kind of language or even a new use of language but rather of a shift of perspective that reveals the importance of something we tended to dismiss as utterly trivial and unworthy of thought: our 'habits' and 'trite words'. In other words, what we must still learn to think is not some very difficult thought but the disappearance of the very object of thought:

> [We] can cease to hold language, the voice, in suspense. If thought is thought in the voice, it no longer has *anything* to think. Once completed, thought has no more thought. We came as close as possible to language, we almost brushed against it, held it in suspense: but we never reached our encounter and now we turn back, untroubled, toward home. So, language is our voice, our language. As you now speak, that is ethics.[28]

What does this enigmatic passage mean? Earlier in the text, Agamben remarks in parentheses that 'the cricket, clearly, cannot think in its chirping'.[29] Thought is only possible by virtue of the negative structure of anthropogenesis, in which the living being is at once negated and conserved, elevated to the status of the subject by placing its life at stake in its words. If this negative structure is itself negated, and thought has nothing left to think, we end up with nothing other than the habitual use of language that no longer means anything but 'simply speaks', the trite words that we have, that we have always had but vainly hoped to replace by words that would be more meaningful or effective because we had put our lives at stake in them.

The anthropogenetic process of subjectivation by oaths and curses is thereby reversed into a plenitude of speech that, however, no longer has anything at stake in it, that does not even think while it speaks, just like the cricket that does not think in its chirping but simply chirps away. To speak that way is to speak vainly and haphazardly, and even to speak blasphemously, with a caveat that there is no longer any authority that could accuse us of blasphemy. Rather than return to the origin, we arrive at a place before the origin, before any scission and any articulation between the living and the speaking. The reversal of the anthropogenetic apparatus leaves us with a language that is strictly equivalent to that of the cricket or the donkey, the language wholly contained in our voice.

On the final page of *The Sacrament of Language* Agamben appears to backtrack from these admittedly radical conclusions by isolating another possible experience of language, in which it would retain its performative efficacy without, however, becoming reducible to the ordering formulae of religion and law. This experience of speech, '[abiding] in the risk of truth as much as of error, forcefully pronounced, without either swearing or cursing, its yes to language, to the human being, as speaking and political animal'.[30] This experience is of course nothing other than philosophy, which is 'constitutively a critique of the oath', ceaselessly questioning the very link between words and actions that constitutes both religion and law without abrogating it entirely. It thereby 'puts in question the sacramental bond that links the human being to language, without for that reason simply speaking haphazardly, falling into the vanity of speech'.[31]

While it is perfectly understandable that a philosopher would seek to elevate the status of their own discourse, this otherwise elegant solution does not really work, especially in the light of the concluding claims of *Language and Death*. The critique of the oath, taken to its logical conclusion, cannot but end in the taking leave of language and thought and the return to purely habitual, trite speech. As a critique of the oath, philosophy must necessarily presuppose its end in the accomplishment of this critique, which at once deprives the oath of its efficacy and philosophy of any meaning. In the language, where an oath is no longer possible, where everything is speakable without effect or responsibility, philosophy has nothing to say and can only retrace its history, the history of its own arriving at an end. Similarly to the famous examples of ritualised arts in Alexandre Kojève's account of the end of history,[32] we would be dealing with a purely ritualised discourse that has long lost its meaning but whose reproduction may still be enjoyable, much as chirping is enjoyable for the cricket and braying is for the donkey. Words that have ceased to be meaningful or effective may nonetheless remain pleasant to speak and this pleasure of speaking is in fact the only reason to go on speaking when nothing is any longer at stake in one's speech. It is no coincidence that the prime site of vain speech in the world today is named after the chirping sound habitually made by birds.

Conclusion

While admittedly esoteric at first glance, Agamben's account of the decline of the oath and the performative efficacy of language in contemporary culture is highly instructive for understanding such widely discussed global phenomena as the 'post-truth' condition.[33] As we have seen, truth could not possibly be a property of the natural language of animals, but only emerges in the scission between the speaker and language, things and words, action and speech. In contrast, a language in which an oath is impossible, which is no longer characterised by the disjunctive articulation of speech and action, only offers the experience of enjoyment of speech *as* action. Such a language leaves no place for truth, as the 'hollowed out' space where the human being could emerge as a subject of true and false discourse is now definitively closed. The post-truth era we dwell in is indeed the age of absolutely speakable things, all of which are nonetheless spoken in vain.

The specific contribution of Agamben's analysis to the diagnosis of the post-truth predicament consists in the elaboration of its relation to anthropogenesis. If the faculty of truth is not merely a historical accident that befell humanity at a certain trajectory of its history, but rather follows from the very experience of anthropogenesis as linguistic subjectivation, then the significance of the post-truth predicament exceeds that of a late-modern cultural malaise that it is often viewed as. If we are no longer capable of distinguishing between truth and falsity in our speech acts, then who or what are we when we speak? If the trite words we now speak resemble the natural languages of animals, does this mean that we also become animals? Agamben certainly does not suggest this explicitly, but his analysis of the decline of anthropogenetic subjectivation in *The Sacrament of Language* resonates with his earlier attempts in *The Open* to deactivate the 'anthropological machine' that at once separates and articulates humanity and animality by animalising human beings or humanising animals.[34] Insofar as the engine of this machine is the presupposition of the difference between animals and humans, the nullification of this difference as a result of the suspension of anthropogenetic subjectivation is the most effective way to render the machine inoperative. It is not that humans become animals when they can no longer make oaths and issue curses. They do not start chirping like crickets or braying like donkeys but continue to speak their languages, which, however, no longer differ in kind from the languages of animals: just like chirping is the voice of the cricket, the trite language of habit is only ever the human voice. It is therefore no longer possible to rely on this difference to legitimise the mastery of one by the other:

> [Neither] must man master nature nor nature man. Nor must both be surpassed in a third term that would represent their dialectical synthesis. What is decisive here is only the 'between', the interval or the play between the two terms, their immediate constellation in a non-coincidence. In the reciprocal suspension of the two terms, something, for which we perhaps have no name and which is neither animal nor man, settles in between nature and humanity and holds itself in the mastered relation, in the saved night.[35]

It would nonetheless be incorrect to read Agamben's diagnosis as yet another meditation on the 'end of man'. In the transcendental approach to the origin, the beginning and the end are never too far apart. The reversal of anthropogenesis in the current age of absolutely speakable things is not a momentous and irreversible transformation but rather the extreme point of the *pendulum* that can always swing to the other extreme without, however, necessarily ending up in the ritualised normativity of oaths and curses. We are therefore just as little doomed to chirp like crickets as we are destined to speak truthfully and seriously.

The question is therefore not whether a return to linguistic subjectivation is possible but rather what kind of content of discourse will make the chirping crickets that we have become speak 'in all seriousness' again. Somewhat ironically, the only theme that appears serious enough to make us want to take our words seriously again is the possibility of the extinction of humanity, not merely as a linguistic subject but also as the natural species alongside many others that never had to enter language in the first place. It remains to be seen whether this possibility of extinction not merely of language but also of voice will lead to a new assumption of responsibility or will only yield more trite words spoken in vain until silence falls.

Notes

1. Giorgio Agamben, *Infancy and History*, trans. Liz Heron (London: Verso, 2007), 3–4.
2. See Agamben, *Language and Death: The Place of Negativity*, trans. Karen E. Pinkus and Michael Hardt (Minneapolis, MN: The University of Minnesota Press, 1991); Agamben, *The Sacrament of Language: An Archaeology of the Oath*, trans. Adam Kotsko (Stanford, CA: Stanford University Press, 2009).
3. Agamben, *Infancy and History*, 56.
4. Agamben, *Infancy and History*, 57.
5. Agamben, *The Signature of All Things: On Method*, trans. Luca D'Isanto and Kevin Attell (New York: Zone Books, 2009), 109–10.
6. Agamben, *Infancy and History*, 59.
7. Agamben, *The Sacrament of Language*, 69.
8. Agamben, *The Sacrament of Language*, 68.
9. Agamben, *The Sacrament of Language*, 69.
10. Agamben, *The Sacrament of Language*, 65.
11. Agamben, *The Sacrament of Language*, 69.
12. Agamben, *The Sacrament of Language*, 58.
13. Agamben, *The Sacrament of Language*, 70.
14. Agamben, *The Sacrament of Language*, 70.
15. John L. Austin, *How to Do Things with Words* (Cambridge, MA: Harvard University Press, 1975), 14–45.
16. Agamben, *The Sacrament of Language*, 71.
17. Agamben, *The Sacrament of Language*, 40–1.

18. Agamben, *The Sacrament of Language*, 71.
19. Agamben, *The Sacrament of Language*, 71.
20. Agamben, *Language and Death*, 85, emphasis in the original.
21. Agamben, *Language and Death*, 84–5.
22. Agamben, *Language and Death*, 95.
23. Agamben, *Language and Death*, 92, emphasis in the original.
24. Agamben, *Language and Death*, 94, emphasis in the original.
25. Agamben, *Language and Death*, 95.
26. Agamben, 'Language and History: Linguistic and Historical Categories in Benjamin's Thought', in *Potentialities: Selected Essays in Philosophy*, ed. and trans. Daniel Heller-Roazen (Stanford, CA: Stanford University Press, 1999), 54.
27. Agamben, *The End of the Poem: Studies in Poetics*, trans. Daniel Heller-Roazen (Stanford, CA: Stanford University Press, 1999), 62–75, 87–101.
28. Agamben, *Language and Death*, 108.
29. Agamben, *Language and Death*, 107.
30. Agamben, *The Sacrament of Language*, 92.
31. Agamben, *The Sacrament of Language*, 92
32. Alexandre Kojève, *Introduction to the Reading of Hegel: Lectures on the Phenomenology of Spirit*, trans. James H. Nichols (Ithaca, NY: Cornell University Press, 1969), 158–62.
33. See Sergei Prozorov, *Biopolitics after Truth: Knowledge, Power and Democratic Life* (Edinburgh: Edinburgh University Press, 2021), chapter 2.
34. Agamben, *The Open: Man and Animal*, trans. Kevin Attell (Stanford, CA: Stanford University Press, 2004), 36–8.
35. Agamben, *The Open*, 83.

Works Cited

Agamben, Giorgio. *Language and Death: The Place of Negativity*. Translated by Karen E. Pinkus and Michael Hardt. Minneapolis, MN: University of Minnesota Press, 1991.

Agamben, Giorgio. *The End of the Poem: Studies in Poetics*. Translated by Daniel Heller-Roazen. Stanford, CA: Stanford University Press, 1999.

Agamben, Giorgio. *Potentialities: Selected Essays in Philosophy*. Edited and translated by Daniel Heller-Roazen. Stanford, CA: Stanford University Press, 1999.

Agamben, Giorgio. *The Open: Man and Animal*. Translated by Kevin Attell. Stanford, CA: Stanford University Press, 2004.

Agamben, Giorgio. *Infancy and History: On the Destruction of Experience*. Translated by Liz Heron. London: Verso, 2007.

Agamben, Giorgio. *The Sacrament of Language: An Archaeology of the Oath*. Translated by Adam Kotsko. Stanford, CA: Stanford University Press, 2009.

Agamben, Giorgio. *The Signature of All Things: On Method*. Translated by Luca D'Isanto and Kevin Attell. New York: Zone Books, 2009.

Austin, John L. *How to Do Things with Words*. Cambridge, MA: Harvard University Press, 1975.

Kojève, Alexandre. *Introduction to the Reading of Hegel: Lectures on the* Phenomenology of Spirit. Translated by James H. Nichols. Ithaca, NY: Cornell University Press, 1969.

Prozorov, Sergei. *Biopolitics after Truth: Knowledge, Power and Democratic Life*. Edinburgh: Edinburgh University Press, 2021.

5 Animality and Inoperativity: Interspecies Form-of-Life

Sherryl Vint

The figure of the animal lies at the heart of analysis of biopolitical governance, and yet this image generally remains precisely that: an abstract figuration in which 'the animal' is only that animal capacity within humanity. The animal predominantly figures the element of life that is at risk for the thanatopolitical side of the operation of power on life, the quality of being included only by the exclusion from community in Giorgio Agamben's theorisation of the distinction between *bios* and *zoē*, or the 'biological-type caesura within a population' that Foucault argues 'will allow power to treat that population as a mixture of races, or to be more accurate, to treat the species, to subdivide the species it controls, into the subspecies known, precisely, as races'.[1] Biopolitical thinking about animals, then, is always shadowed by the spectre of racialisation and colonial extraction, as scholars such as Achille Mbembe and Zakkiyah Iman Jackson have explored in detail.[2] Cary Wolfe argues that 'to live under biopolitics is to live in a situation in which we are all always already (potential) "animals" before the law', contending that the human/animal binary is not a 'zoological classification' but a 'discursive resource' that is the central tactic of biopolitical power.[3]

Wolfe's contention that we are 'all always already' in this category of risk ignores material histories of racial capitalism that sediment into differentiated structures of thanatopolitical risk. As Esposito puts this, 'the animal thus became a point of division within humanity, between species of people who were separated by their relation to life—and thus to death, since the easy life of some turned out to be directly proportional to the forced death of others'.[4] Yet despite this limitation of Wolfe's framework, I find the idea of the human/animal boundary as a 'discursive resource' a useful hermeneutic through which to ask: what happens if we take the animal figuration in biopolitics literally, that is, how might we think a politics that might extend beyond the human? How can we imagine the animal not merely as a point of division within humanity (although it is surely that) but also as a point of division between Western notions of the human and the rest of the living world?

Rethinking the place of material, living animals in the human biopolitical frame moves us towards the possibility of an affirmative biopolitics, a biopolitics that is predicated on shared vulnerability and interdependence rather than on a hierarchical structure by which the optimisation and fostering of valued life is accomplished at the expense of devalued and excluded life. This is not to suggest a flattening or totalising approach in which all life must be equally valued in some kind of amorphous vitalism, but rather it is to suggest that the biopolitical logic of division by which some life can be promoted at the expense of other life is faulty: what we need instead is thinking on the level of entanglements and interspecies dependencies which mandate that we understand that we cannot abstract some (valued) life from the embedded network of the living world: truly to foster any kind of life requires a new metaphysics of subjectivity that begins from premises of mutuality and interdependence. This ecologically oriented understanding of affirmative biopolitics requires us to think of animals within its discourse as more than metaphors to explain how the human is set apart from other life, to acknowledge that 'non-human life is not just something that biopolitical discourse ought to be able to speak to, but, more powerfully, that biopolitics necessarily arose alongside the domination and exploitation of animals'.[5] Agamben begins the *The Open* by contemplating an image from a thirteenth century Hebrew Bible in which the righteous at the end of days appear with the faces of animals. He reads this image to suggest the messianic promise of a better world demands that 'the relations between animals and men will take on a new form, and that man himself will be reconciled with his animal nature'.[6] Following from this, I argue that if we seek to rethink affirmative biopolitics in a way that takes animal lives seriously, it must begin with revising the metaphysics of human subjectivity.

In the analysis that follows, I seek to expand this idea of an affirmative, interspecies biopolitics through three stages of analysis. First, I will revisit the extent to which the idea of the human-as-political subject has been predicted on ideas that disconnect the human from lived embodiment and thus make it impossible to imagine politics outside of this frame of abstraction. Next, I will connect my critique of the limitations of the human thus conceived as to similar calls for a new metaphysics in work by Agamben on what he calls inoperativity and work by Roberto Esposito on his notion of the third person. These critiques show how it is specifically Western metaphysics that has created a problematic division within life into two poles (human/animal, valued/denigrated, Western/colonised). In contrast, Indigenous frameworks for knowledge production offer a contrasting metaphysics that reinforces how the biopolitical logics in which we seem trapped are not coterminous with the human species, but rather with the domination of Western traditions of thought, as I will demonstrate through reference to work by Leanne Betasamosake Simpson. Finally, I will turn to Ray Nayler's science fiction novel *The Mountain in the Sea* to show how its speculations about machine sentience and human communication with sentient octopi provide a concrete image of a possible interspecies, affirmative biopolitics and, moreover, show how such a shift in our metaphysics of subjectivity connects to issues of social justice beyond the human relationship with other species.

Anthropology, Zoology, and the Possibility of the Political

The categories of human and animal that emerge from Western metaphysics are both promiscuously intermingled and yet starkly segregated: on the one hand, biopolitics concerns governance of the human body precisely via the capacities that it shares with other kinds of life (propagation, health, mortality); on the other, biopolitics cannot conceive of human life other than via its separation from an originary community of all life. This segregation of life is precisely how biopolitics emerges as a power over life, and Agamben stresses that 'the becoming human of the human being, is not in fact an event that was completed once and for all in the past; rather, it is the event that never stops happening, a process still under way in which the human being is always in the act of becoming human and of remaining (or becoming) inhuman'.[7] Thus, finding ways to include animals within our political community has the capacity not only to disrupt human exploitation of other species but also to short-circuit this anthropogenic ontology that enables biopolitical racism. Esposito suggests that the animal enters Western philosophical tradition specifically as its power is expressed thanatopolitically, that the animal functions as 'the measure of its internal difference'[8] within the human species, a logic that finds its most extreme expression in projects to purify – thus to save – the species from degeneration. And this project begins by expelling those deemed degenerate from the (bio)political community.

The central biopolitical question – once we concede that the territory of politics has become the biological body – is to determine which forms of life are constituted as within the political community and which are not. This also means recognising that liberal frameworks of politics –which suggest we are governed on the terrain of abstract rights and freedoms – are inadequate to a context in which power has already decided in advance which voices and perspectives can appear in a way that recognises their rights, that hears their political claims. Distancing ourselves from liberalism's disembodied notion of political expression can open up the possibility of thinking of politics as not strictly a human affair, just as work in human–animal and posthumanist studies has prompted us to recognise that sentience is not a human-exclusive capacity. Of course, animal sentience and the possibility of animal politics demand that we develop more capacious ideas of these terms: neither will appear in modes that are identical to human styles of expressing these capacities. That is why rethinking these terms also requires rethinking what human subjectivity could be beyond the human as made by what Agamben has called the anthropological machine.

Agamben's later work is interested in returning to this question of what constitutes the political, starting with what has been excluded from it, namely animals and the animalised element within the human. He suggests this segregation traces back to Aristotle, who connects autarchic life, happiness and politics via the notion of the *ergon* or the work that is proper to human being, where 'proper' designates a kind of being separate from the simple facts of living (growth, sensation). Agamben objects that this qualification of what is properly political life has 'no content other than the pure fact of the caesura as such'.[9] The biopolitical *dispositif* he calls the anthropological machine 'has always already captured it [life] within itself by means of a series of divisions and articulations'.[10] Agamben seeks another mode of politics, a non-state form of politics that does not require the division of life from itself that is figured by the position of the animal:

> A political life, which is to say, one oriented toward the idea of happiness and cohering in a form-of-life, is thinkable only starting from emancipation from this scission [biological life/bare life]. The question of the possibility of a non-state politics thus necessarily has the form: is it possible today, is there today something like a form-of-life, namely, a life for which, in its living, one has to do with the living itself, *a life of potential*?[11]

One of Agamben's contentions about form-of-life is that it is something different from the 'bare' life of the biopolitical binary: it is not the remainder of mere animal life left after the proper human has been produced from some prehumanised materiality, but instead is *natural* life. Such natural life, he continues, is 'nothing other than the essence or nature of each being'[12] and thus it can be suspended and contemplated but never divided from the act of living itself. Agamben's ideal of potentiality emerges from this living-through-acting in that the life is never the object of a will or a project, but just of allowing potential to coincide with form-of-life.[13]

While Agamben is interested in this form-of-life as a way for the human to recover what animals retain but humanity has lost – namely, being that is not bound up with a specific task or project of the proper – I want to extend his term in ways that allow us to see animals not simply as analogies for a different mode of human being, but as invitations to inhabit being in ways that put us in community with other species. Form-of-life in this mode is also inherently collective – a unity of life and thought that promises a new ontology of living things, but also a new politics. If we think of politics as related to the question of what might produce the good or happy life, Agamben cautions us that 'those who deny to irrational beings the capacity of living well end up, without realizing it, placing living well in something other than life (for example, in reason)'.[14] His project of reinventing the metaphysics of subjectivity seeks an ideal of living well that could apply to all living beings, happiness routed in the unity of commonality instead of the transcendence of the proper. Such a notion of politics marks a break with liberal tradition, the rationale that Foucault excavates especially in *Security, Territory, Population*.[15] If in our existing tradition of politics is war by other means – the unending struggle between 'the race that holds power and is entitled to define the norms, and against those who deviate from that norm, against those who pose a threat to the biological heritage'[16] – an affirmative biopolitics of the living might be thought of as kinship-making by other means.

In this space, we can begin to think of the category of those excluded from proper political life – what Agamben names instances of the *homo sacer* – as a site of generativity rather than exile: 'laid claim to and assumed as his own' but in a way that it is 'transformed and inverted into something positive [...] a figure of a new and happy intimacy, of an "alone by oneself" as a cipher of a superior politics'.[17] This is the realm of inoperativity that is possible because of the suspension of anthropogenic processes of making the human out of the living. Yet there remains something individualised in Agamben's way of thinking about this suspension, which is why I find it valuable to put these ideas in dialogue with Roberto Esposito's thinking on affirmative biopolitics of the communal, especially his reflection on approaching subjectivity through the idea of the third person. The third person refuses the binary of subject/object, the hierarchy of relationality that is impossible to escape in a grammar of I and you. My hope is that it might additionally offer a way to think this 'superior politics' as enabling the capacity to include nonhuman animals alongside the refigured humans whose politics no longer divide them from their life.

Inoperativity in the Third Person

Liberal tradition often imagines the solution to the crisis of interspecies ethics as an extension of the notion of personhood to species beyond *homo sapiens*. As Esposito notes in his critique of personhood as a concept, it emerged in Western thought as a strategy to bridge the gap between *zoē* and *bios*, between the mere fact of human life and the protected life of those humans recognised as citizens. It is this ideal of the person that grounds frameworks such as human rights as universal without reference to situated historical or national belonging. But this ideal of the person did not eliminate the binary between bare and proper life, but rather created another bifurcation by which humans, in contrast to all other animals, had some quality that meant they must always transcend their mere biological being. Esposito notes that:

> Even when interpreted in secular terms, in short, the idea of person is never entirely reducible to that of the biological substrate of the subject it designates; rather, its most significant meaning is to be found precisely in a sort of excess, of a spiritual or moral character, that makes more of the 'person', yet without letting it coincide completely with the self-sufficient individual of the liberal tradition.[18]

He points out that the concept of the person is etymologically linked to the Latin *persona* or mask, which emblematises the gap that remains between person and natural life.

Rather than expanding the category of the person, to include those previously not recognised as such, Esposito suggests that we should rethink politics and community from the point of view of what all life shares in common. His affirmative biopolitics is a biopolitics of relation, a politics of the affirmative potentiality of *zoē*, not one concerned with the special province of *bios*. Person as model requires an ideal of a spirit or force that can persist beyond a particular (embodied) life, a separate of life itself from the fact of living, and Esposito offers the concept of the third person as a counter to this abstraction. He argues that we should reject 'the logical thread that ties individual self-consciousness to collective consciousness in the grammatical mode of the first person': instead, 'the impersonal is what prevents this transition, what preserves the singular pronoun by protecting it from the simultaneously self-protective and self-destructive slide into the general'.[19] Thus, the third person is connected to Esposito's larger reframing of biopolitics as a crisis of immunity, in which one part of the body politic sees another part as threat and violently expels it in the name of the health of the totality (what Foucault theorises as the foundational racialisation of biopolitics as war by other means). Esposito frames this as autoimmune disease of our body politic, a hypervigilant protective mechanism that divides life from itself. Drawing on the political origin of the term immunity as exception from certain obligations or tasks, an exception from relationality and obligations to others, Esposito draws attention to immunity's opposite: the bonds of reciprocity that link us together, the willingness to accept rather than elude relevant tasks. Immunity in this understanding prevents relationality: immunity's 'semantic focus is more on difference from the condition of others than on the notion of exemption itself'.[20] Thus, Esposito suggests, its opposite is community: what immuntarian biopolitics protect us against is commonality, it is the 'internal limit which cuts across community, folding it back on itself in a form that is both constitutive and deprivative: immunity constitutes or reconstitutes community precisely by negating it'.[21]

In a similar way that immunity deprives or negates the very society it seeks to protect, the concept of the person, intended to bridge the biopolitical gap between human and citizen, instead 'produced an equally profound gap between rights and life'.[22] This gap is of course the place that the animal inhabits in biopolitical tradition as a figuration of 'a distinction, in the human being, between an individual dimension with a moral, rational character and an impersonal dimension with an animal nature'.[23] Esposito's interest in the third person, then, a place of theorising from the impersonal rather than the personal, offers a pathway by which we might begin to think of relationality with other species as part of how we might invent a new, affirmative biopolitics. In Esposito's vision, the impersonal is a 'shifting border' that 'blocks' the 'reifying outcome' of the metaphysics of Western personhood. It 'does not negate the personal frontally, as a philosophy of the anti-person would; rather, the impersonal is its alteration, or its extroversion [turns the personal] into an exteriority that calls it into question and overturns its prevailing meaning'.[24] The impersonal, then, is a call to rethink how we imagine the metaphysics of subjectivity – to overturn the prevailing meaning of how we draw the line between inside and outside the community. The position of the animal in Western thought is precisely on that line, and thus Esposito's interest in the power of the third person as a way to avoid divisions within the human contains, as well, the seeds for thinking about a metaphysics of the human that does not require abjection of the animal.

There are parallels between this idea of the third person as a structure that helps us escape the hierarchical binaries and Agamben's concept of rendering the anthropogenic machine inoperative. Agamben rejects Western notions of subjectivity, epitomised by the Heideggerian *Dasein*, through which 'the human being find[s] itself only by presupposing the not-truly-human'.[25] His interest lies only in rethinking 'the exposition of the central void, of the gap that separates—in the human being—the human and the animal',[26] not with rethinking the interspecies relationship. Nonetheless, he relies almost entirely on analogies with the kind of life still available to animals when he describes form-of-life as a kind of living that escapes the project or task of the proper, something he calls a 'use' of one's body. He approaches this by articulating a specific mode of use conveyed by the term *chresis*, a mode of living in which we constitute ourselves through the world via interaction with it; we do not simply exist apart as 'transcendent title holders of a capacity to act or make'.[27] Use is thus the expressive embodiment of a capacity of one's body, something that exists in the doing of it, not an abstract ability or skill one 'owns' in oneself. This use is akin to an animal's capacity to inhabit its body without abstracting a self from this embedded experience, Agamben suggests, although he remains interested in a notion of *chresis* that is still specific to the human-as-species, which is why he finds Classical notions of the slave a route towards thinking of *chresis* and inoperativity. The slave is a human but not a citizen, a human whose body is available for use by the master, according to Aristotle's rationalisation that it is by nature that some are suited only to be slaves due to their lack of reason. Agamben points out that this is the juridical posturing as the natural, arguing that 'the master/slave relation as we know it represents the capture in the juridical order of the use of bodies as an originary prejuridical relation'.[28] Finding a way to escape the damage of this juridical order and recover this originary, prejuridical capacity for use is his overall aim.

Agamben seems to turn to the slave, rather than remain with images of animals, because he is interested in the particularities of this use of one's body before the juridical order intervenes to separate the human from animality within the human. At the same time, however, he also suggests that animals have their own version of this capacity, that they know how to use their bodies 'emancipated' from a relationship towards any specific end, 'the simple relation of the living thing with its own body'.[29] This use-of-oneself is what grounds our possibilities for a new metaphysics of subjectivity: 'The self is nothing more than use-of-oneself'.[30] He also describes this as a kind of relationality, albeit distinct from relationality in Esposito; Agamben insists on the non-representability of this interaction between *zoē* and *bios* as they are in contact but 'swell in a non-relation'.[31] Use-of-oneself is also a relationality with the world beyond the self. Unlike biopolitical metaphysics in which the subject emerges from a split within the species that denigrates the animality of humans, Agamben offers a vision of dwelling in use in which 'use-of-oneself and use of the world correspond, without remainder',[32] a form-of-life he also describes as 'inappropriable', which he glosses as 'the unthinkable; it is what our culture must always exclude and presuppose to make it the negative foundation of politics' (2016: 238).[33] This unthinkable foundation of the negative within the biopolitical juridical order is animality. It is here, extending beyond Agamben's and Esposito's interest in refusing the divide between human/animal within the metaphysics of human subjectivity, that I return to my opening set of questions to consider what happens if we read this more literally, to think about the human/animal divide that makes politics a wholly human enterprise as part of the problem.

Agamben's interest in use-of-oneself and inoperativity are key concepts in his vision of new possibilities for politics. Dwelling is a non-relation in which forms-of-life 'communicate' via 'contact' that does not allow the gap of distance of relation and remainder, and this contact is what 'the juridical order and politics seek by all means to capture and represent in a relation'.[34] He seeks a politics of contact that embodies 'the deactivation and inoperativity of every representation',[35] that is not an overcoming of opposites but a threshold of indiscernibility in which they 'fall together' but without synthesis or without instituting a different order of hierarchical relationality. Inoperativity is about deactivating the juridical order that captures our capacities and orients them towards the task of the proper human; thus liberating these energies makes the new possible: 'the capacity to deactivate something and render it inoperative – a power, a function, a human operation – without simply destroying it but by liberating the potentials that have remained inactive in it in order to allow a different use of them'.[36] The slave offers a glimpse of what this form-of-life could be only in the sense that, per Classical theory, the slave inhabits a human body but is not part of the *ergon* of the proper. It seems that Agamben does not pursue animals as more than metaphorical figurations of bodies in such use because this capacity for use-of-oneself is species specific, dependent on morphology and other biological specificities that are not entirely shared among all living beings. My suggestion is that we need not theorise community so narrowly as we consider how our escape from the Western metaphysics of subjectivity could serve as ground for a new kind of politics. The implicit idea that community is premised on homogeneity – all humans as a species – is another biopolitical division we might challenge. We are in ecological relation with other species, both microbes within our bodies necessary to their functioning, and the larger ecosystems through which we cannot function without plants that we rely on for oxygen and food; microbes, bees and other fauna which create the possibility for soil, pollination and thus agriculture overall; other species we use for protein or engage with for companionship. What if we imagined this ecological mutuality as a kind of community? How might we think politics outside of Western systems that make it 'unthinkable' for us to see these exchanges *as politics*?

Speculative Politics: Interspecies Form-of-Life as Decolonial Praxis

A model of this kind of politics exists in Indigenous ways of thinking about what it means to be human, modes of thought that frequently understand animals not as the other to humanity but as a distinct kind of people with whom human people are necessarily in relation. Thinking from an Indigenous point of view does not require the contorted work to deactivate or find our way outside of a damaging metaphysics that has separated the human from other life. As Leanne Betasamosake Simpson explains, in reference specifically to her own Michi Saagiig Nishinaabeg heritage, 'Our way of living was designed to generate life— not just human life but the life of all living things [. . .] and this was reflected in our politics and governance, in our diplomacy with other nations, and even in the protection of our land'.[37] Drawing on her own experience and on work by Dene Indigenous scholar Glen Coulthard, she names this a praxis of 'grounded normativity', 'ethical frameworks generated by these place-based practice and associated knowledges' that are premised on 'process-centered modes of living that generate profoundly different conceptualizations of nationhood and governmentality—ones that aren't based on enclosure, authoritarian power, and hierarchy'.[38] Indigenous ways of thinking of subjectivity and governance have been disrupted and repressed by colonial occupations which forced Indigenous people to live within Western knowledge structures – if not to endorse their logics. From this Western point of view, Indigenous peoples were often collapsed into the category of the animal vis-à-vis state governmentality: in the US, the Bureau of Indian Affairs (BIA), created in 1824, was responsible for both Indigenous peoples and land management. During its first 100 years, BIA policies focused on removing Indigenous peoples from the land and on imposing assimilation upon them, programmes that made impossible this form-of-life that encompassed care for all living things. The US historical example is just one of many colonial encounters in which non-Western metaphysics were violently repressed in the process of Western accumulation.

Mark Minch de Leon points out that this process of 'racialized humanization [. . .] renders Indigenous sociopolitical interrelations nonsensical or, at best, a matter of belief'.[39] Thus, we might understand Indigenous metaphysics within colonial modernity as an example of what Foucault calls 'subjugated knowledges', ways of thinking and living that have been disqualified as knowledge: Foucault contends that 'it is the reappearance of what people know at a local level, of these disqualified knowledges, that made the critique [of modernity's institutions and epistemologies] possible'.[40] I have approached my analysis of the need to rethink human metaphysics of subjectivity to create an interspecies community through Western philosophers seeking to disrupt or escape the dominant logics of Western modernity, and I concur with them that this pathway is needed because the hegemony of Western thought dominates our capacity to imagine and inhabit our lives. At the same time, however, the counterexample of Indigenous knowledge reminds us that alternative modes of being human have persisted alongside the destructive effects of Western frameworks. This is why the projects of rethinking the place of animals in human sociality, of decolonising our social and material relations and of resisting capitalist accumulation are necessarily entangled projects. Simpson points out that colonialism's attack on indigenous grounded normativity was motivated by a desire to dispossess indigenous peoples of the land and its resources, while also emphasising that for indigenous peoples the opposite is not possession but 'deep, reciprocal, consensual *attachment*. Indigenous bodies don't relate to the land by possessing or owning it or having control over it. We relate to land through connection—generative, affirmative, complex, overlapping, and nonlinear *relationship*'.[41]

This relationality of grounded normativity is specifically named a politics by Simpson, a politics that requires negotiation and compromise between competing needs and priorities, which recognises that the thriving of any is contingent on an interconnection that is more pressing than these conflicts. Politics for Simpson's people is

> a series of radiating relationships with plant nations, animal nations, insects, bodies of water, air, soil, and spiritual beings in addition to the Indigenous nations with whom we share parts of our territory. Indigenous internationalism isn't just between peoples. It is created and maintained with all the living beings in Kina Gchi Nishnaabeg-ogamig.[42]

Moreover, she points out that this polity and its way of interacting with other species is a deliberate choice: contra that Enlightenment story that indigenous peoples were less technologically advanced than Europeans and thus 'couldn't' develop capitalist social relations, she points out that they had the capacity to develop similar technologies and economies, but 'we had the ethics and knowledge within grounded normativity to *not develop* this system, because to do so would have violated our fundamental values and ethics regarding how we relate to each other and the natural world' (2017: 80).[43] Work by indigenous peoples to live according to their traditional values and knowledges thus stand as embodied examples of another mode of being human. Yet Simpson also warns of the risk of visibilising this knowledge in a way that makes it 'vulnerable to commodification and control by settler colonialism',[44] pointing out that this knowledge emerges in the act of living through grounded normativity as part of a community, through embodied practice of this knowledge, not by 'reading books or obtaining degrees'.[45] I thus want to suggest that there are parallels between the grounded normativity Simpson describes and the embodied form-of-life Agamben seeks to describe which he admits 'does not yet exist in its fullness'[46] within the existing Western metaphysics. Simpson's work exemplifies why it is necessary to yoke attempts to articulate an affirmative biopolitics inclusive of nonhuman life to a commitment to decolonising our thought and our institutions. Simultaneously, however, this must be a praxis of Western subjects dismantling the destructiveness of our own histories, not simply of appropriating Indigenous alternatives.

In this final section, I want to briefly explore how Ray Nayler's *The Mountain in the Sea*[47] offers some help in thinking through this project of remaking our metaphysics along the lines suggested by Agamben's and Esposito's efforts to begin Western metaphysics anew, which requires first disrupting their current force. I turn to speculative fiction in the methodology suggested by Steven Shaviro, who argues that the genre gives us tools for grappling with philosophical problems that 'deeply and unavoidably concern us, but that are intractable to rational argumentation or to empirical verification'.[48] The main setting for Nayler's novel is a future Con Dao, a set of islands off the coast of Vietnam: it has recently been acquired by a technology company, DIANIMA, who claim they have done so to protect the environment from the fishing industry. This purchase has displaced local peoples, who can no longer live in relation to this specific land, and while their previous fishing activities are posited as a risk to endangered species in the region, the fact that DIANIMA's research centre is established in a building that once served as a luxury hotel for tourists suggests another story. A self-aware AI named Evrim is one of the researchers at this station, his ontology serving as a way for the novel to raise a range of philosophical questions about the nature of consciousness and subjectivity as well as about ethical relations with nonhumans. The researchers are there to explore anomalous behaviour in local octopi, and it ultimately emerges that they have evolved to attain a level of culture that enables them to pass knowledge between generations and to develop a writing system that enables halting communication between them and the human researchers. The choice of octopus as model species to explore interspecies politics also enables the novel to raise compelling questions about knowledge, embodiment and the nature of cognition, given that they are a highly intelligent species whose brains work very differently from human ones, distributing their neuronal processing across the limbs which function semi-autonomously from their central nervous system. The octopus, then, offers a model of a species that has individuality but yet not in the liberal model of the centralised I.

Space precludes a detailed discussion of this rich and intriguing novel. My purpose in this conclusion is to sketch out how the range of plot points and themes that Nayler brings together in the novel make it ideal for considering what an interspecies, affirmative biopolitics might entail. The main cephalopod researcher, Dr. Ha Nguyen, is assigned to this research project due to her previous book, *How Oceans Think*, and Nayler uses excerpts from this text-within-a-text as epigraphs throughout the novel in order to draw attention to the zoological and philosophical issues that underpin her orientation towards the octopi as an emergent culture. Repeatedly, Ha's work emphasises reciprocity between humans and the rest of the natural world, to both 'our immersion in and reliance upon nature' in order to live at all, but also to a recognition that 'the nature we are immersed in also communicates, has values, and strives'.[49] Much of the narrative is given to puzzling out how to communicate with the octopi and what they seek to communicate with humans, which ultimately proves to be a message related to territory that insists that other species have a claim on shared territory and ocean resources as much as do humans. Before the symbolic system is decoded, there are numerous violent encounters between octopi and humans, which we glimpse through interviews with survivors who can only describe something monstrous in the ocean since these interactions are also demonstrates of octopi exhibiting tool use, strategy and locomotion in ways not typically observed. One way of reading these encounters is within the paradigm of environmental revenge science fiction, such as *Day of the Animals*,[50] *Prophecy*[51] or *Long Weekend*.[52] Yet it is precisely in the ways that *The Mountain in the Sea* refuses this paradigm of nature's justified revenge on exploitative humans that I think the novel opens up a way that helps us think of an interspecies affirmative biopolitics that recognises that it must necessarily be decolonial as well.

The octopi attack those whose behaviours threaten the wildlife in the Con Dao region: those who use cyanide dumps to harvest fish, park rangers who steal and sell some of the turtle eggs they are meant to defend, crews of boats whose extractive methods entangle multiple creatures in their nets whom they callously discard so that they can capture sought-after fish most efficiently. Yet the attempts to communicate with the researchers also demonstrate that the octopi would prefer to communicate a warning for people to stay away rather than to engage in violent struggle, that is, they prefer politics to outright warfare. The novel also constructs a parallel between Dr. Ha's previous struggle against poachers in an earlier research centre and the threats faced by the ocean creatures in Con Dao. She explains that her younger self was extremely angry at the destruction the poachers wrought and so she turned them in to a police force she knew to be violently abusive towards those in its custody. She has come to regret this choice, reproaching herself for failing to try to see things from the impoverished residents' point of view: 'Did I try to understand what their needs were? Why they were doing what they were doing? Did I establish a relationship with the village elders? Did I reason with them? Did I try to work for a compromise?... No'.[53] She goes on to explain that her love for her research subjects, in that case cuttlefish, allowed her to believe that she was 'someone who cares for everything, and cares too much'; yet this conflict made her realise 'I only cared for some things. Other things, I discarded. I didn't think at all of their struggles for survival, their subsistence living and how it blinded them to any of the magic I saw in my cuttlefish'.[54] Rather than protecting her cuttlefish, this myopia resulted in their deaths, as local residents dumped cyanide into the water, killing the entire population, as retaliation against the brutal treatment of the poachers by the police. The biopolitical metric of protecting some life at the expense of the entire system of life resulted in universal harm, not selective thriving.

Dr. Ha's reflections on this incident point to the potentiality for an affirmative biopolitics that recognises that we are all entangled together but resists the fantasy of a flattening vitality that insists all life is equivalent. A true ecological understanding of our entanglements requires recognising our competing priorities and positionally, our need for compromise and indeed sacrifice in the sense that we cannot take our own priorities as a default for what is just. In multiple ways, the novel reminds us that this is the case for interspecies relations and also for intra-species ones through which some humans are discarded for the sake of those privileged by biopolitical binaries: we see this in storylines about the ethics of displacing villages to create wildlife sanctuaries; about precarious workers kidnapped into a life of bondage as crew on a largely automated fishing vessels, human components 'more expendable'[55] than machinery for specific tasks; and about Evrim and whether he can be incorporated as part of the human community or if his distance necessarily constitutes a threat.

Throughout the novel in these multiple registers, Nayler suggests that his characters need to see beyond their own needs, need to learn to recognise the reality of other people, other selves, need to learn to extend our subjectivity and our politics to be in dialogue across difference. One plotline refers to the historical massacre of dogs by the Ottoman empire during its modernisation project in 1909, when tens of thousands of stray dogs who used to live freely in Istanbul among the humans were captured and confined to an island without food or water, left to slowly starve to death because 'when the Ottomans were trying to modernise themselves, trying to fit the old empire into a European mold, they began to see the animals as an embarrassment'.[56] Fitting into a European mould suggests an encounter analogous to the colonial one, the erasure of ways of living that were not premised on the separation of human from animal, on the repression of what is deemed an animalised contagion within the human. Before this need to aspire to the metaphysics of European modernity, other interspecies configurations for living were possible. In another plotline, one of the enslaved people on an automated vessel learns to see beyond his own depression to truly see his fellow crewmates, a necessary step to being able to come up with a plan for resistance and escape. This insight helps him realise not only that his solipsism made him vulnerable in that moment, but also that his disavowal of spaces of exploitation on which the global economy relies created the structures that ultimately enslaved him. He saw the newspaper stories, he recalls, 'Autotrawlers crewed by slave crews. Another world, a degraded shadow of our own. How was I to know there was a hole in the world that I could fall through [. . .] and end up on the other side, on a planet I don't even recognize?'. This other world, he realizes, 'was always there. [. . .] *The foundation of it all. The truth of it*'.[57]

Thus *The Mountain in the Sea* offers a glimpse of how we might begin to think of an affirmative and decolonial biopolitics, one that begins from another set of foundational assumptions of the nature of what it means to be human, of who might be part of the political community, and most crucially that refuses the caesura of human from animal both across species and as a figuration of fragmented humans into valued and denigrated classes. Dr. Ha's research insists that 'How we see the world matters—but knowing how the world sees us also matters'.[58] An affirmative biopolitics must begin from this mutuality, a reciprocity that accepts that the biopolitical logic that protects some life at the expense of the larger community of the living is doomed to repeat the thanatopolitical histories we have already inhabit. The potentiality for an interspecies community with the octopi which concludes Nayler's novel is similar to the interspecies model of indigenous internationalism that Simpson describes, but it is not yet fully realised as the novel ends. The two species, human and octopus, have established that they can communicate with one another, but what kind of polity they might mutually create remains to be seen. This ending on a note of ambiguity is fitting too, for in the wake of colonisation and extractivism, as the novel also insists, we must first undo the damage of modernity before we can imagine something new in its place. *The Mountain in the Sea* thus offers a concrete image that brings into sharper focus the potentiality that Agamben and Esposito envision in notions of inoperativity and the third person; yet it adds to this as well the indispensable recognition that an affirmative interspecies biopolitics will necessarily be an exercise in decolonial thought.

Notes

1. Michel Foucault, *Society Must Be Defended. Lectures at the Collège de France, 1975–76*, trans. David Macey (New York: Picador, 2003), 255.
2. Achille Mbembe, 'Necropolitics', in *Biopolitics: A Reader*, eds. Timothy Campbell and Adam Sitze (Durham, NC: Duke University Press, 2003), 161–93; Zakkiyah Iman Jackson, *Becoming Human: Matter and Meaning in an Antiblack World* (NYU Press, 2020).
3. Cary Wolfe, *Before the Law: Humans and Other Animals in a Biopolitical Frame* (Chicago, IL: The University of Chicago Press, 2013), 10.
4. Roberto Esposito, *Third Person: Politics of Life and Philosophy of the Impersonal*, trans. Zakiya Hanafi (Cambridge: Polity Press, 2012), 7.
5. Rick Elmore, 'Biopolitics' in *The Edinburgh Companion to Animal Studies*, eds. Lynn Turner, Undine Sellbach, and Ron Broglio (Edinburgh: Edinburgh University Press, 2018), 90.
6. Giorgio Agamben, *The Open: Man and Animal*, trad. Kevin Attell (Stanford, CA: Stanford University Press, 2004), 3.
7. Giorgio Agamben, *The Use of Bodies*, trans. Adam Kotsko (Stanford, CA: Stanford University Press, 2016), 111.
8. Esposito, *Third Person*, 52.
9. Agamben, *The Use of Bodies*, 203.
10. Agamben, *The Use of Bodies*, 203.
11. Agamben, *The Use of Bodies*, 210.
12. Agamben, *The Use of Bodies*, 207.
13. Agamben, *The Use of Bodies*, 208.
14. Agamben, *The Use of Bodies*, 217.
15. Michel Foucault, *Security, Territory, Population. Lectures at the Collège de France 1977–78*, trans. Graham Burchell (Basingstoke: Palgrave Macmillan, 2007).
16. Foucault, *Society Must Be Defended*, 61.

17. Agamben, *The Use of Bodies*, 236.
18. Esposito, *Third Person*, 71.
19. Esposito, *Third Person*, 102.
20. Roberto Esposito, *Immunitas: The Protection and Negation of Life*, trans. Zakiya Hanafi (Cambridge: Polity, 2011), 6.
21. Esposito, *Immunitas*, 9.
22. Esposito, *Third Person*, 74.
23. Esposito, *Third Person*, 75.
24. Esposito, *Third Person*, 14.
25. Agamben, *The Use of Bodies*, 45.
26. Agamben, *The Use of Bodies*, 265.
27. Agamben, *The Use of Bodies*, 62.
28. Agamben, *The Use of Bodies*, 36.
29. Agamben, *The Use of Bodies*, 51.
30. Agamben, *The Use of Bodies*, 54.
31. Agamben, *The Use of Bodies*, 237.
32. Agamben, *The Use of Bodies*, 91.
33. Agamben, *The Use of Bodies*, 238.
34. Agamben, *The Use of Bodies*, 237.
35. Agamben, *The Use of Bodies*, 237.
36. Agamben, *The Use of Bodies*, 273.
37. Leanne Betasamosake Simpson, *As We Have Always Done: Indigenous Freedom Through Radical Resistance* (Minneapolis, MN: University of Minnesota Press, 2017), 3.
38. Simpson, *As We Have Always Done*, 22.
39. Mark Minch de Leon, 'Race and the Limitation of "the Human"', in *After the Human: Culture, Theory and Criticism in the 21st Century*, ed. Sherryl Vint (Cambridge: Cambridge University Press, 2020), 217.
40. Foucault, *Society Must Be Defended*, 8.
41. Simpson, *As We Have Always Done*, 43.
42. Simpson, *As We Have Always Done*, 58.
43. Simpson, *As We Have Always Done*, 80.
44. Simpson, *As We Have Always Done*, 199.
45. Simpson, *As We Have Always Done*, 199.
46. Agamben, *The Use of Bodies*, 227.
47. Ray Nayler, *The Mountain in the Sea* (New York: MCD, 2022).
48. Steven Shaviro, *Extreme Fabulations: Science Fictions of Life* (London: Goldsmiths Press, 2021), 1.
49. Nayler, *The Mountain in the Sea*, 215.

50. *Day of the Animals*, directed by William Girdler (Warner Bros 1977).
51. *Profecy*, directed by John Frankenheimer (Paramount Pictures 1979).
52. Long Weekend, directed by Colin Eggleston (Dugong Films 1978).
53. Nayler, *The Mountain in the Sea*, 306.
54. Nayler, *The Mountain in the Sea*, 425.
55. Nayler, *The Mountain in the Sea*, 39.
56. Nayler, *The Mountain in the Sea*, 258.
57. Nayler, *The Mountain in the Sea*, 280.
58. Nayler, *The Mountain in the Sea*, 95.

Works Cited

Agamben, Giorgio. *The Open: Man and Animal*. Translated by Kevin Attell. Stanford, CA: Stanford University Press, 2004.

Agamben, Giorgio. *The Use of Bodies*. Translated by Adam Kotsko. Stanford, CA: Stanford University Press, 2016.

Eggleston, Colin, director. *Long Weekend*. Dugong Films, 1978.

Elmore, Rick. 'Biopolitics'. In *The Edinburgh Companion to Animal Studies*, edited by Lynn Turner, Undine Sellbach, and Ron Broglio, 80–93. Edinburgh: Edinburgh University Press, 2018.

Esposito, Roberto. *Immunitas: The Protection and Negation of Life*. Translated by Zakiya Hanafi. Polity, 2011.

Esposito, Roberto. *Third Person: Politics of Life and Philosophy of the Impersonal*. Translated by Zakiya Hanafi. Cambridge: Polity, 2012.

Foucault, Michel. *Society Must Be Defended. Lectures at the Collège de France, 1975–76*. Edited by Mauro Bertani and Alessandro Fontana, translated by David Macey. New York: Picador, 2003.

Foucault, Michel. *Security, Territory, Population. Lectures at the Collège de France 1977–78*. Edited by Michel Senellart, translated by Graham Burchell. Basingstoke: Palgrave Macmillan, 2007.

Frankenheimer, John, director. *Profecy*. Paramount Pictures, 1979.

Girdler, William, director. *Day of the Animals*. Warner Bros, 1977.

Jackson, Zakiyyah Iman. *Becoming Human: Matter and Meaning in an Antiblack World*. New York: NYU Press, 2020.

Mbembe, Achille. 'Necropolitics'. In *Biopolitics: A Reader*, edited by Timothy Campbell and Adam Sitze, 161–93. Durham, NC: Duke University Press, 2003.

Minch de Leon, Mark. 'Race and the Limitation of "the Human"'. In *After the Human: Culture, Theory and Criticism in the 21st Century*, edited by Sherryl Vint, 206–19. Cambridge: Cambridge University Press, 2020.

Nayler, Ray. *The Mountain in the Sea*. New York: MCD, 2022.

Shaviro, Steven. *Extreme Fabulations: Science Fictions of Life*. London: Goldsmiths Press, 2021.

Simpson, Leanne Betasamosake. *As We Have Always Done: Indigenous Freedom Through Radical Resistance*. Minneapolis, MN: University of Minnesota Press, 2017.

Wolfe, Cary. *Before the Law: Humans and Other Animals in a Biopolitical Frame*. Chicago, IL: University of Chicago Press, 2012.

PART II
TALES OF BIOPOLITICS AND ANIMALITY

6 Restraining Biopolitics: On Dino Buzzati's Living Animals
Timothy Campbell

Dino Buzzati is hardly an author who comes to mind when considering the relation of the animal to biopolitics. More or less consigned to the ranks of minor literature and its authors, most see Buzzati as the palimpsest of another writer, whose works stand both as the highpoint of Middle European modernity and as one of twentieth century's most important writers, whose writings became a touchstone for philosophical thought. One need only think of Deleuze and Guattari's monograph on *Kafka*, for instance, or Jacques Derrida's musings on Kafka in 'Before the Law' in *Acts of Literature* to measure the distance between Kafka and the lesser Buzzati.[1] Indeed, if Kafka's insights provide the thinker interested in biopolitics and animality with all the material needed to arrive at a critique of the law and the animal, why turn to a lesser version? The project of rehabilitating Buzzati in a context of animal studies and biopolitics might appear to be redundant at best and a waste of time at worst.

There are a number of reasons to take issue with this judgment. First, Buzzati was especially attuned to animal life, both in his writings and personal life. Indeed, animals populate his short stories and novellas in ways different from Kafka.[2] His writings are more animal-specific than Kafka's, more inclined to the animal than to the human, more directed to highlighting the sacrificial economy that humans institute in order to kill animals without guilt. If we are to take the sacrificial economy as one of the central principles underlying biopower today, we will want to highlight the ease with which the sacrifice of animals (principally of their animality, as I argue below) corresponds to a marked increase in contemporary biopower. Second, Buzzati seems particularly attuned to the impact that biopower has on the transformation of the world through the killing of animals. They are the object of forms of knowledge and are featured prominently in a changed milieu in which 'the living animal' can be regimentalised, farmed, experimented on, produced, consumed, industrialised and killed.[3]

I express this another way throughout the pages that follow. Borrowing from Michel Foucault's formulation in Part 3 of the first volume of *The History of Sexuality*, I will be describing Buzzati's writings on the living animal as a measure of when a biological 'threshold of modernity' has been reached and crossed.[4] Buzzati is especially interested in such moments and goes out of his way to frame them as pushing beyond liminality, across a threshold of modernity, Italian modernity to be sure, but equally a modernity less anchored to questions of industrialisation, gross national product, economic miracles – in a word, all of the typical ways that we have come to understand what forms modernity takes. The crossing of modernity is witnessed in Buzzati's writings as consisting of the sacrifices practiced by the human animal on other animals as the former comes to dominate its own animality and as sacrifices some human animals make of themselves. In both instances the media ecology that characterises Buzzati's encounter with modernity is key. Buzzati adds up the cost of the horrendous price animals pay in order for humans to believe that they have dominated their own and another's animality.

This chapter consists of three parts. In the first, I rehearse my reading of biopower in relation to modernity with a series of glosses from Foucault. In the second, I turn to a particularly insightful short story from Buzzati in which the author forces his reader to witness the onslaught of biopower that emerges as the most dangerous consequence of modernity. In the third I turn to the novel *The Tartar Steppe* and how the figure and silence of the Fort are part of a particular ecology of media that steals intimacy and make it possible for humans, but particularly men, to waste away their lives in a desolate place. I conclude with some pointed reflections on what lessons Buzzati's writings on the 'living animal', as Derrida puts it, might have for us today in an era of seemingly never-ending biopower.[5] Buzzati shows us how human forms of being relate to other forms of being that do not necessarily share the same characteristics, namely symbolic thought, cultural context, social construction and ethical reflection as they do.[6] In this, the animal lies beyond the human and rather than making the animal human, which is of a piece with biopower, we need to learn to become more at ease with that radical alterity, which might lessen the potential for sacrifice. We need, in other words, to learn to restrain those practices that would domesticate alterity. In this important project, Buzzati can be of service.

The Living Animals of Biopower

For a number of years, many of us who had been reading Foucault's first volume of *History of Sexuality* were taken by a series of phrases that decisively offered a different definition of modernity than those which had continually characterised approaches to modernity, specifically from disciplines associated with the social sciences. One passage in particular stood out, and it remains one of Foucault's most-cited:

> But what might be called a society's 'threshold of modernity' has been reached when the life of the species is wagered on its own political strategies. For millennia, man remained what he was for Aristotle: a living animal with the additional capacity for a political existence; modern man is an animal whose politics places his existence as a living being in question.[7]

The French is more precise than this English translation: it should read a 'society's biological threshold of modernity' [*le seuil de modernité biologique*].[8] The accompanying adjective helps make the remainder of the phrase clearer: political strategies operate in such a way as to push the life of the species past the 'threshold of modernity'. We know that we move in a space of modernity when politics concerns itself with the life of the species. We know as well from the following passages that Foucault's focus on these wagers concerns the threat of nuclear war and its real possibility at the moment he was writing. Certainly, if today we continue to speak of wagers around species life, our own and others in the ongoing sixth great extinction, then we clearly have crossed another biological 'threshold of modernity'.

'Modern man is an animal' follows in Foucault's formulation, and it functions chiasmatically with the next observation. Before was pre-modernity with man as a living animal and politics as existential supplement, but after crossing the biological threshold of modernity, living gives way to existing. It does so because of a certain kind of politics, specifically the political strategies that now place bets on whether this animal can exist as a living being. In many of the observations that have been offered on these profound passages of Foucault's, not enough attention has fallen on the steps that lead to the biological crossing of the threshold. We know what name Foucault will give to such strategies, namely biopolitics as 'political technologies' that invest 'the body, health, modes of subsistence and habitation, living conditions, the whole space of existence'.[9] It is striking looking back from a distance of four decades just how much of biopolitics as Foucault defines it focuses on man and the transformations that occur thanks to mechanisms and apparatuses that transformed human life in such a way that species life becomes the object of political strategies. Biopolitics calls human life into question in Foucault's justifiably famous line: 'One might say that the ancient right to take life or let live was replaced by a power to foster life or disallow it to the point of death'.[10] Man exists in ways that he did not before having crossed the 'biological threshold of modernity'.

This raises a fundamental question: what kind of animal is it that exists after the threshold has been crossed? It is the animal whose life can be disallowed or fostered, thanks to political strategies that take it as its object. Jacques Derrida anticipated this line of questioning twenty years ago. Writing in *The Animal that Therefore I Am*, he notes how 'it is all too evident that in the course of the last two centuries these traditional forms of treatment of the animal have been turned upside down by the joint developments of zoological, ethological, biological and genetic forms of knowledge, which remain inseparable from techniques of intervention into their object, from the transformation of the actual object, and from the milieu and world of their object, namely, the living animal'.[11] Where Foucault's focus falls directly on man who exists because political strategies target his living status as animal, Derrida refuses the distinction of man from animal; indeed he goes out of his way to refuse the distinction of man and animal or to speak of the human animal in any way that might separate animals from each other. The knowledge-power of Foucault's lexicon that is 'an agent of transformation of human life' here becomes forms of knowledge that transform actual objects by intervening in the milieu and world of 'their object'. In this combination of insights, we no longer need look only to human beings for the effects of biopower in what remains a distinctly humanistic context. Rather we can chart the origin, emergence, and intensification of biopower in interventions that take place in the continuum that joins all animals. In a context of heightened biopower, the animal that therefore I am is, by the title's own admission, the animal that lives.

Buzzati's Dragons

The relation of biopower to animality is a necessary pretext for unearthing the different and often unfamiliar perspective that Buzzati provides in his short stories and novel. As the publication of Buzzati's *Bestiario* shows, Buzzati was a life-long animalist, a lover of animals (if not of humans), and a dedicated dog-owner, who surrounded himself with more than one dog or three for most of his life, and to whom he dedicated stories and painted sketches.[12] Indeed, after growing up an avid hunter, he swore off hunting and then later meat as part of his uncovered personal alliances with animals.

Certainly, examining Buzzati's friendship with dogs might help spell out what Buzzati saw as alliances with animals, but in order to gauge the significance of Buzzati's encounters with modernity in terms of biopower and the living animal, we need to look elsewhere. Not surprisingly it appears in those stories in which humans come face to face not with their own animality so much as their own human propensity for cruelty and domination. That cruelty and domination of the animal by the human (and the human of the human) appear across Buzzati's works comes as no surprise to any reader of his. His short stories are dominated by tales of power exercised over life, especially in the more famous works, 'Seven Floors' (beloved by Albert Camus), 'The Dog Who Saw God', and the more apocalyptic works of, say, 'Catastrophe' and 'Epidemic'. But no animal seems to challenge man more than the animal who in Buzzati's imaginary threatens to take man's place – the dragon.

Dragons have a rich history across European literature as mythological monsters and so my choice to focus on the dragon's animality may strike some as having conflated monster with a 'real' animal.[13] To see why such is not the case, let's consider in more detail 'The Slaying of the Dragon'. The short story appears in Buzzati's best-selling anthology of short stories, *Sessanta Racconti*, which first appeared in 1958.[14] The story recounts the killing – the Italian title is 'Uccisione' – of the dragon during a hunting trip organised specifically to slaughter the 'large animal' by one Count Gerol.[15] The dragon had come to the Count's attention thanks to the description offered by a peasant of the animal that was so believable, so realistic, that Gerol had come to believe that the dragon had to be seen to be believed and thus killed; hence the need for the taxidermist, Fusti, to accompany them.

An entourage of nobility joins Gerol, including the governor of the province, Quinto Andronico, who is in turn joined by the governor's wife, Maria, along with Professor Inghirami, along with Fusti. The narrator informs us that the events to be described took place in a precise year: 1902. The authentic protagonist of the story we meet six pages later, and that of course is the dragon. Here is the first description of the encounter:

> A shudder went through the company, and they held their breath as a live creature emerged from the mouth of the cave. 'The dragon! The dragon!' shouted several of the hunters, though whether in joy or terror it was not clear.
> The creature moved into the light with the hesitant sway of a snake. So here it was, this legendary monster whose voice made a whole village quake.

'Oh, how horrible!' exclaimed Maria with evident relief, having expected something far worse.
'Come on, courage!' shouted one of the hunters jokingly. Everyone recovered their self-assurance.
'It looks like a small Ceratosaurus!' said Professor Inghirami, now sufficiently confident to turn to the problems of science.[16]

Across the story, the dragon of the title changes names, and so it is not surprising that here too in the initial description, it does so as well. First announced as a large animal in the opening paragraph, the dragon is here referred to after immediately as a snake, then a creature, and then a 'small Ceratosaurus'. Soon after, but especially after the drawn-out process of the 'slaying' begins, the dragon is transformed into a creature of advanced age, a reptile, a cockroach, an insect and then once it is shot, an animal:

'How much longer is this going to go on?' he shouted to Gerol. 'It's fearfully hot. Finish off the animal once and for all, can't you? Why torture it like that, even if it is a dragon?'
'It's not my fault', answered Gerol, annoyed, 'can't you see that it's refusing to die? It's got a bullet in its skull and it's more lively than ever'.[17]

Noteworthy for a biopolitical reading of Buzzati's story is how the various steps of the killing bring forth the dragon as animal; this is not just any animal but a specific animal, a living animal, who arrives in relation to another living animal, the human. The transformation of the dragon from monster to animal precedes the events of its last breath, when we learn that the dragon is also a mother. Her offspring too are slaughtered, their heads bashed in by Gerol's men.

The status of the dragon as a living animal merits further reflection. Consider the distinction that Derrida proposes in his dispute with Levinas among killing, murder and dying:

If the animal doesn't die, that is, if one can put it to death without 'killing' it or murdering it, without committing murder, without 'Thou shalt not kill' concerning it or regarding me in the context of it [*sans que . . . le regarde ou me regarde a son sujet*], it is because the animal remains foreign to everything that defines sanctity, the separation and thus the ethics of the person as face.[18]

Buzzati's dragon does not have a face in 'The Slaying of the Dragon' and so Derrida's insight into the importance of the face for sanctity and indeed for ethics, finds its confirmation. Furthermore, the Count along with the others maintain a significant distance from the dragon. Indeed, Gerol will fire a bullet into its skull and then later pack a goat – meant for the dragon as a sacrifice – full of explosives, after which he will light a fuse. The distance between the dragon and the humans allows the latter to ignore the possibility that the dragon might well have a face, and here we note that such a possibility appears as reality in another of Buzzati's short stories featuring a dragon, 'L'opportunista'.[19] Interestingly, there the dragon not only remains safe but indeed is sovereign over humans to the degree that it can eat them.

Other conclusions can be drawn from the transformations of the dragon. First, only after it has been shot does the dragon become a living animal and this only occurs when its sanctity has been removed. 'The animal remains foreign to everything that defines sanctity' and of course the principal definition of sanctity is precisely the maintaining of proper distance linked to *religio*:

> A number of Roman learned men tell us that *religiosus* could be used with reference to the cult itself: *religio sum quodpropter sanctitatem aliquam remotum ac sepositum a nobis sit* 'a thing is said to be *religiosum* which, because of some sanctity, is remote and set apart from us' (Masurius Sabinus apud Aulus Gellius N.A. 4, g).[20]

Earlier, Benveniste, in marking the distinction between *sacer* and *sanctus* writes that '*sanctus* is a state resulting from a prohibition for which men are responsible, from an injunction supported by law'.[21] The dragon is *sanctus* not because it cannot be killed but because it is set apart from the human realm. Furthermore, there are sanctions surrounding what is considered *sanctus*; the dragon is defended by certain sanctions around potential human behaviour, and these include slaughter. In other words, one slays a dragon but does not slaughter it. And here we return to the Italian that Buzzati uses: 'uccissione'. The word ironically captures what Gerol and the others do. It is an antiseptic name that alters the biopolitical stakes and atmosphere in which the slaughter takes place as a mere killing. It may look like a slaughter, but it is only a killing.

Biopolitical Media

What is it that makes possible the move from slaying to slaughtering? 'The Slaying of the Dragon' provides clues on what has changed biopolitically in order for a slaughter not to qualify as such; a killing for which no sanctions are in place. The first occurs in the opening paragraph when the narrator details how Gerol and the others learned of the dragon's existence. Indeed, the short story begins with a specific month and date, May 1902 (concrete dates are an anomaly in Buzzati's opus) and then proceeds to remark upon how Count Gerol has come to learn of the 'monster' from a peasant by the name of Longo who in his service. The legend had been reported for quite some years but 'no one had ever taken it seriously'. The narrator notes the following difference from previous reports.

> Yet on this occasion Longo's obvious sanity, the exactitude of his account, the absolutely accurate and unwavering repetition of details of the event, convinced people that there might be something in it, and Count Martino Gerol decided to go and find out. Naturally he was not thinking in terms of a dragon; but it was possible that some huge rare serpent was still living in those uninhabited valleys.[22]

'Exactitude', 'absolutely accurate', 'unwavering repetition' along with the peasant's sanity change the previous calculus by which the dragon was left alone. If we were to speak of a biological 'threshold of modernity' in which slaying gives ways to slaughter, then one of the conditions for passing that threshold concerns the ways by which an account comes to be believed as true. Another way of saying this, to borrow from a beloved term of German media theorists of twenty years ago, is to speak of a media ecology and how particular communication media alter human perception. Understood broadly, media compete with each other; thus, writing competes with orality, the telephone with the telegraph, and in this instance legend with realism. Friedrich Kittler said it, concisely of course: 'Media determine our situation'.[23]

Buzzati's short stories make clear how media determine our biopolitical situation, by which I mean that in order for a biological threshold to be passed, media will determine when magical creatures become monsters, then reptiles, and finally living animals that can be slaughtered. At the same time, the human animal emerges as the animal whose power is such that other animals can be made living, which is to say can be hurt and wounded in order to be seen as alive and to count as alive. The process looks something like this. The threshold is crossed when a situation is created in such a way that non-human animals become the object of interest thanks to media of exactitude and repetition. In order for dragons to be killed, a peasant's account begins to count as truth and not merely legend because it competes with other media that are exact, accurate and repeatable.

Here is where Buzzati's contribution to biopolitical reflections is most apparent. He invites us to consider the possibility that the notion of *homo sacer*, which

Agamben famously introduced as central to his understanding of biopolitics, is not limited to the human animal only but can be extended to other animals.[24] The magical animal who is the dragon is subjected not to a de-humanisation but rather to an animalisation that is the precondition for its cruel and brutal killing. But the killing does not end with the dragon's wounding by gun and explosion. We learn that the dragon is a mother whose two offspring are killed by blows to the head and so 'The Slaying of the Dragon' recounts not only the transformation of a dragon into a living animal who can be killed but also describes the specicide of dragons made possible by an earlier situation in which legends must not simply be proven as not accurate. Instead, they are seen as generating a thanatopolitical desire for the killing of a species.

The reference to biological threshold names the impact that modernity has on human animals in a context of biopower and also points to how media play an important part in increasing biopower, particularly with regard to non-human animals. The latter become the object not just of bombs and weapons that can be used against them, but now are seen in ways that they were not before. These animals become the object of accounts which themselves are in competition with media technologies that are more accurate and realistic and repeatable. That the dragon is pathetic, and is not the mythical creature of legend, does not change one bit the situation in which the dragon and its offspring must not simply be killed but must be killed mercilessly, and made extinct. Exploration goes hand in hand with accounts that are repeatable and accurate, which we see every day in mass tourism and its destruction of landscapes. Media competition increases biopower by pushing human technology in such a way that animals are made living.

A Shriek

Yet this is not the entire story. The narrator also relates the dragon's response once it has recognised that its offspring have been seen and then offers an interpretation:

> Finally, the dragon seemed to collect all its remaining strength: it raised its neck toward the sky to emit, first very softly but then with a rising crescendo, an unspeakable, incredible howl [*un urlo indicibile*], a sound [*voce*] neither animal nor human but one so full of loathing that even Count Gerol stood still, paralyzed with horror.
>
> It was asking for help, and for vengeance for its children. But from whom? From the mountains, parched and uninhabited? From the birdless, cloudless

sky, from those men who were torturing it? The shriek [*urlo*] pierced the walls of rock and the dome of the sky, it filled the whole world. Unreasonably enough it seemed completely impossible that there should be no reply.[25]

What are we to make of the passage? In the first, the cry of the dragon is a howl – the Italian has it as 'un urlo indicibile' – which is repeated in the second, as 'shriek'. Here as before with 'uccisione', the English translation can help us see the standardisation of the language of killing which the story is evoking. The dragon emits an incredible howl that is unspeakable, by which we are to understand that it does not involve words (and here we note how the plural 'gli urli' in Italian typically involves animals while humans' howls are 'le urla'). At the same time, the sound of the howl is offered not as a sound as in the English but a voice.

This difference in polarity between voice and the event of meaning can help us mark what is at stake in the dragon and mother's response. For Agamben, citing Paul Valery, 'I or me are the words associated with voice. They are like the meaning of voice itself'.[26] The voice names 'a pure intention to signify as pure meaning' and as such depends on the dragon as having a voice and hence speaking the words 'I', 'me' and with regard to its children, 'mine'.[27] We can say this slightly differently: the howl may be unspeakable, but that does not mean that the dragon lacks a voice, or is without an I. The second passage confirms this tension between unspeakable and voice, remarking on the voice that it should fill 'the whole world'. That it does not, that no help arrives from this event of pure meaning in the dragon's last appeal is precisely what it at issue. There is no appeal that the living animal can make that will alter the course of what is unreasonable. It is an appeal that by any right would be completely impossible to ignore. Yet it is.

One of the most important insights of Buzzati's short story can be found here. The creature who is being slaughtered makes appeals because it has a voice; there *is* an I or me, in Buzzati's rendering of the death agony, one that is part of a meaning of event; the event is the creature's own death and the deaths of her children. The narrator will give a name to this creature by naming the voice, saying it is neither animal nor human, and the reason it is neither is because 'it is so full of loathing'. This is another name for the living animal and mother whose species is being slaughtered.

To return to the question of why such an appeal can be ignored, the narrator's devastating response comes soon after. 'What man had done was right, absolutely in accordance with the law'.[28] This is the power of 'right makes right' contained in the notion of law, which we know is never about what is reasonable or not. In addition, if the voice contains 'I' and 'me' as Agamben puts it in his reading of voice, what matters in the story is precisely that the Count does not have to affirm his presence as 'I', while the dragon does. Derrida's gloss of Kant is helpful on this score: 'This personal subject is capable of its selfness [...] is capable of doing it without saying it, if I can say so; it can affirm itself in its self-ness and in its dignity, which is to say its responsibility, its power to respond, to answer for itself, before others and before the law, even when he cannot yet say "I".'[29] It is not enough for the dragon or the animal more broadly to have a voice that contains or communicates an 'I', but rather to be capable of affirming itself before the law without speaking. The dragon has no way of doing so. This is the point on which 'the massacre' takes place outside of the law or beyond the law.[30] No crime was committed because the issue is not saying 'I' but because it cannot affirm its selfness without saying 'I'.

Of Animals and Intimacy

Animals are few in Buzzati's most famous novel, *The Tartar Steppe*, which makes it an odd choice to follow up on the increase in biopower that turns animals into creatures who can voice an 'I' or 'me' but which does not lead to protection against their own slaughter.[31] Indeed, very few animals appear in the novel: horses, some sheep, but nothing that is as remarkable as the animals that populate many of Buzzati's short stories. The novel instead tells the story of a soldier, Lieutenant Drogo, who through choices of his own and not, wastes his adult life waiting for an enemy to attack (who ultimately does attack but only as the novel closes when Drogo is too infirm to fight).[32] The novel takes place, much like 'The Slaying of the Dragon', in an uninhabited steppe surrounded by mountains on which the armies have outposts. The novel recounts the price Drogo pays for waiting for an event to occur, namely for war to break out, and when it does not, or when it occurs too late for Drogo, the arrival of the event of his death.

The novel contains a number of recognisable existentialist themes, a waiting if not for Godot, then for war and the futility of that wait. Drogo is an every-man whose fate we watch play out across a barren landscape. Clearly, such a setting would seem an odd place for biopower to manifest itself or for a reader to measure Foucault's biological 'threshold of modernity'. And yet if the threshold does not include non-human animals, then we might well ask how the absence of those animals can tell us something we do not yet know about how to measure the ontological features of Buzzati's modernity.

To begin, we might note how often Buzzati describes the Fort across the novel, so much so that it appears as one of the novel's chief antagonists.

Imposing at the beginning, pathetic in the middle, and heroic at the end, the Fort is very nearly always silent:

> The Fort was silent, sunk in the full noonday sun, shadow-less. Its walls – the front could not be seen since it faced north – stretched out yellow and bare. A chimney gave out pale smoke. All along the ramparts of the central building, of the curtain walls and of the redoubts, dozens of sentries could be seen, with rifles at the slope, walking up and down methodically, each on his own little beat. Like the motion of a pendulum, they marked off the passage of time without breaking the enchantment of the immense silence.[33]

The silence of the Fort is repeated and is matched by the solitude of the surrounding environs. Framed by a distant enemy across a desert steppe, those on the other side are called Tartars. Drogo meets his counterpart, Captain Ortiz, in his initial trip to the fort and this is how he characterises the environs:

> 'It is a dead stretch of frontier', Ortiz added, 'and so they never changed it. It has always remained as it was a century ago'.
> 'What do you mean – a dead frontier?'
> 'A frontier which gives no worry. Beyond there is a great desert'.
> 'A desert?'
> 'That's right – a desert. Stones and parched earth – they call it the Tartar steppe'.
> 'Why Tartar?' asked Drogo. 'Were there ever Tartars there?'
> 'Long, long ago, I believe. But it is a legend more than anything else. No one can have come across it – not even in the last wars'.
> 'So the Fort has never been any use?'
> 'None at all', said the captain.[34]

The Fort serves no strategic purpose for most of the novel until the very end when the enemy is about to attack, but that does not mean it holds no purpose for Drogo or the others there. The Fort, much like the hospitals of 'Seven Floors' or the hermit's hut in 'The Dog Who Saw God', functions as a stage on which a hero struggles with earlier decisions and the choices not to act. It lays out what we might call in Foucauldian terms, Drogo's relation to self, or given the number of pages dedicated to that relation, his intimacy with that self. It is precisely the lack of any use afforded to the Fort in the novel that allows the drama of that intimacy with the self to play out, which Buzzati signals surreptitiously at the novel's end: when the Fort becomes of use again, Drogo's own death occurs, when non-use gives way to use marking the end of the drama of the self and intimacy, which to that point had characterised that relation between Drogo and the Fort.

Moreover, the non-use of the Fort extends to the areas surrounding it. In the Tartar steppe, nothing lives. Indeed, in Ortiz's words, a people known as the Tartars lived in the steppe but no longer as he goes on to note that it 'is a legend more than anything else'. In this, the steppe resembles the landscape of 'The Slaying of the Dragon', a place where legends no longer hold, where man is not welcome, the result of a poisonous prior act that we are not privy to. For the drama of intimacy to unfold in the novel, Buzzati requires a space in which intimacy between self and individual can take place.

What is the nature of that relation? While he resides at the useless Fort, in an environment in which no other living is encountered, Drogo grows more intimate with the self, which is not the same to be clear as care. Instead, the Fort with its silences enchants him:

> Down in the courtyard the trumpet was calling, the pure sound of brass and human voice together. It shook once more, warlike and dashing. When it fell silent it left even in the doctor's office an enchantment no words could describe. The silence became such that you could hear someone's long pace crunch on the frozen snow. The colonel had come down in person to take the salute. Three trumpet calls of extraordinary beauty cleft the sky.[35]

Buzzati repeatedly speaks of the relation between the Fort and Drogo in these terms, as mysteries, spells, enchantments. They continue right up to the moment of his death, when they abruptly end:

> He felt as if the flight of time had stopped, as though a spell had been broken. Lately the whirling motion had grown; then suddenly it stopped altogether; the world lay horizontal, listless, apathetic, and the watches ran vainly on. Drogo's road had come to its end; there he is now on the lonely shore of a grey, monotonous sea, and around him there is neither house nor tree nor human beings and so it has been since time immemorial.[36]

Agamben in some of the most insightful pages he has ever written, notes how the biopolitical substance of each individual consists of that which cannot be appropriated in a relation of intimacy:

> That is to say, intimacy is a circular apparatus, by means of which, by selectively regulating access to the self, the individual constitutes himself as the

pre-supposition and proprietor of his own 'privacy' ... [W]hat is vital for the definition of the self is not the inclusion or exclusion of others so much as the capacity to regulate contact when one desires to.[37]

When one no longer is able to regulate contact, the 'lords of intimacy' appear who violently appropriate this privacy, who make the free use of what is proper to the individual their own. This is precisely what *The Tartar Steppe* recounts in the Fort's crevices, its golden sunsets, the martial sounds of trumpets and the slowing down of time.[38] All of these are the tools by which the Fort, an obvious symbol not only for the military, but for institutions generally, appropriate Drogo's intimacy. The fact that the steppe is uninhabited, that the Tartars may have been legend or more simply wiped out, that the other army may attack at any time, that no other creatures outside of other human beings can be seen let alone approached, provides the stage for the 'lords of intimacy' to regulate contact and so co-opt Drogo's relation to what ought to be his 'own' selfhood.

The Tartar Steppe bookends 'The Slaying of the Dragon' by pointing to the ultimate biological 'threshold of modernity'. In a world in which the other is legend because it has been slaughtered, the threshold shifts from the living animal who has been killed, to the human animal who as a result of a threshold having been crossed, is now unable to regulate contact. As a result. he finds that his intimacy has been violently captured. We might, in such an example, speak of the Fort as a kind of biopolitical machine whose job is to create conditions both inside and outside in which intimacy can be appropriated in such a way that the Fort demands. It resembles in many ways the hospital of 'Seven Floors' except that there the physical form of the body takes the place of the relation of the individual to the self as something that remains untouchable. That it is not, is Buzzati's lesson here.

Biopolitical Lessons

What then are the principal lessons we might draw from these readings or more simply, what is it that unites Drogo to the dragon and her children? First, both share a quality of aliveness. In Drogo's case, the games the 'lords of intimacy' play are intended to force Drogo to hand over his intimacy to them without even a forethought. They make Drogo wait a lifetime by substituting authentic care of the self (which would have meant refusing to depart at the onset of the novel or his quick return home when he could).[39] This substitution of an authentic intimacy with an inauthentic and biopolitical one does the work of biopower to the degree that the apparatus (or state or for that matter institution) sucks the potential (and principally social) life of Drogo out across the decades. The stealing of his intimacy makes possible the sacrifice that they require.

Second, if Drogo feels 'alive' in the text, it is because he no longer is able to regulate contact with the outside. We see it in those poignant moments when he returns home or when he sees his friends and in the lack of any form of intimacy with others, sexual or otherwise, romantic or merely friendly. The Fort is an intimate landlord who works by keeping Drogo on a leash, making it appear that some heroic adventure continually awaits him just around the corner, just a binocular view away. The lords speak through the Fort in its silences and in so doing moves him out of the present into some supposedly glorious and deadly future. He believes he is most intimate with himself in those moments when the Fort mediates his desires with its own.

It is the Fort's media that make biopower so decisive for Drogo. There are no telephones, only letters, which arrive but cannot compete with the media of the steppe or the Fort: the empty distances, the cinematographic landscapes, the Fort itself provides him with an intimate visual succour. Poor Drogo has no defences in such a situation; the Fort's media make him feel alive, which is exactly what the Fort and its lords require to make him wait for the end of his life there. The dragon who is ironically slayed occupies a similar position; having crossed over the biological 'threshold of modernity' thanks to accounts that are in competition with inhuman devices that can record more realistically than before, the dragon's aliveness comes to trump its own form of life. No longer dragon or mother who lives in interdependency with its human neighbours who feed it, the dragon now exists in order to highlight the power over life and death that certain humans have given themselves. What, therefore, Drogo and the dragon share is their having crossed over the 'threshold of modernity' into the space of being merely alive.

The consequences of such a reading of Buzzati's writings for contemporary understanding of biological 'thresholds of modernity' are profound. First, it suggests that the seemingly never-ending improvements in technology that exponentially exceed what qualifies as 'realistic' impact dramatically how humans describe what it is they are seeing. It may seem quaint to us today that the peasant's account was so believable that it forced Gerol's hand in seeking out the dragon, but if we let nature stand in for the dragon, then clearly, today we no longer need even human accounts to justify the transformation of animals into living animals who can be ironically or unironically slayed. Second, we continually need to be on the lookout for media which function diabolically, or better there is always a potentially biopolitical function for all media, especially those dedicated to creating inauthentic forms of intimacy that make regulating privacy difficult. Drogo's problem is ours: desires can be manipulated, stolen, replaced. Mine is, I hope, not simply another jeremiad against social media, but instead a reminder that work is continually required if we are to contact and stay in contact with our desires. In other words, biopolitical media of the kind Buzzati describes can be struggled against by adopting a relation to the self that is less tragic, less beholden to images or stories or accounts that demand sacrifice.[40] It is not so far from what some refer to, following a Deleuzian trajectory, as a 'nomadic ethics' or what Derrida in a context of supreme doubt calls 'a lesson in wisdom concerning [. . .] the tracing of traits as the borderly edges of what in sum belongs to us'.[41] Buzzati's fiction allow us to see just where those edges emerge and where thresholds need not be crossed; where a kind of biopolitical restraint can be practiced.[42]

Notes

1. Gilles Deleuze and Félix Guattari, *Kafka: Toward a Minor Literature* (Minneapolis, MN: University of Minnesota Press, 1986); Jacques Derrida, *Acts of Literature* (New York: Routledge, 1992). On Kafka's relation to Italian literature more generally, see Saskia Ziolkowski's recent *Kafka's Italian Progeny* (Toronto: University of Toronto Press, 2020).
2. Dino Buzzati, *Il bestiario di Dino Buzzati. Cani, gatti, e altri animali*, ed. Lorenzo Viganò (Milan: Mondadori, 2015). For a helpful perspective, see Cinzia Posenato, *Il bestiario di Dino Buzzati* (Bologna: Inchiostri Associate, 2009). On the fantastic and the animal in Buzzati's short stories, see Matthew Reza, 'Oltre il confine: La dilatazione dei paradigmi di realtà nei racconti fantastici di Dino Buzzati', in *Italianistica: Rivista di letteratura italiana* 44 (January 2015): 127–39.
3. I am indebted throughout my paper by Nicole Shukin's reading of the intersection of Foucauldian biopower with Derrida's musings on the living animal. See *Animal Capital: Rendering Life in Biopolitical Times* (Minneapolis, MN: University of Minnesota Press, 2009), especially the Introduction.
4. Michel Foucault, *The History of Sexuality: An Introduction, Volume 1* (New York: Vintage Books, 1978), 143.
5. 'It is all too evident that in the course of the last two centuries these traditional forms of treatment of the animal have been turned upside down by the joint developments of zoological, ethological, biological and genetic forms of knowledge, which remain inseparable from techniques of intervention into their object, from the transformation of the actual object, and from the milieu and world of their object, namely, the living animal' (Jacques Derrida, *The Animal That Therefore I Am* (New York: Fordham University Press, 2008), 25).

6. See Eduardo Kohn, *How Forests Think: Toward an Anthropology Beyond the Human* (Berkeley, CA: University of California Press, 2014), 49.
7. Foucault, *History of Sexuality*, 143.
8. Michel Foucault, *Histoire de la sexualité 1: La volonté de savoir* (Paris: Gallimard, 1976), 188.
9. Foucault, *History of Sexuality*, 143–4.
10. Foucault, *History of Sexuality*, 138.
11. Derrida, *The Animal That Therefore I Am*, 25.
12. Carlo Zanda, *Una misteriosa devozione. Storie di scrittori e di cani molto amati* (Milan: Marcos y Marcos, 2014). See too Cesare Cavelleri, 'Una "spiritosa" passeggiata con i cani degli scrittori', *Avvenire*, November 26, 2014. https://www.avvenire.it/rubriche/pagine/una-%C2%ABspiritosa%C2%BB-passeggiata-con-i-cani-degli-scrittori_20141126/ (accessed January 3, 2023).
13. The secondary literature on dragons is of course vast. For a useful bibliography of recent and not so recent, see, Iván Alexander De la Ossa, 'De los poetas de la Antigüedad a la literatura fantástica: una historia general de los dragones en Occidente', *Literatura: teoría, historia, crítica* 22, no. 1 (2020): 13–49.
14. Dino Buzzati, *Sessanta Racconti* (Milan: Mondadori, 1994). For the English translation, see Dino Buzzati, *Catastrophe and Other Stories* (New York: Ecco, 2018).
15. Buzzati, *Catastrophe*, 'The Slaying of the Dragon', ch. 13.
16. Buzzati, *Catastrophe*, 'The Slaying of the Dragon', ch. 13.
17. Buzzati, *Catastrophe*, 'The Slaying of the Dragon', ch. 13.
18. Derrida, *The Animal That Therefore I Am*, 111.
19. The short story is collected in Dino Buzzati, *Il bestiario di Dino Buzzati* (Milan: Mondadori, 2015).
20. Émile Benveniste, *Indo-European Language and Society* (Miami, FL: University of Miami Press, 1973), 520.
21. Benveniste, *Indo-European Language and Society*, 455.
22. Buzzati, *Catastrophe*, 'The Slaying of the Dragon', ch. 13.
23. Friedrich Kittler, *Gramophone, Film, Typewriter* (Stanford, CA: Stanford University Press, 1999), xxxix.
24. Giorgio Agamben: *Homo Sacer: Sovereign Power and Bare Life* (Stanford, CA: Stanford University Press, 1998).
25. Buzzati, *Catastrophe*, 'The Slaying of the Dragon', ch. 13.
26. Giorgio Agamben, *Language and Death: The Place of Negativity* (Minneapolis, MN: University of Minnesota Press, 2006), 32.
27. Agamben, *Language and Death*, 33.
28. Buzzati, *Catastrophe*, 'The Slaying of the Dragon', ch. 13.
29. Derrida, *The Animal That Therefore I Am*, 93.

30. Buzzati, *Catastrophe*, 'The Slaying of the Dragon', ch. 13.
31. Dino Buzzati, *The Tartar Steppe* (Edinburgh: Canongate, 2018).
32. On waiting in Buzzati's novel, see Francesco De Nicola, *Il deserto di Buzzati: Il tempo, l'attesa, il sogno* (Firenze: Nicomp, 2013).
33. Buzzati, *The Tartar Steppe*, ch. 2.
34. Buzzati, *The Tartar Steppe*, ch. 2.
35. Buzzati, *The Tartar Steppe*, ch. 9.
36. Buzzati, *The Tartar Steppe*, ch. 30.
37. Giorgio Agamben, *The Use of Bodies* (Stanford, CA: Stanford University Press, 2016), 92.
38. On the relation of time to borders in the novel, see *Buzzati e il confine: Atti del convegno internazionale*, eds. John Butcher and Marco Perale (Meran: Akademie Meran, 2021).
39. Michel Foucault, *History of Sexuality, The Care of the Self: Volume 3* (New York: Vintage, 1988).
40. On tragic and comic relations to the self, see Grant Farred and Timothy Campbell, *The Comic Self: Toward Dispossession* (Minneapolis, MN: University of Minnesota Press, 2023).
41. Rosi Braidotti, 'Nomadic Ethics', *Deleuze Studies* 7, no. 3 (2013): 342–59; Jacques Derrida, *Aporias* (Stanford, CA: Stanford University Press, 1993), 3.
42. For a terrific example of a threshold that must not be crossed, see Buzzati's 'Il mantello' (The Overcoat) collected in *Sessanta Racconti*. My thanks to Felice Cimatti for drawing my attention to another of Buzzati's biopolitical creatures.

Works Cited

Agamben, Giorgio. *Homo Sacer: Sovereign Power and Bare Life*. Translated by Daniel Heller-Roazen. Stanford, CA: Stanford University Press, 1998.

Agamben, Giorgio. *Language and Death: The Place of Negativity*. Translated by Karen Pinkus and Michael Hardt. Minneapolis, MN: University of Minnesota Press, 2006.

Agamben, Giorgio. *The Use of Bodies*. Translated by Adam Kotsko. Stanford, CA: Stanford University Press, 2016.

Benveniste, Émile. *Indo-European Language and Society*. Translated by Elizabeth Palmer. Miami: University of Miami Press, 1973.

Braidotti, Rosi. 'Nomadic Ethics'. *Deleuze Studies* 7 (2013): 342–59.

Butcher, John, and Marco Perale, eds. *Buzzati e il confine: Atti del convegno internazionale*. Meran: Akademie Meran, 2021.

Buzzati, Dino. *Sessanta Racconti*. Milan: Mondadori, 1994.

Buzzati, Dino. *The Tartar Steppe*. Translated Stuart C. Hood. Boston: D. R. Godine, 1995.

Buzzati, Dino. *Il bestiario di Dino Buzzati. Cani, gatti, e altri animali*. Edited by Lorenzo Viganò. Milan: Mondadori, 2015.

Buzzati, Dino. *Catastrophe and Other Stories*. Translated by Judith Landry. New York: Ecco, 2018.

Cavelleri, Cesare. 'Una "spiritosa" passeggiata con i cani degli scrittori'. *Avvenire*, November 26, 2014. https://www.avvenire.it/rubriche/pagine/una-%C2%ABspiritosa%C2%BB-passeggiata-con-i-cani-degli-scrittori_20141126/ (accessed 3 January 2023).

De la Ossa, Iván Alexander. 'De los poetas de la Antigüedad a la literatura fantástica: una historia general de los dragones en Occidente'. *Literatura: teoría, historia, crítica* 22, no. 1 (2020): 13–49.

Deleuze, Gilles and Félix Guattari. *Kafka: Toward a Minor Literature*. Translated by Dana Polan. Minneapolis, MN: University of Minnesota, 1986.

De Nicola, Francesco. *Il deserto di Buzzati: Il tempo, l'attesa, il sogno*. Firenze: Nicomp, 2013.

Derrida, Jacques. *Acts in Literature*. Translated Derrick Attridge. New York: Routledge, 1992.

Derrida, Jacques. *Aporias*. Translated by Thomas Dutoit. Stanford, CA: Stanford University Press, 1993.

Derrida, Jacques. *The Animal that Therefore I Am*. Translated by David Wills. New York: Fordham University Press, 2008.

Farred, Grant, and Timothy Campbell. *The Comic Self: Toward Dispossession*. Minneapolis, MN: University of Minnesota Press, 2023.

Foucault, Michel. *Histoire de la sexualité 1: La volonté de savoir*. Paris: Gallimard, 1976.

Foucault, Michel. *History of Sexuality, vol. 1: An Introduction*. Translated by Robert Hurley. New York: Vintage, 1978.

Foucault, Michel. *History of Sexuality, Volume 3: The Care of the Self*. Translated Robert Hurley. New York: Vintage, 1988.

Kittler, Friedrich. *Gramophone, Film, Typewriter*. Translated by Geoffrey Winthrop-Young and Michael Wutz. Stanford, CA: Stanford University Press, 1999.

Kohn, Edoardo. *How Forests Think: Toward an Anthropology Beyond the Human*. Berkeley, CA: University of California Press, 2013.

Posenato, Cinzia. *Il bestiario di Dino Buzzati*. Bologna: Inchiostri Associate, 2009.

Reza, Matthew. 'Oltre il confine: La dilatazione dei paradigmi di realtà nei racconti fantastici di Dino Buzzati'. *Italianistica: Rivista di letteratura italiana* 44 (January 2015): 127–39.

Shukin, Nicole. *Animal Capital: Rendering Life in Biopolitical Times*. Minneapolis, MN: University of Minnesota Press, 2009.

Zanda, Carlo. *Una misteriosa devozione. Storie di scrittori e di cani molto amati*. Milan: Marcos y Marcos, 2014.

Ziolkowski, Saskia. *Kafka's Italian Progeny*. Toronto: University of Toronto Press, 2020.

7 Cages and Mirrors: Mr. Palomar and the Albino Gorilla

Serenella Iovino

The literary life of Italo Calvino, one of the most beloved and celebrated Italian authors internationally, is populated by animals.[1] There are spiders and crows in the restless atmosphere of war, dogs that accompany eccentric owners who never come down from the trees, flocks of starlings in the city sky, turtles mating in the garden, whistling blackbirds, geckos, chickens, rabbits, pets, pests and feral creatures.

These animals share a characteristic: even when they are 'wild' or 'free', they always carry traces of a 'culture' that is embodied in their nature as semiotic creatures. Moreover, they sometimes conceal a cipher of violence or otherness, which is often a biopolitical cipher. This happens, for example, in works like *Marcovaldo* (1963), in which animals live a parallel fate of marginalisation and oppression together with marginal humans – the novel's protagonist and his family, in fact. In some of these animals, the biopolitical cipher is coupled with dynamics in which bodily and existential oppression is corroborated by historical and colonial oppression. This is the case in the story 'The Albino Gorilla', included in *Mr. Palomar* (1983).

Set in a zoo, the story lays bare all the ontological and anthropological contradictions implied by the presence of a rare specimen of primate that, from the other side of his cage, looks at us with a face in which we humans can mirror ourselves. Using biosemiotics, multispecies ethnography and postcolonial studies as theoretical coordinates, this chapter takes the cue from Calvino's story for a wider reflection on primates, both nonhuman and human.

Pigeonholing Otherness: Mr. Palomar and the Animal Mirror

Living otherness on display. This is the zoo. A silent observer, always bewildered by the unpredictable forms of reality, Mr. Palomar wanders along cages and glasshouses, where enclosed creatures seem to him at once kin and radically alien. Giraffes, penguins, reptiles, apes: they are brotherly for their pain, their loneliness, the stridor of their anguished presence, which resonates with his incapacity to find patterns of harmony in himself and what he sees. Yet, these animals are alien to him. Alien are their moves and forms. Alien are their original habitats, the remote regions from which they or their ancestors were forcibly subtracted. And alien are their inner worlds, which are inaccessible and lost, reduced to an accident of a museified alterity. In fact, subjugated to reinforce the fantasy of human exceptionalism, these creatures disquietingly demonstrate just the opposite, namely that '[b]eyond the glass of every cage, there is the world as it was before man, or as it will be, to show that the world of man is not eternal and is not unique'. In the 'complicated harmony' of giraffes – graceful despite the apparent gracelessness of their moves – and the 'monstrosity, and necessity, and beauty' of reptiles constrained in 'a motionless mixture of days and nights',[2] Mr. Palomar sees therefore the manifestation of 'an innocent and suffering otherness, a distressing and inscrutable area towards which no self-sufficient exercise of reason is possible or permitted'.[3] All these feelings – of discomfort, sympathy, anxiety, sadness, disorientation – converge vis-à-vis the albino gorilla he sees in Barcelona's Zoo.

To better understand this encounter, we must first consider the nature of *Mr. Palomar*, which is the last volume of fiction Italo Calvino published during his life. 'Fiction' is only partially accurate in this case. Written between 1975 and 1983, this is 'the most autobiographical book I have ever written, a third-person autobiography', he declared in an interview.[4] Although occasionally present, and certainly sublimated in the shape of landscapes and atmospheres, autobiography is not a constant feature in Calvino's writing. Yet this work, which is an exercise in leaving the self aside or letting it disappear in the mystery of its objects, bears traces of his life and experiences – of his cities and places, his travels, his tastes, his family, even his individual traits.

Looked at more closely, the name *Palomar* has a double referent: a famous telescope in California and a dovecote. Observation and the (frustrated) quest for an order by which to 'pigeonhole' phenomena give unity and direction to these twenty-seven episodes, which travel along three experiential paths – description, chronicle and meditation – and gather into three sections: 'Mr. Palomar's Vacation', 'Mr. Palomar in the City' and 'The Silences of Mr. Palomar'. Mediated through the filter of this persona-observatory and certainly not exhaustive of the author's creative and existential universe, a 'Calvino-shadow' emerges in these stories of a taciturn man who lives between Rome, Paris and the Tyrrhenian Sea. From there, he monitors the things that surround him, interrogating himself about their meanings, taxonomies and kinships, and often caught in smaller or bigger frictions with reality.

Animals often appear in Mr. Palomar. In fact, Mr. Palomar's days are filled with nonhuman presences: black birds, turtles, geckoes. And again, starlings flying above his terrace in Rome, a 'brotherly' ox carcass in the butcher shop. All these animals disclose an abyss and a disappointment: an abyss of mystery about their world of meanings, and a disappointment with his efforts to categorise what he sees. His most challenging experiences, however, occur during his three visits to zoos. The first and the last of these, which happen in France at the Vincennes Zoo and Paris' Jardin des Plantes respectively – fall halfway between the aesthetic and the taxonomic. Palomar observes giraffes and reptiles, contemplating the fraternal 'monstrosity' of these captive animals. He tries to locate the place of the human in relation to the 'antediluvian bestiary'[5] of which zoo pythons, boas, iguanas and crocodiles are dismal specimens. But it is the central episode, dedicated to the albino gorilla in Barcelona's zoo, that fully reveals the thickness of the layers – ethical, political, anthropological and semiotic – that lie behind these cages.[6]

Completely eventless, the plot of 'The Albino Gorilla' is built upon the emotional and symbolic density of a meeting. Visiting the primate section, Palomar lingers on Copito de Nieve (Floquet de Neu, in Catalan), a.k.a. Snowflake, a world-famous white gorilla who is one of the zoo's main attractions. And what he finds is a rather depressing – yet thought-provoking – spectacle:

> Beyond a sheet of plate glass, 'Copito de Nieve' [. . .] is a mountain of flesh and white hide. [. . .] The facial mask is a human pink, carved by wrinkles [. . .] Every now and then that [. . .] sad giant [. . .] turns upon the crowd of visitors beyond the glass [. . .] a slow gaze charged with desolation and patience and boredom, a gaze that expresses all the resignation at being the way he is, sole exemplar in the world of a form not chosen, not loved, all the effort of bearing his own singularity, and the suffering at occupying space and time with his presence so cumbersome and evident.[7]

In the 'enormous void of his hours', the gorilla spends his time hugging a car tire. In this space without nature, without games, without a world, surrounded by a ghastly silence, Mr. Palomar perceives the gorilla as kin, sharing a dimension of solitude, incommunicability and the need for meanings.

Already very rich in its rarefied poetic intensity, 'The Albino Gorilla' acquires added depth if considered in its compositional development. Before re-elaborating this episode as a Mr. Palomar chapter, Calvino published it as a short autobiographical feature titled 'Visita a un gorilla albino' ('Visiting an Albino Gorilla') in the newspaper *la Repubblica* on 16 May 1980. Speaking in the first person, he provided a slightly more detailed description of Copito de Nieve's life conditions, mentioning, for example, the many attempts at reproducing his unique genetic material (something to which we will return later) and observing that the source of the sympathy he felt was due to an 'interior situation, also in relationship to the environment, which is completely human, filled with negative human meanings'.[8] He also stressed the 'prison- and concentration-camp-like aspect' of the gorilla's stall, creating an explicit parallel between zoos and these two extreme confinement institutions. The most remarkable difference with the final version, however, is the presence of an occasional interlocutor, the Uruguayan writer and political exile Juan Carlos Onetti (indicated as 'J.C.O.'), with whom Calvino shared the story of the gorilla. The writer's comments and Calvino's unspoken answer, omitted in the end, are worth a mention:

'There's nothing strange about a caged monkey', says O. 'I know a man who's been locked up in a much smaller cage for years'. [. . .] I understand that he wanted to give me a lesson in civil morality: one does not speak of the suffering of a caged monkey to the citizen of a country where so many people are imprisoned and tortured.[9]

In the final version, which omits the presence of J.C.O., the only thing that captures Mr. Palomar's attention is the inhumane condition in which the gorilla is kept: a state of boredom and placelessness, a semiotic desert. By defining this condition as 'inhumane' – an adjective that Calvino does not use – I am not implying that the gorilla is or should be humanised, but that his situation of total withdrawal from a world of meanings, so understandable for a human being, is indeed the most radical form of inflicted pain for other animals, too. And Calvino, who maintained the heuristic usefulness of anthropomorphism to shed light on ethical and ontological similarities across the species, was aware of this.[10]

The *Umwelt* in a Cage

Anthropomorphism is an important concept. The gorilla, in fact, is, like other primates, an anthropomorphic ape. But what does that mean? And where can we go if we follow the thread of these similarities, which are not identities or analogies, but rather deep kinships and affinities?

Frans de Waal, the Dutch ethologist who has brought the social and emotional world of bonobos, chimpanzees and other primates to the general public through his books, also emphasises this. Human and nonhuman primates, de Waal reminds us, are similar not only in their bodily plans, but also in their sensory and cognitive structures: in fact, their brains and neural systems have the same fundamental structure as that of other mammals. Of course, it would be methodologically incorrect to deduce that their worlds overlap. However, a big problem is also *anthropodenial*, the refusal to admit even obvious similarities between us and other primates. After more than a century and a half of evolutionism, this refusal is one of the major obstacles to understanding ourselves as a species: a species with a clear evolutionary history. As Darwin has shown and as genetics and evolutionary biology confirm, in a distant past that we now know to be several million years ago, there was a common ancestor to all primates from which various branches of descent gradually broke away. There is the broader one, which Linnaeus called 'primates'. And then there are the finer branches. Ours, the hominids, also hosts the great anthropomorphic apes, those that, like us, are tailless: chimpanzees, bonobos, gorillas, orangutans. They are our closest relatives. With the first two, the chimpanzee (*Pan troglodytes*) and the bonobo (*Pan paniscus*), we share respectively 98.6% and 99% of our DNA. This is why the American biologist Jared Diamond calls *Homo sapiens* 'the third chimpanzee'. And we are also genetically very similar to gorillas (98%) and orangutans (97%).[11]

This similarity, as Darwin emphasised in his essay *The Expression of the Emotions in Man and Animals* (1872), is not only true for anatomy. Those who have studied these apes – devoting their lives to them, like Jane Goodall, or dying for them, like Dian Fossey – have allowed us to recognise that their world, not unlike ours, is marked by power dynamics and hierarchies, violence, solidarity and altruism. They play, suffer, deceive, kill and love. Thanks to fascinating studies conducted, among others, by the Italian primatologists Elisabetta Palagi and Fausto Caruana, today we can assert that among the things that we have in common with other primates are also laughing or being contagiously affected by someone else's yawn. Reversing the argument, one can even say that laughing is one of the most 'animal' expressions of humanity because it refers to a common ancestral root in which laughter is linked to the social pleasure of play and affiliation. In general, therefore, it is legitimate to argue that if two related species in similar circumstances have similar behaviours, their motivations and their way of perceiving the world are probably similar as well.[12]

Assuming all of this, then the encounter between Mr. Palomar and the gorilla is not only a meeting between two living beings, two mammals, two primates, but it is also a meeting between two ways, in many respects similar, of being in the world: of understanding, experiencing and perceptually relating to environments that are not just material, but also environments of signs, proper to every animal. *Umwelten*, as Jakob von Uexküll used to say. Each animal is in its distinct *Umwelt* as in a sphere of signs and perceptions that includes and helps it live in its habitat, its natural or cultural home. *Umwelt*, in this respect, defines 'the subjective world (*Innenwelt*) of a living being according to what its sensory and physical abilities allow it to know about the objective outside world (or *Umgebung*). Each creature's *Umwelt* is its whole world'.[13]

Mr. Palomar's environment is made up of people and places, objects and things. It is an environment sedimented in the human: an urban, cosmopolitan, natural and cultural environment. The signs that Palomar finds and exchanges in this environment are those that allow him to transform his life into a sequence of coherent experiences, to give meaning to conventions expressed in words and books, symbols and institutions, including the cages of a zoo – and including the zoo itself. This environment also includes, of course, his biological environment of Homo sapiens, and the underground genealogy that connects him to his evolutionary relatives. But what is the environment of a gorilla? Certainly not the zoo. And especially not this zoo: a masonry enclosure, a fake garden without trees that looks like the yard of a prison with an iron gym ladder. Yet this makes up his *Umwelt* as the only realm he can perceive according to his own abilities.

Palomar, although restless and disheartened, understands his environment and is free to use it, explore it, inhabit it, transforming it into new signs, meanings, descriptions, stories and philosophical reflections. On the other side of the cage, Copito de Nieve instead collides with an environment permeated by signs and things that do not belong to him or his species. Confined in an enclosure, in a habitat he does not recognise, the gorilla expresses with his desolate air the pain of an isolation that betrays not only his nature but also his 'culture': that is, his ability to interact creatively and communicatively with the world.

'One can take the ape out of the jungle, but not the jungle out of the ape', writes Frans de Waal.[14] Disentangled from the jungle and its living stories, Copito de Nieve lives suspended in an uncanny void. Now that the signs of his original *Umwelt* are blurred and lost, he spends indefinite spans of time relating to a tire – and this tire, Mr. Palomar infers, becomes in his hands something else: 'What can this object be for him? A toy? A fetish? A talisman?'[15] For a moment, Mr. Palomar puts forward the hypothesis that the tire is an emotional medium, a symbol that helps the gorilla hold on to reality. The tire, one may assume, could be a symbol of Copito's solitude, of his difficult singularity, of his alienated presence in a world poor of signs intelligible to him. But these are only arbitrary interpretations. It would be more accurate to say, as a tour guide does, upon whom Mr. Palomar eavesdrops in Mexico by the ruins of Tula, that we don't know what it means: '*No se sabe lo qué quiere decir*' [sic].[16] What is clear, in the intersection of their two sign-universes, is the need that both Mr. Palomar and Copito de Nieve have of 'investing oneself in things, recognizing oneself in signs, transforming the world into a collection of symbols – a first daybreak of culture in the long biological night'.[17]

Now, that might sound – and perhaps is – an excessively anthropomorphic interpretation. However, the shared need for meaningful signs is a very significant aspect here. Yet, these parallels, although evident, have been for a long time largely underestimated. Consider how powerfully the 'Cartesian scientific practice' of classical behaviourism, with its 'rigidly disciplined experimental regimes in controlled laboratory settings'[18] has confined animals, even those historically and biologically closer to our species, to a limbo of nonmind. In contrast, the so-called 'bi-constructivist paradigm' associated with multispecies ethnography, anthrozoology, modern primatology, zoosemiotics, and the cognitive and phenomenological strands of ethology, 'takes as axiomatic the subjectivity of animals', considering humans not as mere observers, but as partners in a mutual construction of worlds and experiences.[19] It is clear that the type of animal subjectivity at play here is not a total projection, this time incautiously anthropomorphic, of our physical or cognitive characteristics, but rather the recognition of the animal's agency, namely, its capacity for self-determination and for referring to itself as an individual – an agency that also includes violence. Therefore, it is important to always keep in mind that 'affinity' does not mean 'identity' or lower quantitative gradients of the same behaviours and sensitivities, which would lead to seeing other primates as 'failed' or 'imperfect' humans. Affinity rather means the possibility of understanding and working together precisely based on the elements that unite us.[20]

In the research conducted within this framework, humans position themselves as partners of nonhuman animals in the shared construction of worlds and experiences. Think for example of the many successful experiments, such as those with Washoe the chimpanzee, Koko the gorilla or Kanzi the bonobo, who learned hundreds of words and expressions in sign language, even inventing new ones. In some cases, it was the primates who approached our experience, as when Washoe, responding to the sadness of a caregiver who had told her in sign language that she had lost her child, made the sign that means 'crying'. This is even more surprising, considering that chimpanzees do not cry; Washoe, however, had learned the meaning of it in relation to humans. It is not surprising, then, that in her case, as in Koko's, the most significant exchanges with humans were those made of gestures and gazes. Another of these primates, Michael the gorilla, who lived with Koko for a long time and learned sign language from her, was even able to tell the story of the death of his mother, killed by poachers when he was a baby. As shown in the online videos, Michael was reliving and sharing a traumatic memory.[21]

This means that relationships between humans and other animals, while respecting species differences, can be seen as 'intersubjective'. These relationships are built when researchers work alongside nonhuman animals rather than just working on them. The hybrid communities that form are 'semiotic communities', as French ethologist Dominique Lestel calls them. This happens when the nonhuman semiosphere intersects that of the human observer (or better: partner in action), shaping an actively storied dimension that brings together subjects, places and their experiences, allowing for forms of communications.

Exploring these similarities from the viewpoint of the primates' emotions, Frans de Waal insists that '[o]ur species shares many emotions with the other primates because we rely on approximately the same behavioral repertoire. This similarity, expressed by bodies with similar design, gives us a profound nonverbal connection with other primates. Our bodies map so perfectly onto theirs, and vice versa, that mutual understanding is close behind'.[22] It is for this reason that Calvino's description of the gorilla's boredom, his solitude and need for semiotic fulfilment, is so anthropomorphic and yet so realistic – and so accurate. Palomar understands Copito de Nieve because he reads his discomfort in his body and expressions. And he recognises himself in it.[23] The problem is that, in the zoo, humans and nonhumans do not always form a 'semiotic community' in Lestel's terms, and certainly not in zoos like the one where Copito de Nieve is. Among the environments of signs that intersect here, there is no intersubjectivity, but a one-way relationship. The gaze between Mr. Palomar and the gorilla, in fact, is not a reciprocal gaze. The structure of a zoo like the one where they meet makes any real encounter impossible.

As John Berger wrote in his seminal 1977 essay, 'Why Look at Animals?', any connection between humans and nonhuman animals in the zoo is thwarted. Created in an epoch in which animals were disappearing from the sphere of everyday experience, the zoo 'to which people go to meet animals, to observe them, to see them, is, in fact, a monument to the impossibility of such encounters'.[24] In the zoo, animals are marginalised both culturally and physically, and this marginality is not only, Berger continued, connected to the general disappearance of animals – what we now call the 'Sixth Extinction'. Instead, it is linked to breaking the reciprocity of the gaze between human and animal:

> nowhere in a zoo can a stranger encounter the look of an animal. At the most, the animal's gaze flickers and passes on. [. . .] Therein lies the ultimate consequence of their marginalization. That look between animal and man, which may have played a crucial role in the development of human society, [. . .] has been extinguished. [. . .] This historic loss, to which zoos are a monument, is now irredeemable for the culture of capitalism.[25]

This loss also entails the very density of the presence of the animal as a sentient, carnal, living being. Especially in a postmodern culture in which the dominating medium is the image (and this is the culture to which Calvino relates in these years), the animals in flesh and blood are reduced to phantasms, abstract figures whose 'frailties and stress' vanish 'along with our sympathy'.[26]

Colonial Stories and Darwinian Zoos

This consideration takes us to another aspect of this story that has both an individual side, totally embodied by the singular persona of Copito de Nieve, and a larger historical narrative. The story of Copito de Nieve is indeed a real story. And it is a colonial story. It hit the headlines in March 1967, when international newspapers and magazines such as *Life*, *Paris-Match* and *Stern* started reporting the case of a curiously white gorilla cub, found in Equatorial Guinea and soon transported to Spain. *National Geographic*, which featured him on the cover in 1967 and 1970, reports the facts in detail. In the first of his two articles, Dr. Arthur J. Riopelle, a primatologist from Louisiana, triumphally described the humanisation path of 'Snowflake' with expressions such as 'Jungle Ape Adopts Civilized Ways', relating the initial slowness in 'taming' an (evidently traumatised) cub, that 'allowed himself to be touched on the head, ears, arms, legs, and back' only after sixteen days, which is also when he was first 'permitted to leave his cage'. In the second article, however, Riopelle went so far as to describe the gorilla's comfort around people ('his public'), implying that the roles were reversed: 'Time and again I have seen him stand erect to look at us through the window glass of his cage. [. . .] Are we on display?' That nonchalant 'we' and the cruelly ironic game suggesting an impossible place swap confirm the abyssal divide separating Copito, caught in his singularity, and 'his public'.[27]

But how did this little gorilla become a celebrity? Here the personal story also reveals its bitter colonial flipside. In 1966, in Equatorial Guinea, a Fang tribe farmer named Benito Mañé killed a pack of gorillas, that – he claimed – were attacking his banana orchard. Clinging to the female's dead body, he spotted a curiously white cub. Aware of the exceptional discovery – and even more so of its monetary value – Mañé spared the baby gorilla and promptly sold him to Jordi Sabater Pi, a Catalan primatologist who took him to Spain. Before ending up in Barcelona's zoo in 1967, Copito de Nieve lived for some time with the family of the zoo's veterinarian, Román Luera Carbó, looked after by his wife and playing with their eight-year-old son Francisco and their basset hound Pompeia. A photo-reportage in Life shows, with captions in sheer Disney rhetoric, the 'natural' integration of Copito within the fabric of his human 'family'.[28] During these months, he was strongly humanised – with toys, 'boyish roughhousing' with his human 'brother', 'human' food and shoes. After this forced anthropomorphic infancy, even filled with large displays of affection, he was transferred to the zoo. There, he became not only a major attraction, but also the bearer of a genetic pool which had to be preserved at all costs. As Calvino also wrote in his *Repubblica* article, many ways were tried to have him generate white cubs, including mating with his own daughters. At the end of his life, Copito de Nieve had fathered twenty-two offspring by three different mates. Only six children survived to adulthood. However, they – and their children and grandchildren – were all black.[29] Finally, in 2003, Copito fell ill with skin cancer and was euthanised. In Spain he was literally a superstar, inspiring books and films. After his death, an asteroid was named after him.[30]

A few years ago, Spanish newspapers announced that the cause of Copito de Nieve's albinism had finally been discovered. It was apparently due to a case of inbreeding: his parents were genetically related. More than this, however, it is striking that his DNA is still preserved in the 'frozen zoo' of Barcelona, also for future reproductions or cloning.[31] With the genetic makeup of particularly rare animals, this is common practice. However, the reductionism of operations of this kind is appalling. In our case, it is the last dematerialisation of the semiotic world of the gorilla. One wonders if DNA alone is enough to reproduce a living creature without any relationship with its natural habitat. In this spirit, the de-extinction of species lost for millennia, which is often debated, forces us to admit that bringing these animals 'back to the world' is literally impossible because their world, in fact, no longer exists.

The thing that strikes one most, when reading the reports about Copito – and those from the *National Geographic* magazine are no exception – is the candour with which his humanisation and entry into the zoo are presented, almost as if they were the ineluctable destiny of such a unique 'specimen'. As many primatologists have pointed out, humanising practices often increase the previous trauma experienced by formerly wild apes – the trauma of capture, loss of parents and siblings and detachment from the original *Umwelt* – by adding to it the trauma of forcefully leaving their adoptive family once their physical strength becomes a threat to people. 'They're stuck between two worlds', Jane Goodall commented on chimpanzees caught in a similar situation: 'They've never learned to be a chimpanzee and they can never become a human'.[32] And this is often a mutual trauma even for the little humans of the family, as Karen Joy Fowler's stirring book *We Are All Completely Beside Ourselves* (2013) highlights in a lyrical and powerfully evocative way. In this novel, a mysteriously lost sister becomes the cipher of the life of a woman, Rosemary, who finally finds her as a chimpanzee in a zoo cage: 'I didn't know what she was thinking or feeling. Her body had become unfamiliar to me. And yet, at the very same time, I recognized everything about her. My sister, Fern. [. . .] As if I were looking in a mirror'.[33] As Louise Westling noted in her examination of the 'dangerous intersubjectivities' between humans and other primates, 'Rosemary confesses both her incomprehension and her profound identification, trapped in a middle space between species and robbed of what had seemed a full sibling relationship in their very young childhood'.[34] Although not a lost 'family member' for Mr. Palomar, Copito de Nieve is also a mysterious mirror that reveals the hubris of creating cultural gulfs between evolutionary kin that are prevented from recognising each other as brotherly subjects.

The colonial side of Copito's story – a story, where the animal is, materially and by definition, disempowered and 'othered' – is not limited to his case, though. In fact, it prompts a further and more general consideration. Although zoos today have changed from Calvino's time, it is undeniable that modern zoos are, historically, colonial institutions. As Randy Malamud explained in his monumental *Reading Zoos* (1998), the zoo is originally an expression of imperialist capitalism and of its systematic attempt to commodify the living world by transforming all conquered subjects into subaltern beings. The biopolitical dimension of this phenomenon is evident in the fact that these collections of exotic animals, which along with their habitat have suffered the onslaught of colonial predators, speak of a power that is at the same time material and cultural: the power to rewrite the natural world in terms of authoritarian master narratives and more reassuring representations, imposing alien cultural models upon it.

We do not need to mention the imaginary behind the garden of Eden to state that zoos are 'as ancient as humans are'.[35] By and large, the possession of captive animals has always been a distinctive trait of political grandeur: 'Potentates demonstrate their power by appearing to sustain a cosmos', writes Yi-Fu Tuan in his history of animal domestication.[36] Modern zoos are preceded by a long record of animal collecting that dates back to the empires of Assyria and Babylonia and includes Egyptian as well as Chinese dynasties. It seems that the oldest testimony is the one found at the ruins of Hierakonpolis, in Egypt: a small zoo with 112 animals including bulls, dogs, baboons, wild cats, cows and even two elephants. Dating back to 3500 BC, it was reserved for the city's elite and probably also a place of sacrifices and religious rites. The first testimony of a park where 'a large number of beasts were kept for the exclusive contemplation and enjoyment of the monarch', comes from China, dated around 1150 BC.[37] Prepared by the thriving of the geopolitical structures of mercantilism of the Renaissance, which made it possible to further develop the practice of trading and collecting animals, zoos became public institutions in the first decades of the nineteenth century and in the Victorian age. One of the first of its kind, the London Zoological Society, for example, was founded in 1826 by Sir Stamford Raffles with the purpose of collecting the animals he had captured in Southeast Asia while working as a trader for the East India Company. 'He plundered exotic commercial goods in his professional employment, and plundered the animal world as a hobby', writes Malamud, who adds: 'The zoos and the animals thus became part of the discourse that reinforced the hegemonies of imperialism'.[38] An integral part of this discourse is the fact that, in the late nineteenth century, the animals displayed in the zoo cages of all the great European and American cities, were, in some cases, also human animals. As Oliver Hochadel writes in 'Darwin in the Monkey Cage', 'Humans staged as strange and exotic were exhibited alongside lions and monkeys'.[39] Based on the often-racist biases of the zoology and anthropology of the time, this 'zoo Darwinism' reinforced the hegemonic narrative according to which Africans and Asians were closer to animals than were Europeans. Popular attractions included Eskimos exhibited along with their sled dogs, Sudanese people with their camels, and Sri Lankans with elephants. The most infamous – and tragic – case is that of the Congolese pygmy Ota Benga, who in 1906 was exhibited at the Bronx Zoo in the same cage as an orangutan. Following visitors' protests, he was released. He committed suicide in 1916, surrounded by a hostile environment and frustrated at not being able to return to the Congo – even in his case, a lost existential *Umwelt*.[40] One cannot help noticing that in zoos, life is never *bios*, but rather a 'bare life' completely disentangled from its web of meanings and socioecological complexity, something to be put on display in its nakedness and completely left at the mercy of a sovereign power, as Giorgio Agamben (1998) would say. With his poetic rendering of Copito's captive existence as 'bare life', Calvino is implicitly claiming his right to be inscribed as a full-fledged citizen in the realm of *bios*, a social life teeming with meanings.

Today, after so much debating and researching, we may say that zoos look less like concentration camps than they did a few years ago. [41] As Elisabetta Palagi points out, without zoological gardens, often at the forefront and specialising in few species, zoologists would not have the opportunity to observe and study animals 'in the wild'. In addition, in some cases their actions are important for preserving threatened species: the same Copito de Nieve probably would not have survived in the jungle.[42] However, it is equally crucial to note that in no form can the zoo – an expression of the imperialism that is at the roots of this era that many call 'Capitalocene' – serve as an alibi for the damage that the Sixth Extinction inflicts on the living dynamics of our planet. Still, where it survives in its 'classic' form, the zoo is 'a cultural fossil'.[43] It is an institution that hardly allows us to recognise the Other as embodied in a kindred being, despite the fact that this Other has a face that, like the face of the albino gorilla, so closely resembles our own. This is the mark of what we call the Anthropocene: the fact that the environment that creates new ecological proximities in the city is not always able to create an ecosystem, because it cuts all possible ties, including cognitive ones. To be endangered here is not only the ecology of biological systems, but also the ecology of mind, mined by this forcefully schizophrenic relationship with an Other who belongs to our evolutionary family. Still, it is surprising that in (and perhaps despite) this very landscape of concrete and cages, crisscrossed by the dynamics of power, Mr. Palomar is able to cultivate what Roberto Marchesini calls 'animal epiphanies'.[44] These epiphanies allow him to feel compassion for the animals we encage and for those we eat, and surprise and wonder for the animals whose sign-world he does not understand: birds, turtles, geckos and a gorilla. In the nonbinary and yet mysterious vision that Calvino delivers to us, the living world lies and lives in these crossings, these hybrid compositions.

These singular beings in particular are Calvino's response to a generalised faceless vision of nonhuman subjectivity. In his stories, nonhuman beings regain their faces, their uniqueness, situating themselves in the same moral territory of the human observer and inviting us to take 'a sideways glance of a vast nonhuman world that has been denigrated by the concepts, institutions, and practices associated with "the human"'.[45]

Calvino's animals do have a face, a face that coincides with their own bodies, and that, also thanks to his fictional artifice, we can picture as surprised, perplexed, depressed or desperate. As Charles Darwin has taught us, it is a face whose expressions, though different from ours, we are invited to recognise, more than ever now that the mechanisms and assemblages of our power over other species make these species 'killable' as individuals, groups or multitudes.[46]

At the end of 'The Albino Gorilla', Calvino writes:

> Leaving the zoo, Mr. Palomar cannot dispel the image of the albino gorilla from his mind. [. . .] At night, both during the hours of insomnia [. . .] the great ape continues to appear to him. 'Just as the gorilla has his tire, which serves as tangible support for a raving, wordless speech', he thinks, 'so I have this image of a great white ape. We all turn in our hands an old, empty tire through which we try to reach some final meaning, which words cannot achieve'.[47]

This image that Calvino/Mr. Palomar carries with him, out of the zoo, is now ours, too. By passing it on to us, Calvino forces us to think about the singular losses – infinite extinctions taking place in the cages of the world's zoos. They are joint extinctions of habitats, individuals and evolutionary plots, but they are also extinctions of communities of signs, of languages, of kin. Curing these extinctions is what must keep us awake.

Notes

1. This chapter is a substantially revised version of the chapter 'The Gorilla' in my book *Italo Calvino's Animals: Anthropocene Stories* (Cambridge: Cambridge University Press, 2021).
2. Italo Calvino, *Mr. Palomar* (San Diego: Harcourt Brace Jovanovich, 1985), 86.
3. Gian Carlo Ferretti, *Le capre di Bikini: Calvino giornalista e saggista 1945–1985* (Rome: Editori Riuniti, 1989), 151.
4. Italo Calvino, 'L'occhio e il silenzio', in Italo Calvino, *Sono nato in America . . . Interviste 1951–1985*, ed. L. Baranelli (Milan: Mondadori, 2012), 552.
5. Calvino, *Mr. Palomar*, 87.
6. Calvino, *Mr. Palomar*, 87. On *Mr. Palomar*'s zoo animals, see Carrie Rohman, 'On Singularity and the Symbolic: The Threshold of the Human in Calvino's *Mr. Palomar*'. *Criticism* 51, no. 1 (2009): 63–78.
7. Calvino, *Mr. Palomar*, 81.
8. Italo Calvino, 'Visita a un gorilla albino', *la Repubblica* (16 May 1980).
9. Calvino, 'Visita a un gorilla albino'. Excerpts from this article are in Italo Calvino, *Romanzi e racconti*. 3 vols., ed. Claudio Milanini (Milan: Mondadori, 2003), II, 1430. As zoologists know well, and as Frans de Waal repeatedly stresses, 'monkeys' and

'apes' are not the same. In Italian, the word 'scimmia', however, roughly translates both terms ('apes' would be 'grandi scimmie'). I have chosen to translate 'una scimmia in gabbia' as 'caged monkey' to convey the feeling of nuisance emerging from J.C.O.'s answer.

10. On a reappraisal of anthropomorphism in evaluating the primates' emotions, see Frans de Waal, *Mama's Last Hug: Animal Emotions and What They Tell Us about Ourselves* (New York: W. W. Norton, 2019).

11. See Jared Diamond, *The Third Chimpanzee: The Evolution and Future of the Human Animal* (New York: Harper Collins, 1992).

12. These are topics that de Waal treats extensively in his books. See, in particular, *Mama's Last Hug* and *Our Inner Ape: A Leading Primatologist Explains Why We Are Who We Are* (New York: Riverhead, 2006). On laughter and contagious yawning, see the special issue of the *Philosophical Transactions of the Royal Society (B)*, 'Cracking the Laugh Code: Laughter Through the Lens of Biology, Psychology and Neuroscience', edited by Fausto Caruana and Elisabetta Palagi and the article by Elisabetta Palagi, Fausto Caruana, and Frans de Waal, 'The Naturalistic Approach to Laughter in Humans and Other Animals: Towards a Unified Theory', *Phil. Trans. R. Soc.*, 2022. http://doi.org/10.1098/rstb.2021.0175.

13. Louise Westling, 'Interweaving Landscapes: Merleau-Ponty's Counter to Heidegger's Human Exceptionism', unpublished. I thank the author for sharing her paper and thoughts with me.

14. de Waal, *Our Inner Ape*, 1.

15. Calvino, *Mr. Palomar*, 82.

16. Calvino, *Mr. Palomar*, 97.

17. Calvino, *Mr. Palomar*, 83.

18. Louise Westling, 'Dangerous Intersubjectivities from Dionysos to Kanzi', in *Thinking about Animals in the Age of the Anthropocene*, eds. M. Tønnessen, K. Armstrong Oma, and S. Rattasepp (Lanham: Lexington Books, 2016), 28–9.

19. Daniel Lestel, Jeffrey Bussolini, and Matthew Chrulew, 'The Phenomenology of Animal Life', *Environmental Humanities* 5 (2014), 127.

20. I have discussed these aspects with primatologist Elisabetta Palagi. To her, my gratitude. As the Dutch philosopher and multispecies artist Eva Meijer writes, 'Humans and other primates are similar in many respects, and different in others. If we want to know what these similarities and differences are, we need to develop research based on their view of the world' (*Animal Languages: The Secret Conversations of the Living World* (London: John Murray Publishers, 2019), chapter 'Koko and Kanzi').

21. See Meijer, *Animal Languages*, chapter 'Koko and Kanzi'. There are, of course, less happy stories, like that of Nim Chimpsky (whose name mimicked that of

linguist Noam Chomsky). Nim learned some words of sign language, but at the end of the study, he was transferred to a research institute and then sold to a pharmaceutical laboratory. In the first ten years of his life, Nim had never interacted with his own kind. One can see Michael recounting the death of his mother in a video on the website: https://www.koko.org/kokoflix-video-blog/3900/michaels-story/.

22. de Waal, *Mama's Last Hug*, 19–20.
23. For another interpretation of anthropomorphism, see Felice Cimatti, *Filosofia dell'animalità* (Rome-Bari, Laterza, 2012).
24. John Berger, *About Looking* (New York: Vintage, 1980), 21.
25. Berger, *About Looking*, 26.
26. Stephen Spotte, *Zoos in Postmodernism: Signs and Simulation* (Madison: Farleigh Dickinson University Press, 2006), 15.
27. A. J. Riopelle, 'Snowflake: The World's First White Gorilla', *National Geographic* 131 (1967), 446–8; and 'Growing Up With Snowflake', *National Geographic* 138 (1970), 492 (emphasis in the original).
28. 'Unique in All Gorilladom: Román Luera Carbó's Snowflake', *Life* 62 (31 March 1967): 69–70.
29. To examine this 'fixation' with the gorilla's whiteness from the point of view of race theory and coloniality at large would disclose further significant aspects of this story. Not coincidentally, Copito is the white animal that comes from a black country that was a Spanish colony until 1968.
30. Alessandro Oppes, 'Il lungo addio a Fiocco di neve: Barcellona piange il gorilla bianco', *la Repubblica* (30 September 2003).
31. Miguel G. Corral, 'El genoma de Copito de Nieve revela las causas de su albinismo', *El Mundo* (4 June 2013): https://www.elmundo.es/elmundo/2013/06/04/ciencia/1370341229.html.
32. A. Yuhas, 'Jane Goodall Hails "Awakening" as US Labels All Chimpanzees Endangered', *The Guardian* (12 June 2015).
33. Karen Joy Fowler, *We Are All Completely Beside Ourselves* (New York: G. P. Putnam's Sons, 2013), 308.
34. Westling, 'Dangerous Intersubjectivities from Dionysos to Kanzi', 33.
35. Felice Cimatti, 'Zoo', in *A come Animale. Voci per un bestiario dei sentimenti*, eds. Felice Cimatti and Leonardo Caffo (Milan: Bompiani, 2015), 291.
36. Yi-Fi Tuan, *Dominance and Affection: The Making of Pets* (New Haven, CT: Yale University Press, 1984), 75.
37. Tuan, *Dominance and Affection*, 21.
38. Randy Malamud, 'The Problem with Zoos', *The Oxford Handbook of Animal Studies*, ed. Linda Kalof (New York: Oxford University Press, 2018), 402.

39. Oskar Hochadel, 'Darwin in the Monkey Cage: The Zoological Garden as a Medium of Evolutionary Theory', in *Beastly Natures: Animals, Humans, and the Study of History*, ed. D. Brantz (Charlottesville, VA: University of Virginia Press, 2010), 99.
40. An earlier and equally notorious example of 'anthropological showcasing' (although not in specific connection to zoos) is the case of the South African Kohikohi woman Sarah Baartman (c.1775–1815). She was exhibited as a freak-show attraction in nineteenth-century Europe under the name 'Hottentot Venus'. After her death, she was displayed at Paris's Musée de l'Homme. Her body was only repatriated in 2002, upon Nelson Mandela's request. The case is often cited for its scientific racism, sexism and colonialism. See C. C. Crais and P. Scully, *Sara Baartman and the Hottentot Venus: A Ghost Story and a Biography* (Princeton, NJ: Princeton University Press, 2009).
41. See the essays in *Metamorphoses of the Zoo: Animal Encounter after Noah*, ed. Ralph Acampora (Lanham, MD: Lexington, 2010).
42. Palagi, personal communication. On a documented case of a baby albino chimpanzee killed in Uganda, see M. Marshall, 'First known wild chimpanzee with albinism was killed by other chimps', *New Scientist*, 29 July 2021.
43. Spotte, *Zoos in Postmodernism*, 17
44. See Roberto Marchesini, *Epifania animale. L'oltreuomo come rivelazione* (Milan: Mimesis, 2014). On nonhuman subjectivities, see also Roberto Marchesini, *Etologia filosofica. Alla ricerca della soggettività animale* (Milan: Mimesis, 2016).
45. Matthew Calarco, 'Identity, Difference, Indistinction', *The New Centennial Review* 11 (2011): 56.
46. Calarco, 'Identity, Difference, Indistinction', 56. See Ralph Acampora, 'Toward a Properly Post-Humanist Ethos of Somatic Sympathy', and Lori Gruen, 'Navigating Difference (Again): Animal Ethics and Entangled Empathy', both in *Strangers to Nature: Animal Lives and Human Ethics*, ed. G. R. Smulewicz-Zucker (Lanham: Lexington Books, 2012).
47. Calvino, *Mr. Palomar*, 83.

Works Cited

Acampora, Ralph, ed. *Metamorphoses of the Zoo: Animal Encounter after Noah*. Lanham, MD: Lexington, 2010.

Acampora, Ralph. 'Toward a Properly Post-Humanist Ethos of Somatic Sympathy'. In G. R. Smulewicz-Zucker, ed. *Strangers to Nature: Animal Lives and Human Ethics*, 235–48. Lanham, MD: Lexington Books, 2012.

Agamben, Giorgio. *Homo Sacer: Sovereign Power and Bare Life*. Translated by Daniel Heller-Roazen. Stanford, CA: Stanford University Press, 1998.

Berger, John. *About Looking*. New York: Vintage, 1980.

Bolongaro, Eugenio. 'Calvino's Encounter with the Animal: Anthropomorphism, Cognition and Ethics in *Palomar*'. *Quaderni d'italianistica* 30, no. 2 (2009): 105–28.

Calarco, Matthew. 'Identity, Difference, Indistinction'. *The New Centennial Review* 11 (2011): 41–60.

Calvino, Italo. 'Visita a un gorilla albino'. *la Repubblica*, 16 May 1980.

Calvino, Italo. *Mr. Palomar*. Translated by William Weaver. San Diego, CA: Harcourt Brace Jovanovich, 1985.

Calvino, Italo. *Romanzi e racconti*. 3 vols., ed. Claudio Milanini. Milan: Mondadori, 2003.

Calvino, Italo. *Sono nato in America . . . Interviste 1951–1985*, ed. L. Baranelli. Milan: Mondadori, 2012.

Caruana, Fausto, Elisabetta Palagi and Frans de Waal, eds. *Cracking the Laugh Code: Laughter Through the Lens of Biology, Psychology and Neuroscience*. Special Issue of *Philosophical Transactions of the Royal Society of London. Series B, Biological sciences*, vol. 377, 1863 (2022): 20220159.

Cimatti, Felice. *Filosofia dell'animalità*. Rome-Bari, Laterza, 2012.

Cimatti, Felice. 'Zoo'. In *A come Animale. Voci per un bestiario dei sentimenti*, eds. Felice Cimatti and Leonardo Caffo, 291–304. Milan, Bompiani, 2015.

Corral, Miguel G. 'El genoma de Copito de Nieve revela las causas de su albinismo'. *El Mundo* (4 June 2013). https://www.elmundo.es/elmundo/2013/06/04/ciencia/1370341229.html.

Crais, Clifton C., and Pamela Scully (2009). *Sara Baartman and the Hottentot Venus: A Ghost Story and a Biography*. Princeton, NJ: Princeton University Press, 2009.

de Waal, Frans. *Mama's Last Hug: Animal Emotions and What They Tell Us about Ourselves*. New York: W. W. Norton, 2019.

de Waal, Frans. *Our Inner Ape: A Leading Primatologist Explains Why We Are Who We Are*. New York: Riverhead, 2006.

Diamond, Jared. *The Third Chimpanzee: The Evolution and Future of the Human Animal*. New York: Harper Collins, 1992.

Ferretti, Gian Carlo. *Le capre di Bikini: Calvino giornalista e saggista 1945–1985*. Rome: Editori Riuniti, 1989.

Fowler, Karen Joy. *We Are All Completely Beside Ourselves*. New York: G. P. Putnam's Sons, 2013.

Gruen, Lori. 2012. 'Navigating Difference (Again): Animal Ethics and Entangled Empathy'. In *Strangers to Nature: Animal Lives and Human Ethics*, ed. Gregory R. Smulewicz-Zucker, 213–34. Lanham, MD: Lexington Books, 2012.

Hochadel, Oskar. 'Darwin in the Monkey Cage: The Zoological Garden as a Medium of Evolutionary Theory'. In *Beastly Natures: Animals, Humans, and the Study of History*, ed. Dorothee Brantz, 81–107. Charlottesville, VA: University of Virginia Press, 2010.

Lestel, Daniel, Jeffrey Bussolini, and Matthew Chrulew. 'The Phenomenology of Animal Life'. *Environmental Humanities* 5 (2014): 125–48.

Malamud, Randy. *Reading Zoos: Representations of Animals and Captivity.* New York: New York University Press, 1998.

Malamud, Randy. 'The Problem with Zoos'. In *The Oxford Handbook of Animal Studies*, ed. Linda Kalof, 397–413. New York: Oxford University Press, 2018.

Marchesini, Roberto. *Epifania animale. L'oltreuomo come rivelazione.* Milan: Mimesis, 2014.

Marchesini, Roberto. 2016, *Etologia filosofica. Alla ricerca della soggettività animale.* Milan: Mimesis, 2016.

Marshall, Michael. 'First Known Wild Chimpanzee with Albinism Was Killed By Other Chimps', *New Scientist*, 29 July 2021.

Meijer, Eva. *Animal Languages: The Secret Conversations of the Living World.* London: John Murray Publishers, 2019.

Oppes, Alessandro. 'Il lungo addio a Fiocco di neve: Barcellona piange il gorilla bianco'. *la Repubblica*, 30 September 2003.

Palagi, Elisabetta, Fausto Caruana, and Frans de Waal, eds. *The Naturalistic Approach to Laughter in Humans and Other Animals: Towards a Unified Theory.* Special issue of *Philosophical Transactions of the Royal Society of London. Series B, Biological Sciences.* 2022 Nov. 377 (1863): 20210175.

Riopelle, A. J. 'Snowflake: The World's First White Gorilla'. *National Geographic* 131 (March 1967): 442–8.

Riopelle, A. J., 'Growing Up with Snowflake'. *National Geographic* 138 (October 1970): 490–503.

Rohman, Carrie. 'On Singularity and the Symbolic: The Threshold of the Human in Calvino's *Mr. Palomar*'. *Criticism* 51, no. 1 (2009): 63–78.

Spotte, Stephen. *Zoos in Postmodernism: Signs and Simulation.* Madison, NJ: Farleigh Dickinson University Press, 2006.

Tuan, Yi-Fu. *Dominance and Affection: The Making of Pets.* New Haven, CT: Yale University Press, 1984.

'Unique in All Gorilladom: Román Luera Carbó's Snowflake', *Life* 62 (March 31, 1967): 69–70.

Westling, Louise. 'Dangerous Intersubjectivities from Dionysos to Kanzi'. In *Thinking about Animals in the Age of the Anthropocene*, ed. Morton Tønnessen, Kristin Armstrong Oma, and Silver Rattasepp, 19–36. Lanham, MD: Lexington Books, 2016.

Westling, Louise. 'Interweaving Landscapes: Merleau-Ponty's Counter to Heidegger's Human Exceptionism'. Unpublished.

Yuhas, A. 'Jane Goodall Hails "Awakening" as US Labels All Chimpanzees Endangered'. *The Guardian*, 12 June 2015.

8 Bunnies and Biopolitics: Killing, Culling and Caring for Rabbits

David Redmalm and Erica von Essen

Torturing Rabbits

In 2009, four young men bought two rabbits in a pet shop in a large Swedish city to torture them, videorecording the process. After taping the legs together, they set one of the rabbits on fire. The rabbit can be seen struggling to break loose for several minutes before dying. The other rabbit is thrown repeatedly into a wall. Laughter can be heard in the background of the video. A man tries to make a dog attack the rabbit, but the dog refuses. Finally, the rabbit is stamped to death. When this case went to trial around a year later, it was extensively covered by the Swedish news media because of the unusual cruelty of the acts. Animal rights activists who attended the trial protested loudly, shouting 'scum' at the men before they were led out of the courtroom. A regional animal protection case manager who had seen the video recording observed that the dog seemed to experience strong discomfort from the situation, and the men were consequently also prosecuted for abusing the dog.[1] The police described it as 'one of the most horrendous animal abuse cases' that they had ever encountered.[2] Three of the men were sentenced to three, four and six months in jail, and the fourth and youngest one was fined.[3]

Beginning an essay with a torture scene, like Michel Foucault in *Discipline and Punish*, highlights an ambivalence of violence – it is at once direct and absolute, but at the same time, there are different kinds of violence following different logics and rationales. The men's abhorrently cruel actions are unintelligible to both humans and nonhuman witnesses; yet, violence against rabbits is widely accepted: they are culled in large numbers, used in the fur and food industry and are intensively bred to ensure a steady production of family pets as well as laboratory animals. This essay draws on news articles, scholarly work and examples from the authors' study of municipal hunting and wildlife management, building on interviews with hunters, municipal officials and wildlife rescuers in Sweden, to discuss the biopolitics of killing, culling and caring for rabbits.[4] Foucault argued that state-sanctioned torture and executions have been replaced in the West during modernity by a form of rule that focuses on life instead of death, thus framing life as both something inherently valuable and at the same time a resource for governing.[5] Scholars have used the concept of biopolitics to study how nonhuman animals are bred, used and killed in the interest of humans.[6] However, while biopolitics is exerted by subjecting people to the impending threat of turning them into mere resources for governing, the lives of nonhuman animals rarely transcend a status of mere resources and thus cannot be bereaved of such an elevated position.

Rabbits are an especially interesting topic of biopolitical study as they are a common pet, while they are also widely considered to be expendable, lacking the same organisational support and profiled spokespersons as cats, dogs and other charismatic megafauna.[7] Thinking with rabbits makes it possible to interrogate the blind spots of biopolitics and further a theoretical understanding of the management of nonhuman life. By doing so, the essay suggests that there is a close connection between human exceptionalism and biopolitical governing. While humans are governed biopolitically through an optimisation of life – a governing where violence is the exception – for animals, in contrast, violence is the rule and an elevated political status is the exception, attributed selectively to some animals, in 'zones of distinction' like homes, animal shelters and sanctuaries. However, when rabbits enter a zone of distinction, the wider workings of the biopolitical and anthropological machines are exposed and challenged. By bringing focus to such zones, the essay points towards a way out of the biopolitical rabbit hole.

Bunnies and the Boundaries of Biopolitics

Foucault developed the concept of biopower in the first volume of his *History of Sexuality* to point out a development in many Western nation states where a sovereign power that uses violence to control its subjects is replaced by a power that instead focuses on the reproduction, health and wellbeing of its population. Biopower is the power associated with control over life itself, a decentralised kind of power exerted through biopolitical interventions by societal institutions such as schools, hospitals and psychiatric institutions, as well as citizens themselves who are encouraged to practice self-control and engage in continuous self-scrutinisation. At the same time, the biopolitical strategy is twofold: it aims not only 'to make live' but also 'to let die' through the unequal distribution of means that prolongs and optimises some lives but not others – often those belonging to marginalised and oppressed groups.[8]

Biopower presupposes that life is worth protecting. Taking the life of one subject to protect others becomes impossible as it would undermine biopower's own foundation – it would reinstate a rule through direct violence. At the same time, the affluence of the West has been dependent on colonisation, slavery and war throughout modernity. This kind of organised violence is not a passive 'letting die' but a structured oppression and an active killing of human beings[9] – a thanatopolitics, after the Ancient Greek god of death.[10] Such direct violence is broadly and passively accepted within a society as long as it is directed at those considered to be outsiders to the biopolitical order that the violence aims to maintain.

If reproduction is at the center of attention in biopolitics, rabbits may seem like the biopolitical animal *par excellence* – at least according to the popular understanding of the animal's mating habits. Rabbits have been used in idiomatic expressions describing excessive sexual activity and prolific breeding for hundreds of years—humans can for example 'breed like rabbits' – and Playboy has cemented the association between bunnies and sexuality in popular culture.[11] Rabbits do reproduce quickly: they become sexually mature relatively early, and they have short pregnancies with large litters.[12] Subjected to a 'natalist policy',[13] this makes them a reliable source of food and fur, and they can efficiently be bred as laboratory animals as well as pets. Pure-bred show rabbits are subjected to a 'breedism' that relatively arbitrarily accentuates some traits while minimizing others. Nonhuman animals are also subjected to health-focused interventions similar to those directed at humans, such as medication, veterinary treatments, and diets – interventions that could be seen as a biopolitical measure through which the wellbeing of pets is turned into a wider social concern.[14] However, no welfare state provides its non-human 'citizens' with these services as part of their fundamental rights – because they are not in fact citizens. Although they are covered by animal welfare laws, their owners may kill them without juridical consequences, as long as the correct methods are used. They are thus not so much a biopower resource as a tool for the biopolitical governing of humans and are valuable only insofar as they enrich humans' lives.

Giorgio Agamben, expanding on Foucault's biopolitics, regards the distinction between two kinds of life, *zoē* and *bios*, as the foundation upon which the distinction of citizen and non-citizen is construed. In the Ancient Greek worldview, *zoē* was life itself, or biological life, and *bios* was the life led within a societal context associated with certain rights and responsibilities – in other words, political life.[15] Here lie the roots of biopower: by making use of human lives as if they were mere biological life, their *bios* is put at stake, and violence against those lives is justified. It is biopolitics that produces the very idea of a pure 'life itself' – a product Agamben denotes as 'bare life' – as it would not be thinkable without the notion of *bios*.[16] According to Agamben, all state formations are built on a latent threat that any citizens can lose their status as *bios*, be rendered outlaws, and be reduced to bare life.

While not literally excluding nonhuman animals, when Agamben suggests that bare life 'now dwells in the biological body of every living being'[17] it is quite clear that Agamben refers to beings of the human species. It is only humans who are attributed *bios*, and it is therefore only humans who risk losing it. The human, while recognised as an animal, is made exceptional through the exclusion of all other animals – a conceptual manoeuvre Agamben refers to as the 'anthropological machine'.[18] This machine can be used as a powerful weapon in structured oppression, colonization and war, through the dehumanisation and reduction of human beings to bare life. To be rendered bare life has historically also been a legal punishment, as in Roman law where a *homo sacer* was an outlaw who could no longer be put to trial but could be killed by anyone. Animals, however, are already *zoē* and can therefore not be subjected to the threat of dehumanisation; they are not outlaws as they were never legal subjects to begin with. Nonhuman animals are consequently per definition excluded from the sphere of biopolitics.

Pet rabbits are an especially interesting animal in this case as they refuse to enter the typical anthropocentric power nexus that Foucault aimed at conceptualising. In Clare Palmer's terms, they are constitutively domesticated, but not dispositionally so.[19] Rabbits are not domesticated to the same extent as many other pet animals – they have not been bred with a focus on behavioural traits and are 'wild' in a way that for example dogs are not.[20] Rabbits are usually kept in cages and are therefore not disciplined in the same way as dogs. Anyone who has kept a rabbit knows that they can be deeply indifferent to your presence, and many pet rabbits do not like to be petted. As we shall see, when non-human animals are drawn into power relations with humans, the arbitrariness of the anthropological machine is put into the limelight, which in turn opens up a challenge against animals' perpetual relegation to a status of *zoē*.

Figure 8.1 Feral rabbit in Stockholm. Photograph by Erica von Essen.

Culling Rabbits

Around the turn of the millennium, Stockholm saw an increase in the number of feral rabbits. Truly wild rabbits have never lived in the Stockholm area – the population consists of abandoned rabbits, rabbits that have escaped from breeders and rabbits that have been released for hunting. New rabbits are added to the population when owners let out their rabbits in parks and other green areas. After a few generations, the characteristic colours of the rabbits bred in captivity are replaced by a brownish grey colour. The biggest colony was located in a small patch between two motorways, where rabbits thrived in the thousands, building complex tunnel systems under the highway. Fearing that the motorway would collapse due to the cavities beneath it, the city decided to eliminate the rabbit colony. Another place under threat was Stockholm's national urban park where, according to the park's webpage, animals such as squirrels, deer, hares, foxes, toads and minks thrive.[21] Rabbits, however, are not mentioned. A mass shooting of rabbits was organised in Stockholm in 2007, which gained some media attention. The operation was expanded, and in 2008, around 6,000 rabbits were killed. Rabbits have been culled regularly since then.

During 2009 and 2010, the culling began drawing media attention. The journalist Erik Ohlson was appalled over the way the rabbits in Stockholm are 'culled, slaughtered, gassed and poisoned with rat poison'.[22] He asked rhetorically: 'What is it about rabbits that evokes bloodlust and barbaric territorial thinking even in otherwise sane people?' Another journalist, Lars Epstein, pointed out that when a rabbit with cubs is shot, the cubs are left to starve, leading to a prolonged and painful death, and suggested that feeding the rabbits contraceptive pills could be a way of making the population decrease in a humane way.[23] The culling also drew attention internationally, as the Daily Mail reported that the culled rabbits were mass cremated in a heating plant. This led the British newspaper to refer to Swedes as 'bunny boilers' – a misogynist expression used to refer to mentally unstable and violent women, originating from the film *Basic Instinct*, in which a woman takes vengeance on a man by boiling his family's pet rabbit.[24]

The strong reactions against the culling are reminiscent of the disdain shown by the public in the case of the rabbit torture described at the beginning of this essay. Yet, when interviewed, Swedish municipal hunters in regions with large populations of wild rabbits do not generally express 'bloodlust' or 'barbaric territorial thinking'. Instead, while the news articles focus on the rabbits as a species, the threat it poses as well as its more amiable characteristics, hunters are usually critical of the unequal attention that different species get. A hunter in a large Swedish city points out that rabbits and rats both damage properties and spread diseases, but while the public generally has no problem with the culling of rats, people have much more mixed feelings about rabbits – something that he thinks is unfair to rats, who also fill a function in the ecosystem.

A municipal geologist in a large Swedish city explains that the question of rabbits is not one of 'to be or not to be'. Rabbits themselves are not the issue, but their geographical distribution. Rabbits can increase biodiversity, as the holes they dig also become homes to animals of other species. But if the holes are dug in city parks, gardens or football fields, humans' and rabbits' interests collide. Besides being both wanted and unwanted, rabbits are also juridically ambivalent: they are the purview of Swedish county administrative boards when it comes to pet regulation but fall under the jurisdiction of the municipality in their 'wild' state. Municipal hunters are only allowed to cull rabbits on municipal land – a territorial division that rabbits care little about. Rabbits can run across legal boundaries, making it impossible to cull a population. However, anyone can cull rabbits on their private land – as if they were Roman outlaws – so crossing one of these invisible boundaries can have fatal consequences.

Margo DeMello has noted the parallel 'sacred or sacrificial' modality in which rabbits exist[25] – something that is well demonstrated in Swedish cities. Some cities in Sweden are known for their rabbits, and seeing rabbits grazing is for many an expected feature of a summer picnic. Others find the rabbits to be a nuisance and contact the municipality to have them culled when they destroy garden patches. The line between these two groups is sometimes drawn within one and the same family. One hunter, responsible for all wildlife-related issues in his municipality, recounted an incident when he was asked by a house owner to cull a few rabbits who were eating plants in his garden. When he arrived at the house, a teenage girl came out of the house and shouted at him to go away, and never listen to her dad again – the rabbits were there to stay. The hunter did as he was asked. In this way, one is not simply born a rabbit but becomes either a charmingly bucolic feature of urban life or a destructive pest, depending on where one happens to end up. This also conditions the ownership or responsibility towards rabbits. Rabbits stand for pure liveliness, *zoë*, and are not associated with a particular status, a set of rights, or an inherent value, other than that they should not be allowed to suffer. This means that wildlife managers typically have a 'numeropolitical'[26] approach to rabbits by which certain populations become cullable through constructions of overabundance.

As the interviewed hunters underline, rabbits are also culled for humane reasons: when rabbit populations grow, the risk of the spreading of myxomatosis increases – a highly lethal disease with a painful anamnesis during which rabbits suffer from swellings that makes it difficult for them to eat and to see. Some die of starvation, others become easy prey. This disease was in fact originally intentionally introduced into Europe during the 1950s and later in Sweden to reduce the population of wild rabbits.[27] In Australia and New Zealand, where rabbits are considered an invasive species to be culled *en masse*, such 'technofixes' to overabundance have a pronounced and bloody history.[28] Much like myxomatosis, the Australia-used toxin 1080 has no antidote and is banned in several countries because of the painful death it causes – the poisoned rabbit suffers three to four hours before dying. Unlike in Australia, however, where rabbit-proofing and rabbit-poisoning continue in the countryside, Sweden's strategy of an infectious 'letting die' has been replaced by an active intervention to cull rabbits, whenever a perceived balance is threatened.

The most common way to hunt rabbits is to shoot them while sitting in a car, as it stops them from sensing the hunter's smell – a hunting method that is illegal for leisure hunters. However, a hunter in a large Swedish city taking municipal culling assignments on a case-by-case basis regards the method as inefficient, as rabbits often start to run away after the first shot. Instead, he explains that a common method when culling rabbits in larger colonies is to drive them into a net and then club them to death, often in a secondary location, away from the public eye. Another hunter agrees, but says that he would feel uneasy doing it, as it would raise controversy if it became known to the wider public: 'Clubbing a rabbit to death is very effective, and it dies right away, but it sure does look bad'. On one occasion, a hunter brought his netted rabbits to club them to death in an alley outside a hospital – the biopolitical stronghold – and was scolded by a nurse for doing so.

In *Zoopolis*, Sue Donaldson and Will Kymlicka develop a political theory for a more equal multispecies community, in which domesticated animals are considered as 'co-citizens', and wild animals are given sovereignty in the wild.[29] However, a large number of animals live close to humans without sharing their lives – urban pests are typical examples. Donaldson and Kymlicka view these as 'liminal animals' inhabiting a 'parallel plane', as from the perspective of the animals they live in relative independence in a city spatially and temporally different from that of humans.[30] Rabbits' parallelity is spatial, as they are drawn to green areas where humans do not normally walk, such as motorway intersections, and circadian, as they are crepuscular – they are awake at dawn and dusk. Donaldson and Kymlicka argue that these animals are 'denizens' and compare their status to that of refugees, migrant workers or people in disputed territories with multiple citizenships. Denizens live within the state and must obey its laws, but they do not have the full rights associated with citizenship. Donaldson and Kymlicka's suggestion is to let the denizens be in this in-between state: 'If we operate on the idea that adaptive animals are illegal aliens in our cities who need to be apprehended and deported, we are going to fail'.[31] There will always be wild animals in cities – to which the interviewed municipal hunters also testified. Central to Donaldson and Kymlicka is finding a way to live with these animals in a balanced way, without killing them.

While Agamben writes about the liminal zone between *zoē* and *bios* in perilous terms, Donaldson and Kymlicka suggest that the position be re-evaluated and circumscribed with rights and privileges that protect beings ending up in a liminal position – including nonhuman animals. It would not mean that human beings need to completely surrender their cities to rabbits. Nonlethal interventions can still be made to guide animals to areas where they do not harm urban flora or human-built structures. However, rabbits do not take up a steady position as denizens, as rabbits taken up by the feral colony can pass from pet to pest and from domesticated to wild. According to Agamben's conceptualisation of biopolitics, it is not the existence of a liminal position per se that is problematic, but the way beings are pragmatically moved between the categories of insider-liminal-outsider. This pragmatism is also typical of the way nonhuman animals are treated. Studies have shown that dog-walkers, for example, often permit their dogs to go after rabbits who are 'fair game' but reprimand them for pursuing animals that are more firmly positioned in the wild/domestic spectrum, like sheep.[32] This flexibility ensures that humans have sovereign control over other animals. However, Donaldson and Kymlicka's suggestion is interesting: if there is a way to let rabbits remain denizens, they would be neither governable *bios* nor expendable *zoē*. We will now look closer at rabbits traversing the dichotomies the other way, from pest to pet.

Saving Rabbits

Tiny Furries United (pseudonym) is an animal rescue organisation with a network spanning southern Sweden and with a focus on small mammals, in particular rabbits, it rehomes between four and five hundred animals each year. While sanctuaries and rescues often operate on the logic that a captive life is better than a death in the wild,[33] Tiny Furries United also seeks to spare animals from problematic domestic conditions. In an interview, the CEO laments how animals are treated by humans. Some are given to them by owners who do not want to or cannot take care of them, others are found abandoned outdoors, sometimes still in their closed cages. Rabbits live around ten years, far longer than hamsters and rats, and therefore run a higher risk of abandonment, when their owners grow tired of them after a few years. Many of the rabbits they house suffer from abscesses, infections, bad teeth and issues with their eyes. Some have clearly been abused – one time the CEO found a rabbit cub in a container for glass recycling (the rabbit survived with only minor injuries).

Excessive breeding is another reason for the rabbit surplus – a 'natalist policy' run amok. Sometimes the organisation takes care of rabbits that the county administrative board has seized from fur or pet breeders – on one occasion, Tiny Furries United received almost 100 rabbits from one single breeder. While for example dog breeding is under strict control, rabbit breeders are never screened, and breeders can practically breed as many litters as they want. It is also quite common, according to Tiny Furries United's CEO, that people come in who have purchased a male and a female rabbit for their children, to let them see rabbits being born. After birth, they want to get rid of the litter. Based on their accumulated experiences of irresponsible pet owners, Tiny Furries United always carefully screens prospective adopters. The rabbits they take care of are spayed or neutered and given veterinary treatment when needed.

Tiny Furries United occasionally captures feral rabbits – a tricky operation that usually involves around ten people who cooperate, some herding the rabbits while others capture them with a net. It is virtually impossible to lure rabbits into traps with food outdoors as they 'have food everywhere', the CEO explains. She continues to account for the purpose of the operation:

> We usually aim at the cubs, and it's partly for the rabbits' sake, because the municipal hunters come and shoot them when they become too many. Then it's also because they destroy our ecosystem too, you know, they don't belong in this nature, so they destroy the ecosystem, and they undermine buildings when they live in bigger cities.

The boundary between wild and tame is not clear cut when it comes to European rabbits. The CEO says that most of the time she can spot the difference between a wild and a tame rabbit partly based on colour, and partly based on how they act in proximity to humans. Taming a feral rabbit takes time, the CEO explains, but it is feasible: there is no great genetic difference between the most feral rabbits in Sweden and tame ones. In fact, she has a feral rabbit in her home, originally born in the wild, that she successfully relocated. Rabbits usually become increasingly accustomed to human presence and can after a while learn to accept being handled by human hands. Her ex-feral rabbit keeps away from humans and is not cuddly – far from all rabbits are, whether tame or not – but thrives among the other rabbits, as the CEO can tell from following the rabbit through a webcam.

Taming rabbits inevitably implies disciplining them, as they need to adapt to certain limitations and inhibitions.[34] According to Foucault, biopolitical interventions are partly dependent on a disciplinary power acted out through the regulation of behavioural patterns.[35] Disciplinary power is the link between biopolitical governing and the individual, making it possible to turn an individual life into a resource for governing.[36] Training animals to perform tricks and tasks is an obvious kind of disciplining, but at the Tiny Furries United's headquarters the disciplining is more subtle: as rabbits have not been bred to be susceptible to training, the focus is on getting rabbits used to human presence and touch. Dinesh Wadiwel points out that 'animal touching interconnects with disciplinary regimes that must be read in concert with the overarching forms of domination that frame human relationships with companion animals'.[37] Wadivel argues that even if petting may seem to be a purely positive and affirmative human-animal interaction, it is performed against a historical background of disciplining, forced breeding, killing and other kinds of domination. Yet this history is also 'a history of living together and coshaping techniques and practices of touching'.[38] Therefore, petting can be used to build an 'exceptional friendship' in a sphere separate from the prevailing anthropocentric dominance over all other animals.[39] Touch is thus both a means of control and a central form of human–rabbit communication, as touching and smelling are more important to rabbits than sight and sound.[40]

Taming wild rabbits is a way to spare them from a painful death from a lack of food, predators, parasites or diseases. Proponents of rewilding, de-domestication and an abolitionist approach to humans' involvement in nature take objection to such interventions, even if they are based on an idea of care for other animals. Conceptually, to these scholars, micromanagement of wild animal lives may mean 'colouring outside the lines' of Zoopolis, resulting in a hybrid, neither wild nor domestic population that may be understood as a 'rabble' or problematic leftover.[41] Recently, however, other scholars have taken offence to idealisations of wildness in animal states and environments. Based on the ideas of Bernard E. Rollin,[42] Tyler Joshua Kasperbauer and Peter Sandøe[43] suggest that wild animal nature is not valuable on its own; hence, on a biocentric utilitarian rationale there is no moral harm in keeping animals in an enclosure if they enjoy a greater aggregation of positive mental states: 'what at the end of the day matters for animals [. . .] seems to be happiness [. . .] rather than natural living'.[44]

But beyond conceptual and animal welfare considerations, Tiny Furries United's CEO recognizes that taming every single wild rabbit in Sweden would not be practically possible—there are not enough homes for the thousands and thousands of wild rabbits. It would also be impossible to capture each and every single rabbit – just a few 'seed' rabbits remaining in the wild would be enough for the population to start growing again. While trap-neuter-return initiatives are common among cat activists, it is difficult to do this with rabbits, partly because of the limited functionality of traps, and partly because they are sensitive and often die when sedated. The CEO's approach is thus not as far from that of municipal hunters as one might initially think, as she points out that 'we'll never get away from this problem, it's something we will have to live with'. This might also occasionally include culling rabbits, she adds, if they suffer from parasites or diseases. As long as humans want to have rabbits in their lives, there will always be superfluous, feral rabbits roaming the green areas and margins of cities, where they or their ascendants have been let out into a precarious and perilous freedom.

Tiny Furries United approaches rabbits as individuals who matter, exposing the relative arbitrariness of the distinction between domestic and feral rabbits. Taking care of a feral rabbit shows that rabbits are not destined to have the status of denizens but can move between different categories imposed on them by humans. Here, we are confronted with the thin veil between, on one hand, the protected biopolitical sphere of the shelter, and the wild on the other, where illness, starvation and municipal hunters lurk. Rescued rabbits are subjected to disciplinary power and medical interventions that are in line with a biopolitical form of control over their health and reproduction. One can either draw the conclusion that domestic rabbits were after all just like any rabbits and should be treated as expendable and disposable. Or one can make the opposite move and transfer the approach from domestic rabbits to feral rabbits. But in that case, is there a way of living equally with rabbits – to once and for all elevate them to the status of *bios*? And to what extent can such a way of life be understood as 'bunny biopolitics'?

Living and Dying with Rabbits

Julie Ann Smith has written two papers about rabbits: one about living with them,[45] and one about how rabbits die.[46] In the first paper, Smith, a rabbit advocate engaged in the House Rabbit Society, describes how her engagement with abandoned rabbits led her to adopt several individuals. Surely, she claims, if one wants to live with rabbits, one must accept 'that domestic animals will never be equal partners to humans only because they live in arrangements for another

Figure 8.2 Tamed but shy feral rabbit, photograph taken by the CEO of Tiny Furries United. Used with permission.

species'.[47] Yet, she decided to explore ways of living less unequally with rabbits. To allow them to roam freely, Smith rabbit-proofed her house, although, as she puts it, '[r]abbit ideas of space management often conflicted with my own aesthetics'.[48] She bought metal furniture and made tubing from wood strips to cover wiring and also baseboards, cupboards and windows. She built 'free corridors' along the walls where the rabbits liked to run, built places for them to excavate, and decided to encage her bookcases. As a sanitary precaution that still respected the rabbits' habits, Smith put litterboxes wherever the rabbits defecated and urinated. Her rabbit Mattie built tunnels inside of her mattress, and while some House Rabbit Society members usually solve this problem by fencing off their bed – quite literally sleeping in a cage – she decided to regard her bed as an 'excavation opportunity'[49] for her rabbit, sharing even this, the most private of spaces. In the network of the House Rabbit Society, 'humans were the ones having to radically alter their behaviour'.[50]

Although the members of the House Rabbit Society allow their rabbits to 'discipline' them, thus inverting some key tenets of the captivity involved in domestication, Smith recognises that she has the ultimate power over the rabbits' lives and sets the outer boundaries of their existence. She is the one in control of the food supply, she does not allow the rabbits to leave the premises and she lets a veterinarian neuter and spay them. She is bothered by this decision, but she points out that all pet keepers inhibit their animals from different kinds of behaviours. If she were to allow the rabbits to procreate freely, they would soon be afflicted with diseases, or the house would be overcrowded, and the rabbits would suffer from stress and could potentially be subjected to abusive breeding practices if they ever were to leave her care.[51]

Smith turns her home into a biopolitical micro-universe where interventions addressed towards rabbits' health and reproduction are aimed at creating an equilibrium where rabbits can thrive. In Smith's home, every single rabbit matters, while she also tends to the good of the whole colony. This compassionate and 'pastoral'[52] care approach combines a view of life as invaluable and technologies aimed at maintaining the population that correspond to Foucault's view of biopolitics. The aim is not to create a 'natural' miniature rabbit habitat, as Smith realises that the very word 'natural' is in the way of her explorative lifestyle: 'Once one accepts the unnatural as a new kind of naturalness, one no longer confuses the issue by evaluating behaviour in terms of wild animals'.[53] Smith interacts with them as long as they appear to be comfortable with it, so they are far from wild, but Smith does not demand that they be perfectly tame.

Smith's double role as both caretaker and biopolitical administrator of 'life itself' has ramifications for the way she approaches the rabbits' demise: if rabbits should be allowed to live their own lives, they should also be allowed to die their own deaths. Smith provides the rabbits with palliative care so that they may grow old; for example, she kept the rabbit Hattie for another year after her back legs had been paralysed. To the extent possible, she also allows the rabbits to encounter death. She describes one event, where she allows the rabbit Arlo to see his partner Hattie's body after she has been given a lethal injection by a veterinarian in Smith's home. Arlo repeatedly grooms and nudges the body, moves away, and continues to engage with the body for two hours, after which he stretches out beside Hattie – an intimate gesture used sparingly among rabbits. Smith reminds us that nonhuman animals have traditionally been regarded as incapable of having a concept of death[54] but based on this and other observations made by House Rabbit Society members of rabbits confronted with dead peers, she argues that rabbits understand the 'permanent change' that death implies.[55]

Taking living with rabbits seriously has also made Smith push the boundaries of our idea of a valuable nonhuman life. Instead of euthanising rabbits as soon as they show signs of old age, she allows them to age. And instead of protecting rabbits from death, quickly removing the corpse of a dead rabbit, she allows them to face the demise of their partners. This challenges the strong norm in the West not to let animals suffer – especially not companion animals.[56] Paradoxically, companion animals are ideally euthanised while still flourishing.[57] Euthanasia poses a challenge against biopower, according to Agamben, as it is a form of benevolent but active killing – as opposed to a passive 'letting die' – aimed at human beings included in the biopolitical state as citizens. Thus, as Agamben puts it, '[e]uthanasia signals the point at which biopolitics necessarily turns into thanatopolitics'.[58] Agamben argues that biopolitical states regularly establish thanatopolitical 'zones of indistinction', such as concentration camps and 'ghettos', where the inhabitants are reduced to a state of 'bare life' – lives that can be ended without legal consequences.

In Smith's home, rabbits' lives and deaths matter. Smith thus turns her home into an inverted zone of indistinction – a 'zone of distinction' – where rabbits are given a special status in contrast to the wild rabbits roaming outside, whom anyone may kill without any repercussions. Rabbits are here viewed as individuals with their own meaningful relationships, and are valued as unique beings, while also being subjected to disciplinary and biopolitical measures, thus opening up for a benevolent bunny biopolitics. In contrast to Donaldson and Kymlicka's suggestion to allow rabbits to exist in the margins, Smith places rabbits in the centre, establishing clearly demarcated biopolitical spheres where nonhuman animals transcend their status as 'mere animals' and are attributed *bios*. Yet, this does not mean that Smith uses the rabbits as surfaces for anthropomorphic projections or regards them as human-like 'persons'. Smith warns against over-individualising rabbits, and points out that in a colony, each rabbit is 'in close and fluctuating relationship to other bodies' as part of a 'communal rabbit body'.[59] Smith and the other members of the House Rabbit Society accept that there is an unintelligibility in the way rabbits are that humans can never do away with completely, and therefore they approach rabbits through an 'active suspension of interpretation'.[60] Through this compromise, the House Rabbit Society claims to have found a way to lead less unequal lives together with rabbits while still respecting their alterity. By allowing rabbits to remain 'other' to their humans, they are also to some extent independent of the disciplinary and biopolitical power nexus usually structuring human relations.

The Rabbit Collapse

In 2010, the same year as rabbit culling in Stockholm became a major talking point, the genetic makeup of the rabbit population in Nyköping in Sweden may have been changed when the roof of a gymnasium collapsed where a national rabbit exhibition was being held with 1,600 rabbits present.[61] Many rabbits escaped, which led to numerous unplanned rabbit broods. Some people we have spoken to in the municipality are convinced that the rabbits also bred with feral rabbits, as they witnessed a sudden change in colour among wild rabbits. Others suggest that this is an urban myth, as the number of escaped rabbits cannot have been large enough to affect the wider population. The regional museum advertised an embroidery contest in 2022 to memorialise 'kaninraset', which translated means 'the rabbit collapse' – the word 'ras' both meaning collapse and breed.[62] In the call, the contestants were asked to consider questions like: 'What happens with a rabbit that is suddenly set free after years in captivity? How does a rabbit with Sweden's most beautiful fur tackle the urban environment?' The rabbit collapse has indeed become part of Nyköping's local mythology; everyone knows about the event, regardless of its actual genetic impact (although the rabbit population of Nyköping *is* unusually large for a Swedish city).

Agamben speaks of a quite different collapse, that of 'the democratic principle of the separation of powers', and argues that 'the executive power has in fact, at least partially, absorbed the legislative'.[63] This is the consequence of the politicisation of life itself, through which *bios* is increasingly treated as a mere resource. Thus, he argues, this collapse is caused by the way 'the realm of bare life – which is originally situated at the margins of the political order – gradually begins to coincide with the political realm' in modern Western societies.[64] Rabbits cannot be subjected to such a biopolitical collapse because they are members of the category of 'animals' – this absurdly wide-ranging category, including everything from molluscs and mosquitoes to bears and bonobos[65] – defined through its separation from the human, and made expendable through this separation. In their status as *zoē*, nonhuman animals cannot be used to build the biopolitical momentum needed to rule through frameworks of norms and threats of exclusion.

The cases we have used to illuminate the management of rabbits' lives cast light on the thin veil between *zoē* and *bios* – moments when rabbits' expendability is implicitly or explicitly questioned. Some interventions in rabbit lives appear to be aimed at 'thickening' this veil: by subjecting wild rabbits and pet rabbits to different legislations and jurisdictions; by seeing pet rabbits as individuals with personalities and wild rabbits as a biomass at which a critical threshold triggers culling; and by prosecuting pet rabbit killers while (mostly) accepting the organised and large-scale culling of feral rabbits.

There are also ruptures in this veil where these boundaries blur. For one, the rescue of, or interventions into, the lives of feral rabbits may be understood to produce a displaced, liminal, 'rabble' population of beings who are not quite counted as wildlife, but are definitely not tame, to whom duties are unclear. We can try to approach these rabbits as 'denizens', as per Donaldson and Kymlicka's suggestion, which would mean an end to culling and a focus on preemptive interventions to find a balanced existence between humans and rabbits. Rabbits would however still have an ambivalent status because of their mobility – they can move from their marginal position into people's homes, as in the case of Tiny Furries United's action programme. Once inside, a 'zone of distinction' can be established in which rabbits are given a *bios*-like status under specific conditions. Smith's care of rabbits in her home approximated both pastoral-administrative forms of biopower, operating at the level of the individual, through disciplinary measures and caregiving, and at the welfare of the flock, through medication, sterilisation, and rabbit-proofed housing. While biopolitics is exercised on humans through the potential threat of reducing them to bare life, biopolitics is exercised on some animals through a temporary elevation of them to the status of *bios*. However, these rabbits' status remains an exception to the large number of unwanted and feral rabbits denied such a status.

The fact that non-human animals are at least partly indifferent to the normative pressure that is part and parcel of biopolitical governing suggests that there is a life to be lived that is not politicised. Such a life could potentially be generative of an 'affirmative biopolitics'[66] or a 'positive biopolitics'[67] where life itself has an impact on politics rather than the other way around. An affirmative biopolitics can take the form of interspecies co-living, where humans and other animals establish a way of life, optimised in its own way, that challenges established family formations and life course ideals, enabling Wadiwel's 'exceptional friendships', or what Susan McHugh has called 'biopolitical potentials of love'.[68]

James Stanescu has suggested that all animals – human as well as nonhuman – share a fundamental precariousness. The gut reaction that most people probably feel towards rabbit torturers is indicative of this shared precariousness. Shared animal precariousness is highlighted both when nonhuman animals transcend the status of *zoē* and become 'grievable life', and through the biopolitical governing of humans according to which 'everyone is potentially an animal'.[69] Municipal culling targets marginalised beings who are denied a *bios* and excluded from a societal 'we' but still thrive in the centre of human communities. Through rabbits' boundary skipping, the management of wild rabbits is exposed as thanatopolitics – a killing of beings with whom humans in fact share a fundamental precariousness. Culling rabbits to protect 'culture' (houses and

Figure 8.3 Maud Olsson's submission to the 'Kaninraset' embroidery contest: an imagined crossbreed of a runaway rabbit and an urban rat. Used with permission of the artist.

roads) and 'nature' (parks and other green areas) seems arbitrary after rabbits have shown humans the fragility of these categories.

Tiny Furries United's taming of feral rabbits, Smith's biopolitical micro-universe and the mythologisation of the rabbit collapse highlight feral rabbits' lives as liveable lives, worthy of consideration. In these cases, rabbits are not simply placed in a protective category of 'outlaw' or 'denizen' animals, as the boundaries of such liminal categories are challenged through the way the feral moves into the home and the domestic leaks out into the wild. Rabbits are not simply given a third place, between nature and culture, and between *zoē* and *bios*, but challenge the biopolitical and anthropological machines – the very foundations of these dichotomies. Tiny Furries United and the rabbit collapse have perhaps not radically changed the way rabbits are viewed in wider society, but there is potential here to see these rabbits pulling away the veil itself between *zoē* and *bios*. When feral rabbits are tamed, and when pampered and well-bred exhibition rabbits escape into the wild to become part of a subversive communal rabbit body, there is no longer an easy way to draw a line between pet and pest.

Notes

1. Mikael Stengård, 'Plågade ihjäl kaniner – kräktes sen av äckel', Aftonbladet, 15 April 2010, https://www.aftonbladet.se/nyheter/a/xRMJLV/plagade-ihjal-kaniner-kraktes-sen-av-ackel. (accessed 1 February 2023).
2. Daggers Nyheter, 'Ihjälplågade kaniner gavs fängelse', 23 April 2010, https://www.dn.se/sthlm/ihjalplagade-kaniner-gav-fangelse/ (accessed 1 February 2023).
3. Anna Åberg, 'Skärpta straff för unga djurplågare', Daggers Nyheter, 1 July 2010, https://www.dn.se/sthlm/skarpta-straff-for-unga-djurplagare/ (accessed 1 February 2023).
4. The project is called 'License to Cull: Investigating the Necropolitics of Countryside Culling and Urban Pest Control'. It was funded by Formas 2020–2 (grant number 2019-01168), and the results are based on interviews with thirty hunters, municipal officials and people engaged in animal rescue organisations, as well as participant observations during four hunts.
5. Michel Foucault, *The History of Sexuality, Volume I: An Introduction*, trans. Robert Hurley (New York: Pantheon Books, 1978), 140ff.
6. For an overview and several examples of how the concept of biopolitics has been applied to empirical cases involving nonhuman animals, see Kristin Asdal, Tone Druglitrø and Steve Hinchliffe, *Humans, Animals and Biopolitics: The More-Than-Human Condition* (London: Routledge, 2016).

7. Jamie Lorimer, 'Nonhuman Charisma', *Environment and Planning D: Society and Space* 25, no. 5 (2007): 911–32.
8. Michel Foucault, *Society Must Be Defended: Lectures at the Collège de France, 1975–1976* (New York: Picador, 2003), 241.
9. Achille Mbembe has further discussed this other side of the biopolitical coin, with a focus on colonisation, in *Necropolitics*, trans. Steven Corcoran (Durham: Duke University Press, 2019).
10. Michel Foucault, 'The Political Technology of Individuals', in *Power: Essential Works of Foucault, 1954–1984*, ed. James Faubion, vol. 3 (New York: The New Press, 2000), 416.
11. Susan E. Davis and Margo DeMello, *Stories Rabbits Tell: A Natural and Cultural History of a Misunderstood Creature* (New York: Lantern Books, 2003), 143 and 214.
12. Davis and DeMello, *Stories Rabbits Tell*, 13f.
13. Foucault, *Society Must Be Defended*, 243.
14. See for example Cary Wolfe's discussion on veterinary prescriptions of anti-depressants for dogs as a biopolitical strategy in *Before the Law: Humans and Other Animals in a Biopolitical Frame* (Chicago, IL: University of Chicago Press, 2013), 54. For an analysis of how companion animals' bodies are biopoliticised through a widespread pet obesity discourse, see Garrett Bunyak, 'Fat Cats and Porky Pooches: "Pet Obesity," Moral Panic, and Multi-Species Possibilities', *Society & Animals* 30, no. 1 (2022): 3–22.
15. Giorgio Agamben, *Homo Sacer: Sovereign Power and Bare Life*, trans. Daniel Heller-Roazen (Stanford, CA: Stanford University Press, 1998), 7f,
16. Giorgio Agamben, *State of Exception*, trans. Kevin Attell (Chicago, IL: University of Chicago, 2005), 87f.
17. Agamben, *Homo Sacer*, 140.
18. Giorgio Agamben, *The Open: Man and Animal*, trans. Kevin Attell (Stanford, CA: Stanford University, 2004), 26f.
19. Clare Palmer, *Animal Ethics in Context* (New York: Columbia University Press, 2010).
20. Davis and DeMello, *Stories Rabbits Tell*, xiii.
21. Nationalstadspark, 'Små och stora djur', accessed 31 January 2023, https://www.nationalstadsparken.se/om-parken/djur/sma-och-stora-djur/.
22. Erik Ohlsson, 'Hellre kaniner än tråkiga plantor', Dagens Nyheter, 17 October 2010, https://www.dn.se/arkiv/sondag/hellre-kaniner-an-trakiga-plantor-2/ (accessed 1 February 2023).
23. Lars Epstein, 'Utfodra vildkaninerna i stan med preventivmedel!', Dagens Nyheter, 26 September 2010, https://www.dn.se/blogg/epstein/2010/09/26/utfodra-vildkaninerna-i-stan-med-preventivmedel-8154/ (accessed 1 February 2023).

24. Allan Hall, 'Rabbit Bodies "Used as Heating Fuel" in Sweden', Mail Online, 13 October 2009, https://web.archive.org/web/20130117051128/https://www.dailymail.co.uk/news/article-1220119/Rabbit-bodies-used-heating-fuel-Sweden.html (accessed 1 February 2023).
25. Margo DeMello, *Animals and Society: An Introduction to Human-Animal Studies* (New York: Columbia University Press, 2012), 55.
26. Susan Boonman-Berson, Clemens Driessen and Esther Turnhout, 'Managing Wild Minds: From Control by Numbers to a Multinatural Approach in Wild Boar Management in the Veluwe, the Netherlands', *Transactions of the British Institute of British Geographers* 44, no. 1 (2018): 2–15.
27. Statens Veterinärmedicinska Anstalt, 'Kaninpest', https://www.sva.se/amnesomraden/djursjukdomar-a-o/kaninpest/ (accessed 31 January 2023).
28. Jean Hillier, 'No Place to Go? Management of Non-Human Animal Overflows in Australia', *European Management Journal* 35, no. 6 (2017): 712–21.
29. Sue Donaldson and Will Kymlicka, *Zoopolis: A Political Theory of Animal Rights* (Oxford: Oxford University Press, 2011).
30. Donaldson and Kymlicka, *Zoopolis*, 251.
31. Donaldson and Kymlicka, *Zoopolis*, 250.
32. Katrina M. Brown, 'The Role of Landscape in Regulating (Ir)responsible Conduct: Moral Geographies of the "Proper Control" of Dogs', *Landscape Research* 40, no. 1 (2015): 39–56.
33. Rosemary-Claire Collard, 'Putting Animals Back Together, Taking Commodities Apart', *Annals of the Association of American Geographers* 104, no. 1 (2014): 151–65.
34. For an extended discussion on pets and disciplinary power, see further Clare Palmer, 'Taming the Wild Profusion of Existing Things? A Study of Foucault, Power, and Human/Animal Relationships', *Environmental Ethics* 23, no. 4 (2001): 339–58.
35. Foucault, *Society Must Be Defended*, 28f.
36. Foucault, *History of Sexuality, Volume 1*, 139. For an extended discussion concerning the disciplining of nonhuman animals as a way of subjecting them to biopolitical interventions, see Matthew Chrulew 'Animals as Biopolitical Subjects', in *Foucault and Animals*, eds. Matthew Chrulew and Dinesh J. Wadiwel (Leiden: Brill, 2017), 222–38.
37. Dinesh J. Wadiwel, 'Animal Friendship as a Way of Life: Sexuality, Petting and Interspecies Companionship', in *Foucault and Animals*, eds. Matthew Chrulew and Dinesh J. Wadiwel (Leiden: Brill, 2017), 299.
38. Wadiwel, 'Animal Friendship as a Way of Life', 307.
39. Wadiwel, 'Animal Friendship as a Way of Life', 311.
40. Julie Ann Smith, '"Viewing" the Body: Toward a Discourse of Animal Death', *Worldviews* 9, no. 2 (2005): 198f.

41. Erica von Essen and Michael P. Allen, 'A Rabble in the Zoopolis? Considering Responsibilities for Wildlife Hybrids', *Journal of Social Philosophy* 47, no. 2 (2016): 171–87.
42. Bernard E. Rollin, *Animals Rights and Human Morality* (Amherst: Prometheus Books, 1992).
43. Tyler Joshua Kasperbauer and Peter Sandøe, 'Killing as a Welfare Issue', in *The Ethics of Killing Animals*, ed. Tatjana Višak and Robert Garner (Oxford: Oxford University Press, 2015), 17–31.
44. Kasperbauer and Sandøe, 'Killing as a Welfare Issue', 20.
45. Julie Ann Smith, 'Beyond Dominance and Affection: Living with Rabbits in Post-Humanist Households', *Society & Animals* 11, no. 2 (2003): 182–97.
46. Smith, '"Viewing" the Body'.
47. Smith, 'Beyond Dominance and Affection', 182.
48. Smith, 'Beyond Dominance and Affection', 189.
49. Smith, 'Beyond Dominance and Affection', 196.
50. Smith, 'Beyond Dominance and Affection', 185.
51. Smith, 'Beyond Dominance and Affection', 186.
52. See further Michel Foucault, 'The Subject and Power', in *Michel Foucault: Beyond Structuralism and Hermeneutics*, eds. Hubert Dreyfus and Paul Rabinow (Chicago, IL: University of Chicago Press, 1982), 208–26.
53. Smith, 'Beyond Dominance and Affection', 187.
54. Smith, '"Viewing" the Body', 185f.
55. Smith, '"Viewing" the Body', 189.
56. David Redmalm, 'Pet Grief: When Is Non-Human Life Grievable?', *The Sociological Review* 63, no. 1, 19–35.
57. David Redmalm, 'To Make Pets Live, and to Let Them Die: The Biopolitics of Pet Keeping', in *Death Matters: Cultural Sociology of Mortal Life*, eds. Tora Holmberg, Annika Jonsson and Fredrik Palm (Basingstoke: Palgrave Macmillan, 2019), 241–63.
58. Agamben, *Homo Sacer*, 142.
59. Smith, '"Viewing" the Body', 198.
60. Smith, '"Viewing" the Body', 184.
61. Sveriges Radio P4 i Sörmland, 'Kaninungar födda efter takraset i Nyköping', 9 April 2010, https://sverigesradio.se/artikel/3615388 (accessed 1 February 2023).
62. 'Broderiutmaning: Kaninraset', Facebook event created by Sörmlands Museum, accessed 31 January 2023, https://www.facebook.com/events/s%C3%B6rmlands-museum/broderiutmaning-kaninraset/408747757606022/ (Accessed 1 February 2023).
63. Agamben, *State of Exception*, 18.
64. Agamben, *Homo Sacer*, 9.

65. Jacques Derrida, *The Animal That Therefore I Am*, trans. David Wills (New York: Fordham University Press, 2008), 40f.
66. Asdal, Druglitrø and Hinchliffe, *Humans, Animals and Biopolitics*.
67. Dinesh J. Wadivel, 'Biopolitics', in *Critical Terms for Animal Studies*, ed. Lori Gruen (Chicago, IL: University of Chicago Press, 2018), 79–98.
68. Susan McHugh, *Animal Stories: Narrating across Species Lines* (Minneapolis, MN: University of Minnesota Press, 2011).
69. James Stanescu, 'Species Trouble: Judith Butler, Mourning, and the Precarious Lives of Animals', *Hypatia* 27, no. 3 (2012): 573.

Works Cited

Åberg, Anna. 'Skärpta straff för unga djurplågare'. Dagens Nyheter. 1 July 2010. https://www.dn.se/sthlm/skarpta-straff-for-unga-djurplagare/.

Agamben, Giorgio. *Homo Sacer: Sovereign Power and Bare Life*. Translated by Daniel Heller-Roazen. Stanford, CA: Stanford University Press, 1998.

Agamben, Giorgio. *The Open: Man and Animal*. Translated by Kevin Attell. Stanford, CA: Stanford University Press, 2004.

Agamben, Giorgio. *State of Exception*. Translated by Kevin Attell. Chicago, IL: University of Chicago Press, 2005.

Asdal, Kristin, Tone Druglitrø and Steve Hinchliffe (eds). *Humans, Animals and Biopolitics: The More-Than-Human Condition*. London: Routledge, 2016.

Boonman-Berson, Susan, Clemens Driessen and Esther Turnhout. 'Managing Wild Minds: From Control by Numbers to a Multinatural Approach in Wild Boar Management in the Veluwe, the Netherlands'. *Transactions of the British Institute of British Geographers* 44, no. 1 (2018): 2–15.

'Broderiutmaning: Kaninraset'. Facebook event created by Sörmlands Museum. Accessed 31 January 2023. https://www.facebook.com/events/s%C3%B6rmlands-museum/broderiutmaning-kaninraset/408747757606022/.

Brown, Katrina M. 'The Role of Landscape in Regulating (Ir)responsible Conduct: Moral Geographies of the 'Proper Control' of Dogs'. *Landscape Research* 40, no. 1 (2015): 39–56.

Bunyak, Garrett. 'Fat Cats and Porky Pooches: "Pet Obesity," Moral Panic, and Multi-Species Possibilities'. *Society & Animals* 30, no. 1 (2022): 3–22.

Chrulew, Matthew. 'Animals as Biopolitical Subjects'. In *Foucault and Animals*, edited by Matthew Chrulew and Dinesh J. Wadiwel, 222–38. Leiden: Brill, 2017.

Collard, Rosemary-Claire. 'Putting Animals Back Together, Taking Commodities Apart'. *Annals of the Association of American Geographers* 104, no. 1 (2014): 151–65.

Dagens Nyheter. 'Ihjälplågade kaniner gavs fängelse'. 23 April 2010. https://www.dn.se/sthlm/ihjalplagade-kaniner-gav-fangelse/. (Accessed 1 February 2023).

Davis, Susan E., and Margo DeMello. *Stories Rabbits Tell: A Natural and Cultural History of a Misunderstood Creature*. New York: Lantern Books, 2003.

DeMello, Margo. *Animals and Society: An Introduction to Human-Animal Studies*. New York: Columbia University Press, 2012.

Derrida, Jacques. *The Animal That Therefore I Am*. Edited by Marie-Louise Mallet, translated by David Wills. New York: Fordham University Press, 2008.

Donaldson, Sue, and Will Kymlicka. *Zoopolis: A Political Theory of Animal Rights*. Oxford: Oxford University Press, 2011.

Epstein, Lars. 'Utfodra vildkaninerna i stan med preventivmedel!'. 26 September 2010. https://www.dn.se/blogg/epstein/2010/09/26/utfodra-vildkaninerna-i-stan-med-preventivmedel-8154/ (accessed 1 February 2023).

von Essen, Erica, and Michael P. Allen. 'A Rabble in the Zoopolis? Considering Responsibilities for Wildlife Hybrids'. *Journal of Social Philosophy* 47, no. 2 (2016): 171–87.

Foucault, Michel. *The History of Sexuality, Volume I: An Introduction*. Translated by Robert Hurley. New York: Pantheon Books, 1978.

Foucault, Michel. 'The Subject and Power'. Translated by Leslie Sawyer. In *Michel Foucault: Beyond Structuralism and Hermeneutics*, edited by Hubert Dreyfus and Paul Rabinow, 208–26. Chicago, IL: University of Chicago Press, 1982.

Foucault, Michel. *Society Must Be Defended: Lectures at the Collège de France, 1975–1976*. Translated by David Macey. New York: Picador, 2003.

Hall, Allan. 'Rabbit Bodies "Used as Heating Fuel" in Sweden'. 13 October 2009. https://web.archive.org/web/20130117051128/https://www.dailymail.co.uk/news/article-1220119/Rabbit-bodies-used-heating-fuel-Sweden.html (accessed 1 February 2023).

Hillier, Jean. 'No Place to Go? Management of Non-Human Animal Overflows in Australia'. *European Management Journal* 35, no. 6 (2017): 712–21.

Kasperbauer, Tyler Joshua, and Peter Sandøe. 'Killing as a Welfare Issue'. In *The Ethics of Killing Animals*, edited by Tatjana Višak and Robert Garner, 17–31. Oxford: Oxford University Press, 2015.

Lorimer, Jamie. 'Nonhuman Charisma'. *Environment and Planning D: Society and Space* 25, no. 5 (2007): 911–32.

Mbembe, Achille. 'Necropolitics'. Translated by Libby Meintjes. *Public Culture* 15, no. 1 (2003): 11–40.

McHugh, Susan. *Animal Stories: Narrating across Species Lines*. Minneapolis, MN: University of Minnesota Press, 2011.

Nationalstadspark. 'Små och stora djur'. Accessed 31 January 2023. https://www.nationalstadsparken.se/om-parken/djur/sma-och-stora-djur/.

Ohlsson, Erik. 'Hellre kaniner än tråkiga plantor'. 17 October 2010. https://www.dn.se/arkiv/sondag/hellre-kaniner-an-trakiga-plantor-2/ (accessed 1 February 2023).

Palmer, Clare. 'Taming the Wild Profusion of Existing Things? A Study of Foucault, Power, and Human/Animal Relationships'. *Environmental Ethics* 23, no. 4 (2001): 339–58.

Palmer, Clare, *Animal Ethics in Context*. New York: Columbia University Press, 2010.

Redmalm, David. 'Pet Grief: When Is Non-Human Life Grievable?'. *The Sociological Review* 63, no. 1 (2015): 19–35.

Redmalm, David. 'To Make Pets Live, and to Let Them Die: The Biopolitics of Pet Keeping'. In *Death Matters: Cultural Sociology of Mortal Life*, edited by Tora Holmberg, Annika Jonsson and Fredrik Palm, 241–63. Basingstoke: Palgrave Macmillan, 2019.

Rollin, Bernard E. *Animal Rights and Human Morality*. Amherst: Prometheus Books, 1992.

Smith, Julie Ann. 'Beyond Dominance and Affection: Living with Rabbits in Post-Humanist Households'. *Society & Animals* 11, no. 2 (2003): 182–97.

Smith, Julie Ann. '"Viewing" the Body: Toward a Discourse of Animal Death'. *Worldviews* 9, no. 2 (2005): 184–202.

Stanescu, James. 'Species Trouble: Judith Butler, Mourning, and the Precarious Lives of Animals'. *Hypatia* 27, no. 3 (2012): 567–82.

Statens Veterinärmedicinska Anstalt. 'Kaninpest'. Accessed 31 January 2023. https://www.sva.se/amnesomraden/djursjukdomar-a-o/kaninpest/.

Stengård, Mikael. 'Plågade ihjäl kaniner – kräktes sen av äckel'. 15 April 2010. https://www.aftonbladet.se/nyheter/a/xRMJLV/plagade-ihjal-kaniner--kraktes-sen-av-ackel (accessed 1 February 2023).

Sveriges Radio P4 i Sörmland. 'Kaninungar födda efter takraset i Nyköping'. 9 April 2010. https://sverigesradio.se/artikel/3615388.

Wadiwel, Dinesh J. 'Animal Friendship as a Way of Life: Sexuality, Petting and Interspecies Companionship'. In *Foucault and Animals*, edited by Matthew Chrulew and Dinesh J. Wadiwel, 286–316. Leiden: Brill, 2017.

Wadivel, Dinesh J. 'Biopolitics'. In *Critical Terms for Animal Studies*, edited by Lori Gruen, 79–98. Chicago, IL: University of Chicago Press, 2018.

Wolfe, Cary. *Before the Law: Humans and Other Animals in a Biopolitical Frame*. Chicago, IL: University of Chicago Press, 2013.

9 Deading Life and the Undying Animal: Necropolitics After the Factory Farm
James K. Stanescu

In the Spring of 2020, as the Covid-19 pandemic swung into full force in the United States, several animal processing plants had to close. Nearly 90% of meat processing plants in the US were sites of Covid transmission in its first year,[1] which led to the deaths of 269 workers. This is another example of the routine way that workers at factory farms and meat processing plants are forced to work in terrible conditions. But another, almost paradoxical, event occurred as well. Because of how sick the workers were, at one point roughly 40% of the American meat packing and processing capacity was shut down.[2] One would suppose that this decreased capacity would cause there to be less farmed animals being slaughtered. However, that turned out to not be the case. JBS and Smithfield, two hog producing companies, 'euthanised' over 160,000 pigs, dumping their bodies into landfills. A single chicken producer, Allen Harim, had to euthanise over two million chickens.[3] Why did lowering the capacity of the processing plants not decrease the number of animals slaughtered? As agricultural economist Jayson Lusk has explained, most animal 'production operates on a just-in-time basis'.[4] That means if a 'finished' pig does not go to the processing plant, it sets off a chain reaction affecting every part of the life-cycle of an industrial pig, beginning with the new piglets being bred. Animals in the factory farm are segmented throughout their short lives. There is the place they are born, the nursery where they are kept right afterwards, the finishing unit where they are quickly forced to put on weight, and then to the slaughterhouse. If one doesn't slaughter the pigs, then there would be buildup in the place for 'finishing' the pig. If that built up, there would be overcrowding in the nursery. If that filled up, there would be overcrowding in the part of the facility for pregnant sows.

Then overcrowding in the place for breeding, and on and on.[5] To put it another way, the only way to understand the economics of the factory farm is to imagine the animal as a corpse, backwards. The perverse logic of the factory farm sees the animal as already dead. As such, even if the meat processing plants are closed and you cannot process the carcass of the dead animal, turning their body into sellable meat, the system of the factory farm still requires the animals to be killed on time, or throw off the exhausting and exacting schedule for the industrial animal.

Previously, I called this logic 'deading life', and in this chapter I return to my analysis of deading life. First, I will summarise the arguments I previously made about deading life and biopolitics. Then I will explore the work on necropolitics by Achille Mbembe. Following Mbembe, I will explore how Hegel and Heidegger come to understand the strange relationship of the animal, the colony and death. There I will find a strange claim, that the animal cannot die. In the figure of the undying animal I will finally discover a provocation for the idea of a new tomorrow: I will discover the promise of an outside to the totalising logics of the necropolitics of the factory farm.

**

Years ago, I proposed the concept of deading life in my article 'Beyond Biopolitics'.[6] The claim of the article was that much of our understanding of the biopolitical, particularly in Agamben and Esposito, but also in Foucault, was inspired by the Nazi *Lager*. And that while there was some great work being done on the biopolitical realities of our treatment of other animals, there was something about the animal, particularly in the factory farm, that exceeded the understanding of the biopolitical. If the biopolitical is not simply a generalisable, metaphysical condition, then it needs to be understood within a historical context. And that context helps us to understand the factory farm, but is not sufficient. My argument was that whereas the biopolitical tended to focus, following Foucault's famous formulation, on the making live and letting die, it struggled with the realities of the factory farm. Because in the factory farm the making live is not just one side of the same coin as the letting die; to make live and make die belong both to one and the same process. We have life, but only insofar as it is already death. So, in contradistinction to the figurations of the living dead, the ghosts and zombies and *Muselmänner* of Derrida and Agamben, we have deading life. If the living dead are beings that should be dead but were somehow alive, then animals in the factory farm are beings that should be alive, but are already dead. Cicero once said that the pig's 'life [. . .] was given it but as salt to keep it from putrefying'.[7] The factory farm took this same insight and made it a generalisable condition. A living being, in the factory farm, is but a yet nonputrefying corpse.

The concept of deading life explains why so many animals were still slaughtered even if their bodies could not be sold, because they are simply already corpses, and room must be made for the next animals. Indeed, the animal is seen just as a machine. For decades, industry journals have encouraged farmers to see the animal as a machine that converts feed into meat, eggs or milk. As Richard Twine has shown, this has intensified, with the animal increasingly being intervened with at the biological level, and being seen as just a form of biopolitical technology to extract surplus value out of.[8] I want to return to this concept of deading life to first rethink its relationship to necropolitics, and then to explore the bizarre philosophical addition to deading life, the idea that animals also cannot die, that they are undying.

***

Necropolitics is a term coined by the Cameroonian scholar Achille Mbembe. The first clue to the meaning of this term is how close it is to *necropolis*, a term that means literally 'city of the dead' and is used as a synonym for cemetery. In his famous essay of the same name, Mbembe uses the reality of the colonial situation in order to rethink the biopolitical. For Mbembe,

> contemporary forms of subjugating life to the power of death (necropolitics) are deeply reconfiguring the relations between resistance, sacrifice, and terror. I have demonstrated that the notion of biopower is insufficient to account for contemporary forms of the subjugation of life to the power of death. Moreover, I have put forward the notion of necropolitics, or necropower, to account for the various ways in which, in our contemporary world, weapons are deployed in the interest of maximally destroying persons and creating death-worlds, that is, new and unique forms of social existence in which vast populations are subjected to living conditions that confer upon them the status of the *living dead*.[9]

Necropolitics names the principle of organisation of existence within what Mbembe, echoing Edith Wyschogrod,[10] names a death-world. While he does not use the terminology of death-world or necropolitics in his earlier work *On the Postcolony*, a passage there might allow us to make more sense of what Mbembe means:

First, [the postcolony] is a place and a time of *half-death* – or, if one prefers, *half-life*. It is a place where life and death are so entangled that it is no longer possible to distinguish them, or to say what is on the side of the shadow or its obverse: 'Is that man still alive, or dead?' What death does one die 'after the colony'? 'There are so many deaths. One no longer knows which one to die'.[11]

This idea of a place or time where it is no longer possible to distinguish between life and death is the very substance of the death-world, and the very logic of necropolitics. The death-world is exactly a description of the factory farm. For if no other reason, the factory farm generates its profit through the inability to distinguish between life and death. But in my original essay, I pushed against the idea that necropolitics explained what was happening in the factory farm. Why?

First, I agreed that we both seemed to be describing a death-world, but I wanted to highlight the difference between the living dead of those in the colonies and the deading life of animals in the factory farm. Second, I was worried of carelessly drawing upon a concept that came from the experience of racialised colonialism. Advocates for the interests of other animals have a history of using sloppy ethical and conceptual allegories about slavery, the Holocaust and other atrocities in order to try and make people take seriously the harms done to other animals. Or as Alexander Weheliye has mockingly and accurately put it, we have tended to engage in the 'not so dreaded comparison'.[12] Furthermore, as Bénédicte Boisseron has pointed out, the 'black-animal analogy inherently and inevitably reenacts this interspecies battle, as it perpetuates a rivalry that traps the contenders in a paradigm that precludes any chance for the escape of either from this hierarchical measuring system'.[13] In other words, the analogies are not just offensive and wrong-headed, but they short-circuit the crucial work of liberation and coalition building. So, I did not want to engage in another sloppy comparison. So, why am I returning to the concept of necropolitics and Mbembe writings on colonialism?

First, I was struck by a recent article by Marina Gržinić. Gržinić combines my work on deading life with Mbembe's necropolitics to explore the contours and realities of refugee camps. It is a brilliant essay that forced me to rethink distancing my work from Mbembe. As Gržinić argues, it is important to distinguish the necropolitical not just from the biopolitical, but also the thanatopolitical:

> On the other hand, I also postulated above the formulaic description of necropolitics as 'let live and make die', exposing the elements of a supposedly historically 'passé' sort of sovereignty in the current regulation of life and death in neoliberal global capitalism. Why so? As opposed to thanatopolitics,

necropolitics is the mode of life and death that neoliberal global capitalism actively maintains, as described above regarding the implementation of the war machine and its co-propriety with capital. This results in the superimposition of what might seem a 'passé' form of sovereign power by a despotic ruler ('to let live and make die') over biopower; this is not a situation where they simply overlap.[14]

The necropolitical reverses Foucault's famous formulation – now we are in a situation of letting live and making die – but somehow we have not returned to the classical model of sovereignty as Foucault describes it, but what we have is a superimposition of sovereignty onto the biopolitical. The necropolitical is not oppositional to the biopolitical, but a supplementary understanding of how life can be organised in certain situations under 'neoliberal global capitalism'. The other reason I turn now to Mbembe is how central the question of the animal is in *Necropolitics* and *On the Postcolony*. Rather than engaging in any sort of analogies of the animal and the colonised, in the next section I want to tease out Mbembe's own engagement with the animal. After that, we will discover how the confrontation with the animal and necropolitics might change our conceptual understanding of the animal.

***

Early in his essay on necropolitics, Mbembe turns to the Hegelian understanding of death. His reading is explicitly influenced by Kojève's work. Therefore Mbembe writes: 'the human being thus truly *becomes a subject* – that is, separated from the animal – in the struggle and work through which death (understood as the violence of negativity) is confronted. [. . .] Becoming a subject therefore supposes upholding the work of death'.[15] The idea of subjecthood here is contrasted to the animal. An animal, for Hegel, is not a self-conscious subject. The human being's struggle is one of overcoming animalness, and thus carving, by negativity, the human out of the animal. One of the consequences of this is that it is impossible to have something like a generalisable humanism. Those beings who have not sufficiently carved out their animality, however the coloniser wishes to see that, means that they are not really human:

> In [. . .] the Hegelian tradition, the native subjected to power and to the colonial state could in no way be another 'myself'. As an animal, he/she was even totally alien to me. His/her manner of seeing the world, his/her manner of being, was not mine. [. . .] In such circumstances, the only possible relationship with him/

her was one of violence and domination. [. . .] They could be destroyed, as one may kill an animal, cut it up, cook it, and, if need be, eat it.[16]

For this reading of Hegel, the human becomes human to the degree they are willing to risk death, to willingly put their lives on the line knowing that they might die. Only in this way does one become fully a subject. That is, one becomes a subject only when one is willing to die for something and still fight for one's life. Why? Because the part of the human that is still animal will always seek to save itself. So, if you are willing to risk your own death, consciously choose the possibility of your own death, you are cutting away the animal essence from within yourself. You stop being a human animal and become simply human. The attempt to create human mastery and domination over the land, over other animals and over the colonised are all part of the same process, the process by which the human reasserts its own sovereign subject. Indeed, what a fragile creation it must be to become human. One must constantly prove again and again that you are human:

> Let us return to the animal killed in the hunt. Once killed, the animal is no more than a mass of flesh that has to be cut up. For the flesh to become meat, it must undergo a series of procedures. First, it must be cut into pieces or quarters. These may be cleaned; they may also be salted, dried, or smoked before being cooked. Above all, they must be eaten. But flesh is not transformed into meat only when it comes from an animal. Where power has a carnivorous aspect, killing a human being and killing an animal proceed from the same logic. Like that of the animal whose throat is cut, the death inflicted on a human being is perceived as embracing nothing. It is the death of a purely negative essence without substance, the emptying of a hollow, unsubstantial object that, falling back into loss, 'finds itself only as a lost soul'. In other words, the hollow object dies of its own accord. It vanishes 'as a shapeless vapour that dissolves into thin air'. At the end of the act of killing, what remains is, in all cases, practically the same. [. . .] What meat in fact is this? [. . .] The fact is that power, in the postcolony, is carnivorous. It grips its subjects by the throat and squeezes them to the point of breaking their bones, making their eyes pop out of their sockets, making them weep blood. It cuts them in pieces and, sometimes, eats them raw.[17]

The desire to become human is fragile and constantly needs to prove itself again and again. It is unsatiated and unsatiable. When will enough be enough? When the world is arid, broken and empty? Perhaps not empty, for it surely must be filled with corpses. Will the desire's carnivorous demand end when there is no one left to recognise or be recognised? Or even then will it look at its own hands, its own legs, and think, 'Isn't this more meat to be consumed?' And finally, having turned on its self, no one is left.

The factory farm then is a kind of efficiency, dedicated to transforming the living world into feed for the carnivorous power. It is a new technology shaping and consuming an unprecedented number of lives based upon older techniques and concepts of the necropolitical. For as we have seen in Cicero and Hegel and colonialism, the idea of deading life predates the factory farm, even if the factory farm is the apotheosis of deading life and has expressed it in horrifying new regularity and gargantuan size.

***

Is not the claim that the animal never risks its own life kind of strange? Don't animals risk their own life all the time? We can find any number of examples of animals coming to the aid of others at the risk of their own lives. We can also point towards any number of struggles and fights between other animals that occur at the risk of their own lives. Claims like the ones that Hegel makes leave one wondering if these philosophers have ever met an animal. But perhaps the way to understand Hegel's strange stance is to explore an even weirder claim by Heidegger, namely, that animals cannot die at all. Mbembe understands this odd claim in the relationship to the Native as well. As he explains:

> how is it possible to live while going to death, while being somehow already dead? And how can one live in death, be already dead, while being-there – while having not necessarily left the world or being part of the spectre – and when the shadow that overhangs existence has not disappeared, but on the contrary weighs ever more heavily? Heidegger raised similar questions in speaking of the Dasein, which can 'end without dying, strictly speaking' and, it may be added, without being, strictly speaking, finished.[18]

For Heidegger, to have an authentic existence, one must have the capacity for being-towards-death. That is to say, one must know and accept that one day one will die. One must embrace one's own finitude. But not all death is death to Heidegger. Death and finitude for Heidegger individualises. One's death is one's ownmost, it is the thing one cannot give away, but belongs most personally to the Dasein. To paraphrase Kierkegaard, as soon as one is born one is old enough to die. This is one person's death, and no one else's. To live, for Heidegger, means to own one's death. This analytic, explained in *Being and Time*, would carry on throughout Heidegger's work. It would not be a surprise, then, that Heidegger struggled to understand mass death. Not just the in colony and the factory farm, but most shockingly in his few references to the Nazi death camps.

In his 1949 Bremen lectures, we discover some of Heidegger's only remarks about mass death and the Holocaust. They are sparse, elliptical, almost entirely silent. They also show us that Heidegger is unable to philosophically grapple with what has happened. He posits: 'Hundreds of thousands die in masses. Do they die? They perish. They are put down. Do they die? They become pieces of inventory of a standing reserve for the fabrication of corpses. Do they die?'[19] There it is, almost in its entirety, Heidegger's insultingly short discussion of man-made mass death. And in the face of that atrocity, his major concern is simply: can we say that anyone died? Indeed, he seems mostly concerned that the victims who 'die in masses' have been robbed of a particular death. As Todd Presner remarks in his excellent analysis on Heidegger on this very question:

> Although the inmates in the concentration camps existed every second of every day towards death as a permanent possibility, their death does not count as authentic because it conferred no individuality. Dying is a permanent potentiality for being, my ownmost, insuperable possibility, which individualizes the conduct of my life. In the final analysis, the victims of the Nazi death camps did not die and, hence, they have no 'truth of being'. Heidegger will not even name the victims as Jews because masses of corpses who did not die have no individual or group identities.[20]

This idea that death is fundamentally individuating goes back at least to *Being and Time*, where Heidegger also has a formulation that distinguishes between perishing and dying. But in *Being and Time* the issue is not about the modalities of dying, but rather whether an animal can die. As Matthew Calarco clearly summarises:

> When Heidegger turns to a discussion of Dasein's unique mode of being-toward-death, animals reappear briefly in order to highlight a contrast between animal death and Dasein's specific modality of finitude. [...] Inasmuch as Dasein has a relation to death as such and to death in terms of its own finitude, it never simply perishes or comes to an end. By contrast, animals (as instances of the kind of beings that merely have life but have no relation to finitude) never properly die or demise; they can only perish. Demise and dying are modalities of finitude to which animals simply do not have access on Heidegger's account.[21]

Animals cannot die, they can merely perish. For Heidegger, the same forces that keep him from understanding the violence of mass death also prevent him from understanding the death of other animals. The very reality of these deaths is unthinkable for Heidegger.

In Hegel, the animal cannot confront their own death. In Heidegger, the animal cannot die. At the beginning we examined the ways that within deading life the animal is somehow already dead. But here, in the philosophical justifications of Hegel and Heidegger, the animal becomes strangely undying. One way to understand this is that the animal is undying because they are already dead. In other words, because the animal cannot be seen fully as a subject, they can be thrown into death-worlds. This desubjectification is what ties together certain kinds of atrocities – the colony, the camp, the abattoir – without any sort of moral analogy. Those beings who are denied the capacity to become subjects can become exposed to the most systematic and extreme forms of violence. Thus, for Hegel and Heidegger, those who cannot risk their death, those who cannot even die, are subjected to a politics of death, to necropolitics. So, the perverse logic can be brought to its apotheosis, one cannot die because one is essentially already dead. And while all of the above strikes me as true, I think it misses an important aspect of the undying animal that I want us to consider here at the end.

※※※

Two thinkers who worked on similar trajectories as my work on deading life made overlapping objections. First, Dinesh Wadiwel:

> Insofar as these techniques of violence tend toward making living things die, they conform to Achille Mbembe's [. . .] understanding of necropolitics, as the 'subjugation of life to the power of death' [. . .] The food animal is caught in the terrain between these two forces of life and death, as if the dream of these production processes is to bring animals to life on mass, only to 'depopulate' them in the shortest possible time. Within this intoxicating intersection of hostile force, resistance for the food animal becomes equivalent to the will to persevere despite the aversive environment around them. Insofar as these animals can at least be said to prefer to live, against production systems that aim to make them die ever more quickly, life is experienced as essentially resistant, against an apparatus that looms with the continued and actualized threat of life extinguishment in the name of value.[22]

As Wadiwel points out here, just living is a kind of resistance. In a capitalist system that dreams of frictionless processing, anytime a being forces the machinery to recognise it, to understand that we are dealing with living subjects and not just interchangeable parts of the machine, there is resistance. If, within the factory farm, the animal is already dead, any reminder that they are alive is a counter-force to the necropolitical reality. As Deleuze noted in his work on Foucault: 'Life becomes resistance to power when power takes life as its object. [...] When power becomes bio-power resistance becomes the power of life, a vital power that cannot be contained within species, environment or the paths of a particular diagram'.[23] While I am not sure I want to sign off on the full vitalistic tendencies here, I think the fundamental point is correct. When everything is created so that one does not have life, then the reality of life can become revolutionary. The radical option is not that we die, or how we die, but rather that part of us remains undying.

The second objection comes from Kathryn Gillespie. And she makes it in an article thinking through the reality of the cull yards of cattle and the notion of lively commodities:

> In these soon-to-be-dead lives, they inhabit what Achille Mbembe calls death-worlds: 'new and unique forms of social existence in which vast populations are subjected to conditions of life conferring upon them the status of living dead' [...]. This is the sense I had sitting in the audience at the cull market auctions, that I was witnessing the living dead, or 'future corpses', to use James Stanescu's [...] language [...]. One of the consequences of commodification, of materially and conceptually rendering animals as commodities, and even writing critically about their commodification is that who they are, as living, feeling, social beings (who they are in spite of and exterior to their commodification) can be easily obscured. So, yes, they are the soon-to-be-dead, living dead, and future corpses, but they are not only that, and keeping this tension in mind may help to avoid the persistent erasure of their still-aliveness and their suffering, an erasure that is so easily accomplished through the commodification process.[24]

As Gillespie explains here, there is a way that the language of necropolitics, death-worlds and deading life all end up erasing the very subjects we are concerned with. In the case of deading life, I sought to show the ontological reality that power within the factory farm created. But I also partially ventriloquised the stance of those in power of the factory farm. In other words, they wish the animals were already dead, simply future corpses. But the animals are not just future corpses, they are still alive. And part of the horror of the factory farm is to forget this very point. A point that, if we follow Gillespie, Wadiwel and Deleuze, is absolutely key to thinking resistance to deading life.

From the standpoint of necropolitics, the animal is already dead. Life has been reduced simply to salt, to simple perseveration for the future carcass of the animal. But as our long sidetrack with Hegel and Heidegger has shown us, this view is unable to imagine either the life or the death of the animal. Both become obscured within the parallax of deading life. As I have pointed out, this has created the strange paradox whereby the animal is both already dead and undying. In the past I have argued that we need to see our shared finitude, vulnerability and precarity with other animals.[25] Against the Heideggerian view of finitude, which sees our death as individuating, I followed Judith Butler in understanding our precarity as the very basis of our sociality. In other words, the fact that we are vulnerable mean we need each other. We may be, as Heidegger put it, thrown into this world. But we are thrown into this mess together and need one another. But our finitude is, perhaps, not enough. We must recognise that we share life together. Against the idea that our subjecthood depends on learning to die properly, as Hegel and Heidegger have it, we must learn to properly live together. So, rather than a being-towards-death, we must have a kind of being-towards-immortality. Not immortality as individuating either, but rather as what is at stake in community to build the possibility of a tomorrow.[26]

Social theory these days is burdened with a kind of pessimism. We are told to accept that, in this time of the Anthropocene, we must learn to die. We are told that the hyperobject of global warming is one where the world has already ended. But if the undying animal teaches us anything, it must be that the world is not over. We too are, perhaps, undying animals. Just more earthlings together. As Calarco has sought to show us, this shared reality is the basis for constructing something out of our current impasse:

> Consequently, we cannot characterize ontologies solely as human or cultural constructs; ontologies are co-constituted in deep and fundamental ways in our ongoing entanglements with animals and various more-than-human others. To practice a deep ethological form of life is to commit to a continual revision and multiplication of ontological perspectives as we learn to inhabit more charitably and more respectfully the worlds and schemas not just of other 'human' groups but those of more-than-human others as well. This practice of *syn-theōria*, of seeing-with others who are both human and more-than-human, brings ontology back to its practical calling; it also aligns – and even identifies – the task of doing ontology with living well.[27]

Yes, we must learn to live well. What we are fighting for together is not a particular future, but futurity itself. We are striving after the very possibility of a future. The alternative to deading life is the undying, the life that always escapes the stratagems and violence of necropolitics. It is only as earthlings together that we get out of the current crises. No spaceships, no arks, but perhaps just a simple social promise. A promise we make to fight for there to be a tomorrow, together.

Notes

1. Leah Douglas, 'Nearly 90% of Big US Meat Plants Had Covid-19 Cases in Pandemic's First Year – Data', *Reuters*, 14 January 2022, available at https://www.reuters.com/business/nearly-90-big-us-meat-plants-had-covid-19-cases-pandemics-first-year-data-2022-01-14/ (accessed 20 March 2023).
2. Dylan Matthews, 'The Closure of Meatpacking Plants Will Lead to the Overcrowding of Animals. The Implications Are Horrible', *Vox*, 4 May 2020), https://www.vox.com/2020/5/4/21243636/meat-packing-plant-supply-chain-animals-killed (accessed 20 March 2023).
3. Matthews, 'The Closure of Meatpacking Plants'.
4. Matthews, 'The Closure of Meatpacking Plants'.
5. For an excellent overview of this vertical integration, see Alex Blanchette, *Porkopolis: American Animality, Standardized Life, & the Factory Farm* (Durham, NC: Duke University Press, 2020).
6. James Stanescu, 'Beyond Biopolitics: Animal Studies, Factory Farms, and the Advent of Deading Life', *PhaenEx* 8, no. 2 (2013): 135–60.
7. Marcus Tullius Cicero, *On the Nature of the Gods; On Divination; On Fate; On the Republic; On the Laws; and On Standing for the Consulship*, trans. Charles Duke Yonge (London: G. Bell & Sons, 1902), 61.
8. Richard Twine, *Animals as Biotechnology: Ethics, Sustainability and Critical Animal Studies* (London and New York: Routledge, 2010).
9. Achille Mbembe, *Necropolitics*, trans. Steve Corcoran (Durham, NC: Duke University Press, 2019), 92.
10. Edith Wyschogrod, *Spirit in Ashes: Hegel, Heidegger, and Man-Made Mass Death* (New Haven, CT: Yale University Press, 1990).
11. Achille Mbembe, *On the Postcolony* (Berkley, CA: University of California Press, 2001), 197.
12. Alexander G. Weheliye, *Habeas Viscus: Racializing Assemblages, Biopolitics, and Black Feminist Theories of the Human* (Durham, NC: Duke University Press, 2014), 10.

13. Bénédicte Boisseron, *Afro-Dog: Blackness and the Animal Question* (New York, NY: Columbia University Press, 2018), xv.
14. Marina Gržinić, '"Afterwards": Struggling with Bodies in the Dump of History', in *Body between Materiality and Power: Essays in Visual Studies*, ed. Nasheli Jiménez del Val (Newcastle upon Tyne, UK: Cambridge Scholars Publishing, 2016), 163–82, 174.
15. Mbembe, *Necropolitics*, 68.
16. Mbembe, *On the Postcolony*, 26–7. For a discussion of why Hegel's famous Master/Slave dialectic does not apply to the native, see pp. 292–4.
17. Mbembe, *On the Postcolony*, 200–1.
18. Mbembe, *On the Postcolony*, 201–2.
19. Martin Heidegger, *Bremen and Freiburg Lectures: Insight into That Which Is, and Basic Principles of Thinking* (Bloomington, IN: Indiana University Press, 2012), 53.
20. Todd S. Presner, *Mobile Modernity: Germans, Jews, Trains* (New York: Columbia University Press, 2007), 227.
21. Matthew Calarco, *Zoographies: The Question of the Animal from Heidegger to Derrida* (New York: Columbia University Press, 2008), 16–17.
22. Dinesh Wadiwel, 'Chicken Harvesting Machine', *South Atlantic Quarterly* 117, no. 3 (2018): 527–49.
23. Gilles Deleuze. *Foucault*, trans. Sean Hand (Minneapolis, MN: University of Minnesota Press, 1988), 92–3.
24. Kathryn Gillespie, 'The Afterlives of the Lively Commodity: Life-Worlds, Death-Worlds, Rotting-Worlds', *Environment and Planning A: Economy and Space* 53, no. 2 (2020): 280–95, 291.
25. James Stanescu, 'Species Trouble: Judith Butler, Mourning, and the Precarious Lives of Animals', *Hypatia* 27, no. 3 (2012): 567–82.
26. My thanks to Joseph Trullinger, whose many discussions on immortality helped shape my current views. He might not fully agree with what I am saying, but I could not have gotten here without his insights.
27. Matthew Calarco, *Beyond the Anthropological Difference* (Cambridge: Cambridge University Press, 2020), 44–5.

Works Cited

Blanchette, Alex. *Porkopolis: American Animality, Standardized Life, & the Factory Farm*. Durham, NC: Duke University press, 2020.

Boisseron, Bénédicte. *Afro-Dog: Blackness and the Animal Question*. New York: Columbia University Press, 2018.

Calarco, Matthew. *Zoographies: The Question of the Animal from Heidegger to Derrida*. New York: Columbia University Press, 2008.

Calarco, Matthew. *Beyond the Anthropological Difference*. Cambridge: Cambridge University Press, 2020.

Cicero, Marcus Tullius. *On the Nature of the Gods; On Divination; On Fate; On the Republic; On the Laws; and On Standing for the Consulship*. Translated by Charles Duke Yonge. London: G. Bell & Sons, 1902.

Deleuze, Gilles. *Foucault*. Translated by Seán Hand. Minneapolis, MN: University of Minnesota Press, 2016.

Douglas, Leah. 'Nearly 90% of Big US Meat Plants Had Covid-19 Cases in Pandemic's First Year – Data'. Reuters, 14 January 2022. https://www.reuters.com/business/nearly-90-big-us-meat-plants-had-covid-19-cases-pandemics-first-year-data-2022-01-14/. Accessed 20 March 2023.

Gillespie, Kathryn. 'The Afterlives of the Lively Commodity: Life-Worlds, Death-Worlds, Rotting-Worlds'. *Environment and Planning A: Economy and Space* 53, no. 2 (2020): 280–95.

Gržinić, Marina. '"Afterwards": Struggling with Bodies in the Dump of History'. In *Body between Materiality and Power: Essays in Visual Studies*, edited by Nasheli Jiménez del Val, 163–82. Newcastle upon Tyne: Cambridge Scholars Publishing, 2016.

Heidegger, Martin. *Bremen and Freiburg Lectures: Insight into That Which Is, and Basic Principles of Thinking*. Bloomington, IN: Indiana University Press, 2012.

Matthews, Dylan. 'The Closure of Meatpacking Plants Will Lead to the Overcrowding of Animals. The Implications Are Horrible'. Vox, 4 May 2020. https://www.vox.com/2020/5/4/21243636/meat-packing-plant-supply-chain-animals-killed. Accessed 20 March 2023.

Mbembe, Achille. *On the Postcolony*. Berkley, CA: University of California Press, 2001.

Mbembe, Achille. *Necropolitics*. Translated by Steve Corcoran. Durham, NC: Duke University Press, 2019.

Presner, Todd S. *Mobile Modernity: Germans, Jews, Trains*. New York: Columbia University Press, 2007.

Stanescu, James. 'Species Trouble: Judith Butler, Mourning, and the Precarious Lives of Animals'. *Hypatia* 27, no. 3 (2012): 567–82.

Stanescu, James. 'Beyond Biopolitics: Animal Studies, Factory Farms, and the Advent of Deading Life'. *PhaenEx* 8, no. 2 (2013): 135–60.

Twine, Richard. *Animals as Biotechnology: Ethics, Sustainability and Critical Animal Studies*. London and New York: Routledge, 2010.

Wadiwel, Dinesh. 'Chicken Harvesting Machine'. *South Atlantic Quarterly* 117, no. 3 (2018): 527–49.

Weheliye, Alexander G. *Habeas Viscus: Racializing Assemblages, Biopolitics, and Black Feminist Theories of the Human*. Durham, NC: Duke University Press, 2014.

Wyschogrod, Edith. *Spirit in Ashes Hegel, Heidegger, and Man-Made Mass Death*. New Haven, CT: Yale University Press, 1990.

10 Factory Farms for Fishes: Aquaculture, Biopolitics and Resistance
Dinesh Wadiwel

Human relations with fishes globally are arguably one of the central sites of conflict and tension occurring at planetary scale. In describing our current geological epoch with the term 'Anthropocene', Paul J. Crutzen and Eugene F. Stoermer point to a number of human–animal relationships that mark out the proposed geological epoch: the growth in global cattle populations and species extinction are listed.[1] Notably, wild capture fisheries – or 'mechanized human predation' as they are described – are also singled out for attention. Fisheries are today an important component of the global economy, with seafood products one of the world's most traded food commodities.[2] Today, fisheries have been positioned as a central pillar of human food supplies; it is estimated that annually up to 2.3 trillion fishes are captured from the oceans.[3] Leaving aside the impact upon the trillions of animals who are the target of this industry, the environmental impact of the growth of industrialised fisheries is deeply concerning. In 1990, around 10% of global fish populations (or 'fish stocks'[4]) were extracted from the seas at unsustainable levels; by 2019, this figure rose to 35.4 percent.[5] From this perspective, the last 50 years of industrial fisheries might be understood as a slow process of emptying the oceans of sea life; for example, Daniel Pauly claims that over the last half century populations of large fish such as bluefin tuna and Atlantic cod have been reduced by 90%.[6] These extraordinary statistics are more depressing when wastage data is taken into account; for example catch reconstructions suggest that unreported 'discards' from industrial fisheries – that is, nonmarketable fish species who are killed and thrown back into the oceans – account for a significant proportion of annual wild fish capture, more than total global subsistence fishing.[7]

While Crutzen and Stoermer draw attention to industrialised wild fish capture as a showcase example of human devastation of planetary systems, they fail to take note of another transformation which is also planetary scale in nature: namely the arrival of industrial scale aquaculture or 'fish farms'. Aquaculture relies on the use of expansive sea pens in waterways where sea animals are contained, and intensively managed, in order to transform these living animals into food for consumption by humans. The progress in the expansion of fish farms globally has been breathtaking. In 2014 the United Nations Food and Agriculture Organisation notified the world that for the first time more than half of the fish consumed by humans were derived from aquaculture.[8] We should not underestimate the full significance of the achievement of this milestone in terms of human, or at least Anthropocene history. Where domestication of land-based animals took millennia to achieve, recent humans have managed to apply domestication to fish on a mass scale in a mere matter of decades.

The rise of aquaculture marks an important development in biopolitical relations with nonhuman life. On the one hand, in so far as aquaculture has enabled changing human diets, including rising global per capita consumption of sea food, this transformation in food supplies marks an alteration in the relation between humans and fishes at the level of population, where sea life more centrally serves a function in the reproduction of human life. On the other hand, intensification of domesticated fish production requires the development of biopolitical techniques in the management of nonhuman life to extract, contain, regulate and slaughter sea animals, with attendant technological developments around sea pens, feeding, transport and behavioural intervention.

This chapter seeks to examine the rise of industrial aquaculture – factory farms for fishes – using a biopolitical lens. I will firstly take a global view of fisheries as a problem of the biopolitics of population; as I shall argue, the industrialisation of wild capture fisheries, followed by the development of intensive aquaculture, represents a systemic process of establishing fish as a population that is placed in the service of human populations as a means of subsistence. Secondly I will look at the modalities of techniques and technologies within aquaculture, noting the ways in which these sites are intensifying as a means to more precisely produce 'bare life' amongst the beings contained within aquaculture facilities. Finally, I will consider the limits of the control apparatus of intensive aquaculture, and possibilities for fish resistance. As I shall note, as overwhelming as these changes have been for refining modalities of biopolitical domination over animals, aquaculture also opens up different problems for power and resistance. Intensification of fish production within sea pens creates new problematics of visibility and control and thus establishes different patterns for animal insubordination to rule.

The Global Biopolitics of Fisheries

In Raj Patel and Jason W. Moore's *A History of the World in Seven Cheap Things*, 'cheap food' is singled out as one of the important global developments in the history of capitalism, in so far as it proved an engine for both holding down wages and expanding profit. Patel and Moore describe the rationale as follows:

> The cheap food model worked like this. Capitalism's agricultural revolutions provided cheap food, which lowered the minimum-wage threshold: workers could be paid less and not starve. This in turn reduced employers' wage bills as the scale of proletarianization increased, allowing the rate of exploitation to rise. Accumulated capital could continue to grow only insofar as a rising food surplus underwrote 'cheap' workers. It is a simple model.[9]

For Patel and Moore, the meat industry was shaped by these 'cheap food' dynamics: 'the industrial labor techniques of simplification, compartmentalization, and specialization first developed in sugar production have found their way into meat production too'.[10] An example of these processes, and one Patel and Moore focus on, is the dramatic increase in global chicken populations during the twentieth century; these birds were leapt upon by capitalist agriculture as a means to dramatically expand the production of animal-based food. In this context, we are reminded that chicken bones are likely to be one geological marker of the Anthropocene; Patel and Moore argue that:

> The chickens we eat today are very different from those consumed a century ago. Today's birds are the result of intensive post-World War II efforts drawing on genetic material sourced freely from Asian jungles, which humans decided to recombine to produce the most profitable fowl. That bird can barely walk, reaches maturity in weeks, has an oversize breast, and is reared and slaughtered in geologically significant quantities (more than sixty billion birds a year).[11]

In effect, Patel and Moore are paying attention to a number of processes that describe the interaction of capitalism and biopolitics. On one hand, there is the relation that is constructed at a population level between chickens and humans. Capitalist agriculture will mass 'produce' and 'reproduce' chickens as a population, whose cycles of life and death coincide with their functionality as a means of subsistence for human populations. This is thus not only the story of chicken bodies overproduced as a mechanism to drive down the reproductive costs of human labour in order to enable expanded extraction of surplus. It is also the story of one biological population placed in proximity with another, and with this, the establishment of a life and death relation, where one population must be born and made to die in order to enable another population to survive. The rise of chicken as global food staple, from the perspective of human–animal studies, is the story of the construction of a global standing population, whose biopolitical function is to secure the life of another population (i.e., humans). In this sense, as James Stanescu has pointed out, within capitalist agriculture a conception of biopolitics that involves fostering life meets brutally with a thanatopolitics of deadening life at the same time.[12]

There is a second sense in which the discussion by Patel and Moore usefully highlights the relation between capitalism and biopolitics, and this relates to the refinement of processes that sculpt the body of the chicken to become a means of subsistence for human life. As described by animal studies scholars, industrial animal agriculture establishes a zone of 'bare life' in which animal bodies are contained, surveyed, subject to bodily modifications, deep controls over nutrition, lighting, movement, relationality, reproduction and sexuality.[13] The biological lives of these animals are bent to conform with the rhythms of the production process, and as Patel and Moore argue, production time (that is birth to death time) is subject to continuing efficiencies, as is relative 'yield'; all of which aim at maximisation of profit.

We might apply a similar lens to understanding the biopolitics of fisheries globally. However, in doing so, we will have to depart from previous analyses of the biopolitics of land-based animal agriculture. This is because industrial fisheries differ in form. In part this is because fishes killed for human food supplies are derived from two very different modalities of production: namely industrial wild fish capture and intensive aquaculture. On the one hand, wild fish capture fisheries operate in a way that is completely unlike the factory farm model of capitalist food production; as discussed, wild fish capture is a modality of 'mechanised human predation' and thus presents a very different problem for biopolitical analysis. Wild fishes are not contained by agricultural systems; they are instead hunted in the vast 'commons' of the sea. On the other hand, as will be the focus further below, the growth in industrial aquaculture globally has created a completely new model of the factory farm. While industrial aquaculture mirrors intensive agriculture involving land-based animals, the techniques and technologies of violence differ, and thus require a different analysis. I shall discuss each – wild fish capture and aquaculture – below as a modality of population biopolitics, before turning to look at the fish farm in more detail as a site for the production of 'bare life'.

In line with Patel and Moore's analysis presented above, industrialisation of wild capture fisheries has led to the 'cheapening' of seafood: that is, through the application of technologies and efficiencies, more animals are able to be captured for a lower relative cost, thus driving down the consumer costs of seafood in the long run and incentivising growing per capita consumption by humans as a means of subsistence. However, as I have indicated above, this is not just the story about cheap food; instead, from a biopolitical standpoint, this is a narrative at the level of population, or in this case, several populations – fishes – being placed at the service of the life and functioning of another population: namely humans. Where this narrative of population biopolitics differs from land-based agriculture is that wild capture fisheries do not install these living animals within the factory farm; instead, fish populations, who are otherwise self-sustaining, are hunted down by humans to be transformed into food commodities.

I have previously argued that the factory farm establishes a juridical zone of exception, which produces a concentrated site for biopolitical violence.[14] This violence is not merely concerned with the process of slaughter, but also relies upon a ruthless management of life – through controls over movement, lightening, temperature, nutrition, reproduction and sociality – in a 'bare' state in order to produce a saleable food commodity. However, in industrialised wild capture fisheries, the zone of exception is not internal to the nation state. Wild capture fisheries operate within zones that have juridically been treated as 'outside the political reach of any one state'.[15] Roberto Esposito has argued that property in a modern context operates as a form of juridical immunisation, where what was previously held in common is immunised from this claim through the transfer of proprietary rights.[16] Notice here that in so far as wild capture fisheries operate within the 'commons' of the sea,[17] they represent a large scale, unique and ongoing form of biopolitical immunisation. These fisheries reach into these commons established by international law – or perhaps more appropriately in this context, zones of exception[18] – and directly employ a Lockean process of transforming what was previously held in common to what is now immunised as property, to become a raw commodity within the global food system.[19] While various quota regimes have been established to try and regulate wild capture fisheries, these have by and large not been successful in preventing the 'race for fish' which has wrought havoc in the oceans, decimating wild fish populations and systematically debilitating the capacity of some fish species to reproduce as a collective.[20] This means that during the twentieth century, there was an attempt to lock wild fish populations into a biopolitical relation with human populations as part of an ongoing means of subsistence; however, by the close of the twentieth century it was clear that this project was failing.

The solution was the development of industrial aquaculture. At the level of population, aquaculture innovates and addresses the limitations of wild fish capture in its ability to achieve biopolitical dominance over sea animals. Firstly, at a population level, the unsustainable debilitation of wild fish populations, and the resistance of fishes themselves to being caught,[21] is addressed by placing sea animals within perpetual enclosure. Thus, an episodic biopolitical violence is replaced by a continuous form; and there is subsequently a reorientation of the human relation with sea animals from hunter to 'shepherd'. Secondly, as I shall discuss below, wild fish capture provides an opportunity to completely internalise production, by containing fishes, and deploying intensive 'husbandry' techniques including controls over reproduction. These biopolitical processes are interconnected with the development of capitalism as an economic system. In his draft chapter 6 of *Capital*, volume one, Karl Marx used the word 'subsumption' ('*Subsumtion*') to describe the process by which forms of production and labour are drawn into the value circuits of capitalism.[22] Here Marx delineated between 'formal' subsumption, where capitalism co-opts and engulfs an existing process that was previously outside of capitalist value production, and 'real' subsumption, where a production process is integrated into capitalist production in a deep and inseparable way so that labour, production techniques and raw materials become integral to the value and production chains around ('the *application of science*, that *genera* product of social development, to the *direct production process*, has the appearance of a *productive power of capital*, not of labour, or it only appears as a productive power of labour in so far as the latter is identical with capital'[23]). These processes are relevant to the development of aquaculture. The triumph of aquaculture represents a movement from formal subsumption to real subsumption. A previously 'wild' population, whose own self reproduction occurred through its own processes, is parasitically fed upon – for both sustenance and profit – by human populations through industrial predation until the point at which it is no longer possible to sustain this mode of formal subsumption. Aquaculture solves this problem by internalising whole fish populations within the rhythms of capitalist production, deploying continuous techniques to control reproduction and intensively manage fish life. Under this model of real subsumption, fish lives are molded so that they conform absolutely to the production process in ways that transform these beings into organisms that are no longer fit for the 'wild'.[24] Here, we might note that this story about the establishment of fish as a population that is made fit for purpose for capitalist production, is in perfect alignment with Michel Foucault's understanding of the relation between biopower and capitalism:

> This bio-power was without question an indispensable element in the development of capitalism; the latter would not have been possible without the controlled insertion of bodies into the machinery of production and the adjustment of the phenomena of population to economic processes. [. . .] The adjustment of the accumulation of men to that of capital, the joining of the growth of human groups to the expansion of productive forces and the differential allocation of profit, were made possible in part by the exercise of bio-power in its many forms and modes of application. The investment of the body, its valorization, and the distributive management of its forces were at the time indispensable.[25]

Here, no doubt, Foucault is explicit about the meaning of biopower for the alignment of 'human groups' with capitalism; however, these processes might simultaneously describe the 'controlled insertion' of nonhuman life into the machinery of capitalism. Arguably the development of industrial aquaculture has achieved this.

Taking a global perspective then, the last century has seen a remarkable transformation in the population biopolitics of global fisheries. The initial project aimed at using mechanised predation to chase down, capture and kill trillions of fishes annually, placing wild fish at the service of the subsistence of human populations. As this project reached its sustainability limits – that is, when fish populations at the level of reproduction could no longer withstand the onslaught of industrial predation – then a change of strategy emerged. A process of real subsumption began, where the containment and husbandry techniques that were commonplace in land-based agriculture were adapted in earnest to fish populations. Again, human populations are placed into a relation of domination with respect to fish populations; however, here, life is captured in a total sense. The fish farm takes charge of reproduction, of bare biological needs through the life course, and of course, transforms these living beings to dead commodities through a precise control over the means of life extinguishment. The commons of the sea is now not the only zone of exception for the production of fish for food; more prominently today the sea enclosure is now preferred as a means for the concentrated production of bare life.

The Aquatic Factory Farm

The intensive aquaculture facility is a factory farm of sorts; but differs in form and processes from intensive animal agriculture involving land-based animals. As discussed above, there is a body of theoretical work that understands the factory farm as a site for biopolitical violence.[26] I have previously argued, following the work of Agamben, that the factory farm produces bare life through techniques that systematically hold the living beings within on the threshold between life and death.[27] This is starkly apparent where the conditions and resources provided to animals in production facilities debilitate key areas of animal capability in order to 'efficiently' produce a food commodity – for example, systematic injuries that are the result of crowding and inability to exercise, or selective breeding for maximisation of yield at the cost of life expectancy. Arguably, as I shall discuss below, we see strong resonances in intensive aquaculture, where ruthless controls aim at precisely mapping biological life to the production cycle in order to maximise profit.

Aquaculture systems could be broken into at least three categories: open systems, semi-closed and closed.[28] In an open system, a suitable site is located within a natural body of water and a permeable cage is installed. In these systems, enclosed fishes share waters with other sea life outside the cage, tides and currents are relied upon to dissipate waste and nutrients are available either 'naturally' in the cage environment or through the addition of feed by producers.[29] Oxygen levels, water temperatures and waste are thus left to the vicissitudes of the surrounding environment. In a semi-closed system, natural waters may still be accessed, but there is an effort towards 'supplementing or enhancing natural processes'[30] through more intensive controls over water temperatures and oxygen levels, as well as the design of enclosure systems to improve feed efficiency and prevent predation and poaching. Finally, in closed systems, we see the whole production process controlled so that across every aspect of the aquaculture system 'there is human intervention of some type and at some level'.[31] Here as James Tidwell describes:

> the major advantage of closed systems is that they provide the operator complete control over all of the environmental variables in the culture system. The major disadvantage of closed systems is that the operator now has complete responsibility for all aspects of the animals' environment.[32]

From the standpoint of Marx's theory of subsumption, described above, moving through each type of aquaculture system, from open, to semi-open to closed, describes the progress from formal subsumption to real subsumption. In the open aquaculture system, the 'natural' activities of fish are formally subsumed by capitalist production through the capture of fish within the sea pen. In closed systems, on the other hand, animals are completely integrated into the production system, so much so that these fish can no longer be returned to the 'wild'. From the standpoint of biopolitical theory, the transition of open to closed systems reveals a progressive intensification of the powers of life and death, and a transition from a power that was perhaps episodic, to one that is increasingly continuous in its scope.

Regardless of type of aquaculture system, there are a number of features of these fish factory farms that are distinctive. Firstly, like all factory farm systems, enclosure is a prominent modality of domination.[33] In open systems, this enclosure occurs in the landscape of the sea, as it were, and functions in a similar way to a fenced paddock. In closed systems, the entire living area of the contained being is constructed by human artifice, with tanks manufactured from plastic, fibreglass or stainless steel. Movement to other enclosures as part of the production cycle is commonplace in more complex production systems;[34] however, in some systems fishes may spend their entire lives within the same enclosures. The point of enclosure is to lock these beings into the desired stage of production and limit mobility within the confines of the cage or the tank. In some systems, sea cages are located in close proximity to each other, either littered across seas or inland water systems, or alternatively, in closed terrestrial aquaculture, multiple tanks are sequestered within a larger enclosed factory. These systems are now pervasive: there are now more than 3000 sea cages along the coast of Norway,[35] and by the turn of the twenty-first century, some 30% of lakes and reservoirs in China were used for aquaculture.[36] To an extent, these represent a growing archipelago of confinement;[37] though their form – either in sea cages or in closed terrestrial systems – does not directly resemble other forms of carcerality. Aside from the obvious difference in form – land-based animals require air; fishes must be immersed in water – an important difference between the aquaculture system and the factory farms involving land-based animals relates to the different techniques used in relation to partitioning and sequestration, or perhaps more accurately, as Foucault would describe it, '*quadrillage*'.[38] Unlike the typical factory farm for land animals, within aquaculture there is no close range partitioning of single animals or small groups of animals as one finds in a battery cage. Instead, large numbers of fish – sometimes over 100,000 in the case of commercial salmon sea cages[39] – are congregated together in a single enclosure. Indeed, while 'stocking densities' are central to all forms of animal agriculture, within aquaculture they are very much overtly informed by a central measure of potential congregate productivity.[40] This produces a unique carcerality that is by and large, managed at the level of the collective (and perhaps 'population') rather than at the level of individual. As I shall discuss below, this has a shaping effect on the patterns of resistance by fish to these systems of containment.

Control over reproduction is a central aspect of almost all systems of animal domestication. It is therefore not accidental that controls over reproduction are an irreplaceable aspect of industrial aquaculture systems. 'Hatcheries' are an important part of the value chain, providing juvenile animals to aquaculture systems.[41] In some hatchery systems, a 'natural' process of reproduction is managed within ponds and closed enclosures to enable the production of eggs which will be extracted from the system.[42] In other systems, fish are 'strip spawned', a process of egg extraction that may involve the injection of an 'ovulation-inducing hormone, manually expressing the eggs at ovulation, and fertilizing the eggs with sperm'.[43] These hatchery systems then feed aquaculture with the raw materials – that is the living bodies – that will mature into a future consumption commodity. In this context, as in industrial agriculture involving land-based animals, the life and death processes that are required to transform living animals into dead meat require an attendant biopolitical process for the creation of life; that is, a standing army of bodies who are exploited for their reproductive capacity in order to enable 'the controlled insertion of bodies into the machinery of production'.

The space of the enclosure is a site of varying degrees of intensive biopolitical management. As described above, the enclosure delimits movement. In more intensive systems, water temperature and oxygen levels are ruthlessly controlled. In a closed system, manipulation of light can be utilised to shape behaviour.[44] Of particular note are the controls over food and nutrition, as these are subject to concentrated management as systems intensify. A characteristic of all intensive animal agriculture is control over nutrition through the use of manufactured feed; in the case of aquaculture, as fish farms expand, so does the global utilisation of manufactured feed.[45] Though some forms of aquaculture rely on plant-based inputs, in many cases, fishes in aquaculture are fed fish meal and fish oil that is derived from wild fish capture.[46] Note that this has led to the perverse situation where trillions wild fish are hunted down in the oceans beyond sustainable limits, and a portion of this capture – approximately 20 million tonnes – is used to create products to feed livestock, including fish in aquaculture.[47] However, despite what appears prima facie as example of extraordinary inefficiency, manufactured feed is deployed because, at least within the logic of capitalist agriculture, it enables efficient administration of nutrition and means that 'consumption and conversion are accurately recorded'.[48] Here, as in other sites of intensive animal agriculture, feed is an input to production, and must be ruthlessly controlled to maximise 'yield' within a given production period in a way that enables profit maximisation. Precise control over feed is thus one way in which a balance is struck to enable fish within a system to be held at a point of nutrition (and energy utilisation) that minimises feed expenditure and simultaneously maximises yield. It is worth contemplating the different techniques and technologies that are being implemented within aquaculture systems globally to meet this challenge. In the past, models were used to estimate 'via regression analysis and other mathematical methods' feed availability[49]; alternatively, 'bioenergetic' models were used to calculate energy usage by fish so as to determine appropriate feed levels to fit the business model.[50] However, more sophisticated technologies are emerging, including the use of video and acoustic surveillance systems to provide real-time monitoring of fish feeding behaviour, and more recently 'intelligent feeding systems' have been deployed that make use of artificial intelligence.[51] Zhou *et al.* describe a system in Norway that:

> has feedback mechanisms that detect the feeding behaviour of fish until the feed is finished, which allows fish to be fed to satiation without overfeeding and the consequent feed waste. Computer vision and acoustic sensors are commonly used feedback methods to determine feeding conditions in practice. They collect environmental, behavioural and other data as input variables to the control programme to achieve intelligent feeding.[52]

Here, a host of technologies attempt to zero in on the exact point at which feeding practices are efficient; less than this point risks the yield that is possible from the system; more risks wastage that cannot recovered through sales of the 'finished' commodity.

The use of artificial intelligence and developments in 'internet of things' based aquaculture,[53] are part of a general movement that has expanded the capital intensity of fish farms, simultaneously reducing human labour power as a direct input to production. In this regard, intensive aquaculture is working in lockstep with agriculture systems centred on land based animals, where full automation of production appears to be the long-term trajectory.[54] In a sense, this trajectory brings together a number of tendencies within capitalist agricultural production, including a demand to deploy technologies of surveillance and artificial intelligence and to ruthlessly control nutrition, movement and environment to make efficient inputs, reduce turnover times, reduce human labour time and maximise possible surplus. Here, as Wang *et al.* suggest, a kind of dream of the 'intelligent' automated fish farm is being realised:

the intelligent fish farm is an all-weather, full-process and full space automated production mode, that is, in the case of workers not entering the fish farm, the new generation of information technology such as IoT [internet of things], big data, artificial intelligence (AI), 5G, cloud computing and robots are used for remote measurement and control of fish farm or robot independent control of fishery facilities, equipment, machinery, so as to complete all production and management operations of the fish farm. [...] intelligent fish farms rely on digital and intelligent technology to solve the problems of aquaculture labor shortage, water pollution, high risk and low efficiency. Intelligent fish farm is the industrial transformation of fishery production mode and the development direction of fishery in the future.[55]

I have previously argued that a tendency within capitalist animal agriculture is that as human labour power is replaced by machines, there is a rise in the mass of animal labour power which stands in relation to enclosures and machines.[56] From a biopolitical standpoint, we see here that intensification – that is the process of expanding the use of enclosures, machines and technologies – is accompanied by an expansion in animal populations caught within agricultural systems, subject to ever tightening regimes of control. Perhaps because of the generally limited applicability of welfare precautions within fisheries, arguably the most intensive forms of containment and control accompany the aquaculture; further, arguably given growing per capita consumption of seafood products, and an exponentially expanding aquaculture sector, the fish factory farm perhaps represents the full realisation of the biopolitical dream of the factory farm itself as an idealised model of domination. This is a dream to establish an environment where inputs to production are perfectly calculated to ensure maximum profitability; the body of the animal is the site for this bare calculation.

Conclusion: No Escape?

Human relationships with fish have altered dramatically over the last century. As discussed above, industrialised fisheries mechanised hunting, seeking to position populations of wild fishes as a mass-scale means of subsistence for global human populations. When this project reached its limit, industrialisation of aquaculture offered a new strategy, by utilisation of the containment and husbandry techniques associated with land-based animal agriculture and intensifying this process to create factory farms for fishes. Like wild capture fisheries, this new modality of biopolitics again seeks to place fish populations at the service of survival of human populations, but aquaculture instead utilises mass containment and controls over reproduction and nutrition as means to maintain this mode of dominion. As I have described above, the direction of aquaculture is towards increasing intensification with the utilisation of technologies and techniques to make efficient production. This trajectory arguably perfects the model of the factory farm, which aims to hold in place life at precisely the meeting point of efficiency, productivity and profitability. Life is contained here in a bare state, and every aspect of the environment is deployed to squeeze maximal surplus from productive processes.

It is here that I wish to conclude by thinking about fishes themselves and the capacity these beings possess within industrial aquaculture to resist these processes. We might note that one aspect of the transition I have descried above from open to closed aquaculture systems reflects the development of techniques to counter the resistance of fish themselves to their capture.[57] One deficiency of open aquaculture systems is the capacity of fish to escape, a situation that is not merely a cause for concern for producers in relation to lost profitability, but also a potential concern for environments.[58] Escapes are a significant aspect of some aquaculture systems, representing 'average production losses between 1 and 5% [. . .] either caused by persistent low-level leakage or massive events when millions of fish are released'.[59] In this respect, we could argue that within open aquaculture systems, fish resistance to capture is a continuing site of friction and marks the insubordination of fishes to an otherwise total system of life domination.

However, closed aquaculture systems largely solve the problems associated with escape, since within closed systems, particularly terrestrial systems, there is minimal possibility of 'escape' for fish. The closed system produces an environment that is completely managed by producers and establishes the infrastructure for continuing development in surveillance and monitoring. However, even in the complete and austere context of closed systems, there remains ongoing challenges for producers in maintaining continuous domination and control. This is because, despite the deployment of surveillance technologies within intelligent facilities – visual surveillance, sonar, etc. – there are limits to what can be 'seen' within the space of the sea cage or tank. This means, as discussed above, techniques of monitoring and control tend towards collectives of fishes rather than the individual: 'although the processing speed of software and hardware has improved in recent years, it is very difficult to track and identify individual fish in a large group within fast-moving populations. Therefore, trying to avoid individual tracking and research on group behaviour has become a focus of study'.[60] It is for this reason that John Law has noted, with respect to salmon farms, that within these aquaculture environments fish defy systems of control and detection:

> The salmon in the pen are more or less invisible. Sometimes you can see what's going on, but most of the time you can't. Instead, all that you can see is a few dozen salmon out of 50,000. This is the paradox. Even though they are being controlled, the salmon are also dissolving themselves into invisibility. So this is the argument. If salmons are animals this is precisely because in relation to human beings they are also elusive. Down there in the water, so far as the people are concerned, they are also doing their own sweet salmon thing.[61]

While this might perhaps signal cause for hope for the capacity of fish to innovate in their attempts to resist, it would be a mistake on this basis to assume that fish resistance in aquaculture systems is an ever-present reality. The 'more or less visible' status of fish within aquaculture does not preclude adaption of technologies to counter fish resistance, but on the contrary arguably enables redoubled enthusiasm in the design of techniques. And as I have suggested above, the almost zero presence of animal welfare regulation accompanying current fish farming practices creates opportunities for significant ingenuity. Consider the problems associated with transport of live fish. Transportation of fish, including the processes of capture and handling of fish prior and after transport, is typically highly stressful and can lead to injury and death for some fish. One solution to this dilemma explored by producers is the use of mass anaesthesia, which knocks the fish unconscious during the period of transport. Ideally such an anaesthetic 'should produce rapid anaesthesia (1–5 min) and rapid recovery (<5 min), and be cheap, practical to use, water soluble, and leave no residue in fish, humans, or the environment'.[62] In some respects, being able to knock animals out during key phases of the production cycle reveals a further extension of the dream of the factory farm, which continually seeks to smooth all possibility of tussle and friction from the processes that animals are subject to. In this case, fish are knocked insensible for periods of time when an alteration of the living environment is required, only to recover once again to the horrific boredom and daily hostility of a densely packed sea pen.

I raise this final example to highlight the diabolical assembly of powers within contemporary aquaculture facilities. Intensive animal agriculture involving land animals, in many respects, represents one example of biopolitical violence at its most calculating, its most developed, its most intense. Arguably, industrial aquaculture further refines this project.

Notes

1. Paul J. Crutzen, and Eugene Stoermer, IGBP Newsletter 41 (Royal Swedish Academy of Sciences, Stockholm, 2000); see also Paul J. Crutzen. 'Geology of Mankind', *Nature* 415, (2002): 23.
2. Food and Agriculture Organisation, *The State of World Fisheries and Aquaculture 2022: Towards Blue Transformation* (Rome: Food and Agriculture Organisation, 2022), 5.
3. 'Numbers of Fish Caught from the Wild Each Year', 2019, at: http://fishcount.org.uk/fish-count-estimates-2/numbers-of-fish-caught-from-the-wild-each-year (accessed 20 March 2023).
4. The United Nations Food and Agriculture Organisation defines 'fish stocks' as follows: 'A group of individuals in a species occupying a well defined spatial range independent of other stocks of the same species. Random dispersal and directed migrations due to seasonal or reproductive activity can occur. Such a group can be regarded as an entity for management or assessment purposes. Some species form a single stock (e.g., southern bluefin tuna) while others are composed of several stocks (e.g. albacore tuna in the Pacific Ocean comprise separate Northern and Southern stocks). The impact of fishing on a species cannot be fully determined without knowledge of this stock structure'. See Food and Agriculture Organisation, 'Glossary', The United Food and Agriculture Organisation, Rome, 2002, at: https://www.fao.org/3/y3427e/y3427e0c.htm (accessed 20 March 2023).
5. Food and Agriculture Organisation, *The State of World Fisheries and Aquaculture 2022*, 46.
6. See Daniel Pauly, *Vanishing Fish: Shifting Baselines and the Future of Global Fisheries* (Vancouver/Berkeley: Greystone Books, 2019).
7. Daniel Pauly and Dirk Zeller, 'Catch Reconstructions Reveal that Global Marine Fisheries Catches are Higher than Reported and Declining', *Nature Communications* 7 (2016): 5. See also Glenn Simmons et al., 'Reconstruction of Marine Fisheries Catches for New Zealand (1950–2010)', *Sea Around Us*, Global Fisheries Cluster, Institute for the Oceans and Fisheries, University of British Columbia, Vancouver, BC, Canada, at: http://www.seaaroundus.org/doc/PageContent/OtherWPContent/Simmons+et+al+2016+-+NZ+Catch+Reconstruction+-+May+11.pdf (accessed 20 March 2023).
8. FAO, *The State of World Fisheries and Aquaculture, 2016* (Rome: FAO, 2016), 2. See also Michael Marshall, 'Farmed Fish Overtakes Farmed Beef for First Time', *New Scientist*, 19 June 2013, http://www.newscientist.com/article/dn23719-farmed-fish-overtakes-farmed-beef-for-first-time.html (accessed 20 March 2023).

9. Raj Patel and Jason W. Moore, *A History of the World in Seven Cheap Things: A Guide to Capitalism, Nature, and the Future of the Planet* (Collingwood, VIC: Black, 2018). See also Jason W. Moore, *Capitalism in the Web of Life: Ecology and the Accumulation of Capital* (London: Verso, 2015).
10. Patel and Moore, *A History of the World in Seven Cheap Things*, chapter 5.
11. Patel and Moore, *A History of the World in Seven Cheap Things*, 'Introduction'.
12. See James Stanescu, 'Beyond Biopolitics: Animal Studies, Factory Farms, and the Advent of Deading Life', *PhaenEx* 8, no. 2, (2013): 135–60.
13. See Dinesh Joseph Wadiwel, *The War against Animals* (Leiden, Brill 2015); Stanescu, 'Beyond Biopolitics'; Chloë Taylor, 'Foucault and Critical Animal Studies: Genealogies of Agricultural Power', *Philosophy Compass* 8 (2013): 539–51; and Cary Wolfe, *Before the Law: Humans and Other Animals in a Biopolitical Frame* (Chicago, IL: The University of Chicago Press, 2013).
14. See Wadiwel, *The War against Animals*, 65–9.
15. Keyuan-Zou, 'Chapter 1 Global Commons and the Law of the Sea: An Introduction', in Keyuan Zou ed., *Global Commons and the Law of the Sea* (Leiden, The Netherlands: Brill/Nijhoff, 2018), 1.
16. See Roberto Esposito, *Bios: Biopolitics and Philosophy*, trans. Timothy Campbell (Minneapolis, MN: University of Minnesota Press, 2008).
17. See W. Gullett and Q. Hanich, 'Rethinking High Seas Fishing Freedoms: How High Seas Duties Are Catching Up', in *Global Commons and the Law of the Sea*; see also Denise Russell, *Who Rules the Waves?: Piracy, Overfishing and Mining the Oceans* (London: Pluto Press, 2010).
18. Note though that this zone of juridical exception operates differently from the exceptional powers of the sovereign state as described by Giorgio Agamben (see *Homo Sacer: Sovereign Power and Bare Life*, trans. Daniel Heller-Roazen (Stanford, CA: Stanford University Press)). 1998; *State of Exceptioni*, trans. Kevin Attell (Chicago, IL: University of Chicago Press, 2005)). The difference lies in the abandonment of wild fish populations outside of the reach of nation state sovereignty to a global commons mediated by international law which enables an almost unlimited free for all capture of animal lives by private interests.
19. According to Esposito, this process protects against 'the potential risk of a world given in common – and for this reason exposed to unlimited distinction' (Esposito, *Bios*, 67). See my discussion of Esposito, Locke and property in Wadiwel, *The War against Animals*, 129–38 and 147–73.
20. On recent development in quota regimes and neoliberal policy settings, see Fiona McCormack, *Private Oceans: the Enclosure and Marketisation of the Seas* (London: Pluto Press, 2017).

21. See Dinesh Joseph Wadiwel, 'Do Fish Resist?', *Cultural Studies Review* 22, no. 1 (2016): 196–242.
22. Karl Marx, 'Results of the Direct Production Process', *Economic Works of Karl Marx 1861–1864*, 2002, at: https://www.marxists.org/archive/marx/works/1864/economic/index.htm (accessed 20 March 2023).
23. Marx, 'Results of the Direct Production Process'.
24. Although there is significant controversy over the environmental impact of aquaculture escapes, there is some suggestion that these fish lack the capacity to survive in 'the wild'. One fact sheet from the National Oceanic and Atmospheric Administration claims: 'Typically, domesticated fish raised in captivity are poor performers and have low fitness in the wild. Escapees quickly become prey to other predators, lessening their potential for food and habitat competition. In the case of Atlantic salmon, there is no evidence that the species is able to create a self-sustaining population in the Pacific Ocean, despite both accidental and intentional releases in the past', NOAA, 'Potential Risks of Aquaculture Escapes', fact sheet, 2022, at: https://media.fisheries.noaa.gov/2022-03/Fact-Sheet-Potential-Risks-of-Aquaculture-Escapes.pdf (accessed 20 March 2023).
25. Michel Foucault, *The Will to Knowledge: History of Sexuality vol. 1* (London: Penguin, 1986), 140–1.
26. See Wadiwel, *The War against Animals*; Stanescu, 'Beyond Biopolitics'; Taylor, 'Foucault and Critical Animal Studies'; and Wolfe, *Before the Law*.
27. See Wadiwel, *The War against Animals*, 83–6.
28. See James Tidwell, *Aquaculture Production Systems* (Ames, IA: Wiley-Blackwell, 2012), 6–78. It could be argued that open systems could be further divided between those that require 'active feeding' – that is, provision of fish meal – and 'passive feeding', where animals are contained, but nutrients are available within the environment of the enclosure to meet sustenance needs. See for example C. E. Boyd, 'Overview of Aquaculture Feeds: Global Impacts of Ingredient Use', in *Feed and Feeding Practices in Aquaculture*, ed. Allen Davis (Amsterdam: Woodhead Publishing, 2015), 3–25.
29. See Tidwell, *Aquaculture Production Systems*, 65–8.
30. Tidwell, *Aquaculture Production Systems*, 68.
31. Tidwell, *Aquaculture Production Systems*, 73.
32. Tidwell, *Aquaculture Production Systems*, 73–4. It should be added that the actual main advantage of semi-closed or closed systems is increased productivity. Tidwell notes of semi-closed systems: 'Compared to open systems, semi-closed systems have several advantages. One is much higher production rates, as much as 1,000 times the productivity of an open system. This is due to the greater control and inputs into these systems and the fact that their physical parameters can be maximized for greater productivity' (68).

33. On animals and carcerality, see Karen M. Morin, *Carceral Space, Prisoners and Animals* (London: Taylor and Francis, 2018).
34. On live transport within the context of fisheries and aquaculture, see Malcolm Beveridge, *Cage Aquaculture*, 3rd ed. (Hoboken: Wiley, 2008), 201–8.
35. P. G. Fjelldal, S. Bui, T. J. Hansen, et al. 'Wild Atlantic Salmon Enter Aquaculture Sea-Cages: A Case Study', *Conservation Science and Practice* 3 (2021): e369.
36. R. Newton, W. Zhang, Z. Xian, et al., 'Intensification, Regulation and Diversification: The Changing Face of Inland Aquaculture in China', *Ambio* 50 (2021), 1739–56, here 1741.
37. See Wadiwel, *The War against Animals*, 200. See also Michel Foucault, *Discipline and Punish: The Birth of Prison* (London: Penguin, 1990).
38. Michel Foucault, *Abnormal: Lectures at the College de France 1974–1975* (London: Verso, 2003), 44–8. Here Foucault outlines the model for control over the plague, which unlike the management of leprosy (which is centred on exclusion) is instead concentrated upon an inclusive exclusion: 'A certain territory was marked out and closed off: the territory of a town, possibly that of a town and its suburbs, was established as a closed territory. However, apart from this analogy, the practice with regard to plague was very different from the practice with regard to lepers, because the territory was not the vague territory into which one cast the population of which one had to be purified. It was a territory that was the object of a fine and detailed analysis, of a meticulous spatial partitioning (*quadrillage*)' (44–5).
39. See Fjelldal et al., 'Wild Atlantic Salmon Enter Aquaculture Sea-Cages'.
40. See for example Baoliang Liu, Ying Liu, and Guoxiang Sun, 'Effects of Stocking Density on Growth Performance and Welfare-related Physiological Parameters of Atlantic Salmon *Salmo Salar L.* in Recirculating Aquaculture System', *Aquaculture Research* 48, no. 5 (2017): 2133–44.
41. See Geoff L. Allan and Gavin Burnell, eds., *Advances in Aquaculture Hatchery Technology* (Oxford: Woodhead, 2013).
42. Here control over sex characteristics is essential to management of the 'broodstock'. See P. Martínez et al., 'Genetic Architecture Of Sex Determination in Fish: Applications to Sex Ratio Control in Aquaculture', *Front Genet* 5 no. 340 (2014).
43. Note that for some species such as salmon, death follows spawning.
44. See P. J. Ashley, 'Fish Welfare: Current Issues in Aquaculture', *Applied Animal Behaviour Science* 104 (2007): 214.
45. See C. J Shepherd and A. J. Jackson, 'Global Fishmeal and Fish-Oil Supply: Inputs, Outputs and Marketsa', *Journal of Fish Biology* 83, no. 4 (2013): 1046–66; see also R. L. Naylor, R. W. Hardy, A. H. Buschmann, et al., 'A 20-Year Retrospective Review of Global Aquaculture', *Nature* 591 (2021): 551–63.
46. Boyd, 'Overview of Aquaculture Feeds'.

47. See Tim Cashion, Frédéric Le Manach, Dirk Zeller, and Daniel Pauly, 'Most Fish Destined for Fishmeal Production Are Food-Grade Fish', *Fish and Fisheries (Oxford, England)* 18, no. 5 (2017): 837–44. Note that, as Cashion *et al.* observe, 90% of the fish caught in oceans and converted to other products could actually be used for direct human consumption instead of being used to feed 'farmed fish, pigs and chickens' (840). See also Naylor *et al.*, 'A 20-year Retrospective Review of Global Aquaculture'.
48. Tidwell, *Aquaculture Production Systems*, 74.
49. Chao Zhou, Daming Xu, Kai Lin *et al.*, 'Intelligent Feeding Control Methods in Aquaculture with an Emphasis on Fish: A Review', *Reviews in Aquaculture* 10, no. 4 (2018): 975–93, here 977.
50. Zhou *et al.*, 'Intelligent Feeding Control Methods in Aquaculture with an Emphasis on Fish', 978.
51. See Zhou *et al.*, 'Intelligent Feeding Control Methods in Aquaculture with an Emphasis on Fish', 986.
52. Zhou *et al.*, 'Intelligent Feeding Control Methods in Aquaculture with an Emphasis on Fish', 986.
53. See Anamika Yadav, Md Tabish Noori, Abhijit Biswas, and Booki Min, 'A Concise Review on the Recent Developments in the Internet of Things (IoT)-Based Smart Aquaculture Practices', *Reviews in Fisheries Science* 31, no. 1 (2023): 103–18.
54. On robotic dairy production, see Lewis Holloway, Christopher Bear and Katy Wilkinson, 'Robotic Milking Technologies and Renegotiating Situated Ethical Relationships on UK Dairy Farms', *Agriculture and Human Values* 31, no. 2 (2014).
55. Cong Wang, Zhen Li, Tan Wang *et al.*, 'Intelligent Fish Farm – the Future of Aquaculture', *Aquaculture International* 29, no. 6 (2021): 2681–711.
56. See Dinesh Wadiwel, 'Chicken Harvesting Machine: Animal Labor, Resistance, and the Time of Production', *SAQ: The South Atlantic Quarterly* 117, no. 3 (2018): 527–49. See also Dinesh Joseph Wadiwel, *Animals and Capital* (Edinburgh: Edinburgh University Press, 2023).
57. See Wadiwel, 'Do Fish Resist?'
58. See Heidi Moe Føre and Trine Thorvaldsen, 'Causal analysis of escape of Atlantic salmon and rainbow trout from Norwegian fish farms during 2010–2018', *Aquaculture* 532 (2021), 736002; and Mostafa Rachwani, 'Fears for environment after 50,000 fish escape salmon farm in Tasmania', *The Guardian*, 24 November 2020, at: https://www.theguardian.com/australia-news/2020/nov/24/fears-for-environment-after-50000-fish-escape-salmon-farm-in-tasmania (accessed 20 March 2023). Note there is some disagreement about the survivability of fish who escape aquaculture facilities. See T. Skilbrei Ove, Mikko Heino, and Terje Svåsand, 'Using Simulated Escape Events to Assess the Annual Numbers and Destinies of Escaped Farmed

Atlantic Salmon of Different Life Stages From Farm Sites in Norway', *ICES Journal of Marine Science* 72, no. 2 (January/February 2015): 670–85.
59. Javier Atalah and Pablo Sanchez-Jerez, 'Global Assessment of Ecological Risks Associated With Farmed Fish Escapes', *Global Ecology and Conservation* 21 (2020): e00842, 5.
60. Zhou *et al.*, 'Intelligent Feeding Control Methods in Aquaculture with an Emphasis on Fish', 980. Note that more individualising surveillance is possible through some experimental techniques, such as individually tagging fish. See Lidia Muñoz, Eneko Aspillaga, Miquel Palmer *at al.*, 'Acoustic Telemetry: A Tool to Monitor Fish Swimming Behavior in Sea-Cage Aquaculture', *Frontiers in Marine Science* 7, no. 645 (2020).
61. John Law, 'Notes on Fish, Ponds and Theory', *Norsk Antropologisk Tidskrift* 23, no. 3–4 (2012): 9.
62. Ninik Purbosari, Endang Warsiki, Khaswar Syamsu, and Joko Santoso, 'Natural versus Synthetic Anesthetic For Transport of Live Fish: A Review', *Aquaculture and Fisheries* 4, no. 4, (2019): 129–33, 130.

Works Cited

Agamben, Giorgio. *Homo Sacer: Sovereign Power and Bare Life*. Stanford, CA: Stanford University Press, 1998.

Agamben, Giorgio. *State of Exception*. Chicago, IL: University of Chicago Press, 2005.

Allan, Geoff L., and Gavin Burnell. *Advances in Aquaculture Hatchery Technology*. Oxford: Woodhead, 2013.

Ashley, P. J. 'Fish Welfare: Current Issues in Aquaculture'. *Applied Animal Behaviour Science* 104 (2007): 214.

Atalah, Javier, Pablo Sanchez-Jerez. 'Global assessment of ecological risks associated with farmed fish escapes'. *Global Ecology and Conservation*, 21 (2020): e00842.

Beveridge, Malcolm. *Cage Aquaculture*. 3rd ed. Hoboken: Wiley, 2008.

Boyd, C. E. 'Overview of Aquaculture Feeds: Global Impacts of Ingredient Use'. In *Feed and Feeding Practices in Aquaculture*. Edited by Allen Davis, 3–25. Amsterdam: Woodhead Publishing, 2015.

Cashion, Tim, Frédéric Le Manach, Dirk Zeller, and Daniel Pauly. 'Most Fish Destined for Fishmeal Production Are Food-grade Fish'. *Fish and Fisheries* 18, no. 5 (2017): 837–44.

Crutzen, P. J. and E. F. Stoermer, E. F. *IGBP Newsletter* 41, Royal Swedish Academy of Sciences, Stockholm, 2000.

Crutzen, P. J 'Geology of Mankind'. *Nature* 415 (2002): 23.

Esposito, Roberto. *Bios: Biopolitics and Philosophy*. Minneapolis, MN: University of Minnesota Press, 2008).

FAO. 'Glossary'. The United Food and Agriculture Organisation. Rome, 2002. At: https://www.fao.org/3/y3427e/y3427e0c.htm.

FAO. *The State of World Fisheries and Aquaculture, 2016*. Rome: Food and Agriculture Organisation, 2016.

FAO. *The State of World Fisheries and Aquaculture 2022: Towards Blue Transformation*. Rome: Food and Agriculture Organisation, 2022.

fishcount.org.uk. 'Numbers of Fish Caught from the Wild Each Year', 2019. At: http://fishcount.org.uk/fish-count-estimates-2/numbers-of-fish-caught-from-the-wild-each-year.

Fjelldal, P. G., S. Bui, T. J. Hansen *et al*. 'Wild Atlantic Salmon Enter Aquaculture Sea-Cages: A Case Study'. *Conservation Science and Practice* 3 (2021): e369.

Føre, Heidi Moe, Trine Thorvaldsen. 'Causal Analysis Of Escape Of Atlantic Salmon And Rainbow Trout From Norwegian Fish Farms during 2010–2018'. *Aquaculture*, 532 (2021): 736002.

Foucault, Michel. *The Will to Knowledge: History of Sexuality Vol.1*. London: Penguin, 1986.

Foucault, Michel. *Discipline and Punish: The Birth of Prison*. London: Penguin, 1990.

Foucault, Michel. *Abnormal: Lectures at the College de France 1974–1975*. London: Verso, 2003.

Gullett, W., and Q. Hanich. 'Rethinking High Seas Fishing Freedoms: How High Seas Duties Are Catching Up'. In *Global Commons and the Law of the Sea*. Leiden: Brill | Nijhoff, 2018.

Holloway, Lewis, Christopher Bear and Katy Wilkinson. 'Robotic Milking Technologies and Renegotiating Situated Ethical Relationships on UK Dairy Farms'. *Agriculture and Human Values* 31, no. 2 (2014).

Law, John. 'Notes on Fish, Ponds and Theory'. *Norsk Antropologisk Tidskrift* 23, no. 3–4 (2012).

Liu, Baoliang, Ying Liu, and Guoxiang Sun. 'Effects of Stocking Density on Growth Performance and Welfare-related Physiological Parameters of Atlantic Salmon Salmo Salar L. in Recirculating Aquaculture System'. *Aquaculture Research* 48, no. 5 (2017): 2133–44.

Marshall, Michael. 'Farmed Fish Overtakes Farmed Beef for First Time'. *New Scientist*, 19 June 2013, http://www.newscientist.com/article/dn23719-farmed-fish-overtakes-farmed-beef-for-first-time.html.

Martínez, P., A. M. Viñas, L. Sánchez, N. Díaz, L. Ribas, F. Piferrer. 'Genetic Architecture of Sex Determination in Fish: Applications to Sex Ratio Control in Aquaculture'. *Frontiers in Genetics* 5 (2014): 340.

Marx, Karl. 'Results of the Direct Production Process'. *Economic Works of Karl Marx 1861–1864* (2002). At: https://www.marxists.org/archive/marx/works/1864/economic/index.htm

McCormack, Fiona. *Private Oceans: the Enclosure and Marketisation of the Seas*. London: Pluto Press, 2017.

Moore, Jason W. *Capitalism in the Web of Life: Ecology and the Accumulation of Capital*. London: Verso, 2015.

Morin, Karen M. *Carceral Space, Prisoners and Animals*. London: Routledge, 2018.

Muñoz Lidia, Aspillaga Eneko, Palmer Miquel, Saraiva João L., Arechavala-Lopez Pablo. 'Acoustic Telemetry: A Tool to Monitor Fish Swimming Behavior in Sea-Cage Aquaculture'. *Frontiers in Marine Science*, 7 (2020): 645.

Naylor, R. L., R. W. Hardy, A. H. Buschmann, *et al*. 'A 20-year retrospective review of global aquaculture'. *Nature* 591 (2021): 551–63.

Newton, R., W. Zhang, Z. Xian, *et al*. 'Intensification, regulation and diversification: The Changing Face of Inland Aquaculture in China'. *Ambio* 50 (2021): 1739–56.

NOAA. 'Potential Risks of Aquaculture Escapes'. Fact Sheet. 2022. At: https://media.fisheries.noaa.gov/2022-03/Fact-Sheet-Potential-Risks-of-Aquaculture-Escapes.pdf.

Patel, Raj, and Jason W. Moore. *A History of the World in Seven Cheap Things: A Guide to Capitalism, Nature, and the Future of the Planet*. Collingwood: Black, 2018.

Pauly, Daniel. *Vanishing Fish: Shifting Baselines and the Future of Global Fisheries*. Vancouver: Greystone Books, 2019.

Pauly, Daniel, and Dirk Zeller. 'Catch Reconstructions Reveal that Global Marine Fisheries Catches are Higher than Reported and Declining'. *Nature Communications* 7 (2016): 10244, 5.

Purbosari, Ninik, Endang Warsiki, Khaswar Syamsu, Joko Santoso. 'Natural Versus Synthetic Anesthetic for Transport of Live Fish: A Review'. *Aquaculture and Fisheries* 4, no. 4 (2019): 129–33.

Rachwani, Mostafa. 'Fears for Environment After 50,000 Fish Escape Salmon Farm in Tasmania'. *The Guardian*, 24 November 2020. At: https://www.theguardian.com/australia-news/2020/nov/24/fears-for-environment-after-50000-fish-escape-salmon-farm-in-tasmania.

Russell, Denise. *Who Rules the Waves?: Piracy, Overfishing and Mining the Oceans*. London: Pluto Press, 2010.

Simmons, Glenn, Graeme Bremner, Hugh Whittaker, Philip Clarke, Lydia Teh, Kyrstn Zylich, Dirk Zeller, Daniel Pauly, Christina Stringer, Barry Torkington, and Nigel Haworth. 'Reconstruction of Marine Fisheries Catches for New Zealand (1950–2010)'. *Sea Around Us*. Global Fisheries Cluster, Institute for the Oceans and

Fisheries, University of British Columbia, Vancouver, BC, Canada. At: http://www.seaaroundus.org/doc/PageContent/OtherWPContent/Simmons+et+al+2016+-+NZ+Catch+Reconstruction+-+May+11.pdf.

Shepherd, C. J., and A. J. Jackson. 'Global Fishmeal and Fish-Oil Supply: Inputs, Outputs and Marketsa'. *Journal of Fish Biology* 83, no. 4 (2013): 1046–66.

Skilbrei, Ove T., Mikko Heino, Terje Svåsand. 'Using Simulated Escape Events to Assess the Annual Numbers and Destinies of Escaped Farmed Atlantic Salmon of Different Life Stages From Farm Sites in Norway'. *ICES Journal of Marine Science*, 72, no. 2 (2015): 670–85.

Stanescu, James. 'Beyond Biopolitics: Animal Studies, Factory Farms, and the Advent of Deading Life'. *PhaenEx* 8, no. 2 (2013): 135–60.

Taylor, Chloë. 'Foucault and Critical Animal Studies: Genealogies of Agricultural Power'. *Philosophy Compass* 8 (2013): 539–51.

Tidwell, James. *Aquaculture Production Systems*. Hoboken, NJ: Wiley-Blackwell, 2012.

Wadiwel, Dinesh J. *The War against Animals*. Leiden, Brill 2015.

Wadiwel, Dinesh J. 'Do Fish Resist?' *Cultural Studies Review* 22, no. 1 (2016): 196–242.

Wadiwel, Dinesh J. 'Chicken Harvesting Machine: Animal Labor, Resistance, and the Time of Production'. *SAQ: The South Atlantic Quarterly*, 117, no. 3 (2018): 527–49.

Wadiwel, Dinesh J. *Animals and Capital.* Edinburgh University Press, 2023.

Wang, Cong, Zhen Li, Tan Wang, Xianbao Xu, Xiaoshuan Zhang, and Daoliang Li. 'Intelligent Fish Farm—the Future of Aquaculture'. *Aquaculture International* 29, no. 6 (2021): 2681–711.

Wolfe, Cary. *Before the Law: Humans and Other Animals in a Biopolitical Frame*. Chicago, IL: The University of Chicago Press, 2013.

Yadav, Anamika, Md Tabish Noori, Abhijit Biswas, and Booki Min. 'A Concise Review on the Recent Developments in the Internet of Things (IoT)-Based Smart Aquaculture Practices'. *Reviews in Fisheries Science* 31, no. 1 (2023): 103–18.

Zhou, Chao, Daming Xu, Kai Lin, Chuanheng Sun, and Xinting Yang. 'Intelligent Feeding Control Methods in Aquaculture with an Emphasis on Fish: A Review'. *Reviews in Aquaculture* 10, no. 4 (2018): 975–93.

Zou, Keyuan. 'Global Commons and the Law of the Sea: An Introduction'. In *Global Commons and the Law of the Sea*, edited by Keyuan Zou. Leiden: Brill | Nijhoff, 2018.

PART III
RECONCEPTUALISING BIOPOLITICS

| | Imagining Liberation beyond Biopolitics:
The Biopolitical 'War against Animals'
and Strategies for Ending It
Zipporah Weisberg

The biopolitical turn in animal studies has enriched and deepened the analysis of animal exploitation in several significant ways.[1] Building on the biopolitical framework introduced by Michel Foucault, and later developed and transformed by Giorgio Agamben, Roberto Esposito and Achille Mbembe, among others, scholars of biopolitics reveal how modern politics is primarily concerned with the administration and regulation of biological life (and death), a relentlessly invasive process of bodily manipulation and surveillance of which other animals are the most abject victims. Unlike liberal political theories which tend to downplay or ignore the role of capitalism in perpetuating violence against animals, biopolitical analyses lay bare the relationship between capitalism, biopower and systemic violence. Biopolitical approaches also uncover the 'exclusionary' logic of modern politics and, relatedly, how animals are relegated to a permanent state of exception in factory farms and laboratories and other sites of organised violence.

No account of the biopolitical nightmare to which tens of billions of other animals are condemned every year is as powerful and impactful as Dinesh Wadiwel's *The War against Animals*.[2] Published almost a decade ago in 2015, *The War against Animals* is as relevant and timely as ever, not least because the mass production and destruction of animal life has only increased ten-fold in the intervening years. Unlike some scholars of biopolitics who are unduly preoccupied with abstruse philosophical concepts, Wadiwel remains sharply focused on the issues at hand. In a relentlessly honest analysis, he confronts the problem of domination head on, without diluting his analysis or critique.

Wadiwel's detailed biopolitical analysis of human tyranny over other animals offers several crucial and potentially game-changing insights. Among the many strengths of his book is the *totality* of his critique: by revealing the connections between intersubjective, institutional and epistemic violence, Wadiwel captures the universality, ubiquity and enormity of human beings' historic crimes against animals. While Wadiwel is not the first to characterise human–animal relations as a war, he is the first to elaborate on what being at war with animals means in both theoretical and practical terms. He explores the origins of the war, its aims and the strategies and weapons deployed to ensure it continues indefinitely. He reveals with painful acuity the biopolitical nature of the war against animals and demonstrates just how brutally humans' self-proclaimed sovereignty plays itself out on the bodies of other animals.

As valuable as Wadiwel's analysis is, however, his proposals for ending the war are less convincing. Wadiwel's discussion of political veganism as a meaningful form of Foucauldian 'counter-conduct' is certainly compelling but limited in scope. Wadiwel's suggestion to seek a one-day 'truce' in the war against animals might be appealing at first blush but is ultimately implausible and even counter-productive. Although for the idea of a truce Wadiwel draws on the radical feminist tradition, Wadiwel's difficulty in imagining more compelling liberatory possibilities may be partly due to his reliance in this text on the Foucauldian and biopolitical frameworks, which, although perhaps suited to imagining *resistance*, do not seem well equipped for theorising *liberation*. Indeed, some of the core features of Foucauldian thought and the biopolitical framework more generally, especially the view of the subject as always already 'subjection', and the tendency to reduce all relations, including relations of care, to relations of power, pose substantial barriers to envisioning liberation. Other traditions such as Left humanism, the critical theory of the early Frankfurt School and critical pedagogy are more amenable to the task of developing a robust theory and praxis of multispecies liberation.

The Biopolitical War against Animals: A Total Critique

One of the most important contributions of Wadiwel's analysis is that it offers a *total* critique of human violence against other animals. The war against animals is *universal*. It has been fought across space and time, irrespective of culture or creed, and with unparalleled efficiency and cruelty for thousands of years. The form the violence takes may vary, but the fact of the violence does not. From the 'everyday violence that characterizes many of our relations with animals',[3] to the 'monstrous deployment of violence and extermination',[4] we are caught up in a protracted 'war with measurable effects in suffering and death for billions'.[5] The war against animals permeates every aspect of human life. The war is being fought on 'inter[s]ubjective, institutional, and epistemic' fronts.[6] Intersubjective warfare constitutes 'individual acts against animals' and includes things like 'human contact in containment, slaughter, experimentation, and "sport"'.[7] A final distinguishing feature of the war against animals is that, like many wars from the twentieth century onwards, it is being fought against noncombatants. The aim of the war is not to acquire territory or riches but is 'a phenomenon of mass or corporate organised violence that aims at total domination'. It is a war that seeks to bend other animals to our will by any means possible.[8]

The significance of Wadiwel's insights cannot be overstated. If the entire ideological and institutional infrastructure of human life is designed to fight and remain victorious in a war without end, our pleasures, achievements and aspirations are all stained with blood. The recognition that virtually all human activity, all human thought, even, has been unfolding in the context of a war, a zoocidal war on a colossal scale over the course of millennia, is truly chilling. It throws into question what it means to be human, and it dispels any myth of humans' inherent benevolence we may hold dear. In the war against animals, just as in other genocidal wars, some people are more or less consciously involved in the violence, more or less consciously hateful towards the targeted group, more or less consciously committed to the dominant ideology. But all members of the oppressive group are culpable. One might go so far as to say that human beings are zoocidal war criminals. Even people who harbour no active hatred against animals per se are, by virtue of being human, committing war crimes against animals on a daily basis. We are all participants in the war and we all partake of its spoils. We are all guilty of trying to bend the will of animals to our own, whether by chaining or muzzling dogs, eating a hamburger, gawking at tigers in zoos. Even political vegans who are committed to ending violence against animals are beneficiaries of the war.[9] Our freedoms and our pleasures come directly at the expense of other animals' freedoms and pleasures, and much, much worse.

Humans' comportment on earth is nothing other than that of triumphant plunderers: 'We eat, hunt, torture, incarcerate and kill animals because it is our sovereign right won from total victory; our sovereign pleasure'.[10] Certainly, 'the scale by which we kill and harm animals would seem to confirm that our mainstay relationship with animals is combative or at least focused upon producing harm and death'.[11] According to Wadiwel, a deep-seated human hostility towards animals undergirds and sustains the war,[12] although perhaps it would be more accurate to suggest it is fuelled by contempt. Hostility connotes dislike and unfriendliness, whereas contempt connotes a fundamental lack of respect for the other, a disdain, a belief that the object of contempt is worthless or beneath consideration.

The characterisation of human–animal relations as a one-sided war reveals connections between seemingly disparate and innocuous activities such as drinking a cappuccino, taking a Tylenol or taking a dog for a walk. These activities not only link the consumer to the violence of the industries that produced the products (viz., the dairy, pharmaceutical and pet industries), but to other apparently disconnected industries such as, say, the entertainment, fashion and home-decorating industries. The connections are sometimes material, but they are always political: any activity in which animals are harmed, and all activities that depend on animals having been harmed are acts of war. They are made possible by a complex and sophisticated apparatus of violence that spans the planet, a gargantuan animal–industrial complex from which it is nearly impossible to escape. Most attempts at resistance are overcome by the adjustment of the apparatus to anticipate and thwart them.[13]

Wadiwel observes that one of the most pernicious aspects of this war against animals is that it takes place 'under the guise' of peace.[14] As the war against animals rages, most people are none the wiser: 'many enjoy a life of peaceful civility, indeed they may have the luxury of never hearing the canons of war'. Little do people realise that 'these spaces of reprieve are quite literally bordered by zones of absolute terror'.[15] Because the exploitation and killing of animals has been so normalised, because we have all internalised the logic of the war so deeply, because it is bolstered by an all-pervasive 'violent rationality', even exposing people to violence is not necessarily an effective strategy for overcoming it.[16] They will not see the violence as violence, the torture as torture, the killing as killing or the exploitation as exploitation. They certainly will not see the war as war – they will see it as the fulfilment of humans' natural right to total domination, our undisputed claim to species sovereignty.

In the tradition of Agamben and Derrida, Wadiwel emphasises the relationship between sovereign power and biopower.[17] This is an important corrective to theories of biopolitics which displace the role of the sovereign or tyrant in power relations and, as a result, also tend to elide the problem of domination. Wadiwel has no difficulty integrating biopolitical critiques of relations of power with critiques of domination. Following Locke, Wadiwel argues that sovereign power is established through force, and only after it has been acquired are justifications developed to support and sustain it.[18] Determining which came first is perhaps less important than recognising that the war's primary aim is to maintain and reinforce human sovereignty, while sovereignty's aim is, in turn, to perpetuate the war: 'Sovereignty is a means to fix a pattern of domination, through institutions, practices, law and knowledge, which allows for the continuation of war by other means'.[19] Sovereignty institutionalises domination and normalises war to the point of making it invisible to all but the victims. Our appropriation of other animals' bodies and lives was not a one-time occurrence, of course, but is continually re-enacted: 'The war on animals is located upon a violent form of continual appropriation, and an equally violent form of conversion of the lives of animals into value within a human exchange system; property and commodity cohabit as artefacts of war'.[20] Here, Wadiwel emphasises the role that capitalism plays in the biopolitical war against animals, an issue he stresses throughout his analysis. Indeed, one of the strengths of Wadiwel's approach is his seamless integration of a Foucauldian and Marxian perspective.

While a form of primitive accumulation is the founding act of human sovereignty, the exclusion of animals from 'civil political space' is the founding act of politics. This assertion changes the nature of the debate entirely. From this perspective, it is no longer a question of developing individualised ethics. Nor is it a question of reforming ultimately benevolent, if misguided, institutions to better protect other animals, as liberal political theorists seek to do.[21] Because they are built on the substratum of human sovereignty, liberal political institutions are necessarily violent and are necessarily instruments of domination. In Wadiwel's words: 'sovereignty is a means to fix a pattern of domination, through institutions, practices, law and knowledge, which allows for the continuation of war by other means'.[22]

Finally, Wadiwel illuminates the distinctly biopolitical nature of the war against animals. Enormous resources have been dedicated to the precise science of administering billions upon billions of lives and death, so much so that '[o]ur relations with animals appear as biopolitical in an almost archetypal way, in so far as they perfectly and efficiently use violence to locate an exact line between life and death'.[23] In order to supply the world with animals' flesh, we need to keep bringing them into existence: 'industrialised slaughter – the power to make die – also relies on an attendant ability to bring to life – a power to make live'.[24] No life is more seamlessly integrated into 'the systems of efficient and economic controls' than animal life. And no century has been bloodier than the current one. More animals than ever before are being made to live in the most appalling conditions only to be made to die the most terrifying deaths. Lists, genetic codes, tables of figures, statistics, measurements, doses and other calculations are what enable systemic atrocities to be committed with remarkable efficiency and without passion. The situation for those subjugated to such bureaucratised, mechanised violence is particularly hopeless because they are abandoned to an indifferent machinery, an apparatus of destruction, over which individual human agency can have little sway.

In terms of the scale and methods of killing, the war against animals resembles the Holocaust. And, as Charles Patterson has demonstrated in his arresting book, *Eternal Treblinka*, there are concrete historical parallels and connections between the Nazis' war against the Jews and humans' war against animals.[25] However, Wadiwel correctly points that there are substantive differences that cannot be overlooked. In the Nazi Holocaust there was a discernible goal to eliminate the Jewish population to preserve the purity of the German 'race'. In the war against animals, a similar logic is at play on the face of it: animals are killed (ostensibly) so humans can eat, be cured of illness and live long, healthy lives. But the Jews were not 'granted' life only to be disallowed it, nor has any other human population been brought into existence only to be killed. This is something unique to humans' administration of animals' lives and deaths. So, when we compare the experience of humans and other animals under biopolitics, we must be very careful not to conflate the two. Much emphasis is placed on how other human populations have been reduced to 'bare life', have been 'animalised' and reduced to bodies, but they have never been mass produced in order to be annihilated.

The war against animals, the animal holocaust, is not only continuing but accelerating and intensifying. What can be done to slow or stop it? To end the war against animals, human sovereignty must be renounced, but, as Wadiwel aptly notes, one cannot assume this is simply 'a matter of storming the Winter Palace'.[26] Nor can the war be halted simply by 'ending an economic system of power, such as, for example, legislating against animals as property'.[27] Because 'we are dealing with a set of violences that are deeply embedded into almost every conceivable facet of human organisation, life and knowledge', Wadiwel argues, resistance must seek to confront conduct: how we are governed, how we govern ourselves, what we know about ourselves, and what we know about others.

Imagining Liberation

After taking such care to explain how the war against animals plays out, Wadiwel moves to exploring possibilities for resisting it, if not ending it entirely (a much more daunting task). First, Wadiwel suggests that veganism could (or already does) function as a meaningful form of Foucauldian 'counter-conduct' or as a form of insubordination against the 'conduct of conduct', an intervention into the epistemic violence, the false truths, fuelling the war. Veganism is a refusal to accept accepted truths, it is a rejection of the faulty and dangerous 'knowledge systems' perpetuated by doctors, scientists and even family and friends who have internalised the myth that humans 'need' meat and other animal products to survive and thrive and also that animals are ours to use and abuse at will: 'Vegan practitioners run headlong into truth, particularly where personal experiences of how it might be possible to remove oneself from an animal-based diet run against prevailing public advice and medical knowledge'.[28] Far from rejecting science as such, however, vegans construct counter-truths about the health benefits of veganism.

At the same time, Wadiwel properly underlines the 'internal limits of veganism as a strategy'.[29] If treated as an individual moral choice alone, or as a form of personal asceticism, it may have little political impact at all. Turning the focus inward and remaining preoccupied with extracting oneself from the violent system can be self-absorbed (and therefore apolitical) and also self-deceptive because, as noted above, it is impossible to remove oneself entirely from the war against animals, to not somehow benefit from it. (As Lori Gruen and Robert Jones point out, veganism is ultimately aspirational, which is to say it is impossible to fully realise given how virtually every aspect of life – from painting the walls, to taking the bus – is linked to some form of violence against animals.[30]) One might add that if not overtly politicised and treated as an essential component of (multispecies) social justice, veganism runs the risk of reinscribing problematic liberal notions of 'tolerance' and individualism rather than catalysing systemic change. Although it is fair to say that the majority of vegans are committed to political transformation, in wider consumer society veganism is typically regarded as just another dietary choice among many, a view that robs veganism of its political potency as a form of refusal, as a boycott and as an affirmative praxis geared towards building new, nonviolent relations with other animals.

Curiously, Wadiwel limits his exploration of counter-conduct to veganism and does not examine other existing or potential forms of counter-conduct, such as animal sanctuaries and interspecies communities, which could be, and in a sense already are, 'operationalised as a collective or communal form of resistance'.[31] As among the only places on earth where ensuring other animals' wellbeing and flourishing is the primary goal, where the infrastructure, the organisation of personnel and the distribution of resources are aimed squarely at creating the conditions for other animals to thrive, where all forms of exploitation and violence are prohibited, where human supremacism is vehemently rejected, and where new forms of multispecies relationality are actively cultivated, sanctuaries seem like exemplary forms of operationalised, collective counter-conduct.

It goes without saying that sanctuaries are extremely varied and diverse, and some are more successful than others at putting their stated aims into practice, or even at clarifying in a theoretically and philosophically nuanced way what their core principles and objectives are. As Sue Donaldson and Will Kymlicka have pointed out, some sanctuaries subscribe to a rescue and rehabilitation model that reinforces animals' positioning as helpless moral patients, rather than active moral, political and social agents.[32] Some sanctuaries adopt a paternalistic approach to care, while others are too poorly funded to provide adequate care to all animals. These shortcomings and the substantive differences between sanctuaries notwithstanding, broadly speaking sanctuaries' shared raison d'être is to cultivate peaceable relations among the human and nonhuman sanctuary residents and the society at large. One might argue that sanctuaries are manifestations of the Great Refusal, 'the protest against that which is', as defined by Marcuse.[33] They mark a 'historical break' with human supremacism/sovereignty and usher in a new way of being-with other animals. They help initiate 'a change in the "infrastructure of man"' by grounding human–animal relationality in care as opposed to violent domination, something ecofeminists have long been arguing for.[34] Sanctuaries also push back against the biopolitical war against animals (and against weak welfarist reforms, which only perpetuate the war) 'in refusing quantification metrics for success that prioritize the most cost-effective promotion of abstract notions of animal wellbeing, instead insisting on radical care for particular individuals, beings with distinctive histories, associated vulnerabilities, and unique relationships'.[35] Sanctuaries reject the reduction of animals to calculations and instead honour their rich subjectivity and membership in families and communities.

Some sanctuaries, like VINE sanctuary in Springfield, Vermont, are explicitly committed to radical refusal and transformation. VINE is an LGBTQ+ run sanctuary that consistently questions its own assumptions and practices to ensure animals' autonomy and agency are maximised. As Alice Crary and Lori Gruen point out, politically conscious sanctuaries like VINE are examples of the 'revolutionary commons' proposed by Sue Ferguson, 'alternative, prefigurative spaces like workers co-ops or communal kitchens',[36] which, Crary and Gruen explain, are 'valuable for building new forms of political consciousness' even if on the face of it, they 'have limited reach'.[37] VINE and other politicised sanctuaries 'offer a collective refusal of the life-denying social and economic forces that view [animals] as disposable and replaceable'.[38]

Another form of collective counter-conduct that unfolds in sanctuaries is intra- and interspecies friendship. If our relations with other animals are (over-)determined by an underlying hostility and/or contempt, then forming meaningful friendships with them is a powerful form of resistance against the war. Creating the conditions for other animals to form friendships among themselves, something they are deliberately and cruelly prevented from doing in the animal–industrial complex, enables their participation in counter-conduct. Wadiwel argues that most friendships that develop in the context of war are inevitably tainted by that war. Though not free of the war's contamination, friendships that develop in sanctuaries push back against the war inasmuch as they involve former 'enemies' embracing one another as companions and offer a glimpse into what peaceable, respectful, life-affirming and mutually reinforcing relations between humans and other animals could look like. With each new friendship between humans and animals built consciously – with the human party always checking their inherited sense of supremacy – a small dent is made in the bulwark of the war.

In 'Animal Friendship as a Way of Life', Wadiwel explores the meaning of interspecies friendship, especially between humans and companion animals, in the context of war. He suggests that despite the oppressive relations in which they have developed, friendships between humans and companion animals have some potentially redeeming factors. Following Foucault, Wadiwel maintains that all friendships comprise a form of (non-genital) 'sexuality', by which he means 'shared pleasures' generated through consensual forms of non-genital touch, including 'petting', caressing and other forms of touch and affection.[39] This is an interesting take on friendship. The focus on touch is especially important given that touch is such a central element to nonhuman animal life and such a neglected part of human animal life, especially in the digital age. However, perhaps it is more fruitful to explore the possibility of friendship as grounded in Eros more broadly. Taken as a whole, Eros encompasses sensuality, touch, perceptual attunement, physical and emotional affection, physical and emotional intimacy, pleasure-seeking and giving, desire, playfulness and play, love, nurturing, wonder, enchantment, aesthetic sensibility and creativity, among many other things. Most importantly, perhaps, Eros is the counterforce of Thanatos, the death drive. While Eros and Thanatos are intertwined, the aggressive impulses inherent to Thanatos and so fundamental to perpetuating the war against animals can be thwarted by the nonrepressive desublimation of the Erotic drives.[40] If we organise ourselves in such a way as to cultivate the conditions for the free expression of Erotic forces, including intra- and interspecies friendship, we might begin to drain the war of the bellicosity that drives it.

The sanctuary movement could be developed to be more overtly political, with the goal of moving beyond the problematic rescue and rehabilitation model to build dynamic multispecies communities.[41] At the moment, sanctuaries are isolated enclaves, spaces of relative safety, amidst the wider 'topography of enmity', but if further operationalised as forms of refusal, they could begin to transform society more broadly.[42] Of course, sanctuaries cannot stop the war on their own but could form an essential part of a larger coordinated effort, a mass mobilisation across the planet, to dismantle the apparatus of war and usher in a new way of being and being-with other animals (and each other).

Sanctuaries and their liberatory dimension may be problematic from a Foucauldian perspective because they too could be considered biopolitical spaces where every aspect of animals' lives and deaths are managed (by humans).[43] And to an extent this is true. Animals' lives and deaths are micromanaged in sanctuaries, from the kind and quantity of food they are given to their ability to procreate. But the reasons for the biopolitical interventions that take place in sanctuaries are in direct contradistinction to their equivalent in the animal–industrial complex. Their aim is not to exploit animals, but to maximise their flourishing. Their aim is not to accelerate animals' growth and propel them towards premature and violent deaths, but to let them grow and develop naturally, to lead fulfilling lives and to die dignified and peaceful deaths when they reach old age or when they can no longer continue living due to debilitating pain, injury or disease. There is no question that human intervention into animal lives is problematic, especially when it comes to invasive procedures like sterilisation that curb animals' capacity to explore or express their sexuality or make and have babies. But there is a substantive difference between violent and nonviolent forms of biopolitics, which cannot be overlooked.

Ultimately, the Foucauldian, biopolitical framework does not seem to lend itself particularly well towards imagining liberatory politics. If power works productively as well as destructively, if we are always already entangled in complex power relations, does this not cancel out the liberatory nature of sanctuaries altogether? It is fair to say that the Foucauldian and biopolitical approach leaves little (perhaps no) room for 'negativity', which is to say, dialectical tension between what is and what ought to be and attempts to bridge the two. Although the biopolitical framework is very useful for understanding how the war against animals is being fought today, it may be best treated as a critical and descriptive framework, rather than a proscriptive one.

Wadiwel's second and most far-reaching proposal for disrupting the war against animals, a one-day truce in the killing of animals, a 24-hour reprieve in hostilities, is inspired not by Foucault or other scholars of biopolitics, but by the radical feminist tradition. In her 1983 speech at the Midwest Regional Conference of the National Organization for Changing Men in Minnesota, Andrea Dworkin made plea for a 'twenty-four-hour truce during which there is no rape'.[44] The aim was not only to give women a break from the risk of rape, but to create the conditions for true peaceability and equality to develop. The logic behind Dworkin's proposal is that as long as women are kept down by the threat of rape, as long as men feel entitled to carry it out, any attempt to foster equitable relations will be futile. Wadiwel wonders if a similar truce in the war against animals might not also create the conditions for meaningful reflection. Like Dworkin, Wadiwel recognises that a truce cannot end the war, but it may help to clear the way for meaningful change: 'A truce is one way to consider a strategic space where new allegiances might be formed and which provides the foundation for a different sort of friendship, a different politics'.[45] Most importantly, 'a call for a one-day truce would actually intervene in the production process of killing animals and, all things holding equal, reduce the number of animals killed'.[46] A pause in the killing, Wadiwel maintains, would have important ramifications for institutional, intersubjective and epistemic violence. First, 'the intervention thus operates explicitly on an institutional level, in so far as it aims to challenge a systemic practice of violence'. Next, 'while institutional violence is the focus, the intervention nevertheless will impact intersubjective practices where they connect to this institutional violence of mass killing, not only in relation to the practices of workers whose labour involves killing, but also in the global impact for markets and consumers of a reduced supply of meat'. Finally, '[b]y focusing on the site of the production of killing, and not the site of consumption, we might be able to shift the normalising truths that underpin systemic violence against animals'.[47] For Wadiwel, the truce in the war against animals could correspond with a general strike by workers who, through the development of 'alliance politics', may recognise the relationship between their exploitation and the exploitation of animals. Cultivating alliance politics is definitely essential to the struggle for animal liberation, but a truce may not be the best way to go about it.

Indeed, although appealing at first blush – who would not want to grasp at any opportunity to stop the killing for even a day?! – the idea of a truce seems misguided. There are five major problems with it. The first is that, by definition, a truce is an agreement between two or more warring parties to suspend aggressions for a given period. So how could it apply to the war against animals, in which there is only one aggressor: the human species? Second, although a truce may have tremendous symbolic significance (which is not to be sneezed at), its practical impact is questionable and could, in fact, prove counterproductive and harmful. As Wadiwel has himself so poignantly demonstrated, killing is but one part of the organised system of violence against animals. If this is the case, how would stopping systemic killing so abruptly without also stopping the processes that precede it do anything but exacerbate animals' suffering? Does one more day in a veal crate not merely prolong a calf's agony? Would the killing not need to speed up the following day to relieve the 'backlog' and possibly lead to even more cruelty in the ensuing chaos?[48] This is of course not to say that it is better to kill than not to kill a calf languishing in a veal crate. The point is that within the larger scheme of things, holding off on killing the calf for one day would not alleviate his suffering or prevent his violent death the next day. Another problem with the idea of a truce in the killing of animals is that it does nothing to stop the torture and killing of animals in other sites of violence, such as laboratories, circuses, zoos, rodeos and so on. To focus on slaughterhouses alone as the object of the truce seems unnecessarily limited.

The fourth problem with a truce concerns the line of reasoning used to justify it. It seems odd to wait for (an unlikely) pause in violence against women or animals to try to change oppressive attitudes and practices. Certainly, the idea of building solidarity between workers and the animals they are required to kill is compelling and should certainly form a central part of any organised resistance movement against the war against animals. And perhaps calling for a general strike partially on behalf of other animals would inspire a sense of solidarity between the workers and animals. But what would happen when the workers have to go back to the kill floor the next day? Perhaps some would refuse, but most would probably have to return to work out of sheer economic necessity. This could cause confusion, shame and even trauma. Perhaps if the slaughterhouse strike were coordinated with other strikes, with a much larger general strike across all the industries that harm animals and destroy the earth, it could be more impactful. As I suggest below, a mass mobilisation against the capitalist system, against its exploitative and parasitic tendencies, might be more effective in initiating structural (and ideological) change. The fifth problem with the truce as envisioned by Dworkin and Wadiwel inadvertently hands more power over to the perpetrator by depending on their willingness to cease hostilities for a day. As noted above, in the war against animals (and the war against women), the violence is one-sided; it is directed by humans against animals, who are targets of zoocidal atrocities or crimes against animality. Granted, in Wadiwel's proposal, the workers would be responsible for halting the violence for a day, not the CEOs. Although the workers do the actual killing, they are not responsible for it per se, at least not to the extent that CEOs are, and indeed are also victimised. Still, why should we wait for workers to walk out before we collectively mobilise against the war? Shouldn't the work against intersubjective, epistemic and institutional violence start now in homes, schools and elsewhere? Would our energy not be better spent on developing a mass mobilisation for interspecies social justice? Slaughterhouse workers would of course be invited to participate, but we should not waste our time by seeking a truce.

A mass mobilisation for interspecies social justice seems both more feasible and more attractive than a truce. Alliance building would be at the core of this effort but would not depend on a truce for its realisation. As it is becoming increasingly difficult to deny that factory farming, the destruction of the Amazon rainforest and extractive industries are accelerating climate change, it might be the most opportune moment yet for animal liberationists to join forces with climate activists, Indigenous activists and other social justice activists. Animal liberationists are especially attuned to the inextricable links between racism, sexism, classism, ableism and speciesism, so could take the lead in this effort to build a global movement for peace. Wide-scale nonviolent civil disobedience in the form of the occupation of institutions governing the violence could be an effective tactic. Mass sit-ins or 'die-ins' in the offices of the ministries of agriculture could be organised on the same day across the globe. People who were willing and able to participate could camp out in front of and inside the offices and institutions from where atrocities against animals are orchestrated. Meanwhile, rescue operations from all sites of violence could be ramped up and an 'animal underground railroad' could be constructed, linking laboratories, circuses, factory farms and other places where animals are harmed to sanctuaries and other safe spaces.

Another fundamental element of mass mobilisation would be critical pedagogy. With the development of a critical animal pedagogy, new truth systems – a challenge to all three aspects of war (intersubjective, institutional, epistemic) – could be built, truth systems that uncover the 'dehumanisation' of workers and points to ways workers may 'liberate themselves and their oppressors as well from the hellish scenarios the distorted sense of the human (as sovereign) has enabled.'[49] Critical animal pedagogy, like the critical animal theory Crary and Gruen propose, would involve, among other things, 'making the lives of animals perceptible and comprehensible'.[50] What if children were not lied to with storybooks full of 'happy' farm animals and instead told the truth about farming, the inherent violence and wrongness of it? What if children were taught ecofeminist principles and praxes of care? What if children were taught that reason is not bifurcated from emotion, that the worth of a being is not grounded in its 'capacities' but in the fact of its existence as a conscious, embodied being? Imagine if children learned how to nurture, love and form lifelong relationships with other animals. The epistemic and institutional bulwark of the war against animals might finally collapse and the war finally end.

Another reason Foucauldian and biopolitical perspectives may need to be put aside when constructing the liberatory project is for its failure to offer a positive account of subjectivity. On the one hand, biopolitical analyses open up space for reconceptualising subjects as vulnerable embodied beings. Cary Wolfe, for example, celebrates the 'biosubject' as an alternative to the 'rational' subject of 'rights'.[51] But, instead of exploring in any detail what liberated human-animal subjectivity might look like, Wolfe and other biopolitical thinkers (e.g., Matthew Chrulew) offer a stripped down and ultimately impoverished view of the subject.[52] Phenomenology and cognitive ethology offer much richer accounts of human and nonhuman animal subjectivity than biopolitics. Phenomenologists such as Maurice Merleau-Ponty provide insight into the shared embodiment and vulnerability of human and nonhuman animals and of the intimate relationship between the subject to its 'world' (*umwelt*) and other subjects (intersubjectivity).[53] Animal ethologists such as Marc Bekoff and Jonathan Balcombe describe the complex emotional, psychological, social and sexual lives of other animals and in so doing dispel the myth that animals lack emotional and social intelligence and are driven by 'instinct'.[54] Together, phenomenologists and ethologists' respective forays into human and nonhuman animal subjectivity provide a fortuitous defence against one of the ideological positions driving the war against animals (i.e., that animals are necessarily deficient in ethically meaningful ways and are only partially formed subjects at best, automatons at worst) and the contempt this view breeds.

What phenomenology and ethology do not offer is a political framework for envisioning the unfolding of human and nonhuman animal subjectivity. For a political 'programme', we might turn to Left (Marxist, socialist, ecological) humanism(s) as propounded by Erich Fromm, Raya Dunayevskaya, Jean-Paul Sartre, Frantz Fanon and Paolo Freire, among others. Left humanism is important for its challenge to the alienation of the subject under capitalism, for its emphasis on ethical and political responsibility, both personal and collective, and for its vision of reconciliation.[55] Left humanism reinvented as more-than-humanism could be aimed at liberating both humans and other animals from the apparatus of warfare, which not only causes terrible suffering to its victims, but also degrades the perpetrators. The problem of alienation, for example, is rife in the war against animals. Indeed, one might argue that humans' commission of atrocities depends upon our radical alienation from other animals and from ourselves as animals. Drawing on a tradition that affirms the subject, considers it an entity worth salvaging rather than abandoning and explores pathways for overcoming its alienation – an alienation which only seems to be intensifying in the twenty-first century with the technologisation of everyday life – is paramount. Developing the Left humanist project into a project for interspecies liberation may not have the appeal of immediacy, but worked towards over the long term could lead to lasting change, a sea change in our way of thinking about and being-with other animals.

To conclude, Foucauldian thought in general and biopolitical theories in particular, especially as interpreted by Wadiwel, may help us to better understand how the war against animals is playing out, but they may not necessarily help us bring it to an end, something to which Wadiwel attests and attempts to address in his new book, *Animals and Capital*.[56] Other traditions, especially Left humanism, critical pedagogy and the critical theory of the early Frankfurt School provide much more effective tools for imagining and achieving liberation. Radical feminism is certainly an important foundation for imagining liberation, but Dworkin's concept of truce is not convincing for ending violence against women or animals. The war against animals will undoubtedly continue into the future, but it need not carry on indefinitely if we start building effective ways to mobilise against it. To do this, we ought to look beyond biopolitics.

Notes

1. I want to thank Dinesh Wadiwel and Carlo Salzani for their comments and suggestions on early drafts of this chapter.
2. Dinesh Wadiwel, *The War against Animals* (Leiden: Brill, 2015).
3. Wadiwel, *The War against Animals*, 9–10.
4. Wadiwel, *The War against Animals*, 6.
5. Wadiwel, *The War against Animals*, 10.
6. Wadiwel, *The War against Animals*, 31.
7. Wadiwel, *The War against Animals*, 35.
8. Wadiwel, *The War against Animals*, 16, emphasis in the original.
9. Dinesh Wadiwel, 'Counter-Conduct and Truth', in *Philosophy and the Politics of Animal Liberation*, ed. Paola Cavalieri (Basingstoke: Palgrave Macmillan, 2016), 208.
10. Wadiwel, *The War against Animals*, 29.
11. Wadiwel, *The War against Animals*, 5–6.
12. Wadiwel, *The War against Animals*, 28.
13. Wadiwel notes, for example, how the factory farming industry is continually refining its infrastructure of violence to quash animals' continued resistance.
14. Wadiwel, 'Counter-Conduct and Truce', 192. See also, Wadiwel, *War against Animals*, 23.
15. Wadiwel, *The War against Animals*, 87.
16. Wadiwel, *The War against Animals*, 32–3. It is fair to say that slaughterhouses do have proverbial 'glass walls' inasmuch as most people have by now seen images of factory farms on television or social media. That said, as Timothy Pachirat has noted, the facilities themselves tend to be designed to ensure total concealment,

both from without and within. They are built to be hidden from view, to blend in into the industrial landscape, to appear as any other drab, nondescript building and therefore to avoid arousing concern about the dreadful goings-on inside the walls. They are also equipped with a complex infrastructure of inner concealments to hide from the workers the totality of the destruction in which they are engaged (Pachirat, *Every Twelve Seconds: Industrialized Slaughter and the Politics of Sight*) (New Haven, CT: Yale University Press, 2013). Visible or not, violence against animals is not recognised as such. This is a particularly tragic element of the war against animals. They have been so profoundly diminished in our imagination to commodities and instruments for human use, to bare life, or more accurately to 'lives on the threshold of death' (Wadiwel, *War against Animals*, 59).

17. Giorgio Agamben, *The Open: Man and Animal*, trans. Kevin Attell (Stanford, CA: Stanford University Press, 2004); Jacques Derrida, *The Beast and the Sovereign*, vol. I and II, trans. Geoffrey Bennington (Chicago, IL: The University of Chicago Press, 2009). See also Cary Wolfe, *Before the Law: Humans and Other Animals in a Biopolitical Frame* (Chicago, IL: The University of Chicago Press, 2012).
18. Wadiwel, *The War against Animals*, 223.
19. Wadiwel, *The War against Animals*, 252.
20. Wadiwel, *The War against Animals*, 147.
21. For example, Alasdair Cochrane, *Animal Rights Without Liberation: Applied Ethics and Human Obligations* (New York: Columbia University Press, 2012); Robert Garner, *A Theory of Justice for Animals: Animal Rights in a Nonideal World* (Oxford: Oxford University Press, 2013).
22. Wadiwel, *The War against Animals*, 252.
23. Wadiwel, *The War against Animals*, 27.
24. Wadiwel, *The War against Animals*, 27.
25. Charles Patterson, *Eternal Treblinka: Our Treatment of Animals and the Holocaust* (New York: Lantern Books, 2001), also quoted in Wadiwel, *The War Against Animals*, 80n49.
26. Wadiwel, *The War against Animals*, 277.
27. Wadiwel, *The War against Animals*, 277.
28. Wadiwel, 'Counter-Conduct and Truce', 207.
29. Wadiwel, 'Counter-Conduct and Truce', 208.
30. Lori Gruen and Robert C. Jones, 'Veganism as an Aspiration', in *The Moral Complexities of Eating Meat*, eds. Ben Bramble and Bob Fisher (Oxford: Oxford University Press, 2015), 153–71.
31. Wadiwel, 'Counter-Conduct and Truce', 203.
32. Sue Donaldson and Will Kymlicka, 'Farmed Animal Sanctuaries: The Heart of the Movement?', *Politics and Animals*, 1, no. 1 (2015): 50–74.

33. Herbert Marcuse, *One-Dimensional Man: Studies in the Ideology of Advanced Industrial Society* (Boston, MA: Beacon Press, 1964/1991), 63.
34. Herbert Marcuse, *An Essay on Liberation* (Boston, MA: Beacon Press, 1969), 4–5; for ecofeminism see, among many important publications, Carol J. Adams and Lori Gruen (eds), *Ecofeminism: Feminist Intersections with Other Animals and the Earth*, second ed. (London: Bloomsbury Academic, 2022).
35. Alice Crary and Lori Gruen, *Animal Crisis: A New Critical Theory* (Cambridge: Polity Press, 2022), 142–3.
36. Quoted in Crary and Gruen, *Animal Crisis*, 141.
37. Crary and Gruen, *Animal Crisis*, 141; 142–3.
38. Crary and Gruen, *Animal Crisis*, 142.
39. Dinesh Wadiwel, 'Animal Friendship as a Way of Life: Sexuality, Petting and Interspecies Companionship', in *Foucault and Animals*, eds. Matthew Chrulew and Dinesh Wadiwel (Leyden: Brill, 2017), 286–316.
40. Herbert Marcuse, *Eros and Civilization: A Philosophical Inquiry into Freud* (Boston, MA: Beacon Press, 1974).
41. Donaldson and Kymlicka, 'Farmed Animal Sanctuaries'.
42. Timothy Pachirat, 'Sanctuary', in Lori Gruen (ed.), *Critical Terms for Animal Studies* (Chicago, IL: University of Chicago Press, 2018), 339.
43. Wadiwel, *The War against Animals*, 26.
44. Wadiwel, *The War against Animals*, 287; and Wadiwel, 'Counter-Conduct and Truce', 213.
45. Wadiwel, 'Counter-Conduct and Truce', 213.
46. Wadiwel, *The War against Animals*, 290.
47. Wadiwel, *The War against Animals*, 290. See also, Wadiwel, 'Counter-Conduct and Truce', 214–15.
48. As happened when slaughterhouses had to close down during the COVID-19 pandemic and the animals had to be killed en masse to make place for those who follow them in the unstoppable machine of animal agriculture. See Crary and Gruen, *Animal Crisis*, 20–21.
49. Paolo Freire, *Pedagogy of the Oppressed*, trans. Myra Bergman Ramos (London: Continuum, 2000), 44.
50. Crary and Gruen, *Animal Crisis*, 109.
51. Wolfe, *Before the Law*, 22.
52. Wolfe, *Before the Law*, 33–7; Matthew Chrulew, 'Animals as Biopolitical Subjects', in *Foucault and Animals*, eds. Chrulew and Wadiwel, 222–38. Wolfe claims that we are all animals before the law (2012, 10). There is truth to this, but it is also a problematic claim inasmuch as it erases the fundamental line that, because of human supremacism, detaches 'the human' from 'the animal' and places it in a

different ontological category. No matter how badly human beings are treated, they are treated this way *as human beings*. Their animalisation is that much more degrading because they are humans, which, in our anthropocentric civilization, means they are fundamentally not animals. Indeed, their animalisation only confirms their humanity. Mistreating animals, in other words, never carries the same weight as mistreating humans, and it will not until there is a monumental shift in our thinking.

53. See for example, Maurice Merleau-Ponty, *The World of Perception*, trans. Oliver Davis (London: Routledge, 2004).
54. See for example, Marc Bekoff, *The Emotional Lives of Animals: A Leading Scientist Explores Animal Joy, Sorrow, and Empathy — and Why They Matter* (Novato, CA: New World Library, 2008); Jonathan Balcombe, *Pleasurable Kingdom: Animals and the Nature of Feeling Good* (New York: Macmillan, 2006).
55. For more on humanism and animal liberation see Zipporah Weisberg, 'Reinventing Left Humanism: Towards an Interspecies Emancipatory Project', in *Ethical and Political Approaches to Nonhuman Animal Issues*, eds. Andrew Woodhall and Gabriel Garmendia da Trindade (Basingstoke: Palgrave Macmillan, 2017), 121–48.
56. Dinesh Wadiwel, *Animals and Capital* (Edinburgh: Edinburgh University Press, 2023).

Works Cited

Adams, Carol J., and Lori Gruen (eds.). *Ecofeminism: Feminist Intersections with Other Animals and the Earth*, second edition. London: Bloomsbury Academic, 2022.

Agamben, Giorgio. *The Open: Man and Animal*. Translated by Kevin Attell. Stanford, CA: Stanford University Press, 2004.

Balcombe, Jonathan. *Pleasurable Kingdom: Animals and the Nature of Feeling Good*. New York: Macmillan, 2006.

Bekoff, Marc. *The Emotional Lives of Animals: A Leading Scientist Explores Animal Joy, Sorrow, and Empathy — and Why They Matter*. Novato, CA: New World Library, 2008.

Chrulew, Matthew. 'Animals as Biopolitical Subjects'. In *Foucault and Animals*, edited by Matthew Chrulew and Dinesh Wadiwel, 222–38. Leyden: Brill, 2017.

Cochrane, Alasdair. *Animal Rights Without Liberation: Applied Ethics and Human Obligations*. New York: Columbia University Press, 2012.

Crary, Alice, and Lori Gruen. *Animal Crisis: A New Critical Theory*. Cambridge: Polity Press, 2022.

Derrida, Jacques. *The Beast and the Sovereign*, vol. I and II. Translated by Geoffrey Bennington. Chicago, IL: The University of Chicago Press, 2009, 2011.

Donaldson, Sue, and Will Kymlicka. 'Farmed Animal Sanctuaries: The Heart of the Movement?' *Politics and Animals*, 1, no. 1 (2015): 50–74.

Freire, Paolo. *Pedagogy of the Oppressed*. Translated by Myra Bergman Ramos. London: Continuum, 2000.

Garner, Robert. *A Theory of Justice for Animals: Animal Rights in a Nonideal World*. Oxford: Oxford University Press, 2013.

Gruen, Lori, and Robert C. Jones. 'Veganism as an Aspiration'. In *The Moral Complexities of Eating Meat*, edited by Ben Bramble and Bob Fisher, 153–71. Oxford: Oxford University Press, 2015.

Marcuse, Herbert. *Eros and Civilization: A Philosophical Inquiry into Freud*. Boston, MA: Beacon Press, 1974.

Marcuse, Herbert. *An Essay on Liberation*. Boston, MA: Beacon Press, 1969.

Marcuse, Herbert. *One-Dimensional Man: Studies in the Ideology of Advanced Industrial Society*. Boston, MA: Beacon Press, 1964/1991.

Merleau-Ponty, Maurice. *The World of Perception*. Translated by Oliver Davis. London: Routledge, 2004.

Pachirat, Timothy. *Every Twelve Seconds: Industrialized Slaughter and the Politics of Sight*. New Haven, CT: Yale University Press, 2013.

Pachirat, Timothy. 'Sanctuary'. In *Critical Terms for Animal Studies*, edited by Lori Gruen, 337–55. Chicago, IL: University of Chicago Press, 2018.

Patterson, Charles. *Treblinka: Eternal Treblinka: Our Treatment of Animals and the Holocaust*. New York: Lantern Books, 2001.

Wadiwel, Dinesh. *Animals and Capital*. Edinburgh: Edinburgh University Press, 2023.

Wadiwel, Dinesh. 'Animal Friendship as a Way of Life: Sexuality, Petting and Interspecies Companionship'. In *Foucault and Animals*, edited by Matthew Chrulew and Dinesh Wadiwel, 286–316. Leyden: Brill, 2017.

Wadiwel, Dinesh. 'Counter-Conduct and Truth'. In *Philosophy and the Politics of Animal Liberation*, edited by Paola Cavalieri, 187–237, Basingstoke: Palgrave Macmillan, 2016.

Wadiwel, Dinesh. *The War against Animals*. Leiden: Brill, 2015.

Weisberg, Zipporah. 'Reinventing Left Humanism: Towards an Interspecies Emancipatory Project'. In *Ethical and Political Approaches to Nonhuman Animal Issues*, edited by Andrew Woodhall and Gabriel Garmendia da Trindade, 121–48. Basingstoke: Palgrave Macmillan, 2017.

Wolfe, Cary. *Before the Law: Humans and Other Animals in a Biopolitical Frame*. Chicago, IL: The University of Chicago Press, 2012.

12 Animal Magnetism: (Bio)Political Theologies Between the Creature and the Animal
Diego Rossello[1]

I would suggest that [...] the real precursors to the physician's mesmeric body and hands were not some generic 'healers of old' but rather the French and English monarchs, whose bodies were for centuries thought to be endowed with the 'royal touch', the capacity to heal particular illnesses [...] by the laying on of hands.

Eric Santner, The Royal Remains: The People's Two Bodies
and the Endgames of Sovereignty

To be sure, the moment did come – probably in 1789 – when Louis XVI had to give up exercising the miraculous gift, along with everything else reminiscent of divine right. [...] The royal miracle would seem to have died, along with belief in monarchy.

Marc Bloch, The Royal Touch: Monarchy and Miracles
in France and England

Mesmerism aroused enormous interest during the pre-revolutionary decade; and although it originally had no relevance whatsoever to politics, it became, in the hands of radical mesmerists like Nicolas Bergasse and Jacques-Pierre Brissot, a camouflaged political theory very much like Rousseau's.

Robert Darnton, Mesmerism and the End of the
Enlightenment in France

Introduction

In the last few decades political theology has become a vibrant field of studies with a widening scope of analysis. In the already classic work by Carl Schmitt, political theology is circumscribed to the relation between the divine and the human polity, in particular to the link between theology and the juridical foundations of the sovereign state.[2] Such a link is made clear in the famous analogy between the miracle in theology and sovereign decision on the exception. It is hardly noticed, however, that Schmitt's political theology remains committed to a political community circumscribed to the human being alone, or the *civitas humana*, as he calls it.[3] As an author influenced by the Catholic tradition, Schmitt's decisionism invests in securing the political community as an exclusively human realm: 'to be human remains, nonetheless, a decision', he writes in a script for a radio broadcast.[4] Some theorists call this way of approaching humanity and sovereign authority 'anthropocentric sovereignty' – that is, human beings alone can be sovereign, as neither God nor nature can do so in modernity.[5] But anthropocentric sovereignty is no longer common-sense in the Anthropocene, since non-human animals and nature are seen as making claims of entry into the political community.[6] Moreover, some authors suggest that nonhuman animals should be granted sovereignty over the territories that they inhabit.[7]

This chapter explores alternative approaches to political theology by drawing on Eric Santner and Jacques Derrida as points of departure, to arrive at the work by Kari Weil and Jane Bennett. In their works, Schmitt's decision to be human does not take place, leaving ample conceptual room for the creature, the animal and other nonhuman beings to take centre stage.[8] In particular, the chapter contrasts Santner's exploration of the pressures of sovereignty over life, which render human beings creaturely, and Derrida's investigation of the role played by animal figurations in the philosophical foundations of sovereign authority. Accordingly, the chapter suggests that 'animal magnetism' can be conceived as a fruitful point of intersection between Santner's creature and Derrida's animal for rethinking political theology in the Anthropocene. It will be argued that Santner discusses the mesmeric fluid of animal magnetism when tracking modes of vibrancy and animacy in creaturely life and yet resists assimilating the creature to the animal and animality. Derrida, in turn, construes a thorough and compelling inventory of animal figurations in the canon of political theory, from Machiavelli's centaur to Hobbes's wolf, but does not discuss 'animal magnetism' as an alternative political theory akin to democratic revolutions. Thus, both Santner and Derrida remain inattentive to crucial conceptual implications of their own takes on animality in the political theology of sovereignty. Building on the discussion of Santner and Derrida, I draw on Kari Weil's recent work on animal magnetism and Jane Bennett's work on new materialism, to develop a sketch of an alternative (bio)political theology for the Anthropocene.

The chapter proceeds as follows. The first section reviews contemporary alternative approaches to political theology that pay attention to nonhuman forms of life. It is claimed that contemporary political theologies show interest in different forms of biological life, in particular in the life of nonhuman animals; the animality of human beings; and nature in general, at a new planetary scale. Section two highlights Santner's and Derrida's contribution to the alternative approaches reviewed in the prior section. In particular, it will be argued that, although Santner and Derrida are interested in liminal figures such as the creature and the animal, they remain inattentive to 'animal magnetism' as an alternative (bio)political theology in, and for, the Anthropocene. In section three I draw on the work by Kari Weil and Jane Bennett to show how 'animal magnetism' can provide a novel (bio)political theology attuned to the challenges posed by the *condition* of the Anthropocene – as called by William Connolly.[9]

Towards a New Planetary Scale: (Political) Theology Beyond the Human

We shall begin by exploring alternative (bio)political theologies in the vibrant field of studies dubbed as political theology. As it was anticipated above, recent work in political theology moves towards a more-than-human scale. For some authors, such a scale includes nonhuman animals, in others the animality of the human being and in yet others the planetary scale is introduced. From my perspective, these approaches show a trend in political theology that is consistent with the Anthropocene, namely, with a new geological epoch that marks the impact of human beings on Earth and collapses the distinction between human history and natural history, questioning Schmitt's exclusive focus on the *civitas humana*.

For example, for quite some time now several authors have been exploring the possibility of an animal theology that could secure respect and protection to nonhuman animals. At a distance from mainstream approaches both to animal rights theory and political theology, Oxford-based theologian Andrew Linzey found unexplored resources in the Christian tradition to go beyond the 'dogma of humanism', as he calls it. In his defence of animal rights and vegetarianism, he writes:

I defend the world-transforming designs of the Deity I see revealed in Jesus Christ, and also suggest that the urge to behave 'unnaturaly' in respect of our carnivorous habits can be a sign of grace. Living without killing sentients wherever possible is a theological duty upon Christians who wish to approximate the peaceful kingdom.[10]

Moreover, recent approaches to political theology have been interrogating the status of human beings' own animality. Theologian Eric Daryl Meyer theorises what he calls 'inner animalities', namely, the animality of the human being in the theological tradition. This is an important issue given the tendency, present not only in Christian theologies but also in critical theory, to dismiss the animality of the human, and to exercise consistent pressure to tame it.[11] After an instructive discussion of the notions of sin, redemption, the *imago Dei* doctrine, as well as of eschatology and theological anthropology, Meyer concludes that:

> The distinction between human animality and humanity proper is a conceptual knot that generates, justifies, and perpetuates anthropogenic ecological degradation. This internal distinction produces a categorical distinction between human beings on the one hand and all other animals on the other. When all living creatures are divided into these two categories, the whole natural world [...] is lumped in with the animal side, while the home, the town, and the city are conceptually hived off from the 'natural' world and become the proper space of humanity.[12]

In addition to political theologies that discuss the animal and human being's animality, the work by theologian Catherine Keller is conceived at a new planetary scale. The condition of the Anthropocene brought about by climate change, pollution and the loss of biodiversity requires what Keller calls a political theology of the Earth.[13] After the end of globalisation, and of the idea of Globe associated to it, a new scale of thought is required to grapple with our shared planetary condition.[14] Thus, Keller's discussion of the theological notion of apocalypse to account for the perils of climate change should be conceived less as a sign of a bold millenarianism, and more as a revealing or disclosure (*apo-kalypsis*) of the fragility of our contemporary condition.[15] As we shall seek to show in section 3, animal magnetism may provide an alternative account of fluidity and interconnectedness attuned to the challenges posed by climate change, as well as to the Anthropocene as our novel condition. But before delving into the potential of 'animal magnetism' for rethinking the Anthropocene, we may profit from locating the animal within the still predominant political theology of anthropocentric sovereignty.

Beyond Anthropocentric Sovereignty: Political Theology Between the Creature and the Animal

As was anticipated above, both Santner's and Derrida's contributions to political theology are at a distance from Schmitt's anthropocentric sovereignty. In their works, the political theology of sovereignty remains co-implicated with the animal, and therefore Schmitt's decision for a *civitas humana* remains deferred or suspended. But although both Santner and Derrida are interested in animality, the former relies on the figure of the creature, and of creaturely life, to account for the pressures that modern sovereignty exercises over human life. Derrida, in turn, focuses on how animals are placed under human sovereignty since Genesis, as well as on how the canon of political thought is inhabited by a vast inventory of beastly figurations. In addition, both Santner and Derrida discuss spectrality in the political theology of sovereignty. However, if Santner conceptualises spectrality as a kind of ectoplasm of social and vibrant flesh that 'fattens' the political, Derrida discusses sovereignty as haunted by a beast, specifically by a wolf that is never fully present, and whose menacing spectrality is key for sovereignty's task and legitimation. Thus, as we shall see, although Santner's and Derrida's approaches to political theology are close, they also differ in ways worthy of further examination.

Derrida: from Negative Zootheology to Genelycology

In his 1997 Cerisy-la-Salle conference, published as a book with the title *The Animal that Therefore I Am*, Derrida discusses extensively the question of the animal from the perspective of deconstruction.[16] In the book's initial pages, Derrida goes to the core of anthropocentric sovereignty by focusing on the scene in Genesis where Adam is invited by God to name the animals. According to Derrida, this scene in Genesis reveals the Biblical origins of human sovereignty over nonhuman animals and nature. Derrida writes:

> More precisely, he [God] has created man in his likeness *so that* man will *subject, tame, dominate, train,* or *domesticate* the animals born before him and assert his authority over them. God destines the animals to an experience of the power of man, *in order to see* the power of man in action, in order to see the power of man at work, in order to see man take power over all the other living beings.[17]

By questioning Adamic sovereignty Derrida dislodges a vast tradition of political thought that conceives Adam as the first and only creation in the image of God (*imago Dei* doctrine), deriving from this the grounds of human sovereign power – a tradition that extends well into the seventeenth century in works such as Robert Filmer's *Patriarcha*. But Derrida also puts pressure on the biblical scene of human (male) domination over animals by staging the undoing of human sovereignty in a domestic, quotidian, setting. Derrida stages an encounter between a curious, domestic, female cat and a naked philosopher after taking a shower. The domestic encounter with the cat becomes a re-writing of the scene of Adam in Genesis, as Derrida never names the cat, and fails to be the head of the *domus* – or domestic household. Instead, the philosopher is called into question by the gaze of an animal and falls into a descending spiral of shame: shame of being ashamed in front of a creature that cannot distinguish the clothed from the naked. In the process of addressing the figure of the cat, Derrida speculates briefly, almost in passing, about the possibility of a 'negative zootheology'. Derrida writes:

> I must immediately make it clear, the cat I am talking about is a real cat, truly, believe me, *a little cat*. It isn't the *figure* of a cat. It doesn't silently enter the bedroom as an allegory for all the cats on the earth, the felines that traverse our myths and religions, literature and fables. There are so many of them. The cat I am talking about does not belong to Kafka's vast zoopoetics, something that nevertheless merits concern and attention here, endlessly and from a novel perspective. Nor is the cat that looks at, concerning me, and to which I seem – but don't count on it – to be dedicating a negative zootheology.[18]

Derrida does not come back to 'negative zootheology' in the book, but in many ways the idea is performed in the text as a whole. The conceptual status of the domestic cat in the text is akin to negative theology in two main ways: Derrida refuses to perform the Adamic sovereign practice of naming, and therefore does not name the cat; Derrida underscores the reality of the cat by emptying it out from any rhetorical, figural, allegorical or literary signification – while at the same time obliquely engaging in all of the above. In this sense, the conceptual moves in the text resemble negative theology as conceived by Meister Eckhart, namely, a theology based on the idea of an unnameable God who invites naming and signification but at the same time removes itself from naming and signification altogether. As we shall see, this co-implication between the animal – the unnamed cat – and God – the unnameable God – returns in the 2001–03 seminar *The Beast and the Sovereign* (hereafter TBS), when Derrida explores the role played by God and the animal in Hobbes's theory of sovereignty.

In volume 1 of TBS, Derrida's approach departs from the negative zootheology sketched in the 1997 conference. In TBS Derrida also focuses on the animal, but in this case he attempts what he calls 'a sort of taxonomy of the animal figurations of the political, notably from the point of view of sovereignty (always outside the law: above the laws)'.[19] This taxonomical account of animal figurations of the political is later in the seminar reframed as a genelycology, namely, as a genealogical account of animal figurations in the canon of political theory, with a special focus on the wolf and the lupine. Derrida writes: 'A geneycology that must inscribe in its tree, its genealogical tree, what is called the lycanthrope, the wolf-man, man-made wolf or wolf made man'.[20] As I anticipated above, Hobbes's theory of sovereignty, based on the idea of a contract, becomes part of what is interrogated in, and by, Derrida's idiosyncratic genealogical approach with a focus on the animal.

As it is well known, Hobbes argues that individuals in the anarchic and violent state of nature make a contract between them to create a sovereign authority that could provide order and security. In his original reading of Hobbes, Derrida focuses not so much on the pacifying effect of sovereign authority but on the 'ontological space' of humanity created by the limits of the contract. According to Derrida, the contract not only provides a model for the transference of rights presupposed in the creation of sovereign power but is construed upon the exclusion of two specific potential contractors: God and the animal. Hobbes argues that all contracts made by God with humans are to be found in the scriptures alone, and therefore no one who claims to have made a contract with God is to be believed. At the same time, Hobbes suggests that contracts cannot be made with beasts as they cannot express in a meaningful manner their agreement or consent. This double exclusion from 'below' and from 'above' humanity fuels the leitmotif repeated by Derrida throughout the Seminar: *la bête est le souverain* – a homophony between the beast *and* (*et*) the sovereign, and the beast *is* (*est*) the sovereign, playfully iterated throughout the text. As Derrida underscores, both the beast and the sovereign occupy a similar place regarding the law: they are both placed outside the law as delineated by the Hobbesian contract.

Despite the change of approach from negative zootheology in *The Animal that Therefore I Am* to genelycology in TBS, in both cases Derrida seems to be testing the boundaries of what the tradition of philosophy and political philosophy has allowed itself to claim about the animal. At times the register becomes taxonomical, as Derrida himself suggests, and at times the purpose is to problematise the human–animal divide in order to affirmatively pluralise the limit: 'by making it increase and multiply'. Derrida writes:

Limitrophy is therefore my subject. Not just because it will concern what sprouts or grows at the limit, around the limit, by maintaining the limit, but also what *feeds the limit*, generates it, raises it, and complicates it. Everything I'll say will consist, certainly not in effacing the limit, but in multiplying its figures, in complicating, thickening, delinearizing, folding, and dividing the line precisely by making it increase and multiply.[21]

Interestingly, the question of animal magnetism does not come under Derrida's attention in his interrogation of the link between the beast and the sovereign. Even if in TBS Derrida discusses extensively the figure of the werewolf in Jean-Jacques Rousseau and approaches the horizon of ideas leading to the French Revolution, he does not dwell on animal magnetism, a cluster of ideas that historian Robert Darnton calls 'a camouflaged political theory very much like Rousseau's'.[22] Derrida approaches the question of the animal during the French Revolution mainly through the issue of animal menageries, when revolutionaries decide to finish with royal menageries as a form of 'Asiatic' luxury, to transition towards popular, state-run, menageries that originate the modern zoo: a site conceived by the revolutionary imaginary as contributing to the cultivation of natural history, physiology and scientific research.[23]

Santner: From Creaturely Life to the Science of the Flesh – via Animal Magnetism

Like Derrida, Santner is also interested in the link between animality and sovereign authority. In his book *On Creaturely Life*, Santner tackles the state of exception, where the sovereign makes the paradoxical decision to suspend the law in order to enforce it, leaving citizens in a zone of indistinction neither inside nor outside the legal order. Santner reworks the primal scene of the state of exception in a way that emphasises the traumatic, and at the same time ex-citing, kernel generated by the 'threshold of law and nonlaw'.[24] If Schmitt sees in this threshold the possibility of reinforcing the law, and Agamben the generation of *homines sacri* (i.e., lives that can be killed committing neither sacrifice nor homicide), Santner tracks the agitations provoked by the topological torsions of law – an inside that is also an outside, an inclusion that excludes. Exposure to this threshold is ex-citing, according to Santner, since the subject is cited outside itself in a traumatic but also disturbingly 'creative' fashion. The traumatic ex-citation of law is called by Santner 'sovereign *jouissance*',[25] and its product is creaturely life: a life at the threshold between humanity and animality that is seduced, agitated and captivated by the enigmatic messages of the law. The life of Joseph K., Kafka's main character in *The Trial*, who dies 'like a dog', is for Santner an exemplar of the captivating ex-citation provoked by law's disturbing enigma.[26]

Santner continues to interrogate the political theology of sovereignty in *The Royal Remains: The People's Two Bodies and the Endgames of Sovereignty*. In this book, Santner's approach to the political theology of modern sovereignty is based on tracking the displacement of an excess in the shift from monarchy by divine right to popular sovereignty after democratic revolutions. In order to both conceive and track such excess, Santner draws on Ernst Kantorowicz's account of the political theology of the king's two bodies. As it is well known, according to Kantorowicz the political theology of monarchy – as laid out by medieval jurist Edmund Plowden – relies on the existence of two kingly bodies: a natural body, subject to aging, illness and decay, and a spectral, incorporeal body, removed from the limitations of natural/organic life. It should be noted that Santner does not merely draw on the argument on the king's two bodies, itself inspired by a neo-Kantian approach akin to Ernst Cassirer's *The Myth of the State*, but offers a strong reading of Kantorowicz's thesis instead. A neo-Kantian reading of Kantorowicz's thesis could argue that the double body of the king is part of the fictive aspect of monarchy and that understanding such fiction can help us both dissect and disenchant the symbolic allure of monarchical sovereignty. Disenchantment seems to be the comfort zone of theories of secularisation that include other neo-Kantians such as Max Weber, but also political philosophers interested in political theology with an emphasis on lack, such as Claude Lefort's idea of the empty space of power.

Contrary to narratives of disenchantment and lack, Santner emphasises immanence and excess. From Santner's perspective, the second body of the king becomes available or excarnated after democratic revolutions, generating an excess of somatic, vibrant, materiality that constitutes the flesh of the political. According to Santner, the quasi-scientific theory put forward by German physician Franz Anton Mesmer, often referred to as 'mesmerism', stands for a new (bio)political theology akin to democratic revolutions. Santner writes:

> With mesmerism we find ourselves at that point of transition we have been exploring throughout this study at which a new set of theories, practices, and concepts are put to work to locate and manage the vicissitudes of the flesh at a crucial juncture in the political theology of sovereignty. That is, the mesmeric fluid represents not so much a pseudoscientific condensation of the multiple invisible forces of nature; it functions rather as one of the names of the flesh at the point at which the matter and charisma of the King's sublime body [. . .] becomes dispersed into the new locus of sovereignty, the people.[27]

Interestingly, Santner assumes that the redistribution or dispersion of the king's sublime body into the people, the new bearer of sovereignty, is circumscribed to human beings alone. However, as we have suggested above, recent developments in animal rights theory not only claim citizenship for domestic animals but also territorial rights or sovereignty for wild animals.[28] Thus, although Santner is not interested in animal studies in general, or in animal rights theory in particular, he conceives the link between animality and mesmerism as having elective affinities with democracy. In this context, the animal reappears in his thought with the vibrancy required by a philosophy of immanence, but without the trappings of creaturely life. In the following paragraph what is charged, ex-citing, magnetic, is the animal itself. According to Santner, after the king loses his head, 'the principle of his rule has been excarnated'[29] and therefore:

> It is the substance of this [kingly] responsibility that now circulates in the social space, not as the supernatural aura surrounding a few crowned heads [. . .] but rather under a series of new and in some sense more 'democratic' names, among them 'animal magnetism' and 'mesmeric fluid'.[30]

Interestingly, animal magnetism is identified by Santner with novel democratic ways of naming the excarnated, sublime, body of the king. Thus, although Santner gestures towards the democratic potential of animal magnetism as dealing with 'a universal fluid in which we all ostensibly bathe',[31] he conceptualises this fluid as a type of flesh in need of a new science akin, on the one hand, to Michel Foucault's idea of biopolitics and, on the other, to Freud's 'psychoanalysis qua "philosophy of the flesh"'.[32] This way of conceptualising mesmerism, as well as Santner's consistency in dismissing animal studies,[33] constrains his position to a very species-specific one and makes his argument inattentive to the possibilities of animal magnetism as an alternative political theology for the Anthropocene.

Animal Magnetism: A (Bio)Political Theology for the Anthropocene?

In her recent work, Kari Weil explores the concept of animal magnetism for rethinking the Anthropocene. Considering her prior work on animal studies, it is not surprising that she focuses on further implications of animality in mesmerism for thinking about our contemporary condition. Weil argues that eighteenth-century German physician Anton Mesmer drew on an idiosyncratic understanding of the force of gravitation over bodies, and extended it to similar forces in fluids surrounding humans and animals. Mesmer first called his therapeutic approach 'animal gravitation', Weil suggests, to later shift to the term 'animal magnetism'.[34] According to Weil in her book *Precarious Partners*, Mesmer's main thesis is the existence of

> a magnetic, if unseen, fluid whose flow within and between bodies was vital for health. Its blockage was said to be the cause of a range of physical and emotional ills that could be cured by 'magnetic passes' by hands held near the locus of injury and believed to transmit energy to unblock the fluid, bringing the body back to health and into harmony with nature and even the cosmos.[35]

The idea of bringing human bodies into harmony with nature and the cosmos is an aspiration of mesmerism that Weil finds promising in times of climate change and the risk of a sixth extinction. Thus, Weil's insights respond to our quest for novel ways of conceptualising the human place in nature and the cosmos so as to avoid disrupting the balance of nature and collapsing the very Earth we call home. Since the challenge posed by the Anthropocene is massive, drawing on unusual or unexpected conceptual resources such as animal magnetism may not be so far-fetched. In a recent paper, Weil links animal magnetism with animal studies and with current theoretical forms of ecocriticism. She writes:

> It is in his understanding of a body's embeddedness in the forces and flows that surround it and of the body's ability to affect and to be affected by them – both negatively and positively – that Mesmer can be seen as a precursor to current ecocritical thinking and to acknowledging the alternative meanings or logos to which our fundamental animality may be attuned.[36]

Moreover, Weil finds that the mesmeric fluids surrounding human and non-human bodies have evident affinities with recent innovative conceptual approaches in the critical environmental humanities – in particular with new materialism. Although she is not invested in an alternative political theology for the Anthropocene, Weil finds in animal magnetism conceptual resources for thinking fluidity, affect and contagion. She reminds us how influential mesmeric insights were on later developments in the field of mass psychology, where 'irrational' affects were thought to chaotically circulate, contaminate and ultimately override individual rational judgment to construe a herd-like mass. But Weil departs from the cultural pessimism predominant in the tradition of mass psychology – from Gustav Le Bon to Sigmund Freud – to invest in the potential of fluidity and contagiousness regarding more constructive affects such as sympathy. Reading the work by Jane Bennett, one of the most prominent thinkers of new materialism, Weil explores sympathy's potentiality for contagion, considering that such an affect could bring humans, animals and nature together.

But Weil focuses her discussion on a 2014 chapter by Bennett whose ideas are further elaborated in her latest book *Influx and Efflux: Writing Up with Walt Whitman*, published in 2020.[37] In the book, the reader can still appreciate Bennett's commitment to approaches and orientations she developed in prior works, such as the link between eco-criticism and re-enchantment; the potentiality of non-linear forms of causality; the possibility of emerging properties in and of systems, as well as the idea of assemblages that become more than, and qualitatively different from, the sum of their parts. But in this particular book the accent is placed on what can be called 'fluence', namely, on a distinctive form of causation that is neither internal nor external and that is only partially grasped by the notion of *influence*. Bennett develops the notion of influence by discussing the works of Henry David Thoreau and Walt Whitman but, interestingly enough, her vocabulary is not that far from Mesmer's vernacular. Bennett writes:

> Influence: a tendency for outsiders to ooze, drift, seep, incur across the perimeter of insiders; the propensity to cross over an edge; to cause to flow in; to infuse, inspire, or instill [. . .]. Thoreau wades deep into the great river of natural influence – into what he also calls the 'circulation of vitality beyond our bodies'. We will follow him as he is impressed by, digests, and decants that vitality.[38]

However, the affinities between Bennett and mesmerism do not occur only at the level of vocabulary. Bennett invokes Mesmer's work in a few revealing passages in the book. Some of these references are linked to Whitman's understanding of sympathy; others are concerned with Thoreau's own interest in 'mesmeric influence' in relation to the experience of nature. Like Weil, Bennett is invested in the potential of mesmerism to explain the contagion of sympathy, but in the book Bennett refers to sympathy as a 'more than human atmospheric force',[39] and sees Whitman as particularly attuned to it. According to Bennet, in Whitman this atmospheric or gravitational fluence does not express an ontological preference for the human. She writes:

> The current of sympathy connecting 'Nature' to human beings does not discriminate [. . .]. Whitman flirts with the idea of a sympathy *so* impartial

that, akin to gravity, it exhibits not even an anthropocentric preference. In this limit-concept, sympathy departs not only from moral sentimentalism but also starts to break free from the providentialism of American transcendentalism.[40]

Bennett's conceptualisation of sympathy goes beyond the tradition of Scottish moral sentimentalism – Hutcheson, Hume, Adam Smith – and resonates with the origins of mesmerism considered as 'animal gravitation'. Moreover, Bennett sees Whitman as breaking free from the, so to say, political theology of American transcendentalism. But affinities between Bennett's approach to influence and mesmerism become even more evident in her reading of Thoreau. Thoreau himself resorts to mesmerism to describe his own peculiar encounters with nonhuman forms of life. Bennett quotes and comments on the following revealing journal entry by Thoreau, of April 1852:

> As I turned round the corner of Hubbard's Grove, saw a woodchuck [. . .] in the middle of the field [. . .]. When I was only a rod and a half off, he stopped, and I did the same [. . .]. We sat looking at one another about half an hour, till we began to feel mesmeric influences [. . .]. I walked round him, he turned as fast and fronted me still. I sat down by his side within a foot. I talked to him quasi forest lingo.[41]

In this adorable encounter with a woodchuck we can feel sympathy flowing across the human–animal divide, even as an undercurrent of connection and communication. Drawing on Bennett, it is not hard to describe this scene as one of mutual *influence* in the midst of the forest. It is difficult not to superimpose this encounter with Derrida's encounter with a domestic cat that looks at him. The difference lies not only in the setting where the encounter takes place, the domestic space versus the forest, but also in the way Thoreau engages with language in the scene: whereas Derrida invites a 'negative zootheological' interpretation of the scene by not naming the cat, Thoreau engages not only in an exchange of gazes – just like Derrida does – but mostly in an idiosyncratic chat or conversation in a language that is not precisely human; it is the language offered by, and predominant in, the space where the encounter takes place – a kind of 'forest lingo'.

Before concluding, let me underscore that neither Weil nor Bennett seem to be particularly invested in thinking a (bio)political theology for the Anthropocene. They both draw on affect, contagion and mesmeric influences to foster and cultivate a certain kind of connecting vibrancy with the potential of bringing humans, animals and nature together. And in both cases 'animal magnetism' features prominently as a kind of hybrid approach, neither fully 'scientific' nor fully 'metaphysic' but also deeply embedded in the momentum of democratic revolutions. In the final section I will suggest that 'animal magnetism' can be conceived as a peculiar, although overlooked, (bio)political theology encrypted in the process leading to one of the most influential democratic breakthroughs in history. Perhaps 'animal magnetism' is part of the unrecognised democratic imaginary, a kind of – non-Christian, but also nonevidently Judaic – political theology of democracy, that is still waiting and available to be explored and developed in and for the Anthropocene.

A Few Final Thoughts

Animal magnetism or mesmerism was an idiosyncratic collection of ideas about animal gravitation; invisible but active atmospheric fluids; disruptive therapeutic practices involving hand passes and a kind of underground political theory rivalling monarchy, that reached a peak in France right before the French Revolution but whose legacy remains vibrant. Although Mesmer's theories were dismissed by the scientific standards of the time, as well as by state institutions that enacted such standards, the truth of 'animal magnetism' may reside not so much on its 'scientific' claims but, as Santner cogently argues, on its grasp of the theologico-political mutations provoked by the shift from monarchy by divine right to popular sovereignty. Thus, by relaxing the hierarchy of political representation that went downwards from God to the king by divine right, animal magnetism made available an alternative, enchanted, yet not hierarchical, form of connecting life among humans and across the human–animal divide. From my perspective, this is the reason why Weil and Bennet reintroduce mesmerism for ecocriticism and vital materialism, as they both see the potential of a nontranscendentalist, immanent, (bio)political theology that makes vibrant fluences intelligible and sympathy contagious. In sum, it seems that animal magnetism was always-already an enchanted, horizontal, and popular political theology made available by, and akin to, democratic revolutions. Its legacy, however, became thwarted and misunderstood by one-sided narratives of secularisation, disenchantment and so-called objective scientism. In this context, reclaiming animal magnetism from the dustbin of history could be a promising way of rethinking the links that continue to bind different forms of life together under the condition of the Anthropocene.

Notes

1. The author wishes to acknowledge the financial support of FONDECYT Regular Project 1220403, Chilean National Agency for Research and Development (ANID), Chile.
2. Carl Schmitt, *Political Theology: Four Chapters on the Concept of Sovereignty* (Chicago, IL: University of Chicago Press, 2006).
3. Carl Schmitt, *Roman Catholicism and Political Form* (Westport, CT: Greenwood Press, 1996).
4. Carl Schmitt, *Dialogues on Power and Space* (Cambridge: Polity, 2015), 31. For a discussion of the implications of such phrase for understanding the link between sovereignty and humanism see Diego Rossello, '"To be Human Remains, Nonetheless, a Decision": Humanism as Decisionism in Contemporary Critical Political Theory', *Contemporary Political Theory* 16, no. 4 (2017): 439–58.
5. Alex Wendt and Raymond Duvall, 'Sovereignty and the UFO', *Political Theory* 36, no. 4 (2008): 607–33.
6. On the rights of nature see Paola Villavicencia and Louis J. Kotzé, 'Living in Harmony with Nature? A Critical Appraisal of the Rights of Mother Earth in Bolivia', *Transnational Environmental Law* 7, no. 3 (2018): 397–424; Craig M. Kauffman and Pamela L. Martin, 'Constructing Rights of Nature Norms in the US, Ecuador, and New Zealand', *Global Environmental Politics* 18, no. 4 (2018): 43–62.
7. On animal sovereignty see Robert Goodin, Carole Pateman and Roy Pateman, 'Simian Sovereignty', *Political Theory* 25, no. 6 (1997): 821–49; Sue Donaldson and Will Kymlicka, *Zoopolis: A Political Theory of Animal Rights* (Oxford: Oxford University Press, 2011).
8. Eric Santner, *On Creaturely Life: Rilke, Benjamin, Sebald* (Chicago, IL: Chicago University Press, 2006); *The Royal Remains: The People's Two Bodies and the Endgames of Sovereignty* (Chicago, IL: Chicago University Press, 2011); Jacques Derrida, *The Animal that Therefore I Am* (New York: Fordham University Press, 2008); *The Beast and the Sovereign. Volume 1* (Chicago, IL: University of Chicago Press, 2009); Kari Weil, *Precarious Partners: Horses and their Humans in Nineteenth Century France* (Chicago, IL: University of Chicago Press, 2020); Jane Bennett, *Vibrant Matter: A Political Ecology of Things* (Durham, NC: Duke University Press, 2010); *Influx and Efflux: Writing Up with Walt Whitman* (Durham, NC: Duke University Press, 2020).
9. William Connolly, 'Bodies, Microbes and the Planetary', *Theory & Event* 21, no. 4 (2018): 962–7.
10. Andrew Linzey, *Animal Theology* (Urbana, Chicago & Springfield: University of Illinois Press, 1995), 76.

11. Diego Rossello, 'All in the (Human) Family? Species Aristocratism in the Return of Human Dignity', *Political Theory* 45, no. 6 (2017): 749–71.
12. Eric Daryl Meyer, *Inner Animalities: Theology and the End of the Human* (New York: Fordham University Press, 2018), 174.
13. Katherine Keller, *Political Theology of the Earth: Our Planetary Emergency and the Struggle for a New Public* (New York: Columbia University Press, 2018).
14. William Connolly, *Facing the Planetary: Entangled Humanism and the Politics of Swarming* (Durham, NC: Duke University Press, 2017); Bruno Latour, *Facing Gaia: Eight Lectures on the Climate Regime* (Cambridge: Polity Press, 2017); Dipesh Chakrabarty, *The Climate of History in a Planetary Age* (Chicago, IL: The University of Chicago Press, 2021).
15. Katherine Keller, *Cloud of the Impossible: Negative Theology and Planetary Entanglement* (New York: Columbia University Press, 2015), 311–16.
16. Jacques Derrida, *The Animal that Therefore I Am.*
17. Derrida, *The Animal*, 16, emphases in the original.
18. Derrida, *The Animal*, 6.
19. Jacques Derrida, *The Beast and the Sovereign. Vol. 1*, 14.
20. Derrida, *The Beast*, 64.
21. Derrida, *The Animal*, 29.
22. Robert Darnton, *Mesmerism and the End of the Enlightenment in France* (Cambridge, MA: Harvard University Press, 1968), 3.
23. Jacques Derrida, *The Beast*, 394.
24. Santner, *On Creaturely*, 15.
25. Santner, *On Creaturely*, 22–7.
26. Santner, *On Creaturely*, 22.
27. Santner, *The Royal*, 98.
28. Donaldson and Kymlicka, *Zoopolis*; Sue Donaldson, 'Animal Agora: Animal Citizens and the Democratic Challenge', *Social Theory and Practice* 46, no. 4 (October 2020): 709–35.
29. Santner, *The Royal*, 99.
30. Santner, *The Royal*, 99.
31. Santner, *The Royal*, 99.
32. Santner, *The Royal*, 99.
33. Eric Santner, *Untying Things Together: Philosophy, Literature, and a Life in Theory* (Chicago, IL: Chicago University Press, 2023), 82.
34. Kari Weil, *Precarious Partners*, 160.
35. Weil, *Precarious Partners*, 160.
36. Kari Weil, 'Animal Magnetism as Ecocriticism for a Time of Pandemic', *Contemporary French and Francophone Studies* 25, no. 1 (2021): 133.

37. Jane Bennett, 'Of Material Sympathies, Paracelsus, and Whitman', in *Material Ecocriticism*, eds. Serenella Iovino and Serpil Oppermann (Bloomington, IN: Indiana University Press, 2014), 239–52.
38. Bennett, *Influx and Efflux*, 91.
39. Bennett, *Influx and Efflux*, 27.
40. Bennett, *Influx and Efflux*, 30.
41. Bennett, *Influx and Efflux*, 106.

Works Cited

Bennett, Jane. *Vibrant Matter: A Political Ecology of Things*. Durham, NC: Duke University Press, 2010.

Bennett, Jane. 'Of Material Sympathies, Paracelsus, and Whitman'. In *Material Ecocriticism*, edited by Serenella Iovino and Serpil Oppermann, 239–52. Bloomington, IN: Indiana University Press, 2014.

Bennett, Jane. *Influx and Efflux: Writing Up with Walt Whitman*. Durham, NC: Duke University Press, 2020.

Chakrabarty, Dipesh. *The Climate of History in a Planetary Age*. Chicago, IL: The University of Chicago Press, 2021.

Connolly, William. *Facing the Planetary: Entangled Humanism and the Politics of Swarming*. Durham, NC: Duke University Press, 2017.

Connolly, William. 'Bodies, Microbes and the Planetary'. *Theory and Event* 21, no. 4 (2018): 962–7.

Darnton, Robert. *Mesmerism and the End of the Enlightenment in France*. Cambridge, MA: Harvard University Press, 1968.

Derrida, Jacques. *The Animal that Therefore I Am*. New York: Fordham University Press, 2008.

Derrida, Jacques. *The Beast and the Sovereign. Volume 1*. Chicago, IL: University of Chicago Press, 2009.

Donaldson, Sue. 'Animal Agora: Animal Citizens and the Democratic Challenge'. *Social Theory and Practice* 46, no. 4 (October 2020): 709–35.

Donaldson, Sue, and Will Kymlicka. *Zoopolis: A Political Theory of Animal Rights*. Oxford: Oxford University Press, 2011.

Goodin, Robert, Carole Pateman and Roy Pateman. 'Simian Sovereignty'. *Political Theory* 25, no. 6 (1997): 821–49.

Kauffman, Craig M., and Pamela L. Martin. 'Constructing Rights of Nature Norms in the US, Ecuador, and New Zealand'. *Global Environmental Politics* 18, no. 4 (2018): 43–62.

Keller, Katherine. *Cloud of the Impossible: Negative Theology and Planetary Entanglement*. New York: Columbia University Press, 2015.

Keller, Katherine. *Political Theology of the Earth: Our Planetary Emergency and the Struggle for a New Public*. New York: Columbia University Press, 2018.

Latour, Bruno. *Facing Gaia: Eight Lectures on the Climate Regime*. Cambridge: Polity Press, 2017.

Linzey, Andrew. *Animal Theology*. Urbana, Chicago & Springfield: University of Illinois Press, 1995.

Meyer, Eric Daryl. *Inner Animalities: Theology and the End of the Human*. New York: Fordham University Press, 2018.

Rossello, Diego. 'All in the (Human) Family? Species Aristocratism in the Return of Human Dignity'. *Political Theory* 45, no. 6 (2017): 749–71.

Rossello, Diego. '"To be Human Remains, Nonetheless, a Decision": Humanism as Decisionism in Contemporary Critical Political Theory'. *Contemporary Political Theory* 16, no. 4 (2017): 439–58.

Santner, Eric. *On Creaturely Life: Rilke, Benjamin, Sebald*. Chicago, IL: Chicago University Press, 2006.

Santner, Eric. *The Royal Remains: The People's Two Bodies and the Endgames of Sovereignty*. Chicago, IL: Chicago University Press, 2011.

Santner, Eric. *Untying Things Together: Philosophy, Literature, and a Life in Theory*. Chicago, IL: Chicago University Press, 2023.

Schmitt, Carl. *Roman Catholicism and Political Form*. Westport, CT: Greenwood Press, 1996.

Schmitt, Carl. *Political Theology: Four Chapters on the Concept of Sovereignty*. Chicago, IL: University of Chicago Press, 2006.

Schmitt, Carl. *Dialogues on Power and Space*. Cambridge: Polity, 2015.

Villavicencia, Paola, and Louis J. Kotzé. 'Living in Harmony with Nature? A Critical Appraisal of the Rights of Mother Earth in Bolivia'. *Transnational Environmental Law* 7, no. 3 (2018): 397–424.

Weil, Kari. *Precarious Partners: Horses and their Humans in Nineteenth Century France*. Chicago, IL: University of Chicago Press, 2020.

Weil, Kari. 'Animal Magnetism as Ecocriticism for a Time of Pandemic'. *Contemporary French and Francophone Studies* 25, no. 1 (2021): 126–35.

Wendt, Alex, and Raymond Duvall. 'Sovereignty and the UFO'. *Political Theory* 36, no. 4 (2008): 607–33.

13   Creaturely Biopolitics
Carlo Salzani

There is a crack, a crack in everything
That's how the light gets in
Leonard Cohen, *Anthem*

The Crooked Timber of Humanity[1]

In the Sixth Proposition of his 1784 essay 'Idea for a Universal History with a Cosmopolitan Aim' Kant uses a famous metaphor: 'out of such crooked wood as the human being is made, nothing entirely straight can be fabricated'.[2] Here, Kant is analysing the problem of 'a civil society universally administering right', which in the Fifth Proposition he had defined as 'the greatest problem for the human species'.[3] This problem is 'the greatest' or, in the Sixth Proposition, 'the most difficult of all' precisely because the crooked timber of humanity cannot be entirely straightened, that is, the universal administering of right clashes with, and is hindered by, a 'crooked' human nature. Hence, for this problem a 'perfect solution is even impossible' and '[o]nly the approximation to this idea is laid upon us by nature'.[4] This metaphor will return nine years later in the third part of *Religion Within the Boundaries of Mere Reason*, where the idea of an ethical community is deemed as 'never fully attainable' and 'greatly restricted under the conditions of sensuous human nature': 'how could one expect to construct something completely straight from such crooked wood?'[5]

The metaphor might have a biblical origin, since two passages of *Ecclesiastes* read: 'What is crooked cannot be straightened, and what is lacking cannot be counted' (1:15) and 'Consider what God has done: Who can straighten what he has made crooked?' (7:13). It seems thus to reveal an immemorial geometry of 'rightness' that counterposes what is straight against what is crooked. This contraposition is also expressed by another, cognate image in Proposition Five of 'Idea for a Universal History with a Cosmopolitan Aim',[6] whereby Kant intends to emphasise the need for coercion in civil society, which returns with almost identical wording in a passage of Kant's courses on practical pedagogy, originally given in the 1770s and 1780s but only posthumously published in 1803 as 'Lectures on Pedagogy':

> But a tree which stands alone in the field grows crooked and spreads its branches wide. By contrast, a tree which stands in the middle of the forest grows straight towards the sun and air above it, because the trees next to it offer opposition.[7]

On the one hand, the crooked timber of humanity only allows for an asymptotic approximation to a just society ('straightness'); on the other, it is only social pressure and coercion that can and will (partially) 'straighten' this natural crookedness. A note to the Sixth Proposition importantly adds that human vocation (i.e., 'straightness') can never be fully attained by the individual, only by the species as a whole.[8]

The opposition between straightness and crookedness corresponds explicitly to the opposition between rationality and animality: 'as a rational creature', Kant writes, the human being has a vocation to rectitude, but 'his selfish animal inclination [*Neigung*]' misleads him into crooked ways. Therefore, Kant concludes, the human being 'needs a master, who breaks his stubborn will'.[9] The human being is an animal of the social kind who needs a master and a coercive social organisation in order to attain (although asymptotically and only as a species) a rational vocation to rectitude.[10] Discipline – in the philosophy of history as in the theory of education – is a necessary social technique for moulding and shaping something out of its natural, animal inclinations into straightness.[11] At the very beginning of the 'Lectures on Pedagogy', Kant writes: 'Discipline or training changes animal nature into human nature' and 'The human being can only become human through education. He is nothing except what education makes out of him'.[12] The human being, Allen Wood emphasises (glossing the definition from Kant's 1798 *Anthropology*[13]), is not therefore an *animal rationale* but rather an *animal rationabilis*, a project teleologically but asymptotically tending from animal crookedness towards rational, truly human rectitude and in continuous need of disciplining and coercion.[14]

The dichotomous opposition of straight/crooked can be read through a Foucauldian lens and fits perfectly into Foucauldian categories: it epitomises both the 'orthopaedics' of individuality as defined in *Discipline and Punish*[15] and the 'anatomo-politics of the human body' from *Society Must Be Defended*, which focus on the disciplining and straightening of the individual, and the 'biopolitics of the human race', again from *Society Must Be Defended*[16] and *The Will to Knowledge*, or the apparatuses of 'normalisation' as defined in *Security, Territory, Population*,[17] which focus instead on population and the human species in general.[18] But it can also be taken as a paradigm of a much deeper and immemorial apparatus: an apparatus of verticalisation and straightness that constructs human nature itself and its relationships with the other lifeforms within the dichotomy straight/crooked – with the consequent rejection of crookedness and animality. Our very moral lexicon has internalised this dichotomy and is constructed upon it: 'right', 'righteousness' and 'rectitude' all express the opposition to and rejection of what is bowed and crooked, of what deviates from the straight line of justice, from the 'rule' and the 'norm' (the former comes from the Latin term for 'ruler' (*regula*) and the latter from the set square to measure right angles (*norma*)). As Adriana Cavarero has shown, this geometry of straightness is far from neutral. Rather, it acts as an immemorial criterion of discipline, normalisation and exclusion.[19]

This geometry informs a powerful politics that captures and manages life through the opposition straight/crooked or what I will call the 'biopolitics of rectitude'. This politics works through exclusion, rejection, submission and normalisation and warrants, as in Kant, a coercive hold on life. This chapter will attempt to construct as a counterproposal a politics that deactivates the dichotomous opposition straight/crooked and proposes instead a politics of life that is inclusive and eludes dualisms and contrapositions. To this end I will use the category of the 'creaturely', which in recent years has gained traction in many disciplines as a way of challenging traditional, all-too anthropocentric dichotomies. Specifically, I will propose a 'creaturely biopolitics', a politics that seeks not to straighten human or nonhuman life, or reject its crookedness, but rather to celebrate and nurture its playful multiplicity of forms.

Framing and Figuring

In his influential reading of biopolitics, Cary Wolfe proposed the concept of 'frame' as the structure of rules, norms and laws that 'decides what we recognize and what we don't, what counts and what doesn't'.[20] Wolfe insists that framing is not merely a logical or epistemological problem but a social and material one, and importantly, that the line dividing the proper from the improper, the inside from the outside, is not a natural one but rather a way of framing, 'a discursive resource'.[21] We could apply this structure also to the biopolitics of rectitude and say that the Western tradition has framed straightness as what is 'proper' and what deviates from it as crooked and in need of correction, rectification or rejection. However, something else seems to be at work: the dichotomy straight/crooked orients the frame along a specific axis, it gives the framing a precise orientation, a precise figure, and is thus more a figuring than a framing, or perhaps a figuring that precedes and orients the framing. The concept of *figura* is therefore fundamental for the analysis of the biopolitics of rectitude, not least because it resonates with the biopolitics of *creatura* that will be analysed in the following sections.[22]

As we will see with *creatura*, *figura* comes from the future-active participle of the Latin verb *fingere*, which means to mould or shape, where the suffix -*ura* ('that which is about to occur') marks it with an element of plasticity and potentiality. As Eric Auerbach famously remarked, 'this peculiar formation expresses something living and dynamic, incomplete and playful' and that it is with Ovid that it took on the sense of 'changing form'.[23] It can be argued, therefore, that the vertical orientation imposed by the biopolitics of rectitude is a *figura*, not something *natural* but rather *a way of figuring*, 'a discursive resource'.[24] Though this figuring is immemorial and extremely powerful, its constitutive and ongoing openness also, importantly, implies a plasticity that allows for evolution and change. In her 'critique of rectitude', Cavarero proposes that the vertical geometry that determines Western subjectivity constitutes this immemorial figuring and is therefore an 'ontological question'. The emphasis on (ethical) rectitude reflects the vertical axis that allows the (paradigmatic Kantian) subject to balance itself and to be, consequently, free and autonomous. Autonomy is self-centeredness, it is the product of balance around an internal centre of gravity, and any inclination or deviation from the central axis entails its diminishment or loss.[25] The Western (Kantian) subject follows the individualistic ontological model of an 'egocentric verticality'.[26]

One could push Cavarero's argument further and give this figuring an 'organic', anthropogenetic twist. In two lengthy footnotes in chapter IV of *Civilization and Its Discontents*, Freud famously put forward the hypothesis of an 'organic repression' at the origin of human civilisation that is explicitly linked to the adoption of the upright posture. It is the adoption of this posture, Freud argued, that determined the cultural dominance of vision at the expense of other senses, in particular olfaction:

> The diminution of the olfactory stimuli seems itself to be a consequence of man's raising himself from the ground, of his assumption of an upright gait; this made his genitals, which were previously concealed, visible and in need of protection, and so provoked feelings of shame in him. The fateful process of civilization would thus have set in with man's adoption of an erect posture.[27]

According to Freud, 'the deepest root of the sexual repression that advances along with civilization is the organic defence of the new form of life achieved with man's erect gait against his earlier animal existence'.[28] Through the hypothesis of the 'organic repression' and the consequent feeling of shame, Freud insistently attempted to determine the origins of the moral law; the vertical geometry of this law (rectitude), we could gloss, is thus a reflection of the upright posture – it is the immemorial figuring that 'decides what we recognize and what we don't, what counts and what doesn't'. It is important to remark that this whole construction is erected 'against his earlier animal existence', that is, against animality, which in this figuring is equated, as in Kant, to all that is not straight and 'right'.

The vertical figuring is fully operative not only in conceptualisations of the human that exclude all forms that are not properly or entirely 'straight' – the 'inferior', animalised races, but also the 'not yet' or 'no longer' properly human (children, the senile, women) and the physically and mentally disabled – but also in all those ethical postures that, though attempting to extend ethical consideration to (some) nonhuman animals, still take as a paradigm the human figure as a (straight) 'norm'.[29] Ultimately, racism, ableism and anthropocentrism are all products of the same figuring and framing that take 'normal', adult (male, white) human beings as *the* figure of reference, as norm and paradigm for ethical and political consideration. This problem sometimes contaminates animal studies as well. Preference utilitarianism, animal rights theory and the capability approach are all committed to a rational, liberal tradition that revolves around the figure of the 'normal' – or rather 'normate', according to the neologism popularised by Garland-Thomson[30] – human subject as the Protagorean *homo mensura*, as measure of all things and paradigm of ethical and political conceptualisation. Dinesh Wadiwel takes Peter Singer and Tom Regan to task for their conceptualisation of animal ethics along the lines of a liberal, still all-too humanist paradigm, while Cynthia Lewiecki-Wilson makes a similar critique of Martha Nussbaum's take on disability and animality.[31]

In all these theories, the reference to the (vertical) human figure as norm inherently implies a push toward normalisation: both disability and animality are formulated in relation to regimes of normalisation and are therefore construed as lacking – and here is where they meet. As J. M. Coetzee's Elizabeth Costello puts it, in these theories, as in the whole Western tradition, the animal is treated 'as a mentally defective human being',[32] and likewise people with disabilities are downgraded to a lesser form of humanity that borders on animality.[33] Wadiwel appropriately links these conceptualisations to Foucault's theorisation of racism in *Society Must Be Defended*, which, in turn, Richard Twine expands into a 'dominant approach to difference, one which is to an extent applicable to the naturalization of gender, class, race and species hierarchy'.[34] Racism is not only what allows the (post-)sovereign to keep exercising his right to kill even in biopolitical times, but is also the paradigmatic apparatus that allows for the hierarchisation of forms of life along the lines of a species norm. The figuring and framing of the biopolitics of rectitude create hierarchies of 'normalness' that authorise and naturalise domination and coercive conformity.[35]

The Biopolitics of Vulnerability

The very term 'animal' belongs to the figuring of the biopolitics of rectitude. As we have seen in the examples of Kant and Freud, the human norm is formulated as vertical (straightness, the upright posture) and is explicitly counterposed to the animal as that which is not vertical (crooked, not upright): animal is what is not 'right'. 'Animal' belongs to the logic of a binary opposition, to a dichotomy that positions the human and the 'animal' in mutually exclusive contradistinction to each other, despite the fact that etymologically 'animal' denotes all 'animated' beings and taxonomically it also includes the human being.[36] To insist on the inclusive use of the term animal or to add further specifications ('human vs nonhuman animals') does not seem very effective: the term 'animal' is exactly what structures the figure. We need to move beyond the vocabulary of the 'animal' and its dualistic logic; we need a vocabulary of post-animality.[37]

One term in particular has emerged in the past couple of decades as a possible alternative: 'creature', or, in its adjectival form, 'creaturely'. Though it also presents a certain ambiguity and risks at times getting pulled into the binary logic of the animal (I will return to this in the next section), creature is a more inclusive and capacious term that traverses and deactivates the human–animal divide. The term originates in theology and refers to any being created by a creator. This means that all beings – including human beings – are creatures of God the Creator. This concept is not limited to theology. It traverses disciplinary boundaries and has been adopted in a number of fields, from philosophy and history to literature and film. There are 'creaturely theologies'[38] and 'creaturely cosmologies',[39] 'creatural fiction/poetics'[40] and even 'creaturely rhetorics'.[41]

The advantage of this term is, first, that, as Cora Diamond points out, it is not a biological concept (it is a theological or politico-theological one) and, when combined with 'fellow', it marks the commonality of the living that breaks with the binary logic of the animal.[42] Anat Pick adds that the term provocatively hints at a certain simultaneous animalisation of the human and humanisation of the animal, which implies a rejection of the human species norm that is still dominant in animal ethics.[43] The widespread preference for the adjective over the noun, suggest Pieter Vermeulen and Virginia Richter, further emphasises that this is a condition that does not pertain only to fully individuated beings but cuts across the very boundaries of the individual.[44]

This creaturely commonality is articulated through a series of shared features that are all related to the materiality of life and to the question of embodiment – and thus to the theological emphasis on life as gift, as something fragile and dependent on an external creative force. Pick's deployment of the concept has been very influential and can be taken as paradigmatic of a certain mode of understanding the creaturely. She defines the creaturely as 'the condition of exposure and finitude that affects all living bodies whatever they are'.[45] Exposure and finitude mark every body, human and nonhuman alike, with a sense of fragility, transience and corruption that unmasks and undermines all dreams of human exceptionality and supremacy (i.e., the autonomy of the straight subject): we are all, humans and nonhumans, material, fragile, mortal creatures. These characteristics of the creaturely fall under one overarching trait: vulnerability. Indeed, Pick declares that her whole engagement with this concept grew out of an insight by Simone Weil: 'The vulnerability of precious things is beautiful because vulnerability is a mark of existence'.[46] Vulnerability ontologically marks creaturely embodiment and exposes the body – every body – to forces that control and subject it – and thereby also twist and bend it. From this perspective, vulnerability could be the starting point for an inclusive ethics and politics.

In the past twenty years, a plethora of debates surrounding the ethics and politics of vulnerability have cut across a number of disciplines and discourses, which for reasons of scope cannot be outlined here, save for one. Cavarero's take on vulnerability, which does not stem from the discourse of the creaturely but from the perspective of political philosophy and feminism, especially as articulated by Judith Butler, is particularly interesting: the Italian philosopher defines vulnerability as a negation of the verticality of the human species norm. Vulnerability as a paradigm of subjectivity disrupts the 'myth of autonomy'[47] of the self-centred, vertical subject and consigns subjectivity to a relational ontology, an ontology where the subject is no longer balanced on a vertical axis but is rather inclined towards, exposed to, and dependent on a multiplicity of others.

It is not simply a question of correcting the traditional, individualistic ontology by inserting the category of relation into it, but, instead, of thinking of relation and inclination as originary and constitutive. Here is where Cavarero, despite her unabashed anthropocentrism, mobilises the discourse of the creaturely: we are all always vulnerable, unbalanced creatures consigned to each other. For Cavarero, inclination, not rectitude, is the fundamental concept of ethics, politics and ontology.[48]

The concept of vulnerability adds an important element to the critique of the biopolitics of rectitude, though it has also come under harsh criticism within and without the discourse of the creaturely. From early on, the emphasis on the vulnerable body has been accused of bolstering a 'culture of victimization'[49] and of focusing only on a negative, limited and limiting aspect of embodiment, on a passive conception of existential exposure and on an impoverished notion of relationality.[50] A politics of life defined by the vulnerability and injurability of the body – a biopolitics of vulnerability[51] – risks becoming what Bonnie Honig has defined as 'mortalist humanism' (or posthumanism, if we open it up to all creatures[52]), a politics determined and constrained by the looming spectre of violence, injury, cruelty and death and therefore incapable of articulating a more affirmative perspective grounded on the creative energies of life.[53] However, a different articulation of the creaturely that focuses more on its disruptive and creative potential than on its intrinsic injurability can pave the way to a different politics of life, to a positive and alternative creaturely biopolitics.

Warping the Canons of Creation

Eric Santner has elaborated a different and very influential articulation of the creaturely that inserts a biopolitical vocabulary (mostly borrowed from Agamben) into a Lacanian model of subjectivity. For Santner, the creaturely is life that is exposed to and called into being by what he names the 'excitations of power' or 'sovereign jouissance', that is, a traumatic dimension of (bio) political exposure that he associates with Agamben's theorisation of the 'state of exception'.[54] The exposure and abandonment of life to the constricting and repressive mechanisms of the state of exception, that paradoxical state where the suspension of the law is what upholds the law itself, is what makes life 'creaturely'. Contrary to Pick, Santner does not use this concept to seek a more capacious ethico-political frame that could overcome anthropocentric binaries and divisions but rather, in a somewhat 'perverse', Heideggerian way,[55] he uses the profound debasement of the creaturely to emphasise the difference between the human and nonhuman.[56] It is paradoxically the peculiar proximity to the animal in the exposure to the state of exception that marks creaturely life as specifically human, insofar as it reveals its belonging to a dimension (the political, the Lacanian *jouissance*) that is (supposedly) exclusively human: 'human beings are not just creatures among other creatures but are in some sense *more creaturely* than other creatures by virtue of an excess that is produced in the space of the political and that, paradoxically, accounts for their "humanity"'.[57]

Against this view, Pick, Wolfe and Wadiwel, among others, have convincingly argued that, within the biopolitical frame adopted by Santner, the animal constitutes an exemplary, archetypal 'state of exception' of (species) sovereignty and hence a sort of Ur-form of the exposure to the 'excitations of power'.[58] Ultimately, Santner's lingering anthropocentrism is contradictory and rather 'perverse' (though all-too common[59]). Nevertheless, Santner makes two points that are fundamental for my critique of the biopolitics of rectitude. By defining the creaturely as an excess, as what is included into the norm (the human) through its very exclusion, as an uncanny too-muchness that disrupts traditional ideals and classifications, he shows how this concept cannot be simply domesticated by traditional humanism (i.e., the biopolitics of rectitude). Moreover, in defining the creaturely as the product of the exposure to the excitations of power, he emphasises that it is not a natural dimension but instead a political – or rather biopolitical – one, the effect of a politics of life that captures and manages it through techniques and apparatuses that are historical and contingent.

As excess, the creature is in opposition to the human (as norm) and at times has been conflated into the animal (as for example in Rilke's *Duino Elegies*, where it marks the division between the human and the 'other creatures'). But the creature is not the animal, since the animal 'can be named, assigned a species, and analysed as a living organism'.[60] The creature, on the contrary, 'has no iconography of its own', its excess signifies indeterminacy and bordering, and as such it dwells in the gaps between species and taxonomies, calling classifications into question.[61] The creature in fact is also used to denote those humans who do not entirely adhere to the 'norm' and therefore do not 'fully' qualify as human, like children,[62] women (often as a term of – paternalistic – endearment) and the 'de'-formed, the 'ab'-normal, the pathological; in modern vernacular, 'creature' comes to signify also the hybrid, the amorphous, the monstrous, the unnatural. In a seminal text (an important source for Santner as for most elaborations of the creaturely), Julia Lupton writes that the term is 'increasingly applied to those created things that warp the proper canons of creation', that disturb, confound, trouble and deactivate taxonomies and classifications, that question the 'norm' and 'foil any normative reading'. '[C]aught between mud and mind, dust and dream', the creature 'measures the difference between the human and the inhuman while refusing to take up residence in either category'.[63]

As I have noted above (following Lupton), in Latin *creatura* is the future-active participle of a verb, *creare*, where the suffix *-ura*, just like in *figura*, marks a sense of continual or potential process, an openness to the possibility of future metamorphosis: 'The *creatura* is a thing always in the process of undergoing creation; the creature is actively passive or, better, *passionate*, perpetually becoming created, subject to transformation at the behest of the arbitrary commands of an Other'.[64] This inherent potentiality for change situates the creature in a permanent 'state of emergency'. Lupton's preference for 'emergency' over the Schmittian and Agambenian 'exception' intends to emphasise not exclusion but rather a continuous 'emerging', in which forms are no longer fixed and new possibilities can always arise.[65] For the norm of the biopolitics of rectitude, the creature constitutes the exception, what is rejected as an aberration (as crooked, deformed, distorted) and is thereby captured, subjugated, and controlled through its very exclusion; for a true creaturely biopolitics, it marks the state of permanent emergence that can open up dangerous and liberating possibilities. This means that, unlike the Kantian autonomous subject, the 'creature is never simply sovereign over himself, in a condition of stable autonomy in which the terms would balance each other in a just distribution'[66]: autonomy, the precious balance around a vertical axis that defines the Western subject (the human figure), is deformed and disrupted by a permanent, heterogeneous and metamorphic play of forms, inclinations and orientations by continuous creation as the very driving force of life.

Finally, the permanent emerging of the creature prevents its inclusion into stable groups and categories, into 'species': creatures are singularities that never congeal into a set, that can never be captured by the 'universal', but also refuse to stand for the 'particular', since the singularity can never be resolved into an identity (of species, race, culture, nation). In this respect, creatures are indeed exceptions, but in the sense that all singularities, all living beings are exceptions to all attempts to capture and imprison them into taxonomies and categorisations. If humans are also creatures, then all humans are exceptions to their own humanity,[67] to the human species norm that binds life to a self-centred, vertical and ultimately illusory autonomy. The liberating play of interdependent, crooked and multiform singularities can open instead the path to a form of community (never a totality) constituted by exceptions in a permanent state of creation.

Distortion and Its Self-Sublation

Pick, Santner, Lupton and many other theorists of the creaturely consistently refer to Walter Benjamin's evolving and diverse elaborations of the notion of *Kreatur* in subjects as diverse as the German Baroque Play of Mourning (*Trauerspiel*), Karl Kraus' works or Kafka's strange world. And even Cavarero (with no reference to the discourse of the creaturely) begins her critique of rectitude from an obscure 1918 fragment in which Benjamin criticises Kant's 'vertical' ethics (based on the notion of rectitude) and writes that a change of perspective (*Bedeutungswandel*) could instead turn its opposite, 'inclination' (*Neigung*), into one of the most fundamental concepts of morality.[68] Benjamin's work offers an extremely rich conceptual ground that can be mined to elaborate a positive creaturely biopolitics, and it is with a Benjaminian vignette that I also want to conclude this chapter. However, instead of elaborating further on the notion of creaturely as such, I will briefly explore one of its paradigmatic instantiations, the little hunchback, in order to flesh out its implications for a critique of the biopolitics of rectitude and a positive 'creaturely biopolitics'.

This by-now iconic figure of Benjamin's iconography comes from famous childhood rhymes that were ubiquitous in German folklore and that Benjamin encountered as a child, originally collected (and often re-invented) by the Heidelberg Romantics, Achim von Arnim and Clemens Brentano in their famous edition of folk poems and songs *Des Knaben Wunderhorn: Alte deutsche Lieder.* According to Hannah Arendt, the little hunchback looms over Benjamin's own life as a mark of Saturnian disposition and misfortune,[69] but in Benjamin's oeuvre it appears in three specific works: in his memoirs, *Berlin Childhood around 1900*, in the 1934 essay on Franz Kafka and in his very last work, the theses 'On the Concept of History'. A comprehensive analysis of this figure exceeds the scope of this chapter,[70] so to conclude my critique of the biopolitics of rectitude I will focus on one specific instance: the essay on Kafka, and more precisely the second to last section entitled 'The Little Hunchback'. In this text, Benjamin links this figure to a peculiar trait that for him characterises and defines all Kafka's characters and creatures, human and nonhuman alike: distortion (*Entstellung*). It is in the opposition between distortion and its rectification that Benjamin recapitulates the biopolitics of rectitude but also shows us a way out.

For Benjamin, Kafka's world is a distorted world. Distorted is Odradek, the strange and unidentifiable creature from the story 'The Cares of a Family Man'; distorted is the insect into which Gregor Samsa has morphed in *The Metamorphosis*; distorted is the half-lamb, half-kitten creature from 'A

Crossbreed'; and also distorted are the human characters who bow their heads down: 'the fatigue of the court officials, the noise affecting the doormen in the hotel, the low ceiling facing the visitors in the gallery'.[71] The hunched back of the little folklore figure is taken as a 'prototype of distortion' and in turn is made to link distortion to forgetfulness and guilt – as in another Kafka story, 'In the Penal Colony', where a mortiferous apparatus engraves the sentence and punishment for an unknown crime on the back of the guilty man. These are the moods and feelings that notoriously dominate Kafka's world and that have made of this world a paradigm of nightmarish modernity, where guilt, submission and exception rule. In a way, Kafkan distortion also reflects the Kantian anthropological pessimism of the 'crooked timber of humanity', which is extended here to a universal scale. However, Kafka's (and Benjamin's) response to this universal crookedness is the reversal of Kant's biopolitics of rectitude.

The motif of distortion is a classic of messianic literature: it is only as distortion, de-figuration and parody that the messianic can appear in this world. According to the tradition, the distortion will disappear with the coming of the Messiah. Benjamin explains that the little hunchback 'will disappear with the coming of the Messiah, who (a great rabbi once said) will not wish to change the world by force but will merely make a slight adjustment in it'.[72] The fundamental issue is how Benjamin envisions this disappearing. The 'slight adjustment' in German is rendered with the verb *zurechtstellen*, to rectify, to put (up)right, and it could appear therefore that for Benjamin, too, as for Kant, redemption means the straightening out of the hump, of the distortion and deformity the hunchback represents. Benjamin's strategy would therefore fully fall within the biopolitics of rectitude. In German, as in many other languages, the 'verticalisation' of justice is linguistically evident: *Recht, Gerechtigkeit, Rechtschaffenheit* express the same positioning as 'right', 'righteousness' and 'rectitude', a positioning that takes the upright posture as the 'just' figure, and Benjamin simply abides by the linguistic norm.

However, Benjamin's political strategy can be interpreted as set precisely against this 'orthopaedia of the upright posture', against bourgeois idealism celebrating the 'classical ideal of humanity'.[73] Some preparatory notes for the Kafka essay clarify this point by referring to a specific Kafkan text, the Nature Theatre of Oklahoma, the last chapter of Kafka's unfinished novel *The Missing Person* (*Der Verschollene*, formerly titled *Amerika* by Max Brod). In Kafka's novel, the peculiarity of the Nature Theater of Oklahoma is that everyone is hired by it: there are no standards for admission, 'all that is expected of the applicants is the ability to play themselves' – and this constitutes their final redemption (in Kafka's intention, the chapter would have constituted the 'happy ending' of Karl

Rossman's adventures). Nobody is excluded from this theatre of redemption, there are no exceptions, no inclusive exclusions, no normalisations, no rectifications; this universal acceptance implies, for Brendan Moran, the defying of established and complacent norms (of inclusion/exclusion).[74]

One of Benjamin's preparatory notes connects the Nature Theatre of Oklahoma to the coming of the Messiah: just as the Messiah, as the great rabbi said, will not change the world completely (*durch und durch verändere*) but only 'set it aright' (*rückt sie nur zurecht*), so also the Nature Theatre of Oklahoma 'does not change people completely. It sets them aright by letting them play' (*verändert die Menschen nicht durch und durch. Es rückt sie nur zurecht, indem es sie spielen läßt*).[75] Here the 'slight adjustment' the Messiah will bring about still has a vertical connotation (*zurecht*), but this 'uprightness' seems to be deactivated by the 'free rein' that is given to play, an activity not inclined towards verticality.

Another important preparatory note again relates play to the theme of *Entstellung* in Kafka's creatures: 'The distortion will sublate itself [*sich selber aufheben*] by making its way into redemption. This displacement of axis [*Axenverschiebung*] in redemption manifests itself in that it becomes play (the nature theatre of Oklahoma)'.[76] Here the orthopaedics of 'setting aright' disappear and are replaced by play as a 'displacement of axis', a change of perspective. In another note, quoting from Felix Bertaux's 1928 book *Panorama de la litterature allemande contemporaine*, Benjamin defines *Entsellung* itself as a '*derangement de l'axe*'.[77] Distortion and its disappearance seem to revolve around the positioning with respect to an axis, to a 'figuring'. The Hegelian *Aufhebung* does indeed lead to the disappearance of distortion, but in a dialectical movement that is at the same time also a preservation and a salvation. Moreover, this redemption is not an external imposition (a rectification, a normalisation) on a passive 'subject',[78] but rather a *self*-sublation as a mere geometrical displacement of the axis that 'will not change anything'. We could say, therefore, that the self-sublation of distortion is the change of perspective that shows the complete arbitrariness of the norm that declares something as distorted.

Distortion, crookedness, ab-normality (and, consequently, animality) are not deviations from an originary, natural, undistorted state (straightness) but rather the product of a contingent perspectival positioning, of a figuring, of a politics that captures and manages life according to apparatuses of verticality. These apparatuses imply and lead to the exclusion, rejection, submission and normalisation of what deviates from the vertical norm. In opposition to this politics, distortion as mark of the creaturely in Benjamin's Kafka deactivates exceptionality by challenging hierarchisation and exclusion – a challenge that is brought to humanity itself as construed through the biopolitics of rectitude. Through a radical change of perspective, the messianic self-sublation of distortion, of the hunched back, is the proposal of a different politics of life, a 'biopolitics of distorted life', a creaturely biopolitics that does not 'wish to change the world by force' but promises instead to end exception and exclusion.

Notes

1. I warmly thank Matthew Chrulew, Felice Cimatti, Benjamin Lewis Robinson, Diego Rossello, Kristof Vanhoutte and Zipporah Weisberg for their criticisms, comments and suggestions on early drafts of this chapter.
2. Immanuel Kant, 'Idea for a Universal History with a Cosmopolitan Aim', trans. Allen W. Wood, in *Kant's Idea for a Universal History with a Cosmopolitan Aim: A Critical Guide*, eds. Amélie Oksenberg Rorty and James Schmidt (Cambridge: Cambridge University Press, 2009), 16.
3. Kant, 'Idea for a Universal History with a Cosmopolitan Aim', 14.
4. Kant, 'Idea for a Universal History with a Cosmopolitan Aim', 16.
5. Immanuel Kant, *Religion Within the Boundaries of Mere Reason and Other Writings*, trans. Allen W. Wood and George di Giovanni (Cambridge: Cambridge University Press, 1998), 111. See Paul Guyer, 'The Crooked Timber of Mankind', in *Kant's Idea for a Universal History with a Cosmopolitan Aim: A Critical Guide*, 129–49.
6. Kant, 'Idea for a Universal History with a Cosmopolitan Aim', 15.
7. Immanuel Kant, *Anthropology, History, and Education*, eds. Günter Zöller and Robert B. Louden (Cambridge: Cambridge University Press, 2007), 443.
8. Kant, 'Idea for a Universal History with a Cosmopolitan Aim', 16.
9. Kant, 'Idea for a Universal History with a Cosmopolitan Aim', 15.
10. Despite his anthropological pessimism, Kant is not Montaigne, and the ascertaining of the crookedness of human nature does not tone down his anthropocentrism. If anything, it leads to an even stronger and more contemptuous view of debased animal nature in the name of a 'true' human (i.e., rational, ideal).
11. See David Baumgarten, 'Animality in Kant's Theory of Human Nature', in *Kant and Animals*, eds. John J. Callanan and Lucy Allais (Oxford: Oxford University Press, 2020), 105–22.
12. Kant, *Anthropology, History, and Education*, 437, 439.
13. Cf. Kant, *Anthropology, History, and Education*, 417.
14. Allen W. Wood, 'Kant and the Problem of Human Nature', in *Essays on Kant's Anthropology*, eds. Brian Jacobs and Patrick Kain (Cambridge: Cambridge University Press, 2003), 51. For 'liberal' interpreters like Isaiah Berlin, Kant's anthropological pessimism means that any search for perfection (i.e., socialist utopias) is a 'recipe for

bloodshed' (Isaiah Berlin, *The Crooked Timber of Humanity: Chapters in the History of Ideas* (Princeton, NJ: Princeton University Press, 2013)). However, it does not mean that, since human nature is crooked, then 'anything goes', as Italian journalist Giuliano Ferrara, for example, tried to argue in 2010 by twisting Kant's argument in order to defend his 'master' Silvio Berlusconi, then Italy's Prime Minister, accused of corrupting underage girls and of using his power to cover up his crimes. The acknowledgement of the crookedness of human nature does not lead to the cynical laxness of *così fan tutti*, but, on the contrary, to a stronger sanctioning and justification of discipline and duty: *du kannst, denn du sollst*.

15. Michel Foucault, *Discipline and Punish: The Birth of the Prison*, trans. Alan Sheridan (New York: Vintage, 1995), 294.
16. Michel Foucault, *Society Must Be Defended. Lectures at the Collège de France, 1975–76*, trans. David Macey (New York: Picador, 2003), 243.
17. Michel Foucault, *Security, Territory, Population. Lectures at the Collège de France 1977–78*, trans. Graham Burchell (Basingstoke: Palgrave Macmillan, 2007), especially 55–86.
18. This definition from *Society Must Be Defended* fits perfectly here: 'to say that power took possession of life in the nineteenth century, or to say that power at least takes life under its care in the nineteenth century, is to say that it has, thanks to the play of technologies of discipline on the one hand and technologies of regulation on the other, succeeded in covering the whole surface that lies between the organic and the biological, between body and population. We are, then, in a power that has taken control of both the body and life or that has, if you like, taken control of life in general – with the body as one pole and the population as the other' (253).
19. Adriana Cavarero, *Inclinations: A Critique of Rectitude*, trans. Amanda Minervini and Adam Sitze (Stanford, CA: Stanford University Press, 2016).
20. Cary Wolfe, *Before the Law: Humans and Other Animals in a Biopolitical Frame* (Chicago, IL: The University of Chicago Press, 2013), 6.
21. Wolfe, *Before the Law*, 10. Wolfe's focus is the traditional biopolitical frame that does not 'recognise' the Animal (as worthy of consideration) and thus excludes and puts 'outside the frame' their invisibilised lives.
22. I owe this insight to Benjamin Lewis Robinson.
23. Eric Auerbach, 'Figura', in *Scenes from the Drama of European Literature* (Minneapolis, MN: University of Minnesota Press, 1984), 12, 21.
24. Discussing Quintilian's 'invention' of the figure of speech, Auerbach tellingly writes that '[b]asically all discourse is a forming, a figure' ('Figura', 25–6): the vertical figuring of the biopolitics of rectitude, it bears repeating, is a 'discursive resource'.

25. Cavarero, *Inclinations*, 6. Cf. also Rosemarie Garland-Thomson, *Extraordinary Bodies: Figuring Physical Disability in American Culture and Literature*, Twentieth Anniversary Edition (New York: Columbia University Press, 2017), 45.
26. Cavarero, *Inclinations*, 11. Cavarero's 'egocentric verticality' interestingly resonates with Rosemarie Garland-Thomson's connecting the autonomy of the Western subject to the 'possessive individualism' described by C. B. MacPherson (*Extraordinary Bodies*, 45).
27. Sigmund Freud, *Civilization and Its Discontents*, trans. and ed. James Strachey (New York: Norton and Company, 1962), 46n1.
28. Freud, *Civilization and Its Discontents*, 53n3.
29. 'Straight' or 'vertical' norm is a tautology, since 'norm', it is important to insist, is a vertical metaphor.
30. 'This neologism names the veiled subject position of cultural self, the figure outlined by the array of deviant others whose marked bodies shore up the normate's boundaries. The term normate usefully designates the social figure with which people can represent themselves as definitive human beings. Normate, then, is the constructed identity of those who, by way of the bodily configurations and cultural capital they assume, can step into a position of authority and wield the power it grants them. If one attempts to define the normate position by peeling away all the marked traits within the social order at this historical moment, what emerges is a very narrowly defined profile that describes only a minority of actual people' (Garland-Thomson, *Extraordinary Bodies*, 8).
31. Dinesh Wadiwel, *The War Against Animals* (Leiden: Brill – Rodopi, 2015), 42–55; Cynthia Lewiecki-Wilson, 'Ableist Rhetorics, Nevertheless: Disability and Animal Rights in the Work of Peter Singer and Martha Nussbaum', *JAC* 31, no. 1–2 (2011): 71–101.
32. J. M. Coetzee, *The Lives of Animals*, ed. Amy Gutmann (Princeton, NJ: Princeton University Press, 1999), 26.
33. See Sunaura Taylor, *Beasts of Burden: Animal and Disability Liberation* (New York: New Press, 2017). Singer has been particularly attacked on this point, since he explicitly theorises the legitimacy of euthanising severely handicapped newborns and elderly (e.g. Peter Singer *Practical Ethics*, second edition (Cambridge: Cambridge University Press, 1993), 175–217). For some examples, see Per Sundström, 'Peter Singer and "Lives Not Worth Living": Comments on a Flawed Argument from Analogy', *Journal of Medical Ethics* 21, no. 1 (1995): 35–8; Lewiecki-Wilson, 'Ableist Rhetorics, Nevertheless'; and Jenell Johnson, 'Disability, Animals, and the Rhetorical Boundaries of Personhood', *JAC* 32, no. 1–2 (2012): 372–82. The charge of 'normalising' the human species can also be brought against PETA, which in its campaigns in defence of nonhuman animals always uses healthy, beautiful and

perfectly able human bodies. On this topic, see also issue 51, no. 4 (2020) of *New Literary History* on 'Animality/ Posthumanism/ Disability'.

34. Wadiwel, *The War Against Animals*, 52; Foucault, *Society Must Be Defended*, 255; Richard Twine, *Animals as Biotechnology: Ethics, Sustainability and Critical Animal Studies* (London: Routledge, 2015), 85.
35. Diego Rossello shows how the concept of human 'dignity' in many contemporary debates rests on the verticality of 'standing tall' ('All in the (Human) Family? Species Aristocratism in the Return of Human Dignity', *Political Theory* 45, no. 6 (2017): 749–71).
36. See for example, Felice Cimatti, *Unbecoming Human: Philosophy of Animality After Deleuze*, trans. Fabio Gironi (Edinburgh: Edinburgh University Press, 2020), 1–23.
37. Carlo Salzani, 'From Post-Human to Post-Animal: Posthumanism and the "Animal Turn"', *Lo Sguardo* 24 (2017): 97–109; Felice Cimatti, *Il postanimale. La natura dopo l'Antropocene* (Rome: DeriveApprodi, 2021).
38. Celia E. Deane-Drummond and David Clough, eds., *Creaturely Theology: On God, Humans and Other Animals* (Norwich: Hymns Ancient and Modern, 2009); Stephen D. Moore and Laurel Kearns, *Divinanimality: Animal Theory, Creaturely Theology* (New York: Fordham University Press, 2014).
39. Brianne Donaldson, *Creaturely Cosmologies: Why Metaphysics Matters for Animal and Planetary Liberation* (Lanham: Lexington Books, 2015).
40. David Herman, ed., *Creatural Fictions: Human-Animal Relationships in Twentieth and Twenty-First Century Literature* (New York: Palgrave Macmillan, 2015); Anat Pick, *Creaturely Poetics: Animality and Vulnerability in Literature and Film* (New York: Columbia University Press, 2011).
41. Diane Davis, 'Creaturely Rhetorics', *Philosophy and Rhetoric* 44, no. 1 (2011), 88–94.
42. Cora Diamond, 'Eating Meat and Eating People', *Philosophy* 53, no. 206 (1978): 465–79.
43. 'Interview with Anat Pick, author of Creaturely Poetics', *Columbia University Press Blog*, 19 July 2011, available at https://www.cupblog.org/2011/07/19/interview-with-anat-pick-author-of-creaturely-poetics/ (accessed 2 June 2021).
44. Pieter Vermeulen and Virginia Richter, 'Introduction: Creaturely Constellations', *European Journal of English Studies* 19, no. 1 (2015): 3.
45. 'Interview with Anat Pick, author of Creaturely Poetics'.
46. Pick, *Creaturely Poetics*, 3.
47. Garland-Thomson, *Extraordinary Bodies*, 48.
48. Cavarero, *Inclinations*, 13–14.
49. Quoted in Pick, *Creaturely Poetics*, 16.
50. Dominik Ohrem, 'An Address from Elsewhere: Vulnerability, Relationality, and Conceptions of Creaturely Embodiment', in *Beyond the Human-Animal Divide:*

Creaturely Lives in Literature and Culture, eds. Dominik Ohrem and Roman Bartosch (Basingstoke: Palgrave Macmillan, 2017), 43–76.
51. Ohrem, 'An Address from Elsewhere', 55.
52. Diego Rossello, '¿Hacia el Tanatoceno? Dignidad humana, aunque el mundo perezca', *Mutatis Mutandis: Revista Internacional de Filosofía*, 1, no. 16 (2021): 95–107.
53. Bonnie Honig, *Antigone, Interrupted* (Cambridge: Cambridge University Press, 2013).
54. Eric L. Santner, *On Creaturely Life: Rilke – Benjamin – Sebald* (Chicago, IL: University of Chicago Press, 2006), 24, 15.
55. Dominic Pettman, 'After the Beep: Answering Machines and Creaturely Life', *boundary 2* 37, no. 2 (2010), 141.
56. Santner, *On Creaturely Life*, 26. The creaturely as debasement of the human (in the sense of the proud and autonomous Kantian subject) is of course not intrinsic to the theological concept of creature but depends on the contemporary German-Jewish theologico-political frame that Santner (and many others) adopt. I owe this clarification to Kristof Vanhoutte.
57. Santner further elaborates that 'the "creaturely" pertains not primarily to a sense of a shared animality or a shared animal suffering but to a biopolitical *animation* that distinguishes the human from the animal. To put it again in psychoanalytic terms, what we share with animals is life lived along the spectrum of pleasure and pain. Where we diverge from the animal is in our peculiar capacity for that pleasure-in-pain that Lacan refers to as "jouissance." And as I have furthermore proposed, the psychoanalytic concept of jouissance needs to be correlated with the topology of the state of exception as a crucial dimension of politicosocial bonds, a dimension that is no doubt susceptible to considerable historical mutation' (*On Creaturely Life*, 38–9).
58. Pick, *Creaturely Poetics*, 15, 172; Wolfe, *Before the Law*, 46; Wadiwel, *The War Against Animals*, 27.
59. See Diego Rossello, 'The Creature and the Sovereign: On Eric Santner's New Science of the Flesh', *Political Theory* 42, no. 6 (2014): 739–52.
60. Eugene Thacker, *After Life* (Chicago, IL: University of Chicago Press, 2010), 97.
61. Vermeulen and Richter, 'Introduction', 3.
62. In Portuguese, the word for children is *crianças*, which, like *creatura*, derives from the Latin verb *creare*.
63. Julia Lupton, 'Creature Caliban', *Shakespeare Quarterly* 51, no. 1 (2000): 1, 3, 5.
64. Lupton, 'Creature Caliban', 1.
65. Lupton, 'Creature Caliban', 5–6.
66. Lupton, 'Creature Caliban', 6, emphases added.
67. Lupton, 'Creature Caliban', 21.

68. Walter Benjamin, 'Zur Kantischen Ethik', in *Gesammelte Schriften*, volume VI, edited by Rolf Tiedemann and Hermann Schweppenhäuser (Frankfurt a.M.: Suhkamp, 1985), 55; Cavarero, *Inclinations*, 1.
69. Hannah Arendt, 'Walter Benjamin: 1892–1940', trans. Harry Zohn, in *Man in Dark Times* (New York: Harvest Books, 1968), 153–206.
70. I have carried out this analysis, with an explicit focus on a creaturely biopolitics as critique of the biopolitics of rectitude, in 'A Hunchbacked Political Theology: Creaturely Biopolitics as the Self-Sublation of Distorted Life', in *Walter Benjamin and Political Theology*, eds. Brendan Moran and Paula Schwebel (London: Bloomsbury Academic, 2024).
71. Walter Benjamin, 'Franz Kafka: On the Tenth Anniversary of His Death', in *Collected Writings*, volume 2 – 1927–1934, eds. Michael W. Jennings et al. (Cambridge, MA: The Belknap Press of Harvard University Press, 1999), 811.
72. Benjamin, 'Franz Kafka', 811.
73. Rebecca Comay, 'Benjamin's Endgame', in *Walter Benjamin's Philosophy: Destruction and Experience*, eds. Andrew Benjamin and Peter Osborne (London: Routledge, 1993), 259. In this respect, though, Benjamin's position is not always unambiguous and at times slips into a (very traditional) intolerance of distortion and a patronising and cavalier approach to it. See Brendan Moran, *Politics of Benjamin's Kafka: Philosophy as Renegade* (Basingstoke: Palgrave Macmillan, 2018), 296–7, 307.
74. Moran, *Politics of Benjamin's Kafka*, 285.
75. Walter Benjamin, 'Anmerkungen zu "Franz Kafka"', in *Gesammelte Schriften*, volume II/3, eds. Rolf Tiedemann and Hermann Schweppenhäuser (Frankfurt a.M.: Suhkamp, 1977), 1239.
76. Benjamin, 'Anmerkungen zu "Franz Kafka"', 1201.
77. Benjamin, 'Anmerkungen zu "Franz Kafka"', 1200.
78. Here the concept of subject must be understood in the passive sense of 'subjected to' a (sovereign) subjectification (as normalisation). Moreover, this very subjectification is strongly marked by the verticality of the upright posture that marks out the 'proper' human subject and excludes the distorted creature. (I owe this insight to Benjamin Lewis Robinson.)

Works Cited

Arendt, Hannah. 'Walter Benjamin: 1892–1940'. Translated by Harry Zohn. In *Man in Dark Times*, 153–206. New York: Harvest Books, 1968.

Auerbach, Eric. 'Figura'. In *Scenes from the Drama of European Literature*, 11–76. Minneapolis, MN: University of Minnesota Press, 1984.

Baumgarten, David. 'Animality in Kant's Theory of Human Nature'. In *Kant and Animals*, edited by John J. Callanan and Lucy Allais, 105–22. Oxford: Oxford University Press, 2020.

Benjamin, Walter. 'Anmerkungen zu "Franz Kafka"'. In *Gesammelte Schriften*, volume II/3, edited by Rolf Tiedemann and Hermann Schweppenhäuser, 1153–275. Frankfurt a.M.: Suhkamp, 1977.

Benjamin, Walter. 'Zur Kantischen Ethik'. In *Gesammelte Schriften*, volume VI, edited by Rolf Tiedemann and Hermann Schweppenhäuser, 55. Frankfurt a.M.: Suhkamp, 1985.

Benjamin, Walter. 'Franz Kafka: On the Tenth Anniversary of His Death'. In *Collected Writings*, volume 2 – 1927–1934, edited by Michael W. Jennings *et al.*, 794–818. Cambridge, MA: The Belknap Press of Harvard University Press, 1999.

Berlin, Isaiah. *The Crooked Timber of Humanity: Chapters in the History of Ideas*. Princeton, NJ: Princeton University Press, 2013.

Cavarero, Adriana. *Inclinations: A Critique of Rectitude*. Translated by Amanda Minervini and Adam Sitze. Stanford, CA: Stanford University Press, 2016.

Cimatti, Felice. *Unbecoming Human: Philosophy of Animality After Deleuze*. Translated by Fabio Gironi. Edinburgh: Edinburgh University Press, 2020.

Cimatti, Felice. *Il postanimale. La natura dopo l'Antropocene*. Rome: DeriveApprodi, 2021.

Coetzee, J. M. *The Lives of Animals*. Edited and introduced by Amy Gutmann. Princeton, NJ: Princeton University Press, 1999.

Comay, Rebecca. 'Benjamin's Endgame'. In *Walter Benjamin's Philosophy: Destruction and Experience*, edited by Andrew Benjamin and Peter Osborne, 251–91. London: Routledge, 1993.

Davis, Diane. 'Creaturely Rhetorics'. *Philosophy and Rhetoric* 44, no.1 (2011): 88–94.

Deane-Drummond, Celia E., and David Clough, eds. *Creaturely Theology: On God, Humans and Other Animals*. Norwich: Hymns Ancient & Modern, 2009.

Diamond, Cora. 'Eating Meat and Eating People'. *Philosophy* 53, no. 206 (1978): 465–79.

Donaldson, Brianne. *Creaturely Cosmologies: Why Metaphysics Matters for Animal and Planetary Liberation*. Lanham: Lexington Books, 2015.

Foucault, Michel. *Discipline and Punish: The Birth of the Prison*. Translated by Alan Sheridan. New York: Vintage, 1995.

Foucault, Michel. *Society Must Be Defended. Lectures at the Collège de France, 1975–76*. Translated by David Macey. New York: Picador, 2003.

Foucault, Michel. *Security, Territory, Population. Lectures at the Collège de France 1977–78*. Translated by Graham Burchell. Basingstoke: Palgrave Macmillan, 2007.

Freud, Sigmund. *Civilization and Its Discontents*. Translated and edited by James Strachey. New York: Norton and Company, 1962.

Garland-Thomson, Rosemarie. *Extraordinary Bodies: Figuring Physical Disability in American Culture and Literature*. Twentieth Anniversary Edition. New York: Columbia University Press, 2017.

Guyer, Paul. 'The Crooked Timber of Mankind'. In *Kant's Idea for a Universal History with a Cosmopolitan Aim: A Critical Guide*, edited by Amélie Oksenberg Rorty and James Schmidt, 129–49. Cambridge: Cambridge University Press, 2009.

Herman, David, ed. *Creatural Fictions: Human-Animal Relationships in Twentieth and Twenty-First Century Literature*. New York: Palgrave Macmillan, 2015.

Honig, Bonnie. *Antigone, Interrupted*. Cambridge: Cambridge University Press, 2013.

Johnson, Jenell. 'Disability, Animals, and the Rhetorical Boundaries of Personhood'. *JAC* 32, no. 1–2 (2012): 372–82.

Kant, Immanuel. *Religion Within the Boundaries of Mere Reason and Other Writings*. Translated by Allen W. Wood and George di Giovanni. Cambridge: Cambridge University Press, 1998.

Kant, Immanuel. *Anthropology, History, and Education*. Edited by Günter Zöller and Robert B. Louden. Cambridge: Cambridge University Press, 2007.

Kant, Immanuel. 'Idea for a Universal History with a Cosmopolitan Aim'. Translated by Allen W. Wood. In *Kant's Idea for a Universal History with a Cosmopolitan Aim: A Critical Guide*, edited by Amélie Oksenberg Rorty and James Schmidt, 9–23. Cambridge: Cambridge University Press, 2009.

Lewiecki-Wilson, Cynthia. 'Ableist Rhetorics, Nevertheless: Disability and Animal Rights in the Work of Peter Singer and Martha Nussbaum'. *JAC* 31, no. 1–2 (2011): 71–101.

Lupton, Julia. 'Creature Caliban'. *Shakespeare Quarterly* 51, no. 1 (2000): 1–23.

Moore, Stephen D., and Laurel Kearns. *Divinanimality: Animal Theory, Creaturely Theology*. New York: Fordham University Press, 2014.

Moran, Brendan. *Politics of Benjamin's Kafka: Philosophy as Renegade*. Basingstoke: Palgrave Macmillan, 2018.

Ohrem, Dominik. 'An Address from Elsewhere: Vulnerability, Relationality, and Conceptions of Creaturely Embodiment'. In *Beyond the Human-Animal Divide: Creaturely Lives in Literature and Culture*, edited by Dominik Ohrem and Roman Bartosch, 43–76. Basingstoke: Palgrave Macmillan, 2017.

Pettman, Dominic. 'After the Beep: Answering Machines and Creaturely Life'. *boundary 2* 37, no. 2 (2010): 133–53.

Pick, Anat. *Creaturely Poetics: Animality and Vulnerability in Literature and Film*. New York: Columbia University Press, 2011.

Pick, Anat. 'Interview with Anat Pick, author of Creaturely Poetics'. *Columbia University Press Blog*, July 19, 2011. Available at https://www.cupblog.org/2011/07/19/interview-with-anat-pick-author-of-creaturely-poetics/ (accessed 2 June 2021).

Rossello, Diego. 'The Creature and the Sovereign: On Eric Santner's New Science of the Flesh'. *Political Theory* 42, no. 6 (2014): 739–52.

Rossello, Diego. 'All in the (Human) Family? Species Aristocratism in the Return of Human Dignity'. *Political Theory* 45, no. 6 (2017): 749–71.

Rossello, Diego. '¿Hacia el Tanatoceno? Dignidad humana, aunque el mundo perezca'. *Mutatis Mutandis: Revista Internacional de Filosofía*, 1, no. 16 (2021): 95–107

Salzani, Carlo. 'From Post-Human to Post-Animal: Posthumanism and the "Animal Turn"'. *Lo Sguardo* 24 (2017): 97–109.

Salzani, Carlo. 'A Hunchbacked Political Theology: Creaturely Biopolitics as the Self-Sublation of Distorted Life'. In *Walter Benjamin and Political Theology*, edited by Brendan Moran and Paula Schwebel. London: Bloomsbury Academic, 2024.

Santner, Eric L. *On Creaturely Life: Rilke – Benjamin – Sebald*. Chicago, IL: University of Chicago Press, 2006.

Singer, Peter. *Practical Ethics*. Second edition. Cambridge: Cambridge University Press, 1993.

Sundström, Per. 'Peter Singer and "Lives Not Worth Living": Comments on a Flawed Argument from Analogy'. *Journal of Medical Ethics* 21, no. 1 (1995): 35–8.

Taylor, Sunaura. *Beasts of Burden: Animal and Disability Liberation*. New York: New Press, 2017.

Thacker, Eugene. *After Life*. Chicago, IL: University of Chicago Press, 2010.

Twine, Richard. *Animals as Biotechnology: Ethics, Sustainability and Critical Animal Studies*. London: Routledge, 2015.

Vermeulen, Pieter, and Virginia Richter. 'Introduction: Creaturely Constellations'. *European Journal of English Studies* 19, no. 1 (2015): 1–9.

Wadiwel, Dinesh. *The War Against Animals*. Leiden: Brill – Rodopi, 2015.

Wolfe, Cary. *Before the Law: Humans and Other Animals in a Biopolitical Frame*. Chicago, IL: The University of Chicago Press, 2013.

Wood, Allen W. 'Kant and the Problem of Human Nature'. In *Essays on Kant's Anthropology*, edited by Brian Jacobs and Patrick Kain, 38–59. Cambridge: Cambridge University Press, 2003.

14   A Dog's Life: From the Biopolitical Animal to the Posthuman
Felice Cimatti

The modern fact is that we no longer believe in this world. We do not even believe in the events which happen to us, love, death, as if they only half concerned us.[1]

Somato-Power and Life

What kind of animal is a biopolitical animal? First, it is important to make explicit what is meant by 'biopolitics' in this chapter.[2] According to Foucault, biopolitics is

> the attempt, starting from the eighteenth century, to rationalize the problems posed to governmental practice by phenomena characteristic of a set of living beings forming a population: health, hygiene, birthrate, life expectancy, race [. . . .] We know the increasing importance of these problems since the nineteenth century, and the political and economic issues they have raised up to the present.[3]

This attempt to rationalise problems has characterised the response to the Covid-19 pandemic. The power and pervasiveness of the pandemic and the rationalising forces mobilised to manage it are undeniable: actually, there is no aspect of human life that does not fall under the direct or indirect control of medical and political authorities. What is even more important is that in the existing biopolitical 'governmental practice' it is more and more difficult to distinguish between what pertains to medicine and science and what pertains to politics. That is, politics blends with biology and medicine: political life – for example the question of civil rights – is indistinguishable from simple biological life, as in the case of the restrictive measures that have been imposed to prevent the spread of the Covid-19 pandemic, which severely limit freedom of movement and have effectively blocked unvaccinated people from engaging in public life. In a situation like this, political decisions are wholly indistinguishable from medical ones.

According to this perspective, 'biopolitics' has to do with the political and administrative control over (at least in principle) all aspects of human life, to the point that humans are mainly – if not exclusively – considered animal bodies (according to this definition, nonhuman animals, especially those under human control, are also biopolitical animals[4]). In fact, biopolitics is not concerned with the classical characteristics of the political, such as ideas or speeches through which humans demonstrate their freedom; rather, what is at stake are lungs, the immune system and so on. From the point of view of biopolitics, the only thing that matters is the biological substratum of the classical political animal. Given this context, what would remain from Aristotle's ancient definition of the human being as a *'zōon* politikon' is only the *zōon*, without any further qualification; that is, what remains is only the bare *zoē* instead of *bíos*, instead of a specific form of life as that of fishes or bees.

This notion of 'biopolitics' presents at least two main characteristics: one external and one internal. The former (i.e., political and administrative control over all aspects of human life), as we have just seen, is widely recognised by scholars of biopolitics, while the latter is frequently forgotten. To understand what a biopolitical animal could be, one has to consider especially this second and much less acknowledged character of biopolitics. Take the case of sexuality. According to Foucault, the problem in the concept of 'sexuality' is not, to be precise, the social or religious external power that governs sexuality; what is really at stake is the internal control exerted by the human subject on its 'own' body. In this case one does not need to be controlled by an external device like the Panopticon; to the contrary, every subject is the Panopticon of itself. Therefore, the first and more effective human biopolitical device is the self-conscious subject, whose main object of attention and work is its own body: such a biopolitical practice consists of 'an exercise of the self, by which one attempts to develop and transform oneself, and to attain to a certain mode of being'.[5] For Foucault, therefore, the subject – what he defined as an entity capable of *'self-regulation'*[6] – is a biopolitical device exactly like the Panopticon:

the point of the latter is not simply its being designed in such a way as to assure absolute visibility, at all times, of its subject. The point is also that for it to work, nobody actually needs to occupy the central tower and survey the inmates. In other words, even if nobody occupies the point from which everything can be seen, the mechanism of power and control not only works perfectly, but emerges, so to speak, within each individual cell of the prison.[7]

Both of these devices, the external and the internal, have at the same time a dual function in the body: to make it an object of knowledge and to rule over it 'because the subject constitutes itself in an active fashion through practices of the self [. . .] [that] are [. . .] not something invented by the individual himself. They are models that he finds in his culture and that are proposed, suggested, imposed upon him by his culture, his society and his social group'.[8] One can see that the 'political' in the compound 'bio*political*' represents a power whose function is, at the same time, to institute (in the sense that is instituted as such by a social impersonal dispositive) and control the body. In both cases, what is at stake in biopolitics is the fundamental dualism between a mind/subject on one side, and an object/body on the other. The point that must be stressed is that this dualism is not restricted to Europe; as Foucault's analysis clearly shows, the split constitution of the human being is a consequence of the process through which the human animal acquires knowledge about itself, that is, the process that separates the subject of knowledge from the object of this knowledge, which is a universal phenomenon. As Foucault said, 'what I am trying to show is how power relations can get through to the very depths of bodies, materially, without having been relayed by the representations of subjects. [. . .] There is a network of bio-power, of somato-power from which sexuality is born as a historical and cultural phenomenon within which we both recognize and lose ourselves'.[9] This 'somato-power' is the anthropogenic device that institutes the human being as an animal (being an 'animal', that is an entity which is different from a 'thing', is 'decided' by some biopolitical dispositive, as that of zoological science) whose first object of control is its own body.[10] The 'somato-power' splits the *infans* into two parts – mind and body – a dualism that defines the species-specific character of the human animal. The point that one must not forget is that there is no humanity without some 'somato-power' that 'produces' such a split.[11]

We can now paraphrase the somewhat ambiguous expression 'biopolitical animal' as an animal whose internal constitution is based on a radical separation between the 'controller' – the subject, which in turn is nothing but the internalisation of external political power devices – and the 'controlled', the body.[12] Since such a split is what defines the human animal *qua* animal, there is no human being that is not also a biopolitical animal.[13] However, this paraphrasing appears somewhat redundant since in fact it means 'animal-political animal'. One might rather consider such a strange definition as a line of flight from an animality that is based on the dualism of mind and body. That is, one can read it as a suggestion for an unprecedented experience of becoming-animal on the part of *Homo sapiens*. Since the human animal becomes human at the expense of its body, the becoming animal of such a split living being corresponds to a movement towards the posthuman condition, that is, the condition where the split animal becomes, for the first time in its biological history, a unitary living being; an animal whose nature no longer requires it to be split into a subject and an object. This no-longer split animal, which is to say, an animal that is not divided into mind and body, is frequently referred to as 'posthuman'. On this reading, the posthuman is the only human that is properly *animal*.

Animality and Postsubjectivism

What is really at stake when we speak of posthumanism? What does the 'post' stand for? According to Rosi Braidotti, 'the common denominator for the posthuman condition is an assumption about the vital, self-organising and yet non-naturalistic structure of living matter itself. This nature-culture continuum is the shared starting point for [any] posthuman theory'.[14] While the classical humanistic stance places the human far from nature, the posthumanist stance deactivates the distance imposed and the superior position assumed. In this context, the question concerning Braidotti's definition of 'posthuman subjectivity' arises. As we have just seen, the problem posed by the 'classical' notion of subject is that it is subjected to the action of the devices of 'biopower'. Therefore, the notion of posthumanism could be a tool to develop a 'new' kind of humanity for the time to come, provided a different kind of subjectivity is developed, a subjectivity that is not based on the separation of mind and body. In this perspective, Braidotti proposes a

> critical posthuman subject within an eco-philosophy of multiple belongings, as a relational subject constituted in and by multiplicity, that is to say a subject that works across differences and is also internally differentiated, but still grounded and accountable. Posthuman subjectivity expresses an embodied and embedded and hence partial form of accountability, based on a strong sense of collectivity, relationality and hence community building.[15]

In a similar vein, according to Cary Wolfe, 'posthumanism [. . .] isn't posthuman at all – in the sense of being "after" our embodiment has been transcended – but is only posthuman*ist*, in the sense that it opposes the fantasies of disembodiment and autonomy, inherited from humanism itself'.[16]

Therefore, an initial answer to the question raised by the incipit of this paragraph is that the 'post' in posthumanism first means that the time has come for a no-longer biopolitical animal human being. For both Braidotti and Wolfe, what is at stake is an animal whose 'nature' is no longer based on a separation, neither on the basic metaphysical bifurcation between mind and body nor on the equally basic separation between *Homo sapiens* on one side and an undifferentiated and generic Nature on the other. In Pramod Nayar's words:

> In a radical reworking of humanism, critical posthumanism seeks to move beyond the traditional humanist ways of thinking about the autonomous, self-willed individual agent in order to treat the human itself as an assemblage, co-evolving with other forms of life, enmeshed with the environment and technology. It rejects the view of the human as exceptional, separate from other life forms and usually dominant/dominating over these other forms. Critical posthumanism begins with the assumption that the human incorporates difference in the form of other DNA, species and forms of life, so that its uniqueness is a myth.[17]

This kind of posthumanism rightly points towards a radical extension of the boundaries of humanity but, at the same time, it extends the boundaries of what was once the nonhuman. However, it is not clear at all how such an extension radically puts into question the position of the biopolitical subject. What is at stake is exactly how 'post' this posthumanism is. If 'post' fundamentally means that in order for humans, especially in the West, to maintain their privileged position in the world it is necessary to limit the exploitation of the natural world, this is not the kind of 'post' we need. Consider Richard Grusin's recent assertion: the 'nonhuman turn' is 'generally [. . .] engaged in decentering the human in favor of [. . .] the nonhuman, understood variously in terms of animals, affectivity, bodies, organic and geophysical systems, materiality, or technologies'.[18] Even if this definition explicitly claims the autonomous agency of the nonhuman, it still gathers phenomena that are completely different from each other into the same category. Take the case of the blending or insertion of digital technologies inside the human body. In this case, the 'nonhuman turn' seems to focus on the technological prothesis of human body and life (in this sense it is quite near to those forms of posthumanism that resemble transhumanism). This is a point that it is important to highlight: 'unlike the posthuman turn [...] the nonhuman turn does not make a claim about teleology or progress in which we begin with the human and see a transformation from the human to the posthuman, after or beyond the human'. For this and other reasons, the nonhuman turn must be distinguished from posthumanism. In particular, the nonhuman turn insists that 'the human has always coevolved, coexisted, or collaborated with the nonhuman'.[19] Such a coevolution of the human with artificial devices (the first and most important of which is language) has been always recognised. Since its biological appearance, *Homo sapiens* has been an 'artificial' species,[20] that is, an animal species whose biological development and bodily formation critically depend on the internalisation of external artificial devices. From this point of view, contrary to the concerns outlined by Grusin, what is at stake is precisely a 'transformation from the human to the posthuman, after or beyond the human'. In fact, according to Grusin, 'the nonhuman turn [...] runs the risk of inviting confusion with the posthuman turn'.[21] On the contrary, one takes a risk if one wants to try to cope with the post-Covid-19 world, that is, a world where the agency of the nonhuman (the virus) is absolutely undeniable (what is equally undeniable is the human surprise and astonishment at the former's agency). What this 'nonhuman' does not take into consideration are the possible 'dangerous' biopolitical consequences of 'the impact of our new technical media on the human'.[22] Grusin defines these technologies as 'our media'. However, the problem we have to face is how much these media can be considered 'ours', and to what extent instead they constitute a kind of disembodied rationality that completely overtakes human agency.

The point is that the problems raised by the political and medical interventions put into action all over the world to counter the pandemic not only will not be solved, but the biopolitical grip over human and nonhuman life will expand inexorably. The 'nonhuman turn', at least as articulated by Grusin, clearly does not imply any radical change to the human stance regarding nature and life. To highlight the interconnectedness between the human and the posthuman – for example, acknowledging that 'human cognition has been interdependent with embodied, nonhuman technologies'[23] – does not radically put into question the position of the human in relation to the nonhuman world: paradoxically, not only is there the 'risk' of confusing the nonhuman turn with the posthuman one; there is the much more important risk of simply accepting the transformation of the human body into a biopolitical entity. In fact, the body is completely under the control of the mind – that is, the prototypical biopolitical device – which transforms it into a technical device which is permanently at its disposal. As we have already seen with Foucault, what is worth stressing is that whether control over biological life is exerted by the legal 'owner' of the body or by an external political authority, from the vantage point of the actual body it does not make any difference. In both cases, the living body is nothing but a technical tool serving an external biopolitical force. That is, it is not sufficient to criticise subject-object dualism, for example, as a classical anthropocentric way of imagining the human relationship with nature. What is important is to deactivate that dualism within the human being, where it takes the form of the almost always unnoticed distinction between a ruling mind and a ruled body, between an 'I' and a 'flesh' whose unique 'function' is to be a 'perfect' executor of the subject's desire and will. If one does not question this basic dualism, the 'nonhuman turn' will not break free from a hidden – and for this reason much more powerful – anthropocentric dualism that makes useless any other attempt to avoid stripping 'the world of any ontological or agential status'.[24] That is, what is at stake is less that of putting into question the human than putting into question the human subject. In this sense, posthumanism is, effectively, postsubjectivism, that is, a condition in which the somewhat human animal is no longer subject to the grip of a biopolitical 'subject'. It is this condition that Braidotti defines as 'radical posthuman subjectivity'.[25]

In this context, the question of posthumanism intersects with that of animality.[26] Take the case of a feral cat who has no human 'owner' and has not been sterilised. Such an animal lives a life that can be wonderful or horrible, as can be the life of any living being. However, the cat's life is not under the control of any biopolitical device, neither internal nor external, at least as long as the cat is not brought into a household and domesticated or caught and used for some kind of scientific experiment. This does not mean that the cat is devoid of any subjectivity, but rather that the cat's subjectivity does not have the form of an external 'I' who decides what the cat's body can or cannot do. The cat seeks out what it likes and avoids what it dislikes. There is no gap between this embodied subjectivity and the actual life of the cat. Such a life is not a biopolitical life because it does not obey any biopolitical device, such as, for example, 'self-consciousness', 'scientific animal enclosure', 'pets' affection' and so on. What is worth noticing about this living condition is that it is a 'bare' animal life that is not 'disturbed' by any transcendental issue. Deleuze defines this as a life of 'absolute immanence in itself', that is, 'a pure plane of immanence [. . .] without consciousness'.[27] The main thesis of this chapter is that the posthuman condition is still a human life, which nonetheless has attained the condition of 'absolute immanence', that is, the condition of animality.

Otherwise, if not intended in this radical way, posthumanism (which is not to be confused with the 'nonhuman turn') remains entrapped in what

Christopher Peterson refers to as the 'posthuman error'. This apparently anti-anthropocentric stance does not take into account

> that the human – however misrecognized and misnamed – remains the zero point of our relation to alterity. The phantasm of human exceptionalism cannot be so easily vanquished because its error is also its 'truth'. The human that declares the fallacy of its own exceptionality can do so only from the position of its phantasmatic centeredness. We turn back even as we turn away; or rather, we never turn away from ourselves precisely so that we can turn away from ourselves.[28]

The thesis of this chapter states to the contrary that the posthuman body is a body to which the biopolitical power – internal or external – no longer applies. That is, the posthuman body is a body that has been freed from the biopolitical power that controls its life. Such a body is no longer a human body, since the separation between mind and flesh is the basic social anthropogenic operation which transforms a primate body into a human, that is, a being endowed with self-consciousness and language. Therefore, the posthuman body is a body in which this anthropogenic device has been deactivated. Such a body will be the first human-animal, that is, a human body whose life is completely animal, but at the same time does not cease to be human. The point is to imagine a way of being human which does not entail the splitting of mind and flesh, 'I' and 'lived body' (*Leib*), subject and object. From this perspective, the posthuman body is the becoming-animal of human subjectivity.

On this view, one can also read Nietzsche's famous and too frequently misunderstood assertions about the *Übermensch* as a human being placed beyond humanistic humanity (i.e., a humanity whose mind and body are bifurcated). For this reason, as Nietzsche writes in *Thus Spoke Zarathustra*, 'the overman is the meaning of the earth. Let your will say: the overman *shall be* the meaning of the earth! I beseech you, my brothers, remain *faithful to the earth* and do not believe those who speak to you of extraterrestrial hopes!'[29] This is the key point of the 'overman': he is 'faithful to the earth'. His life remains at the level of the earth's surface, in a condition of 'absolute immanence'. Therefore, the overman is 'a going over and a going under' actual humanity[30]: 'going over' mind and transcendence on one side, and 'going under' the split human condition, that is, towards animality, on the other. The 'overman' does not place himself over humanity, as if he were a special kind of human (as in transhumanism[31]). At the same time, he does not place himself under humanity, in a pure prehuman animal condition, because, as we have already seen, *Homo sapiens* has never been a bare animal species. As Nietzsche wrote in an unpublished note in the autumn of 1887: the actual 'man is the un-animal and the over-animal [*Unthier und Überthier*]' – because he is at the same time less and more than an animal – 'the higher man is the un-man and the overman [*Unmensch und Übermensch*]: so, it belongs together'.[32] One can paraphrase this condition using the notion of 'absolute immanence' that we have already encountered. In the posthuman condition, both possibilities of transcendence and immanence are deactivated, that is, the posthuman (the 'overman') is no longer divided into mind and flesh. He is no longer a dualistic animal.

However, we already know that the dualistic animal is nothing but the biopolitical animal, an animal whose nature is to be split into self-consciousness on one side and bare, tamed body on the other. Therefore, the 'overman', that is, the overcoming of this basic separation, represents a condition where the human being is at the same time human and – for the first time in its natural history – also an animal.[33] The 'overman' is the 'becoming-animal' of the human, dualistic, and therefore biopolitical, being. It is important to stress that the 'overman' is not a new animal species. The point of the 'posthuman' is not that it represents a new stable condition; on the contrary, it is a condition where the human no longer thinks of itself as an entity detached from the world. Being 'faithful to the earth' means nothing more than being open to the contingencies of life. It means no longer enclosing human life in a biopolitical bubble. It means, like the cat we met earlier, living a *human*-animal life, at the ground level, neither below nor above the ground, a life that is neither simply animal nor a dualistic, transcendent life:

> The becoming-animal of the human being is real, even if the animal the human being becomes is not; and the becoming-other of the animal is real, even if that something other it becomes is not. This is the point to clarify: that a becoming lacks a subject distinct from itself; but also that it has no term, since its term in turn exists only as taken up in another becoming of which it is the subject, and which coexists, forms a block, with the first.[34]

A Posthumous Life

In May 1927, D. H. Lawrence wrote to his friend Henry Brewster about a short story he had just finished writing, *The Escaped Cock* (subsequently known with the more explicit title *The Man Who Died*):

> I wrote a story of the Resurrection, where Jesus gets up and feels very sick about everything, and can't stand the old crowd any more – so cuts out – and

as he heals up, he begins to find what an astonishing place the phenomenal world is, far more marvellous than any salvation or heaven – and thinks he needn't have a 'mission' any more.[35]

Lawrence imagines a Jesus that, after dying on the cross, is resurrected as a simple human being, not as God. What does it mean to be reborn as an everyman? Jesus, in his life before crucifixion, was the earthly voice of his Father, God in Heaven. That is, Jesus was a sort of symbol of transcendence; what happened in his actual life was subordinate to what really mattered, to something postponed to another, transcendent life. In Lawrence's retelling, however, the man who died is now simply someone who lived his actual life. There is no more transcendence, no more dualism, no more bifurcation of mind and body; there is simply a life, and nothing else. According to Lawrence, it is only in such a condition that one can fully appreciate 'what an astonishing place the phenomenal world is'. This is exactly what is at stake when one tries to imagine a post-biopolitical life (i.e., a posthuman life). The key feature of any biopolitical life, both human and nonhuman (viz., animals, plants, even nonliving matter), is the subordination of the actual life to a transcendent somato-power (capitalism is nothing but one of the historical forms of such a power over life) that 'decides' how this life must be put to work. Take the case of the human body and the mind that rules over it, in particular the process that transforms a child body into an adult body, that is, a body that 'voluntarily' accepts that it must work (never forget that the most apparent difference between a human being and a nonhuman living being is that the latter does not voluntarily work). The process of humanisation, from an anthropological point of view, essentially consists in the taming of the animal *infans* body to meet the needs of the society. Let us think about how difficult it is to train an *infans* body, such as a nonhuman primate body, to sit still at a school desk. Such training is nothing but a complete transformation of the *infans*' natural way of living into a socially accepted behaviour, a form of training that ultimately consists of transforming the child mind into an adult mind regulated by social norms. By now, there is no longer any need for an external authority to dictate to the child how it ought to behave; it is the child itself that dictates to 'its' own body how to behave. The whole training process attains two interconnected goals: 1) the social institution of the internal controller of the body on one side, which is the child's self-conscious mind (for this reason the 'I' is a biopolitical institution, because it is the internal delegate of an external social dispositive); and 2) the social institution of the controlled body on the other side. The very process of humanisation consists in the splitting of a unitary living body, the *infans* body, into two separate 'entities': the famous mind/body problem is not a philosophical problem. On the contrary, it is the 'natural' result of the process (a process that can only succeed up to a certain point) through which an *infans* transforms itself into an adult human being.

Returning to *The Man Who Died*, Lawrence is of the view that Jesus is exactly the kind of extraordinary figure needed to bring together what the humanisation process has severed. It is for this reason that Jesus can finally appreciate the actual world, without looking for another, transcendent one. What is at stake is a life, a simple life, that does not need to look for any further meaning beyond itself. As Lawrence writes, Jesus, once he found refuge in the guardhouse of a farmer,

> felt the cool silkiness of the young wheat under his feet that had been dead, and the roughishness of its separate life was apparent to him. At the edges of rocks, he saw the silky, silvery-haired buds of the scarlet anemone bending downwards. And they, too, were in another world. In his own world he was alone, utterly alone. These things around him were in a world that had never died. But he himself had died, or had been killed from out of it, and all that remained now was the great void nausea of utter disillusion.[36]

For the first time in his life Jesus realises that until he 'died' he had never properly noticed or appreciated the lushness of earthly existence – a life that was 'in another world' than one he inhabited – or that in 'his own world he was alone'. The reason why in his 'first' life Jesus was alone is connected to the process through which he became a divided human being. When this being was divided into mind and body, the former began to live in a separate world of ideas and desires while the latter remained bound to the condition of a simple object. Living in the world of thoughts means forgetting to live in the actual world of body. Forgetting the body also leads to forgetting the earthly world of flowers, the astonishing presence of which leaves Jesus in a state of awe. In his 'new' life Jesus will never forget these flowers, that is, he will never forget the only life that is now the life on earth. When Madeleine encounters him, Jesus makes explicit this point: 'My triumph, he said, is that I am not dead. I have outlived my mission and know no more of it. It is my triumph. [. . .] The teacher and the saviour are dead in me; now I can go about my business, into my own single life'.[37] It is as if Jesus had said: 'the transcendent mind is dead in me, now I can go about my life, "into my own single life"'. It is as if Jesus, the man who died as a dualistic entity, had taken seriously the epigraph from Deleuze that opens this chapter. What is precisely at stake is to *believe* in the actual world. However, it is important to understand why Lawrence's Jesus, and with him all those who find themselves in a similar posthuman condition, does not trust the world. Because he is, as any human being is, a biopolitical animal, an animal whose nature is divided into two parts, mind and body. This fundamental dualism detaches the living human being from its actual bodily life. The world is no longer the world as it actually is, but how it should be or how one should want it to be. Therefore, what Lawrence's Jesus first and foremost discovered after his death is nothing but the actual existence of the world as it simply is. For this reason, Jesus can now believe in the world. Previously – when he was the Son of God – he did not have any certainty about the existence of the real world:

> The link between man and the world is broken. Henceforth, this link must become an object of belief: it is the impossible which can only be restored within a faith. Belief is no longer addressed to a different or transformed world. Man is in the world as if in a pure optical and sound situation. The reaction of which man has been dispossessed can be replaced only by belief. Only belief in the world can reconnect man to what he sees and hears.[38]

Jesus now believes in the world. The posthuman condition is nothing but such a belief. 'I am a man, and the world is open',[39] Jesus says upon parting with a woman with whom he stayed for a while. The posthumous life of Jesus is a life that is no longer a biopolitical life, no longer a life that must be tamed. This life is a posthuman life because the human being who lives it believes in the world. Such a posthuman being does not need to change the way the world is, starting from what was once 'its' so-called own body, since the world does not need to be changed to accommodate human needs. For this reason, the posthuman life is also a postanthropocentric life. Only a living being who is not amazed by the way the world is can feel the inhuman desire to change it. The world is fine as it is: this is the motto – if such a life still needs one – of the posthuman life. Lawrence's novel ends with Jesus going away on a boat from the temple where he met a priestess: 'so let the boat carry me. To-morrow is another day'.[40] The posthuman life is a life that is driven by life itself. Since there is no longer any biopolitical power to drive life, because it does not need any drive outside its own inner movement, Jesus can adapt to what happens to him. Jesus simply avoids situations that could make his life difficult and dangerous once again – difficulties and dangers that are always generated by biopolitical feelings such as envy or desire (as we have already seen, the basic biopolitical entity is self-consciousness, that is, the social entity that controls the body. The posthuman body no longer needs to be controlled; therefore, there is no more envy or desire, which only exist for the 'I'). The posthuman condition coincides with Nietzsche's *amor fati*:

> My formula for human greatness is *amor fati*: not wanting anything to be different, not forwards, not backwards, not for all eternity. Not just enduring what is necessary, still less concealing it – all idealism is hypocrisy in the face of what is necessary – but *loving* it.[41]

Becoming Animal

Let's try to sum up the path that we have traversed so far. The first step was to specify the peculiar notion of biopolitics used in this chapter. I proposed an 'ontological' definition: the field of biopolitics encompasses 'machines that make one see and talk'.[42] Take the case of an apparatus where a social entity, like the Mother, observes an *infans* and regards it as 'her son'. A Mother is not a biological entity. A Mother is a social construction whose behaviours and feelings are mediated by the peculiar social apparatus of the 'family'. This means that she has learned to take care of the *infans* from social and economic imperatives of which she is completely unaware. Any apparatus 'has its own regimen of light' and discourse whose functions consist in 'generating or eliminating an object, which cannot exist without it'.[43] Taken together, the biopolitical apparatuses 'produce' that particular living being that is the human animal, an animal whose nature is to be divided into two separate entities, mind and body, where the latter is completely subordinated to the former.

Why should these apparatuses be called biopolitical? Because according to Aristotle politics and language are inseparable, and all the apparatuses we have considered cannot exist without language and politics. Therefore, the root of biopolitics ('-politics') collects within itself all those devices that have as their main function to institute the biopolitical body, that is, a power relation between a controller – the mind – and a controlled – the body. At the same time, as Foucault never stops remarking, any power produces a counter-power. This means that the body-object is always on the verge of freeing itself from the grasp of the mind-subject. As Foucault put it:

> a power relationship [...] can only be articulated on the basis of two elements that are indispensable if it is really to be a power relationship: that "the other" (the one over whom power is exercised) is recognised and maintained to the very end as a subject who acts; and that, faced with a relationship of power, a whole field of responses, reactions, results, and possible inventions may open up.[44]

This point is of particular relevance since Foucault makes it clear that a body does not exist without a mind that tries to rule over it, and vice versa.

That the posthuman life is a life that places itself beyond the biopolitical dualism of mind and body signifies the possibility of living life in a posthuman condition. Posthumanism is not a condition that one would attain only in some remote and far future. Quite the contrary, there is a posthumanist possibility each time someone succeeds in remaining undecided between mind and body, that is, each time the power relation between mind and body is made inoperative. The point is that any posthuman life is still linked to the human; therefore the dualism of the mind and the body does not completely disappear. What is important is to deactivate the ancient hierarchy that places the mind over the body. In this sense, such an indecision between mind and body is the typical posthuman feeling.

When a human living being is no longer split into subject and object, that is, when there is not a mind ruling over a body, the living being experiences an unprecedented condition, that of not being a split animal. Such a condition is the typical condition of every nonhuman animal, that is, the 'natural' condition of any animal whose process of formation is not mediated by a biopolitical device – except for the special case of nonhuman animals who are raised and bred for human needs.[45] The process is opposite to humanisation, that is, to the biopolitical splitting into mind and body; the process is what Deleuze and Guattari called 'becoming-animal', those 'acts of becoming-animal [. . .] [that] are absolute deterritorializations'.[46] For the first time in the life of human beings, becoming-animal reassembles what the anthropogenic process originally divided. Since becoming-animal reverses this process, it is nothing but becoming posthuman on the part of the human being. As Deleuze and Guattari explained, while the anthropogenic process territorialises spaces – through the biopolitical institution of the two different and hierarchically defined regions of mind and body – becoming-animal deterritorialises those regions, that is, it makes them indistinguishable. In this regard, becoming-animal is much more radical than Haraway's concept of companion species: 'we are, constitutively, companion species. We make each other up, in the flesh. Significantly other to each other, in specific difference, we signify in the flesh a nasty developmental infection called love'.[47] Love is a relation between two already territorialised entities, while becoming-animal is much more radical, since it entails deterritorialising the pre-existing identities, something Haraway herself seems to have recognised:

> I find that notion [i.e., companion species], which is less a category than a pointer to an ongoing 'becoming with', to be a much richer web to inhabit than any of the posthumanisms on display after (or in reference to) the ever-deferred demise of man. I never wanted to be posthuman, or

posthumanist [...] The partners do not precede their relating; all that is, is the fruit of becoming with: those are the mantras of companion species.[48]

This last point is the key concept: while the concept of companion species leaves the different 'companions' in their own identities – the notion of 'species' is in fact a biopolitical notion – the concept of becoming-animal does not leave them unchanged, as the case of SARS-CoV-2 apparently shows, since it is transforming us while being continually transformed by its encounters with us. From this perspective, the notion of companion species does not seem incompatible with the biopolitical apparatus of subjectivity – an apparatus that this chapter has identified as being at the core of the biopolitical era. As Braidotti insists, 'the posthuman' should be intended as a 'becoming-animal',[49] that is, a becoming that radically questions subjective identity for the first time.

But what does becoming-animal actually entail on the part of the human? Even if Foucault, in the last lectures at the Collège de France, does not refer to the notion of 'becoming-animal', he is describing such a life. What is at stake is the cynical life, a human life resembling a dog's life. To understand what this kind of life could be it is necessary to refer to the Deleuzian distinction between morality and ethics. In a lecture on Spinoza at the University of Paris Vincennes (21 December 1980), Deleuze states that the ethical point of view is 'ethology in the most rudimentary sense'. He goes on to explain that it 'is a practical science, of what? A practical science of the ways of being. The way of being is precisely the status of the being, of the existing, from the point of view of a pure ontology'. Ethics does not have to do with a judgment on life; an ethical life is a life in which there is no separation between what one believes and what one does. In contrast, 'a morality calls us back to the essence [...] which calls us back to it by the values. It is not the point of view of the being. [...] Indeed, morality is the enterprise of judging not only all that is, but the being itself. But we can judge the being only in the name of an authority superior to the being'. While a moral life is a classical biopolitical device, since it is based on the separation between life and a judgment on life, an ethical life is precisely a life where this distinction no longer operates. This life is what Foucault defined as the 'cynical life':

> First, the *kunikos* life is a dog's life in that it is without modesty, shame, and human respect. It is a life which does in public, in front of everyone, what only dogs and animals dare to do, and which men usually hide. [...] Second, the Cynic life is a dog's life because, like the latter, it is indifferent. It is indifferent to whatever may occur, is not attached to anything, is content with what it has, and has no needs other than those it can satisfy immediately. Third, the life of

the Cynic is the life of a dog, it received the epithet *kunikos* because it is, so to speak, [...] a diacritical (*diakritikos*) life, [...] a life which can fight, which barks at enemies.[50]

What is worth stressing is that a *kunikos* life, even if it is like a dog's life, does not stop being a distinctly human life. Becoming-animal does not mean changing or improving our DNA or anything along those lines. What is at stake, rather, is the ability to live a completely different life from the biopolitical life. Take the first of the three points highlighted by Foucault, a life without shame. Shame could be considered the prototypical biopolitical feeling, since it is what one feels when under the gaze of a transcendent power. Shame means that someone/something is looking at you, whether an external device (a biometric camera, for example) or one's self-consciousness – the 'internal' gaze. In both cases, shame is a response to being observed. On the contrary, a *kunikos* life is without shame (in fact dogs are 'artificial' animals constructed by humans to live with them. Shame is the typical biopolitical feeling. A 'true' animal has nothing to be ashamed of); it is a life that is under no one's or no thing's control. It is important to stress that a life beyond shame is not per se a shameless life, like the life of an egocentric or egoistic person. This life is still a biopolitical life, since it is still a dualistic life based on the primacy of the self-conscious subject over the body, whereas the *kunikos* life develops itself in the indistinction between mind and body, between the subjective gaze and the object of such a gaze.

Second, the cynic life is 'indifferent' to what happens to it. This is a point that resonates with Nietzsche's *amor fati* or Deleuze's 'absolute immanence'. Since the *kunikos* life places itself beyond the biopolitical apparatus of subjectivity (therefore also beyond the private property device), it has nothing to care about, except boring or dangerous encounters. The *kunikos* life is an existential position where no hierarchies can be traced, where any one phenomenon of life is at the same level of any other phenomenon of life. At the same time, the *kunikos* life is not the nihilistic life of those who do not believe in anything: quite the contrary, since it is the life of those who believe only in the world.

Third, the *kunikos* life 'barks at the enemies' of life. It can bark because, unlike human beings who use language to produce imagined and transcendent worlds, the *kunikos* life is directly connected to actual life. While the metaphysical ground of language is the transcendent semiotic principle of *aliquid stat pro aliquo*, barking is not a sign; it is an action, an ethical (according to Deleuze's use of the term) behaviour. In the end, the *kunikos* life is the always present virtuality of the becoming-animal of the philosopher, that is, it is the opportunity, always at hand, of the becoming posthuman of the human. In Foucault's words:

In general terms [. . .] we may say that in ancient thought animality played the role of absolute point of differentiation for the human being. It is by distinguishing itself from animality that the human being asserted and manifested its humanity. Animality was always, more or less, a point of repulsion for the constitution of man as a rational and human being. In the Cynics [. . .] animality will play a completely different role. It will be charged with positive value, it will be a model of behavior, a material model in accordance with the idea that the human being must not have as a need what the animal can do without. [. . .] Animality is not a given; it is a duty. [. . .] This animality [. . .] constitutes a sort of permanent challenge in the Cynic life. Animality is a way of being with regard to oneself, a way of being which must take the form of a constant test. Animality is an exercise. It is a task for oneself and at the same time a scandal for others.[51]

Notes

1. Gilles Deleuze, *Cinema 2. The Time-Image* (Minneapolis, MN: University of Minnesota Press, 1989), 171.
2. Laurette Liesen and Mary Walsh, 'The Competing Meanings of "Biopolitics" in Political Science: Biological and Postmodern Approaches to Politics', *Politics and the Life Sciences* 31, nos. 1–2 (2012): 2–15.
3. Michel Foucault, *The Birth of Biopolitics. Lectures at the Collège de France, 1978–1979* (Basingstoke: Palgrave Macmillan, 2008), 317. Cf. Vanessa Lemm and Miguel Vatter, 'Michel Foucault's Perspective on Biopolitics', in *Handbook of Biology and Politics*, eds. Steven A. Peterson and Albert Somit (Cheltenham: Edward Elgar Publishing, 2017), 40–52.
4. As we have explained in the introduction to this volume, 'we are all biopolitical animals'. However, this chapter focuses in particular on the human biopolitical condition and seeks to develop a path towards becoming posthuman on the part of the human animal; that is, on becoming a post-biopolitical animal.
5. Michel Foucault, *Foucault Live: Collected Interviews, 1961–1984* (New York: Semiotext(e), 1996), 433.
6. Robert Mitchell, *Infectious Liberty: Biopolitics Between Romanticism and Liberalism* (New York: Fordham University Press, 2021), 186.
7. Alenka Zupančič, 'Biopolitics, Sexuality and the Unconscious', *Paragraph: Italian Biopolitical Theory and Beyond: Genealogy, Psychoanalysis, and Biology* 39, no. 1 (2016): 55.
8. Foucault, *Foucault Live*, 440–1.
9. Foucault, *Foucault Live*, 209.

10. It is not surprising to discover that nonhuman animals, for example rhesus monkeys in an experimental cage equipped with a mirror, can begin to master their own mirror image to manipulate their body (Virginia Morell, 'Monkeys Master a Key Sign of Self-awareness: Recognizing their Reflections', *Science*, 13 February 2017, available at: https://www.science.org/content/article/monkeys-master-key-sign-self-awareness-recognizing-their-reflections, accessed 16 May 2022). This means that monkeys, through human-fabricated experimental devices, acquire the capacity to focus their attention specifically on their 'own' body. This is the first cognitive step towards what can become a full mind/body dualism. These experiments show that even a nonhuman animal, when raised within a biopolitical apparatus, transforms itself into a biopolitical animal, that is, a living being split into body and mind – a 'who' that observes and controls a 'what', the 'object' of a subjective gaze.
11. Giorgio Agamben, *The Open: Man and Animal*, trans. Kevin Attell (Stanford, CA: Stanford University Press, 2004).
12. Felice Cimatti, *Unbecoming Human. Philosophy of Animality After Deleuze* (Edinburgh: Edinburgh University Press, 2020).
13. Lynton Caldwell, 'Biopolitics: Science, Ethics, and Public Policy', *The Yale Review* 54, no. 1 (1964): 1–16; Glendon Schubert, 'Review: Biopolitical Behavior: The Nature of the Political Animal', *Polity* 6, no. 2 (1973): 240–75; Robert Blank, 'Biology and Politics: An Introduction', in *Politics and the Life Sciences: The State of the Discipline*, eds. Robert Blank et al. (Bingley: Emerald, 2014), 1–34.
14. Rosi Braidotti, *The Posthuman* (Cambridge: Polity Press, 2013), 2.
15. Braidotti, *The Posthuman*, 49.
16. Cary Wolfe, *What is Posthumanism?* (Minneapolis, MN: Minnesota University Press, 2010), xv.
17. Pramod Nayar, *Posthumanism* (Cambridge: Polity Press, 2014), 13.
18. Richard Grusin, 'Introduction', in *The Nonhuman Turn*, ed. Richard Grusin (Minneapolis, MN: University of Wisconsin Press, 2015), vii.
19. Grusin, 'Introduction', ix.
20. André Leroi-Gourhan, *Gesture and Speech* (Cambridge, MA: MIT Press, 1993).
21. Grusin, 'Introduction', ix.
22. Grusin, 'Introduction', xiii.
23. Grusin, 'Introduction', x.
24. Grusin, 'Introduction', xi.
25. Braidotti, *The Posthuman*, 49.
26. Felice Cimatti and Carlo Salzani, eds., *Animality in Contemporary Italian Philosophy* (Basingstoke: Palgrave Macmillan, 2020).
27. Gilles Deleuze, *Two Regimes of Madness: Texts and Interviews 1975–1995* (New York: Semiotext(e), 2006), 385.

28. Christopher Peterson, *Monkey Trouble. The Scandal of Posthumanism* (New York: Fordham University Press, 2018), 6.
29. Friedrich Nietzsche, *Thus Spoke Zarathustra: A Book for All and None* (Cambridge: Cambridge University Press, 2006), 6.
30. Nietzsche, *Thus Spoke Zarathustra*, 233.
31. Cf. Hans Moravec, *Robot: Mere Machine to Transcendent Mind* (Oxford: Oxford University Press, 1999).
32. Nietzsche, *Nachgelassene Fragmente*, Herbst 1887, 9 [154] www.nietzschesource.org (my translation).
33. Kalpana R. Seshadri, 'Between Derrida and Agamben', in *HumAnimal: Race, Law, Language*, ed. Kalpana R. Seshadri (Minneapolis, MN: University of Minnesota Press, 2012), 109–36; Donna Haraway, *Staying with the Trouble: Making Kin in the Chthulucene* (Durham, NC: Duke University Press, 2016).
34. Gilles Deleuze and Félix Guattari, *A Thousand Plateaus: Capitalism and Schizophrenia* (Minneapolis, MN: Minnesota University Press, 1987), 238.
35. David Herbert Lawrence, *The Man Who Died* (London, Heinemann, 1931), viii–ix.
36. Lawrence, *The Man Who Died*, 25.
37. Lawrence, *The Man Who Died*, 42.
38. Deleuze, *Cinema 2*, 171–2.
39. Lawrence, *The Man Who Died*, 155.
40. Lawrence, *The Man Who Died*, 157.
41. Friedrich Nietzsche, *Ecce Homo: How to Become What You Are* (Oxford: Oxford University Press, 2007), 35.
42. Deleuze, *Two Regimes of Madness*, 339.
43. Deleuze, *Two Regimes of Madness*, 339.
44. Michel Foucault, *Power: Essential Works of Foucault*, Vol. 3 (New York: The New Press, 2001), 340.
45. Charles Patterson, *Eternal Treblinka: Our Treatment of Animals and the Holocaust* (New York: Lantern Books, 2001).
46. Gilles Deleuze and Félix Guattari, *Kafka: Toward a Minor Literature* (Minneapolis, MN: Minnesota University Press, 1986), 13.
47. Donna Haraway, *When Species Meet* (Minneapolis, MN: Minnesota University Press, 2008), 16. Cf. Linda Williams, 'Haraway contra Deleuze and Guattari: The Question of the Animals', *Communication, Politics & Culture* 42, no. 1 (2009): 42–54; Robert Leston, 'Deleuze, Haraway, and the Radical Democracy of Desire', *Configurations* 23, no. 3 (2015): 355–76.
48. Haraway, *When Species Meet*, 16–17.
49. Braidotti, *The Posthuman*, 67.

50. Michel Foucault, *The Courage of the Truth (The Government of Self and Others II). Lectures at the Collège De France 1983–1984* (Basingstoke: Palgrave Macmillan, 2011), 243.
51. Foucault, *The Courage of the Truth*, 265–6.

Works Cited

Agamben, Giorgio. *The Open: Man and Animal*. Translated by Kevin Attell. Stanford, CA: Stanford University Press, 2004.

Blank, Robert. 'Biology and Politics: An Introduction'. In *Politics and the Life Sciences: The State of the Discipline*, edited by Robert Blank et al., 1–34. Bingley: Emerald, 2014.

Braidotti, Rosi. *The Posthuman*. Cambridge: Polity Press, 2013.

Caldwell, Lynton. 'Biopolitics: Science, Ethics, and Public Policy'. *The Yale Review* 54, no. 1 (1964): 1–16.

Cimatti, Felice. *Unbecoming Human. Philosophy of Animality After Deleuze*. Edinburgh: Edinburgh University Press, 2020.

Cimatti, Felice, and Carlo Salzani, eds. *Animality In Contemporary Italian Philosophy*. Basingstoke: Palgrave Macmillan, 2020.

Deleuze, Gilles. *Cinema 2. The Time-Image*. Minneapolis, MN: University of Minnesota Press, 1989.

Deleuze, Gilles. *Two Regimes of Madness: Texts and Interviews 1975–1995*. New York: Semiotext(e), 2006.

Deleuze, Gilles, and Félix Guattari. *Kafka: Toward a Minor Literature*. Minneapolis, MN: Minnesota University Press, 1986.

Deleuze, Gilles, and Félix Guattari. *A Thousand Plateaus: Capitalism and Schizophrenia*. Minneapolis, MN: Minnesota University Press, 1987.

Foucault, Michel. *Foucault Live: Collected Interviews, 1961–1984*. New York: Semiotext(e), 1996.

Foucault, Michel. *Power: Essential Works of Foucault, Vol. 3*. New York: The New Press, 2001.

Foucault, Michel. *The Birth of Biopolitics. Lectures at the Collège de France, 1978–1979*. Basingstoke: Palgrave Macmillan, 2008.

Foucault, Michel. *The Courage of the Truth (The Government of Self and Others II). Lectures at the Collège De France 1983–1984*. Basingstoke: Palgrave Macmillan, 2011.

Grusin, Richard. 'Introduction'. In *The Nonhuman Turn*, edited by Richard Grusin, vii–xxix. Minneapolis, MN: University of Wisconsin Press, 2015.

Haraway, Donna. *When Species Meet*. Minneapolis, MN: Minnesota University Press, 2008.

Haraway, Donna. *Staying with the Trouble: Making Kin in the Chthulucene*. Durham, NC: Duke University Press, 2016.

Lawrence, David Herbert. *The Man Who Died*. London: Heinemann, 1931.

Lemm, Vanessa, and Miguel Vatter. 'Michel Foucault's Perspective on Biopolitics'. In *Handbook of Biology and Politics*, edited by Steven A. Peterson and Albert Somit, 40–52. Cheltenham: Edward Elgar Publishing, 2017.

Leroi-Gourhan, André. *Gesture and Speech*. Cambridge, MA: MIT Press, 1993.

Leston, Robert. 'Deleuze, Haraway, and the Radical Democracy of Desire'. *Configurations* 23, no. 3 (2015): 355–76.

Liesen, Laurette, and Mary Walsh. 'The Competing Meanings of "Biopolitics" in Political Science: Biological and Postmodern Approaches to Politics'. *Politics and the Life Sciences* 31, nos. 1–2 (2012): 2–15.

Mitchell, Robert. *Infectious Liberty. Biopolitics between Romanticism and Liberalism*. New York: Fordham University Press, 2021.

Moravec, Hans. *Robot: Mere Machine to Transcendent Mind*. Oxford: Oxford University Press, 1999.

Morell, Virigina. 'Monkeys Master a Key Sign of Self-awareness: Recognizing their Reflections'. *Science*, 13 February 2017. Available at: https://www.science.org/content/article/monkeys-master-key-sign-self-awareness-recognizing-their-reflections. Accessed 16 May 2022.

Nayar, Pramod. *Posthumanism*. Cambridge: Polity Press, 2014.

Nietzsche, Friedrich. *Thus Spoke Zarathustra: A Book for All and None*. Cambridge: Cambridge University Press, 2006.

Nietzsche, Friedrich. *Ecce Homo: How to Become What You Are*. Oxford: Oxford University Press, 2007.

Patterson, Charles. *Eternal Treblinka: Our Treatment of Animals and the Holocaust*. New York: Lantern Books, 2001.

Peterson, Christopher. *Monkey Trouble. The Scandal of Posthumanism*. New York: Fordham University Press, 2018.

Schubert, Glendon. 'Review: Biopolitical Behavior: The Nature of the Political Animal'. *Polity* 6, no. 2 (1973): 240–75.

Seshadri, Kalpana R. 'Between Derrida and Agamben'. In *HumAnimal: Race, Law, Language*, edited by Kalpana R. Seshadri, 109–36. Minneapolis, MN: University of Minnesota Press, 2012.

Williams, Linda. 'Haraway contra Deleuze and Guattari: The Question of the Animals'. *Communication, Politics & Culture* 42, no. 1 (2009): 42–54.

Wolfe, Cary. *What is Posthumanism?* Minneapolis, MN: Minnesota University Press, 2010.

Zupančič, Alenka. 'Biopolitics, Sexuality and the Unconscious'. *Paragraph*: *Italian Biopolitical Theory and Beyond: Genealogy, Psychoanalysis, and Biology* 39, no. 1 (2016): 49–64.

Afterword: Locating Race and Animality amidst the Politics of Interspecies Life
Neel Ahuja

The Biopolitical Animal is essential reading for the current convergence of trans-border crises. On the one hand, the early twenty-first century has witnessed the deepening climate crisis as well as a new pandemic politics, both of which bring the specter of extinction, human and animal, to the fore of geopolitics on a world scale. On the other hand, the climate denialism that has largely dictated responses to environmental movements on the Right is being reconfigured by the emergence of a new Green nationalism, one in which speculation of environmentally driven migration serves the discourse of repeated border crises, requiring a political theory that seeks to address our interspecies relationships to grapple with the specter of fascism. We might take the twin emergence of a new discourse of the 'rights of nature', pioneered by Indigenous activists across Latin America, and the example of a resurgent animal protection vigilantism, fostered by the Hindu nationalist Modi government in India, as reflecting the widening poles of a thoroughly interspecies politics. The expansion of brutal and polluting regimes of industrial animal agriculture and extractivist land arrangements within these poles, supported in hushed tones by the eco- and animal fascists from Europe to Israel to India, displays the violence of capitalist systems' ongoing control of life through a variety of legal, economic and technical interfaces. In some real sense, we are fast losing the battle to disrupt and reverse the capitalist violence against animals and earth referenced across many writings in this volume. And perhaps one of the reasons this is the case is that we have not yet developed adequate political discourses, practices and solidarities that meet the scale of the challenge.

The essays here articulate political theories fit for the interspecies relationships that have, as many of the essays demonstrate, too often been excluded in liberal approaches to the political, including those that turn back to ancient Greek and Roman philosophies to grapple with the animality of the human. In the varied forms of politics envisioned in this volume's analyses of the embodied philosophy of Diogenes and the Cynics (Calarco, Lemm); the literature of Nayler, Kafka and Buzzati (Vint, Salzani, Campbell); and the work of animal advocates who develop deep relationships across species lines (Weisberg, Redmalm and von Essen), it is possible to glimpse alternative forms of intimacy, belonging, communication and even solidarity and resistance that reflect that anthropocentrism is not a simple norm but an imposition that masks the many forms of interspecies relationality and intimacy that offer resources for different ways of living. One of the important nascent contributions of the book is its multiple engagements with disability in relation to animal biopolitics, including the notion of a 'creaturely' biopolitics that allows for a critical reflection on the reproduction of norms and an alternative ethics (Salzani). Many of the essays in the book (including Cimatti and Salzani, Calarco, Lemm, Prozorov and Cimatti), have in turn attempted to grapple with not only the insufficiency of prior biopolitical framings for addressing an interspecies politics, but also with some emergent concepts in political theory derived from the late works of Foucault and Agamben that can extend the biopolitical frame to address the ethico-politics of environmental collapse and mass animal exploitation. It is perhaps no surprise that the ethical turn in Foucault provides a frame for some of these rewritings of conduct and care as interspecies interruptions of biopower, and yet, as I contend in what follows, there are some limits to these late Foucauldian approaches that we should consider as political theories move forward with new models for thinking species and biopower.

One of the difficulties in theorising the current convergence is to more capaciously account for how the current 'posthumanist' turns in politics reflect some particularities of the geopolitics of race and empire. Cimatti and Salzani in the introduction quite correctly diagnose that 'anthropo-*de*centralization will have to be accompanied by . . . an andro-*de*centralization and Euro-*de*centralization that institute a cross-species biopolitics along race, gender, and decolonial lines'. This work is still in progress and is dependent on the willingness of theorists working on biopolitics, posthumanism and animal studies to read and think more slowly and carefully with respect to race, colonialism, gender and related forms of structural domination. Works by Indigenous studies scholars on the animal question, including those by Billy-Ray Belcourt, Kim TallBear, Daniel Heath Justice and Kyle White, have not just pointed out that race and colonialism are 'blind spots' of many works in these fields, but that Indigenous political perspectives actually require a wholesale rethinking of these fields' foundational narratives of the human. As Vint narrates through a discussion of the work of Michi Saagiig Nishnaabeg scholar Leanne Betasamosake Simpson, the anthropocentric political worldview is out of step with many Indigenous cosmologies that have consistently situated humans in relation to animals and land and have refused liberal ideologies of recognition despite the dislocations of colonial settlement, ethnic cleansing and extraction that threaten these interspecies political models. In short, the very notion of the 'post'human reflects a colonial notion of time and embodiment that ignores views of politics that have continuously stressed the interspecies form of life as the site of kinship, reproduction and solidarity. At the same time, Black Studies and critical ethnic studies scholars reflecting on animals specifically and posthumanism more broadly – especially Zakiyyah Iman Jackson, Benedicte Boisseron, Alexander Weheliye, Claire Jean Kim and Mel Chen – have worked to acknowledge that racism draws extensively on figures of animality without resorting to either an anthropocentric refusal of interspecies intimacy or a pitting of animals against minoritised subjects through a comparative weighing of violence, which is discussed as a key obstacle to formulating an interspecies notion of necropower in Stanescu's essay. So if, in contradistinction to situations in which Indigenous persistence and resurgence have maintained a continuous alternative to the alienated, empty container of the human that colonial liberalism serially produces in the guises of property, rights and capitalist exchange, racial power sometimes involves situations in which colonialism and its regimes of slavery and indenture have effectively destroyed the webs of life for minoritised groups (see Iovino), such works have insisted on situated and contextualised analyses that can understand how animalisation is deployed contradictorily. This includes some cases where animals are elevated by structures of power above people of colour. (The examples of continuing racial and colonial biases in some mainstream animal activist organizing are exemplary here.) I point to these lines of argument in part to disentangle some of the threads of our fields' accounts of race that too often get conflated, distorted or compressed, the narrative passing too quickly on to other concerns when the logics of land and labour under racial capitalism often place minoritised publics in very different positions with respect to the question of an animal politics.

Based on these literatures, I want to respectfully offer a question in response to the suppositions in Foucault, Agamben and Wolfe that species difference generates modern racism. What might we learn if we reverse the proposition? What if, as an artefact of an Orientalism that clouds colonial views of nature, it is race that generates our notions of species? This hypothesis, which I discuss in the preface of my book *Bioinsecurities*, might further be extended to the notion of the posthuman, as the figure of the 'nonhuman' (critiqued in Rossello and Cimatti's essays) ends up projecting resistance to anthropocentrism upon an unimaginable variety of bodies, objects and systems. This operation, it could be argued, provides posthumanist theories with an apparent outside to the human that is nonetheless overdetermined by anthropocentric (and, perhaps, anthropomorphic) boundary-drawing. Although we need not discount the ability of animals to act and escape the confines of speciesist violence, we also need not romanticise animal resistance to an order that has totalising aspirations. After all, the type of interspecies intimacies, knowledges and life practices documented throughout this volume can at times diverge from resistant counter-conduct in the direction of fascistic moral imperative. (Without drawing too close a comparison, we might at least note a resonance between the iconoclastic street-life of Diogenes with his dog and the ascetic moralism of the urine-drinking, cow-feeding Brahmanical overlords of cow protection.)

Following Wadiwel's essay on aquaculture and the subsumption of fish reproduction under neoliberal capitalism, as well as Vatter's analysis of the changing views of planetarity that place many species in shared milieus, we can, however, glimpse paths forward for an affirmative biopolitics via a careful reading of the changing regimes of labour, technology and life. For this, it is necessary to maintain contextual geopolitical and materialist methods in our readings of the political, including those that critically examine the relationship between a neoliberal globalisation that has extended the assault on planetary life and the biological frameworks through which we often make sense of these relations. Wadiwel's argument suggesting that the transborder mechanisation of labour witnesses the recession of the human body alongside the increased interactivity of animal bodies with machines is a useful path forward for understanding the conjuncture of ecological and species violence with the current alienated form of capital that is technologising politics in new ways. With the ongoing specter of fascism haunting the highly divergent poles of today's interspecies politics, we might do best by amending and expanding some apparently 'humanist' methods rather than moving too quickly to attempt to transcend the empty container that colonial liberalism has carved for the self-anthropomorphising subject, the so-called human. This is not because such a project would not within its own hermeneutic frame be worthwhile but because we may in the process find ourselves carving out a secondary empty space of the beyond.

Index

abattoir, 183
ableism, 227, 256
actor-network theory, 5
aesthetics, 163
　of existence, 29, 32, 35
Agamben, Giorgio, 2, 5, 6, 8–9, 12n11,
　　13n15, 13n19, 54n42, 60, 76–91,
　　92–110, 121, 122, 125, 144, 153–4,
　　158, 164, 165, 176, 197, 205n18, 215,
　　218, 241, 259, 261, 296, 297
　anthropological machine, 13n19, 88, 95,
　　152, 154, 168
　Homo Sacer, 13n15
　The Human Voice, 76, 77
　Infancy and History, 76, 77, 78
　Language and Death, 77, 83, 84, 85, 87
　The Open, 88, 93
　The Sacrament of Language, 6–7, 77,
　　83, 86, 88
agency, 28, 37n18, 63, 138, 219, 222, 278,
　279
Alexander the Great (Alexander III of
　Macedon), 41
Althusser, Louis, 23
altruism, 136
anatomo-politics, 25, 254
animal
　agriculture, 193, 197, 198, 199, 200, 201,
　　203, 231n48, 295
　becoming, 33, 48, 49, 277, 281, 282,
　　286–90

companion, 160, 164, 169n14, 223
exotic, 142
gregarious, 1
human, 13, 114, 116, 120, 121, 126,
　143, 180, 223, 276, 277, 280, 286,
　290n4
husbandry, 60
liminal, 158
magical, 121
political, 1–3, 4, 6, 12n7, 12n11, 13n19,
　13n21, 16n41, 86, 275
rationabilis, 253
rationale, 253
rights, 236, 243, 256
sanctuary, 221
theology, 236
animalisation, 3, 4, 6, 13n15
Anthropocene, 9, 42, 43, 61, 66, 68, 144,
　185, 190, 191, 192, 235, 236, 237, 243,
　244, 246, 247
anthropocentrism, 5, 8, 11, 24, 27, 32, 33,
　35n4, 36n8, 256, 259, 260, 265n10,
　296, 298
anthropodenial, 136
anthropogenesis, 8, 76–89
anthropological machine, 13n19, 88, 95,
　152, 154, 168
anthropology, 49, 143
　theological, 237
anthropomorphism, 135, 136, 146n10,
　147n23

anthrozoology, 138
Antisthenes, 44
ape, 133, 136, 137, 142, 145
    anthropomorphic, 136
apocalypse, 237
apparatus, 2, 3, 4, 15n30, 41, 77, 78, 80, 81, 82, 84, 86, 116, 125, 126, 183, 191, 218, 219, 224, 254, 257, 260, 263, 264, 286, 288, 289; see also *dispositif*
aquaculture, 10, 190–212, 298
Arendt, Hannah, 262
Aristotle, 1–3, 6, 11n2–3, 12n11, 16n41, 51, 55n47, 79, 95, 99, 115, 275, 286
    The History of Animals, 1
    Politics, 1
Arnim, Achim von, 262
ascetism, 221
askesis, 34, 48
ass, 84
Auerbach, Eric, 255, 266n24
Aufhebung, 264
Austin, J.L. (John Langshaw), 81
autobiography, 133
avian flu, 43

Baartman, Sarah (Hottentot Venus), 148n40
Balcombe, Jonathan, 228
Basic Instinct (film), 156
becoming animal, 33, 48, 49, 277, 281, 282, 286–90
behaviourism, 138
Bekoff, Marc, 38n32, 228
Benjamin, Walter, 85, 262–5
    Berlin Childhood around 1900, 262
    'Franz Kafka', 262
    'On the Concept of History', 262
Bennett, Jane, 235, 236, 245–6
    Influx and Efflux, 245
Benveniste, Émile, 6, 119
Berger, John, 139–40
    'Why Look at Animals?', 139
Berlin, Isaiah, 265n14
Berlusconi, Silvio, 266n14
Bible, 93
    Ecclesiastes, 252
Binswanger, Ludwig, 23
    Traum und Existenz, 23
biology, 2, 3, 61, 62, 136, 275

biopolitics
    affirmative, 6, 9, 27, 34, 93, 94, 96, 97, 98, 103, 104, 105, 166, 298
    animal, 26, 296
    creaturely, 11, 254, 259, 261, 262, 265, 296
    decolonial, 106
    of the human race, 154
    immunitarian, 98
    interspecies, 93, 107
    liberating, 6
    neoliberal, 60, 63
    of rectitude, 11, 254, 255, 257, 259, 260, 261, 262, 263, 265, 266n24
    of relation, 97
    of vulnerability, 259
    planetary, 72n43, 73n65
    positive, 166
biopower, 4, 24, 25, 26, 27, 29, 30, 36n8, 58, 113, 114, 116, 117, 121, 123, 125, 127, 152, 153, 154, 164, 166, 177, 179, 196, 215, 218, 277, 296
bios, 6, 12n11, 30, 31, 92, 97, 99, 143, 144, 153, 154, 158, 159, 162, 164, 165, 166, 167, 168, 275
biosemiotics, 9, 132
biosphere, 9, 60, 62, 63, 65
bird, 83, 87, 134, 144, 192
body, 11, 13n19, 25, 36n8, 46, 47, 50, 54n45, 61, 62, 68, 98, 99, 115, 126, 139, 141, 142, 164, 176, 193, 196, 244, 259, 266n18, 275, 276, 277, 278, 280, 281, 283, 284, 285, 286, 287, 289, 291n10
    animal, 15n30, 61, 201
    biological, 13n19, 94, 154
    human, 4, 13n19, 25, 46, 94, 100, 254, 258, 278, 279, 281, 283, 298
    king's two, 242
    natural, 242
    politic, 98
    posthuman, 281, 285
    species, 25
    sublime, 242, 243
    use of, 8, 50, 51, 99
bonobo, 136, 138, 166
Braidotti, Rosi, 59, 65, 277, 278, 280, 288
Brentano, Clemens, 262
Brod, Max, 263

Butler, Judith, 185, 258
Buzzati, Dino, 9, 113–31, 296
   Bestiario, 116
   'Catastrophe', 117
   'The Dog Who Saw God', 117, 124
   'Epidemic', 117
   'L'opportunista', 119
   Sessanta Racconti, 117
   'Seven Floors', 117, 124, 126
   'The Slaying of the Dragon', 117, 118, 119, 121, 123, 125, 126
   The Tartar Steppe, 114, 123, 126

Calvino, Italo, 9, 132–50
   Marcovaldo, 132
   Mr. Palomar, 9, 132, 133
camp, 5, 135, 144, 164, 178, 183
   death, 182
Camus, Albert, 117
Canguilhem, Georges, 62, 63, 64, 65, 66, 67
   'The Living and Its Milieu', 63
capability approach, 256
capital, 179, 192, 195, 196, 298
capitalism, 92, 140, 142, 178, 179, 192, 193, 195, 196, 215, 219, 228, 283, 297, 298
Capitalocene, 144
carcerality, 198, 199
care, 5, 101, 125, 163, 216, 222, 227, 296
   of the self, 30, 46, 126
Cassirer, Ernst, 242
   The Myth of the State, 242
cat, 161, 239, 246, 280, 282
cattle, 184, 190
Cavarero, Adriana, 254, 255, 259, 262
centaur, 235
Chakrabarty, Dipesh, 68
chicken, 43, 175, 192, 193
chimpanzee, 136, 138, 142
Chomsky, Noam, 147n21
cicada, 84
Cicero, Marcus Tullius, 176, 181
classism, 227
climate change, 227, 237, 244
Coetzee, J.M., 257
colonialism, 67, 102, 103, 148n40, 178, 181, 296, 297
commodity, 194, 197, 199, 200, 219

commons, 193, 194, 196, 222
community, 1, 7, 8, 41–51, 73n65, 92, 94, 97, 98, 100, 101, 103, 105, 185, 261, 277
   Christian
   ethical, 252
   interspecies, 102, 106
   more-than-human, 42–4
   multispecies, 158
   political, 94, 106, 235
   semiotic, 139
Copito de Nieve (gorilla), 9, 134–44
cosmopolis, 44
counter-conduct, 28, 29, 34, 35, 216, 220, 221, 222, 223, 298
COVID-19, 5, 8, 9, 11, 58–75, 175, 274, 275, 279
cricket, 76, 77, 79, 84, 86, 87, 88, 89
Crutzen, Paul J., 190, 191
cuttlefish, 105
cybernetics, 61, 62, 63
cynicism, 41, 42, 46, 47, 48, 50

Darwin, Charles, 64, 136, 143, 145
   The Expression of the Emotions in Man and Animals, 136
Dasein, 99, 181, 182
decision
   sovereign, 61, 235, 238
decisionism, 235
deconstruction, 238
de-extinction, 141
Deleuze, Gilles, 8, 66, 113, 184, 185, 280, 284, 287, 288, 289
   Kafka, 113
democracy, 243, 247
Derrida, Jacques, 6, 10, 11, 12n11, 42, 113, 114, 116, 118, 123, 128, 176, 218, 235, 236, 238–41, 246
   Acts of Literature, 113
   The Animal That Therefore I Am, 116, 238, 240
   'Before the Law', 113
   The Beast and the Sovereign, 12n11, 239
de Waal, Frans, 136, 137, 139, 145n9, 146n12
Diamond, Cora, 258
Diamond, Jared, 136
Diderot, Denis, 41

Diogenes Laertius, 40
Lives of Eminent Philosophers, 40
Diogenes of Sinope, 40, 41, 45–7, 50, 51, 296, 298
disability, 256, 296
discipline, 24, 25, 26, 29, 30, 36n8, 253, 254, 258, 266n18
disenchantment, 242, 247
dispositif, 61, 66, 95; *see also* apparatus
dog, 31, 35, 40, 44, 48, 51, 106, 116, 117, 132, 143, 151, 152, 154, 159, 217, 218, 241, 288, 289, 298
domestication, 5, 143, 163, 191, 199
Donaldson, Sue, 158, 159, 164, 166, 222
  Zoopolis, 158
donkey, 76, 77, 79, 84, 86, 87, 88
dragon, 117–23, 126, 127
Dunayevskaya, Raya, 228

Ecclesiastes, 252
ecocriticism, 244, 247
ecology, 144
  media, 114, 120
economy, 26, 60, 106, 190
  sacrificial, 113
Eden, 143
emergency
  state of, 59, 261
Enlightenment, 102
environmentality, 58, 62, 63, 66
Epicureanism, 30, 52n12
ergon, 1, 95, 100
Eros, 223
eschatology, 237
Esposito, Roberto, 6, 9, 41, 73n65, 92, 93, 94, 96, 97, 98, 99, 100, 103, 107, 176, 194, 205n19, 215
ethics, 12n7, 27, 62, 86, 103, 105, 118, 119, 258, 259, 262, 288, 296
  animal, 256, 258
  individualised, 219
  interspecies–, 97
  nomadic, 128
ethnography
  multispecies, 6, 9, 132, 138
ethnology, 61
ethology, 16n41, 34, 35, 138, 228, 288
  cognitive, 228
  deep, 38n32

evolutionism, 136
exception, 98, 152, 154, 235, 261, 263, 264, 265
  state of, 215, 241, 259, 260, 269n57
  zone of, 194, 196, 205n18
exceptionality/exceptionalism, 264
  human, 2, 133, 152, 258, 281
Existentialists, 68
extinction, 89, 145, 190, 295
  sixth, 115, 140, 144, 244
extractivism, 107

factory farm, 10, 27, 28, 175–8, 181, 182, 184, 185, 191, 193, 194, 197, 198, 201, 202, 203, 215, 227, 229n13, 229n16
Fanon, Frantz, 228
feminism, 229, 258
fish, 10, 104–5, 190–212, 275, 298
form-of-life, 9, 95, 96, 99, 100, 101
Fossey, Dian, 136
Foucault, Michel, 2, 4, 5, 6, 7, 8, 11, 12n5, 13n15, 14n23, 23–39, 46, 61, 62, 63, 66, 92, 96, 98, 102, 114, 115, 116, 123, 151, 152, 153, 154, 160, 163, 176, 179, 184, 196, 198, 207n38, 215, 223, 224, 243, 257, 274, 275, 276, 279, 286, 288, 289, 296, 297
  The Courage of Truth, 7, 30
  Discipline and Punish, 4, 151, 254
  Dits et écrits, 13n15
  History of Sexuality, 114, 115, 152
  Security, Territory, Population, 13n15, 96, 254
  Society Must Be Defended, 4, 25, 36n8, 254, 257, 266n18
Franciscans, 54n42
freedom, 10, 41, 42, 50, 51, 63, 65, 79, 80, 95, 161, 217, 275
  Cynic, 41
  individual, 41, 47
Freire, Paolo, 228
Freud, Sigmund, 23, 243, 244, 255, 256, 257
  Civilization and Its Discontents, 255
friendship, 35, 55n47, 117, 160, 167, 222–3, 225
  interspecies, 222–3
Fromm, Erich, 228

Gaia hypothesis, 63
gender, 4, 6, 257, 296
   blindness, 13n21
Genesis, Book of, 42, 238, 239
global warming, 185
globalization, 67, 68
goat, 119
God, 2, 55n47, 82, 153, 235, 238, 239, 240, 247, 252, 257, 283, 285
Goodall, Jane, 136, 142
gorilla, 9, 133–48
governance, 58, 60, 92, 94, 101
government, 58, 59, 60, 62
   of things, 61
governmentality, 30, 34, 59, 60, 62, 63, 66, 101
Guattari, Félix, 8, 113, 287
   Kafka, 113

habitat, 35, 59, 61, 63, 64, 65, 66, 68, 71n41, 133, 137, 141, 142, 145, 163, 206n24
Haldane, John Scott, 63, 65
happiness, 95, 96, 161
Haraway, Donna, 6, 287
health, 25, 94, 98, 115, 152, 162, 163, 244, 274
   One, 59
   planetary, 58, 59–60
   right to, 58
Hegel, Georg Wilhelm Friedrich, 176, 179–80, 181, 183, 185
Heidegger, Martin, 14n29, 23, 42, 71n41, 176, 181–3, 185
   Being and Time, 182
   Dasein, 71n41, 99, 181, 182
history, 46, 78, 79, 87, 178, 191, 247, 257, 277
   human, 3, 66, 236
   natural, 236, 241, 282
   philosophy of, 253
Hobbes, Thomas, 235, 239, 240
Holocaust, 178, 182, 220
Homer, 2
homo sacer (concept), 96, 120, 154
Homo Sapiens, 3, 24, 97, 136, 137, 277, 278, 279, 281
horse, 123
human exceptionalism, 2, 133, 152, 258, 281

humanimality, 3, 11
humanism, 10, 179, 236, 260, 278
   Left, 216, 228, 229
   mortalist, 259
humanity, 12n7, 14n23, 33, 41, 66, 76, 81, 84, 88, 89, 92, 93, 96, 101, 136, 232n52, 235, 237, 240, 241, 252, 253, 257, 260, 261, 263, 265, 276, 277, 278, 281, 290
Humboldt, Alexander von, 66–7
   Kosmos, 67
Hume, David, 246
husbandry, 60, 195, 196, 201
Hutcheson, Francis, 246
hyperobject, 185

idealism, 286
   bourgeois, 263
immanence, 11, 242, 243, 282
   absolute, 280, 281, 282, 289
immortality, 185
immunisation, 41, 194
immunity, 8, 41, 52n12, 98
imperialism, 67, 143, 144
impersonal, the, 97, 98
individualism, 41, 221
   possessive, 267n26
infancy, 77, 78–9, 84, 85, 141
inoperativity, 9, 93, 96, 99, 100, 107
insect, 7, 83, 102, 118, 262
interdependence, 47, 93
intersubjectivity, 139, 154, 228

Jaspers, Karl, 23
Jesus, 237, 282–5
Jew, 182, 220
jouissance, 260, 269
   sovereign, 241, 259
Jung, Carl, 23
justice, 254, 263
   multispecies, 221, 226–7
   social, 94, 221, 226–7

Kafka, Franz, 113, 239, 241, 262–4, 296
   'The Cares of a Family Man', 262
   'A Crossbreed', 263
   'In the Penal Colony', 263
   The Metamorphosis, 262
   The Missing Person, 263

Kafka, Franz (*cont.*)
   The Trial, 241
Kant, 123, 252–4, 256, 257, 262, 263, 266n14
   'Idea for a Universal History with a Cosmopolitan Aim', 252–3
   'Lectures on Pedagogy', 253
   Religion Within the Boundaries of Mere Reason, 252
Kantorowicz, Ernst, 242
Kanzi (bonobo), 138
Kierkegaard, Søren, 181
knowledge-power, 116
Kojève, Alexandre, 87, 179
Koko (gorilla), 138, 139
Kraus, Karl, 262
Kripke, Saul, 44
Kymlicka, Will, 158, 159, 164, 166, 222
   Zoopolis, 158

Lacan, Jacques, 269n57
Lager (Nazi), 176; *see also* camp
Latour, Bruno, 5, 61, 68
law, 3, 9, 49, 81, 83, 86, 87, 92, 113, 119, 122–3, 153, 154, 158, 194, 218, 219, 240, 241–2, 254, 256, 259
Lawrence, D.H. (David Herbert), 282–6
   The Escaped Cock, 282
   The Man Who Died, 282–6
Le Bon, Gustav, 244
Lefort, Claude, 242
Leib, 281
Lestel, Dominique, 139
Levinas, Emmanuel, 118
liberalism, 63, 95, 297, 298
life
   animal, 4, 7, 27, 29, 31, 32, 34, 49, 51, 95, 113, 215, 219, 223, 280
   bare, 81, 82, 95, 143, 144, 154, 164, 165, 166, 191, 193, 194, 196, 197, 220, 230n16
   biological, 2, 12n11, 59, 95, 154, 197, 215, 236, 275, 280
   contemplative, 50
   creaturely, 235, 238, 241, 243, 260
   cynical, 11, 288, 289, 290
   deading, 10, 176–86
   good, 31, 34
   grievable, 167
   happy, 96
   human, 25, 44, 94, 97, 101, 116, 191, 193, 216, 217, 238, 274, 275, 280, 282, 288, 289
   humanimal, 11, 282
   natural, 49, 95, 97, 242
   nonhuman, 8, 10, 93, 103, 152, 164, 191, 196, 254, 279
   other-than-human, 43, 47, 58
   philosophical, 30, 40, 46, 50
   political, 2, 12n11, 28, 95, 96, 154, 275
   postanthropocentric, 285
   posthuman, 285, 287
   posthumous, 283, 285
   species / of the species, 2, 42, 115, 116
   transcendent, 282, 283
   true, 30, 31, 32
Linnaeus, Carl (Carl von Linné), 136
Linzey, Andrew, 236
lion, 7, 51, 83, 143
Locke, John, 218
logos, 2, 6, 12n4, 12n7, 32, 43, 46, 79, 80, 82, 244
Lovelock, James, 63
Luhmann, Niklas, 42
lycanthrope, 240

MacPherson, C.B., 267
mad cow disease, 43
Mandela, Nelson, 148n40
Marcuse, Herbert, 222
Marx, Karl, 195, 197
   Capital, 195
materialism, 247
   gross, 46
   new, 236, 244, 246
Mbembe, Achille, 5, 92, 176, 177, 178, 179, 181, 183, 184, 215
   Necropolitics, 179
   On the Postcolony, 177, 179
meat, 117, 175, 176, 177, 180, 181, 192, 199, 221, 225
medicine, 58, 59, 62, 274–5
Meister Eckhart (Johannes Eckhart von Hochheim), 239
Merleau-Ponty, Maurice, 228
Mesmer, Franz Anton, 242, 243, 244, 245, 247

mesmerism, 235, 242–7
Messiah, 263, 264
metaphysics, 9, 93, 94, 96, 98, 100, 101, 106
   Indigenous, 102
   non-Western, 101
   of subjectivity, 96, 98, 99
   Western, 8, 94, 100, 103
Michael (gorilla), 139
milk, 177
modernity, 1, 8, 26, 53n12, 68, 68, 77, 102, 107, 114, 115, 117, 121, 152, 153, 235, 263
   colonial, 102
   European, 67, 106, 113
   threshold of, 2, 9, 14n23, 114, 115, 116, 120, 123, 126, 127
   Western, 102
monkey, 135, 143, 145–6n9, 291n10
monster, 46, 117, 118, 120
monstrosity, 133, 134
mouse, 35, 50

nature, 1, 3, 8, 9, 10, 13n19, 24, 30, 32, 35, 38n34, 43, 44, 48, 49, 50, 51, 52n12, 64, 69, 88, 95, 104, 127, 160, 161, 168, 235, 236, 238, 242, 244, 245, 247, 277, 280, 297
   human, 32, 46, 252, 253, 254, 265n10, 266n14
   more-than-human, 32
   rights of, 65, 248n6, 195
   state of, 240
necropolitics, 10, 176–86
necropower, 177, 297
Negri, Antonio, 6
Nietzsche, Friedrich, 45, 50, 52n12, 281, 282
   and *amor fati*, 285–6, 289
   On Truth and Lies in an Extra-Moral Sense, 45
   Thus Spoke Zarathustra, 50, 281
   Übermensch/overman, 281–2
Nim Chimpsky (chimpanzee), 146n21
nomos, 32, 34, 51, 69, 72n54
norm, 46, 47, 51, 63, 64, 96, 166, 254, 256, 257, 258, 260, 261, 264, 283, 296
normalisation, 11, 29, 254, 256, 264, 278n78

normativity, 59, 63, 68, 89, 101, 102, 103
Nussbaum, Martha, 256

octopus, 104, 106
One World One Health, 59
Onetti, Juan Carlos, 135
ontology, 9, 94, 96, 103, 185, 288
   individualistic, 259
   relational, 258
ontotheology, 85
orangutan, 136, 143
Ota Benga, 143
overman, 281–2; see also *Übermensch*
Ovid (Publius Ovidius Naso), 255

pandemic, 5, 8, 11, 58, 59, 60, 175, 274, 275, 279, 295
Panopticon, 275
parrēsia, 15n30, 30
pastoral power, 5, 163, 166
pedagogy, 253
   critical, 216, 227, 229
performative/performativity, 81, 82, 83, 86
Peripatetics, 30
personhood, 97, 98
pest, 132, 157, 158, 159, 168
pet, 132, 152, 153, 154, 158, 159, 166, 168, 218, 280
PETA (People for the Ethical Treatment of Animals), 267
phenomenology, 228
phōnē, 2, 6
physis, 32, 34, 51
pig, 175, 176
Plato, 30, 55n47
Plessner, Helmuth, 8, 65
polis, 1, 2, 3, 6, 12n7, 32, 43, 44, 48, 49, 51
political theology, 10, 235–47
politics, 1, 2, 3, 5, 6, 7, 10, 11, 11n2, 28, 37n18, 51, 62, 68, 93, 94, 95, 96, 97, 100, 101, 102, 115, 166, 215, 219, 224, 225, 254, 258, 259, 264, 265, 275, 286, 296, 297
   anatomo-, 25, 254
   animal, 297
   interspecies, 104, 295, 296, 298
post-animality, 7
postcolonial studies, 9, 132

posthumanism, 259, 277–80, 287, 296, 297
post-truth, 87
potentiality, 79, 96, 97, 105, 106, 107, 182, 245, 255, 261
power, 4, 5, 7, 10, 24, 25, 26, 27, 28, 29, 30, 34, 36n8, 61, 92, 94, 96, 100, 116, 117, 122, 127, 136, 142, 145, 152, 154, 177, 180, 181, 184, 195, 219, 224, 238, 259, 260, 266n18, 276, 297
  biopolitical, 60, 92, 165, 281, 285, 286
  disciplinary, 24, 29, 60, 61, 160, 162
  labour, 201
  pastoral, 5
  somato-, 276, 283
  sovereign, 25, 61, 144, 152, 179, 218, 239, 240
  transcendent, 289
predation, 190, 193, 195, 196, 197
primatology, 138
psychoanalysis, 78, 243
psychology, 16n41, 52n12, 244

Quintilian (Marcus Fabius Quintilianus), 266n24

rabbit, 9, 132, 151–68
race, 4, 6, 96, 147n29, 220, 257, 261, 296, 297
racism, 4, 36n8, 94, 148n40, 227, 256, 257, 297
Raffles, Stamford, 143
rationality, 47, 218, 253, 279
Ray, John, 14n23
reason, 12n4, 31, 42, 43, 44, 46–7, 50, 96, 99, 133, 227
relationality, 96, 98–100, 102, 193, 221, 222, 259, 277, 296
religion / *religio*, 81, 83, 86, 87, 119, 239
Regan, Tom, 256
reptile, 118, 120, 133, 134
resistance, 10, 26, 27, 28, 29, 30, 34, 37n18, 106, 177, 183, 184, 185, 191, 195, 199, 202, 203, 216, 218, 220, 221, 222, 226, 229n13, 296, 298
revolution
  agricultural, 192
  Darwinian, 14n23
  democratic, 235, 242, 247

French, 241, 247
  genetic, 62
rhesus monkey, 291n10
right, 59, 61, 95, 98, 122, 153, 154, 157, 158, 194, 217, 228, 240, 252, 254
  animal, 236, 243, 256
  civil, 275
  divine, 242, 247
  to health, 58, 59
  human, 97
  to kill, 4, 257
  to mobility, 58, 59
  natural, 218
  of nature, 65, 295
Rilke, Rainer Maria, 260
  Duino Elegies, 260
Ritter, Carl, 66
Rousseau, Jean-Jacques, 241
Ryder, Richard, 35n4

sanctuary (animal), 222–3
Santner, Eric, 10, 11, 235–6, 238, 241–3, 247, 259–60, 262, 269n56–7
  On Creaturely Life, 241
  The Royal Remains, 242
SARS-CoV-2, 288
Sartre, Jean-Paul, 228
Schmitt, Carl, 72n54, 235, 236, 238, 241, 261
seafood, 190, 194, 201
secularisation, 242, 247
Secundus the Silent, 44
security, 60, 63, 66
semiotics, 64
sentience, 94, 95
sentimentalism
  moral, 246
Serres, Michel, 35
sexism, 227
sheep, 123, 159
Singer, Peter, 35n4, 256, 267n33
slaughterhouse, 175, 226, 229n16, 231n48
slavery, 27, 153, 178, 297
Sloterdijk, Peter, 5, 8, 46, 61, 65, 67–9, 71n41, 72n54
Smith, Adam, 246
snake / serpent, 117, 118, 120
society, 25, 27, 60, 61, 98, 140, 153, 168, 222, 224, 276, 283

civil, 61, 252, 253
consumer, 221
Socrates, 41, 47
somato-power, 276, 283
sovereign, 119, 218, 227, 235, 240, 241, 257, 261
  authority, 10, 235, 240, 241
  decision, 61, 235
  jouissance, 241, 259
  power, 25, 60, 61, 144, 152, 179, 218, 239, 240
  state, 205n18, 235
sovereignty, 10, 158, 178, 179, 205n18, 216, 218, 236, 238, 239, 240, 242, 243, 260
  anthropocentric, 235, 237, 238
  human, 218, 219, 220, 222, 238, 239
  monarchical, 242
  popular, 242, 247
  species, 218, 260
species, 2, 4, 5, 9, 14n23, 36n8, 89, 92, 94, 104, 136, 144, 145, 156, 190, 253, 260, 261, 282, 296, 297, 298
  blindness, 4, 13n21
  companion, 287–8
  endangered, 26, 103, 144
  egalitarianism, 59
  human, 5, 14n23, 35n4, 36n8, 42, 63, 66, 68, 94, 154, 225, 252, 254, 258, 261, 267n33
  life of, 42, 115
  man-as-, 25, 36n8, 99, 100
  norm, 257, 258
speciesism, 35n4, 36n8, 42, 227
speech act, 81, 88
Spinoza, Baruch, 288
State, 5, 26, 48, 61, 126, 152, 153, 154, 158, 161, 164, 179, 194, 205n18, 235
state
  of emergency, 59, 261
  of exception, 215, 241, 259–60, 269n57
  of nature, 240
Stoermer, Eugene F., 190, 191
Stoics, 30, 32
subject, 10, 12n12, 24, 49, 76, 77, 80, 81, 83, 86, 87, 96, 100, 123, 142, 179, 189, 183, 185, 216, 227–8, 241, 258, 270n78, 275, 276, 277, 282, 286, 289
  animal / nonhuman, 9

autonomous, 261, 269n56
biopolitical, 2, 5, 278, 280
human, 29, 33, 79, 256, 270n78, 275, 280
Kantian, 255, 261, 269n56
legal, 154
of life, 64, 66
of rights, 228
posthuman, 7, 277
sovereign, 180
Western, 3, 103, 261, 267n26
subjectivation / subjectification, 8, 13n19, 16n45, 26, 29–30, 31, 32, 76, 77, 78, 79, 80, 84, 85, 86, 88, 89, 270n78
subjectivity, 1, 3, 7, 8, 11, 29, 32, 96, 101, 103, 106, 222, 227–8, 258, 280, 288, 289
  animal / of animals, 138, 228
  biopolitical, 3
  human, 6, 93, 95, 281
  Lacanian, 259
  metaphysics of, 93, 94, 96, 98, 99, 100, 102
  nonhuman, 144
  posthuman, 277, 280
  Western, 12n12, 99, 255
survival of the fittest, 64
sympathy, 133, 135, 140, 245–6, 247

technosphere, 58, 60, 61, 62, 65, 66
teleology, 279
telos, 29
thanatopolitics, 9, 153, 164, 167, 178, 193
Thanatos, 223
theology, 235, 257
  animal, 236
  negative, 239
  political, 10, 235, 236, 237, 238, 242, 243, 244, 246, 247
Thoreau, Henry David, 245, 246
threshold of modernity, 2, 9, 14n23, 114, 115, 116, 120, 123, 126, 127
tradition, 30, 31, 32, 96, 238–9
  biopolitical, 98
  Christian, 235, 236
  feminist, 216, 224
  Hegelian, 179
  humanist, 10
  liberal, 96, 97, 256

tradition (*cont.*)
  philosophical, 2, 30, 34, 94, 240
  Platonic, 50
  political, 12n5
  Socratic, 50
  Western, 2, 11n2, 12n5, 42, 94, 255, 257
transcendence, 96, 281, 282, 283
transcendentalism, 246
transhumanism, 278, 281
tuna, 190, 204n4
turn
  animal, 8
  biopolitical, 2, 215
  counter-linguistic, 6
  nonhuman, 278–9, 280
  other-than-human, 63
  planetary, 63
  political
  posthuman, 279, 296

Übermensch, 281–2; see also overman
Uexküll, Jakob von, 8, 64, 65, 67, 137
Umwelt, 8, 64, 65, 66, 137, 142, 143, 228
utilitarianism
  preference, 256
utopia
  socialist, 265n14

Valery, Paul, 122
veganism, 216, 220–1
vegetarianism, 236
veridiction, 30, 81
Vernadsky, Vladimir, 63
violence, 3, 4, 10, 24, 27, 132, 136, 138, 151, 152, 153, 153, 179, 180, 183, 186, 193, 215, 216, 217, 218, 219, 221, 226, 227, 229, 230n16, 259, 295, 297
  biopolitical, 194, 195, 197, 203
  epistemic, 216, 220, 225
  institutional, 225, 226
  species/speciesist, 298
  systemic, 215, 225
virus, 5, 58, 59, 60, 279
voice (*phōnē*), 76, 77, 83–6, 88, 89, 122–3
vulnerability, 11, 48, 93, 185, 228, 258–9

war, 115, 123, 132, 153, 154
  against animals, 216–29
  by other means, 96, 98
  World War I, 65
  World War II, 192
Washoe (chimpanzee), 138, 139
Weber, Max, 242
Weil, Simone, 258
werewolf, 241
Whitman, Walt, 245–6
wolf, 235, 238, 240
woodchuck, 246

zoē, 12n11, 92, 97, 99, 153, 154, 157, 158, 159, 166, 167, 168, 275
zōon, 4, 12n11, 275
  politikon, 1, 275
zoo, 9, 28, 132, 133, 134, 135, 137, 139–40, 141–5, 148n40, 217, 226, 241
zoology, 143
zoonosis, 8, 58
zoopoetics, 239
zoo-politics, 6, 12n11
zoosemiotics, 138
zootheology, 239, 240